DISCRIMINATION, COPYRIGHT AND EQUALITY

Opening the E-Book for the Print-Disabled

While equality laws operate to enable access to information, these laws have limited power over the overriding impact of market forces and copyright laws that focus on restricting access to information. Technology now creates opportunities for everyone in the world, regardless of their abilities or disabilities, to access the written word – yet the print-disabled are denied reading equality, and have their access to information limited by laws protecting the mainstream use and consumption of information. The *Convention on the Rights of Persons with Disabilities* and the World Intellectual Property Organization's *Marrakesh Treaty* have swept in a new legal paradigm. This book contributes to disability rights scholarship and builds on ideas of digital equality and rights to access in its analysis of domestic disability anti-discrimination, civil rights, human rights, constitutional rights, copyright and other equality measures that promote and hinder reading equality.

Dr Paul Harpur is Senior Lecturer at TC Beirne School of Law, University of Queensland. He has participated in a number of prestigious research fellowships, including as an International Visiting Fellow, Centre for Disability Law and Policy, Institute for Lifecourse and Society, National University of Ireland, Galway, and as a Distinguished International Visiting Fellow, Burton Blatt Institute, College of Law, Syracuse University, New York. He has led a range of projects, including one with the International Labour Organization, assessing labour rights in the South Pacific, with a particular focus on the rights of persons with disabilities.

CAMBRIDGE DISABILITY LAW AND POLICY SERIES

Edited by Peter Blanck and Robin Paul Malloy

The Disability Law and Policy Series examines these topics in interdisciplinary and comparative terms. The books in the series reflect the diversity of definitions, causes and consequences of discrimination against persons with disabilities while illuminating fundamental themes that unite countries in their pursuit of human rights laws and policies to improve the social and economic status of persons with disabilities. The series contains historical, contemporary and comparative scholarship crucial to identifying individual, organisational, cultural, attitudinal and legal themes necessary for the advancement of disability law and policy.

The book topics covered in the series are also reflective of the new moral and political commitment by countries throughout the world toward equal opportunity for persons with disabilities in such areas as employment, housing, transportation, rehabilitation and individual human rights. The series will thus play a significant role in informing policy makers, researchers and citizens of issues central to disability rights and disability anti-discrimination policies. The series grounds the future of disability law and policy as a vehicle for ensuring that those living with disabilities participate as equal citizens of the world.

Books in the series

Ruth Colker, *When Is Separate Unequal? A Disability Perspective*, 2009

Larry M. Logue and Peter Blanck, *Race, Ethnicity, and Disability: Veterans and Benefits in Post-Civil War America*, 2010

Lisa Vanhala, *Making Rights a Reality? Disability Rights Activists and Legal Mobilization*, 2010

Alicia Ouellette, *Bioethics and Disability: Toward a Disability-Conscious Bioethics*, 2011

Eilionoir Flynn, *From Rhetoric to Action: Implementing the UN Convention on the Rights of Persons with Disabilities*, 2011

Isabel Karpin and Kristin Savell, *Perfecting Pregnancy: Law, Disability, and the Future of Reproduction*, 2012

Arie Rimmerman, *Social Inclusion of People with Disabilities: National and International Perspectives*, 2012

Andrew Power, Janet E. Lord, and Allison S. deFranco, *Active Citizenship and Disability: Implementing the Personalisation of Support for Persons with Disabilities*, 2012

Lisa Schur, Douglas Kruse and Peter Blanck, *People with Disabilities: Sidelined or Mainstreamed?*, 2013

Eliza Varney, *Disability and Information Technology: A Comparative Study in Media Regulation*, 2013

Jerome Bickenbach, Franziska Felder and Barbara Schmitz, *Disability and the Good Human Life*, 2013

Robin Paul Malloy, *Land Use Law and Disability: Planning and Zoning for Accessible Communities*, 2014

Peter Blanck, *eQuality: The Struggle for Web Accessibility by Persons with Cognitive Disabilities*, 2014

Arie Rimmerman, *Family Policy and Disability*, 2015

Anna Arstein-Kerslake, *Restoring Voice to People with Cognitive Disabilities: Realizing the Right to Equal Recognition Before the Law*, 2017

Arie Rimmerman, *Disability and Community Living Policies*, 2017

Paul Harpur, *Discrimination, Copyright and Equality: Opening the E-Book for the Print-Disabled*, 2017

Discrimination, Copyright and Equality

OPENING THE E-BOOK FOR THE PRINT-DISABLED

PAUL HARPUR

University of Queensland

CAMBRIDGE
UNIVERSITY PRESS

University Printing House, Cambridge CB2 8BS, United Kingdom

One Liberty Plaza, 20th Floor, New York, NY 10006, USA

477 Williamstown Road, Port Melbourne, VIC 3207, Australia

4843/24, 2nd Floor, Ansari Road, Daryaganj, Delhi – 110002, India

79 Anson Road, #06–04/06, Singapore 079906

Cambridge University Press is part of the University of Cambridge.

It furthers the University's mission by disseminating knowledge in the pursuit of education, learning, and research at the highest international levels of excellence.

www.cambridge.org
Information on this title: www.cambridge.org/9781107119000
DOI: 10.1017/9781316340516

First published 2017

Printed in the United Kingdom by Clays, St Ives plc

A catalogue record for this publication is available from the British Library.

ISBN 978-1-107-11900-0 Hardback

Contents

Foreword

'No Excuses: Reading for All, Including People with Disabilities'

In the twenty-first century, the world's leaders have repeatedly acknowledged the importance of everyone possessing the right to education, enabled by the right to read and write. Recall that Goal 4 of the United Nation's Sustainable Development Goals enjoins us to: 'ensure inclusive and equitable quality education and promote lifelong learning opportunities for all'. Among the targets to be achieved by 2030 is ensuring that 'all girls and boys complete free, equitable and quality primary and secondary education'. This global aspiration is one expression of a widely held belief across societies around the world: namely, that every person should be able to read and write.

Reading is at the heart of many ancient and most modern societies. Reading interacts with, and underpins, many elements of everyday and public life: education and work; travel and leisure; access to health care, social services and justice; social and political participation; and cultural belonging. Reading is also closely related to gaining access to information, media and communication. A substantial number of the world's population cannot read, have not been afforded the opportunity to learn to read, face significant barriers or challenges with reading (and literacy generally), or read in different ways. Hence the many policies and practices adopted to address such issues, and to ensure that reading is something extended as an opportunity to all.

Against the backdrop of these commonly held views that reading is central to social life, and the prospects of individuals and their communities, what are we to make of the disturbing situation in which the right to read is systematically denied to a large and diverse group of humanity: the 'print-disabled'?

The print-disabled include blind people and those with visual impairments (an estimated 300 million worldwide), but also a wide range of others, including those with other sensory disabilities who are not able to hold or manipulate a book or other printed material, not to mention those with cognitive and other disabilities which preclude or interfere with reading (such as dyslexia, autism, intellectual disability, acquired and traumatic brain injury). Through the history of print culture and the book, since the invention of writing, commemorated in various milestones, especially the advent of the printing press, it has been recognised that many people are not able to read. 'Work-arounds' have been devised, such as providing assistance with people reading to those with print disabilities. Particular media have developed to make books and printed material accessible, including Braille, radio for 'print-handicapped' people; 'talking books' and formats such as DAISY. These efforts to make books accessible to the print-disabled are typically regarded as 'specialised', though most people would have some awareness of their existence.

With the digital age, there has been great excitement generally about the prospects of digital technologies, multimedia, the internet, mobile devices, and the pervasiveness of voice synthesiser and recognition technologies to create new ways for reading to occur – and for many people hitherto denied easy access to finally be able to fully participate in cultures of reading. After all, when mobile phone and tablet computer technology and associated computer operating systems and software support 'reading out aloud' of digital material, including books, are we not on the cusp of book stores, libraries, archives, schools and universities of the world – great repositories of knowledge and educational institutions – supporting a genuine revolution in reading? As we know, digital formats, widely used for electronic reading, can have capabilities and features that greatly extend accessibility, especially for print-disabled people. On the very threshold of the world of letters undergoing a transformative leap forward, there is a real danger than these great but very concrete and feasible hopes will be dashed.

This is the extraordinary story told in full for the first time by Dr Paul Harpur in his luminous book, *Discrimination, Copyright and Equality: Opening the E-Book for the Print-Disabled*. In a distinctive, powerful voice, underpinned by outstanding legal scholarship and analysis, Harpur provides a systematic account of how international and national copyright law has been the principal agent of oppression for people with print disabilities when it comes to their access to books and printed material. Publishers have rarely created and distributed works in accessible formats. One of the most scandalous examples in the world of digital books is the decision by Amazon to quail in the face of copyright advocates such as the American Authors Guild, and enable publishers to turn off accessibility features – so that the Kindle (the most famous name in E-Books) is effectively not accessible for the print-disabled.

When publishers large and small, traditional and digitally in the vanguard, have chosen not to make their books accessible to the print-disabled, the task has fallen to other intermediaries. For decades, there have been ways for organisations (typically charities and disability organisations) and, more recently, individuals (through optical character recognition software, scanners and screen readers) to take inaccessible books and make copies in alternative formats so print-disabled readers can read them. Fair enough, one might think; other people putting in the labour and funds to make books accessible, where the publishers have failed to do so. Enter the central doctrine of copyright when it comes to print disability: the emergence of an exception to copyright to allow such copying of books to make them accessible for the print-disabled. Bizarrely enough, this minor exception has been fiercely resisted by copyright holders and a range of vested interests, including societies of authors. For their part, governments have been reluctant to take action, until recently.

As Harpur lays out, there are two 'game changers' that mean it can no longer be (disabling) business as usual for those denying books to print-disabled people. The more recent is the 2013 *Marrakesh Treaty to Facilitate Access to Published Works for Persons Who Are Blind, Visually Impaired, or Otherwise Print Disabled*, which makes it mandatory for the states who have signed the Treaty to adopt copyright exceptions for the creation and distribution of accessible versions of work for those with print disabilities. This is an epochal step forward, yet it has two major flaws. It does not include people with non-sensory disabilities, and, more troubling still, it also mandates exceptions for the *non-profit* accessible version of works. As Harpur discusses, this latter stipulation means that commercial publishers and organisations are prevented from creating accessible works. Moreover, instead of gaining the benefits of 'universal design', the exception still revolves around converted works into accessible formats only for those with print disabilities. So, why this ban on the harnessing of commerce, when this could otherwise see accessibility become a 'normal', unexceptional part of all books? Harpur provides an elaborated and convincing explanation of why this parlous situation still obtains, as the dominant, 'taken for granted' approach in books and disability – even in the digital age, when accessibility is being taken mainstream in all kinds of other technology.

To understand this situation, Harpur gives a comprehensive account of the other game changer, the 2006 *Convention on the Rights of Persons with Disabilities* (CRPD). As Harpur's analysis shows, extending the work of many other scholars, the *CRPD* greatly advances the rights and obligations governments and other actors now shoulder when it comes to matters of information, communication, media and technology. The right to read can be seen as part of the web of human rights that there is now no doubt are the patrimony of people with disabilities, as of all humanity. There are many complexities to the body of international law, fortified by the *CRPD*, but, especially, there is the overarching question of how such laws, and new dimensions of rights, are conceived, implemented and safeguarded in national contexts. This is laid out by Harpur with careful analysis and argumentation, and impeccable documentation, as he dissects the shortcomings of existing anti-discrimination, equality of opportunity and human rights law across a number of leading Anglophone jurisdictions. It makes for depressing reading, to absorb and be puzzled by the many ways in which narrow concepts of ability, normalcy and justice underpin the framing, interpretation and enacting of law and justice when it comes to laws whose manifest purpose is to remove discrimination against people with disabilities, or to give effect to human rights. Displaying commendable optimism of the spirit as well as pessimism of the intellect, Harpur offers a creative and rigorous set of arguments, based on the resources of actual existing law and legal practice on how we could, and indeed, should, construe and enact copyright, anti-discrimination and human rights law differently – to finally make accessibility of books, especially E-Books, the general condition of culture, no longer an 'exception' to culture (that is, a patronising, charity-based apology that needs to be made amidst the courts and tribunals of copyright law, in order to make a mere fraction of books accessible to print-disabled people).

Harpur lucidly explains the absurd, unjust, disabled dispensation that still prevails, despite the twin peaks of the *CRPD* and *Marrakesh Treaty*, whereby print-disabled people have access only to a fraction of the world's books. Given that copyright is one of the most widely debated, researched and legislated public concerns in digital culture – as evidenced in the Commons debates, the furious arguments about illegal downloading, or the affirmative policy in favour of open-access publishing – it is astounding that the issues of copyright and the print-disabled are not widely known. Why are these issues not routinely raised, in the mainstream, when we talk about the opportunities and discontents of digital technology for society and culture? The continuing oppression of print-disabled readers, and their exclusion from the world of books, can no longer continue – and it is something that should be an integral part of our university courses, research, public debates and public policy discussion on digital technology. A very important addition to this indispensable Cambridge University Press series, this is a book that must be widely read.

Harpur's study deserves an engaged reception across a range of disciplines, not just law and policy studies – but also disability studies, sociology, media and communication studies, literary studies and elsewhere in the humanities and social sciences, as well as engineering and technology sciences. Equipped with Dr Harpur's fine book, we are armed with the resources to take these issues mainstream and secure proper action, so that everyone in the world, by 2030, or sooner, can indeed be a reader.

Gerard Goggin
University of Sydney

Acknowledgements

I would like to dedicate this monograph to my parents, Barry and Joan Harpur, who made my career and education possible. I lost my eyesight at the age of 14 in a commuter train accident. Suddenly the written word was a closed book to me. I could not read Braille and copyright concerns meant instructional materials were not provided in formats that I could use. In the first few years, my parents spent tens of hours each week reading material to me and scanning book content. As technology improved, the burden on them reduced substantially, but even now, as an accomplished academic, they provide me with support. For their lifelong support, I want to dedicate this book to them.

I also want to dedicate this book to my wife, who has provided me much support in more recent times, and to my son, Hayden Harpur, who, at one, is amazing and does not understand the significance of the thousands of E-Books contained in the E-Reader he is holding as I type.

I would also like to acknowledge two academics who have had a profound influence on my development as a lawyer and an academic. The transition from able-bodiedness to blindness in a train accident helped me understand how the world treats people with ability differences, but also led me to wonder about my place in this world. Professor Ron McCallum AO, who has been blind since birth, and who was and remains one of the world's finest legal and academic minds, gave me substantial hope and inspired me to reach for success. Ron made me believe anything was possible and encouraged my dreams of entering law school.

Once in law school, I was privileged to come under the wing of Professor Des Butler. Professor Butler uses an electric wheelchair and made an awkward first-year law student believe it was possible to graduate. He inspired and encouraged me to learn, and ultimately became my PhD supervisor and a man I have the greatest respect and appreciation for.

Within academia, a number of people have made this work possible. Foremost is the fabulous academic and financial support at the University of Queensland.

Within my faculty, I would like to extend my appreciation to Professor Ian Watson, Executive Dean of the Business, Economic and Law Faculty, Professor Sarah Derrington, Head of the TC Beirne School of Law and Dean of Law, Professor Simon Bronitt, Deputy Dean of Law, and Professor Fiona Rohde, Deputy Dean of Law, for supporting my special studies programme application that made this work possible. In addition, I would like to acknowledge for their mentoring and encouragement to apply for this research grant and to write this monograph, Professors Heather Douglas, Graeme Orr and Michael White QC.

The library staff at the University of Queensland are outstanding and provide students and staff with amazing levels of support. In particular, I would like to acknowledge the support of Julie Oates, Thomas Palmer and Pam Schindler.

For editing my work and helping chase down resources, I would like to extend my thanks to my research assistant, Joseph Lelliott. To have a PhD candidate of such high calibre on the team has been a real boon.

Finally, I would like to express my gratitude to Professor Gerard Quinn and Professor Peter Blanck for opening up their respective research centres and homes to me. My fellowships at the Centre for Disability Law and Policy, Institute for Lifecourse and Society, National University of Ireland, Galway, and at the Burton Blatt Institute, College of Law, Syracuse University, New York, provided me with the opportunity to gather critical data and to discuss my work with the brightest minds in the field.

Introduction

If you are reading this monograph then you are engaging in an activity denied to hundreds of millions of print-disabled people across the globe. For most of human history, reading equality has been an unrealised and impossible dream for people who are unable to read and handle standard books, including people with blindness, quadriplegia or dyslexia. Technological advancements have revolutionised what is possible. While books have been born digital for decades, almost exclusively they have been published in standard paper formats. Books are now born digital and are being distributed as E-Books via E-Libraries, and read on E-Readers. There is now no reason that people with print disabilities cannot enjoy full access. People with print disabilities can use adaptive technologies to read digital content, unless that content is published in ways that block the use of adaptive technologies. Reading equality remains an unrealised dream that is technologically, commercially, economically and legally possible.

This monograph contributes to disability rights scholarship and legal advocacy. It builds on international and domestic notions of digital equality and rights to access information. The core thesis of this monograph is that technology now creates the possibility that everyone in the world, regardless of their abilities or disabilities, should be able to access the written word. Why, then, is there still a book famine, where only 5 to 7 per cent of the world's books are available to people with print disabilities in wealthy, advanced economies, and less than 1 per cent in the majority of countries?

While anti-discrimination and equality laws operate to enable access, these laws have limited impact on the overriding impact of market forces and copyright laws that focus on restricting access to information. For decades, the print-disabled have been denied reading equality and have instead had their access to information limited by legal frameworks and resource allocations that tolerated minor exceptions to the mainstream consumption of books and information. The recent United Nations *Convention on the Rights of Persons with Disabilities* (CRPD), and other international developments, have swept in a new disability politics that is altering what is expected from laws and institutions.[1] The human rights paradigm has created the possibility of achieving equality. The challenge is to analyse barriers to this dream of reading equality, and to craft laws and institutions that open the E-Book for the world's print-disabled.

TERMINOLOGY: DISABLEMENT OR HUMANITY FIRST

This introductory chapter, and the remainder of the book, adopts the terms 'persons with print disabilities' and 'print-disabled'. Whether the person or disability is placed first has theoretical and practical significance.[2] Medical professionals describe people by reference to their impairment. Under this approach, a person with an impairment loses their humanity and is described as the 'person with paraplegia' or, even worse, simply as 'the paraplegic'.

To turn the focus away from the medical label and towards the role society plays in disabling people with impairments, social model advocates in the United Kingdom sought to emphasise that it is society that causes the disablement. To emphasise the role society has in causing disablement, the 'disabled person' terminology was adopted.[3] This social model approach, discussed further in Chapter 2 of this monograph, emphasises that the person is disabled by barriers in society.

Advocates in Australia, Canada and the United States predominantly use the person-first approach to emphasise the humanity of the individual over the impairment.[4] The United Nations *Convention on the Rights of Persons with Disabilities* has enshrined a human rights model reflecting a wider civil rights model that places humanity first and uses the term 'persons with disabilities'.[5]

---

[1] *Convention on the Rights of Persons with Disabilities* (CRPD), opened for signature 30 March 2007, 2515 UNTS 3 (entered into force 3 May 2008).
[2] Darcy Granello and Todd Gibbs, 'The Power of Language and Labels: "The Mentally Ill" Versus "People with Mental Illnesses"' (2016) 94(1) *Journal of Counseling & Development* 31; Paul Harpur, 'From Disability to Ability: Changing the Phrasing of the Debate' (2012) 27(3) *Disability and Society* 325.
[3] Colin Barnes, *Disabling Imagery and the Media: An Exploration of the Principles for Media Representations of Disabled People* (1992) The British Council of Disabled People, 43; Michael Oliver and Colin Barnes, *Disabled People and Social Policy: From Exclusion to Inclusion* (1998) Longman, 18.
[4] Gerard Goggin and Christopher Newell, *Disability in Australia: Exposing a Social Apartheid* (2003) University of New South Wales Press, 25.
[5] CRPD; Paul Harpur, 'Embracing the New Disability Rights Paradigm: The Importance of the *Convention on the Rights of Persons with Disabilities*' (2012) 27(1) *Disability and Society* 1, 1.

Despite the debates, Tom Shakespeare argues that 'the person first is the politically progressive choice in America, Australia and other English speaking countries'.[6]

The author has previously argued for the person-first approach,[7] and will predominantly adopt the person with disabilities approach in this monograph. The author believes that in most situations it is more important to emphasise the humanity of the individual over focusing on the role society has in creating disability. There will be situations throughout this monograph, however, where the disablement caused by society is so stark that it requires particular emphasis. For example, if a person who has no eyesight can use adaptive technology to read an E-Book, but the only reason they cannot read the book is a decision by an E-Publisher to use coding that does not follow universal design, then that person can be said to be disabled by that ableist decision. But for the ableist E-Publisher, the existence of the impairment would not be disabling. By employing both terminologies in this monograph, the author is fence-sitting, while leaning towards one side of the debate. The author believes this theoretically uncomfortable position is correct for this monograph, especially considering the fact that the CRPD recognises the role society has in creating disablement (the social model), while engaging with the health aspects of the individual.[8]

WHO ARE THE PRINT-DISABLED?

The terms 'print-disabled' and 'persons with disabilities' both describe an impairment category which constitutes a disability. The notion of disablement is analysed in Chapter 2 of this monograph, and the situations where an impairment is regarded as a disability in the CRPD and anti-discrimination laws is analysed in detail in Chapter 6. At this stage, it is sufficient merely to define when an inability to consume standard print material amounts to a print disability.

The notion of print disability extends wider than the estimated 39 million clinically blind persons and 246 million vision-impaired persons in the world.[9] Until recently, no international legal instrument has provided a definition of

---

[6] Tom Shakespeare, *Disability Rights and Wrongs Revisited* (2014) Routledge, 19.

[7] Harpur, 'From Disability to Ability'.

[8] For a further discussion of the medical model, social model and human rights paradigm adopted in the CRPD, see Chapter 2 of this monograph.

[9] Kaya Koklu, 'The Marrakesh Treaty – Time to End the Book Famine for Visually Impaired Persons Worldwide' (2014) 45(7) *International Review of Intellectual Property and Competition Law* 737, 737; Jingyi Li, 'Reconciling the Enforcement of Copyright with the Upholding of Human Rights: A Consideration of the Marrakesh Treaty to Facilitate Access to Published

what a print disability is. The *Treaty to Facilitate Access to Published Works for Persons Who Are Blind, Visually Impaired, or Otherwise Print Disabled (Marrakesh Treaty)*, discussed in Chapter 3 of this monograph, benefits persons with print disabilities and defines 'beneficiary persons' to include a person who:

(a) is blind;
(b) has a visual impairment or a perceptual or reading disability which cannot be improved to give visual function substantially equivalent to that of a person who has no such impairment or disability and so is unable to read printed works to substantially the same degree as a person without an impairment or disability; or
(c) is otherwise unable, through physical disability, to hold or manipulate a book or to focus or move the eyes to the extent that would be normally acceptable for reading; regardless of any other disabilities.[10]

While the scope of beneficiary disabilities in the *Marrakesh Treaty* extends protection to many well-established disability categories, concerningly, it fails to extend protection to many impairment categories which have historically been recognised as print-disabled.

It is troubling that the scope of beneficiary disabilities in the *Marrakesh Treaty* does not include people who have long been recognised as being people with print disabilities. The scope of print disability in the *Marrakesh Treaty* is limited to sensory and physical impairments. This excludes all persons with print disabilities related to cognitive impairments. Cognitive disabilities include impairments categorised as intellectual and developmental disabilities; acquired and traumatic brain injury, autism, learning and reading disabilities; and attention, perceptual, memory and communication-processing limitations.[11] Many of these impairments are associated with reading difficulties. Copyright exemptions, discussed in Chapter 5 of this monograph, extend exemptions for the print-disabled to impairments relating to comprehension. Moreover, it is widely accepted in scholarship and in the disability community that print disabilities include people experiencing disabilities that impact on their capacity to consume standard

---

Works for the Blind, Visually Impaired and Print Disabled' (2014) 36(10) *European Intellectual Property Review* 653, 655.

[10] *Treaty to Facilitate Access to Published Works for Persons Who Are Blind, Visually Impaired, or Otherwise Print Disabled (Marrakesh Treaty)*, opened for signature 28 June 2013, WIPO Doc. VIP/DC/8 (not yet in force), art. 3.

[11] Peter Blanck, *E-Quality: The Struggle for Web Accessibility by Persons with Cognitive Disabilities* (2014) Cambridge University Press, 27; Tom Campbell, *Dyslexia: The Government of Reading* (2013) Palgrave Macmillan, 105–40.

books.[12] A person with dyslexia, for example, may use a screen reader which reads the content of the screen to them in the same way as a person who is blind. Arguably, it should not be relevant whether the person has a cognitive or physical disability, but whether their impairment prevents them consuming standard print content. The leading authority on the human rights of persons with disabilities, the *CRPD* discussed in Chapter 2 of this monograph, does not define print disability, and encourages an inclusive approach to protecting the rights of persons with disabilities. Accordingly, this monograph regards all impairments that restrict consumption of print as print disabilities, regardless of whether the impairment is categorised as sensory, physical or cognitive.

HOW DO THE PRINT-DISABLED CONSUME DIGITAL CONTENT?

As a group, persons with print disabilities consume information differently from those without any impairments. In addition, persons with print disabilities may consume content differently from each other, depending on their attributes. Technology can be used to enable persons with various disabilities to communicate and consume content to enable them to exercise their rights.[13] To enhance social inclusion, hardware and software are increasingly including universal design features so that disability-specific technology is not required.[14] In addition to universally designed products, persons with print disabilities may utilise adaptive technology to consume content. Examples include:

---

[12] See, for example, Learning Ally, which was founded in 1948 as Recording for the Blind & Dyslexic: <www.learningally.org> (accessed 18 November 2016); for examples discussed in the author's other works: Paul Harpur and Nicolas Suzor, 'The Paradigm Shift in Realising the Right to Read: How E-Book Libraries Are Enabling in the University Sector' (2014) 29(10) *Disability and Society* 1658; Paul Harpur, 'Ensuring Equality in Education: How Australian Laws Are Leaving Students with Print Disabilities Behind' (2010) 15(1) *Media and Arts Law Review* 70; Nicolas Suzor, Paul Harpur and Dylan Thampapillai, 'Digital Copyright and Disability Discrimination: From Braille Books to Bookshare' (2008) 13(1) *Media and Arts Law Review* 1.

[13] Piers Gooding, Anna Arstein-Kerslake and Eilionoir Flynn, 'Assistive Technology as Support for the Exercise of Legal Capacity' (2015) 29(2/3) *International Review of Law Computers & Technology* 245.

[14] Janet E Lord, 'Accessible ICTs and the Opening of Political Space for Persons with Disabilities' in Michael Stein and Jonathan Lazar (eds), *Frontiers in Human Rights: Disability Rights, Law, and Technology Accessibility* (forthcoming) University of Pennsylvania Press; Emily J Steel and Gunnel Janeslätt, 'Drafting Standards on Cognitive Accessibility: A Global Collaboration' (2016) *Disability and Rehabilitation: Assistive Technology* (published online 13 June).

1. For the vision-impaired and the blind – screen readers that provide an audio description of the text content (but not images or complex graphs) of computer screens, and screen magnification, which enables people with low vision to read content;[15]

2. For persons unable to physically handle books, such as people with quadriplegia or tetraplegia, robotic devices which enable movement and use of computers;[16]

3. For people with cognitive impairments, the inclusion of images and multimedia that can aid understanding, as well as screen readers that assist users with low vision.[17]

While such technologies enable people with print disabilities to consume digital content, disability adaptive technologies can be prohibitively expensive and may not work on certain devices.[18] Even where persons with disabilities can utilise adaptive technologies or universally designed products, not all E-Books or E-Libraries are in accessible formats, and many books remain solely in standard formats printed on paper. This denial of the right to read is why there is said to be a book famine.

THE BOOK FAMINE CONFRONTING THE PRINT-DISABLED

Chapter 1 of this monograph will illustrate how technological advances created the possibility that persons with print disabilities could enjoy reading equality for the first time in human history. Rather than enjoying reading equality, however, the denial of reading equality has been labelled a 'book famine'.[19] While this language may appear overly emotive, the adoption of such language has wide support and was not challenged to any notable degree

---

[15] Marion Hersh and Michael A Johnson (eds), *Assistive Technology for Visually Impaired and Blind People* (2010) Springer Science and Business Media.

[16] Michel Busnel et al., 'The Robotized Workstation "MASTER" for Users with Tetraplegia: Description and Evaluation' (1999) 36(3) *Journal of Rehabilitation Research and Development* 217; R Platts and M Fraser, 'Assistive Technology in the Rehabilitation of Patients with High Spinal Cord Lesions' (1993) 31(5) *Spinal Cord* 280.

[17] Blanck, *E-Quality*, 173.

[18] Delia Ferri, G Anthony Giannoumis and Charles Edward O'Sullivan, 'Fostering Accessible Technology and Sculpting an Inclusive Market through Regulation' (2015) 29(2/3) *International Review of Law Computers & Technology* 81; Greg Vanderheiden, Jutta Treviranus and Amrish Chourasia, 'The Global Public Inclusive Infrastructure (GPII)' (Proceedings of the 15th International ACM SIGACCESS Conference on Computers and Accessibility, ACM, 2013).

[19] Brian Watermeyer, 'Freedom to Read: A Personal Account of the "Book Famine"' (2014) 3(1) *African Journal of Disability* 144.

by the copyright lobby in the recent debates in the World Intellectual Property Organization which resulted in the adoption of the *Marrakesh Treaty*.[20]

There are over 129 million book titles in the world,[21] but persons with print disabilities in wealthy developed countries can obtain less than 5 to 7 per cent of these titles in formats that they can consume.[22] The situation in emerging and majority world countries is even grimmer. For example, in India, one of the world's strongest emerging economies, only 0.5 per cent of published books are converted into formats that persons with print disabilities can access.[23] Even if books in accessible formats are available, people who are socio-economically disadvantaged encounter additional barriers in accessing the written word.[24]

---

[20] Lior Zemer and Aviv Gaon, 'Copyright, Disability and Social Inclusion: The Marrakesh Treaty and the Role of Non-Signatories' (2015) 10(11) *Journal of Intellectual Property Law & Practice* 836.

[21] This figure was reported by a Google engineer as part of the Google Books project. See Leonid Taycher, 'Books of the World, Stand Up and Be Counted! All 129,864,880 of You' on *Booksearch Blogspot* (5 August 2010) <booksearch.blogspot.com.au/2010/08/books-of-world-stand-up-and-be-counted.html> (accessed 18 November 2016).

[22] Brook Baker, 'Challenges Facing a Proposed WIPO Treaty for Persons Who Are Blind or Print Disabled' (Research Paper No. 142, Northeastern University School of Law, 21 May 2013); Paul Harpur and Nicolas Suzor, 'Copyright Protections and Disability Rights: Turning the Page to a New International Paradigm' (2013) 36(3) *University of New South Wales Law Journal* 745; World Blind Union, 'June 17 Press Release for WIPO Book Treaty' (17 June 2013) <www.worldblindunion.org/English/news/Pages/JUne-17-Press-Release-for-WIPO-Book-Tr eaty.aspx> (accessed 18 November 2016).

[23] Patrick Hely, 'A Model Copyright Exemption to Serve the Visually Impaired: An Alternative to the Treaty Proposals before WIPO' (2010) 43 *Vanderbilt Journal of Transnational Law* 1369, 1375.

[24] Lea Shaver, 'Copyright and Inequality' (2014) 92 *Washington University Law Review* 117, 127–8.

1

How Technology Has Created the Possibility of Opening the Book: From Hard Copy to E-Books

INTRODUCTION

The written form is one of the primary means of acquiring and communicating knowledge. This monograph argues that the print-disabled are experiencing a book famine created by the operation of law. This introductory chapter analyses how technology enables this book famine to be reversed. Section I analyses how the print-disabled have been excluded from the written word for most of human history. Rock painting, writing on parchment and, later, paper were mediums that the print-disabled could not access without substantial assistance. The advent of Braille and scanning technology enabled persons with print disabilities to gain limited access to books. These approaches, however, have not and will not reverse the book famine experienced by the world's print-disabled in the current regulatory environment.

The expansion of E-Books and E-Libraries creates the possibility that persons with print disabilities might be able to experience reading equality for the first time in human history. Section II of this chapter analyses the growth of E-Books and E-Libraries, the potential of equality, and the reasons persons with print disabilities continue to be denied access to E-Books and E-Libraries, despite the technological capacity now existing to realise reading equality. Reading equality will be achieved when people with print disabilities can access materials independently and on comparable terms with the wider population. This monograph argues that persons with print disabilities have a right to enjoy reading equality, and that E-Books and E-Libraries provide the greatest opportunity to date to achieve reading equality for the world's print-disabled. Finally, Section III explains why many corporations do not ensure that their E-Books and E-Libraries are accessible to persons with print disabilities, and provides the foundation for the analysis for this monograph.

SECTION I THE WRITTEN FORM: INDEPENDENT READING BEYOND THE PRINT-DISABLED

For most of human history, the written word has been inaccessible to the print-disabled, or only available to them as an exception to the norm. Originally, the written word was denied to almost the entire community. With the advent of the printing press, reading became an activity available to the majority of the population. During this time, the print-disabled were excluded from the reading revolution. While Braille improved access, this resource could not provide anything like reading equality. Legal, technological and social changes enabled the print-disabled to access books as an exception to the norm. This section will illustrate that these advances have improved access, but they have not reversed the impact of the book famine on the world's print-disabled.

Days of the Illuminators – Reading as a Noble Activity

For millennia, humans have transcribed meaning into a permanent form. Rock paintings are the oldest form of human written expression, such as the 40,000-year-old paintings of animals on the Indonesian island of Sulawesi, or the 50,000-year-old continuous tradition of Australian Aboriginal rock paintings.[1] After rock paintings, humans began to write on animal skins, papyrus and parchment. In the first millennia following the birth of Jesus Christ, humans across Asia, India, the Middle East and Europe wrote on religion, history and other issues of great import.[2]

A key aspect of all early writing styles is that their creation was extremely labour-intensive, with the materials including gold, silver and precious stones. They remain enormously expensive pieces of artwork. The creation of a manuscript in medieval Europe, for example, would first involve a scribe writing out the content of the work by hand, followed by an illuminator, who would first draw the design in silverpoint, then burnish the drawing with gold dots, add in modulating colours, repeat each step, and then perform the task again with marginal figures. The manuscript would then be bound in covers that were painted and decorated with gold, silver and precious stones.[3]

---

[1] Maxime Aubert et al., 'Pleistocene Cave Art from Sulawesi, Indonesia' (2014) 514 *Nature* 223; George Chaloupka, *Journey in Time: The World's Longest Continuing Art Tradition: The 50,000 Year Story of the Australian Aboriginal Rock Art of Arnhem Land* (1993) Reed.

[2] See, for a wide-ranging discussion: Sarah Foot and Chase F Robinson (eds), *The Oxford History of Historical Writing, Vol. 2: 400–1400* (2012) Oxford University Press.

[3] Robert Calkins, 'Stages of Execution: Procedures of Illumination as Revealed in an Unfinished Book of Hours' (1978) 17(1) *International Center of Medieval Art* 61.

Illuminated manuscripts could take a team of dedicated monks years to create, and were only available to wealthy churches, powerful nobility and royalty.[4]

The Invention of the Printing Press and the Book Revolution

The invention of the printing press by Gutenberg in 1450 transformed reading from the province of a very small elite, to something accessible by the middle classes and, eventually, the masses.[5] The printing press used hand-carved plates covered with ink pressed against paper to create an imprint. The process of etching and engraving was a precise art and any error could result in the entire plate being discarded and the process started again. While it took less man power to create a scribed page than to carve a plate for the printing press, once the plate was prepared the printing press enabled a book to be mass-produced at a rapid rate.[6] A plate enabled a new page to be created every few seconds, in contrast to scribing, which took hours or days per page, depending on the artistic complexity involved.

The cost of printing books continued to decrease as techniques improved. One of the most significant developments was the invention of movable type. Movable type enabled plates to be prepared and corrected quickly, and the materials reused.[7] The invention of the printing press transformed the publishing of books from beautiful works of art to more utilitarian, lower-cost, mass-produced items for work, scholarship and enjoyment. The printing press transformed access to the written word so that members of the middle classes were able to access and create books.[8] Providing a person had moderate means and the capacity to read ink on paper, the printing press was transformational.

The Genius of Louis Braille: The Blind Can Now Read

The printing press enabled large portions of the population to read, but this reading revolution was a closed book for the print-disabled. If a person could not read ink on pages, then they either missed out or had to find a person who was not disabled, able to read and prepared to read to them. Over the centuries

---

[4] J Alexander, *Medieval Illuminators and their Methods of Work* (1992) Yale University Press; Christopher De Hamel, *Scribes and Illuminators* (1992) University of Toronto Press.

[5] Lucien Febvre and Henri-Jean Martin, *The Coming of the Book: The Impact of Printing 1450–1800, Vol. 10* (1997) Verso.

[6] Adrian Johns, *The Nature of the Book* (1998) University of Chicago Press.

[7] Hoda ElMaraghy (ed.), *Changeable and Reconfigurable Manufacturing Systems* (2008) Springer Science and Business Media.

[8] Elizabeth Eisenstein, *The Printing Press as an Agent of Change, Vol. 1* (1980) Cambridge University Press.

there have been attempts to create a script that the blind could read.[9] One of the first attempts to develop a tactile alphabet was made by a fourteenth-century Egyptian scholar who produced raised hieroglyphic writing. Unrelated to this, in Spain in 1517, Francisco Lucas developed carved letters on wood to help the blind, and in 1547 in Italy, Gironimo Cardano had used a raised dot system which resembled an early form of Braille. These efforts and others were isolated events which did not spread into the movement which has become known as Braille.

Lennard Bhickel provides an inspired account of the story of the Braille Code. The story of the Braille Code has its roots in a meeting on a Sunday in November 1771, when a middle-class Frenchman, Valentin Haily, gave a donation to a blind beggar boy and watched as he sorted the coins by touch. Haily realised what the boy was doing, and that he could be taught to read raised letters. Using carved wood blocks, this boy, François Lesueur, was taught to read. A sculpture of the first meeting of Haily and Lesueur appears in stone on the Boulevard des Invalides in Paris.[10]

Following the success of Hailey's efforts, funding was obtained and the first school for the blind was opened in 1784. The school was closed when the French Revolution swept across France in 1789, which resulted in Haily fleeing for his life across Europe. Haily's flight spread the notion of educating the blind and sowed the seed for the rebirth and expansion of schools for the blind in the future.

The blind schools during the 1800s created tactile versions of the letters that sighted people read. This was extremely inefficient and new methods emerged. A French artillery officer, Captain Charles Barbier, developed a code of twelve raised dots.[11] While this was a massive advance, the code contained a number of inefficiencies which were swept away when Louis Braille developed his six-dot Braille Code which subsequently spread across the world.

Louis Braille said in 1841:

> Access to communication in the widest sense is access to knowledge, and that is vitally important for us if we are not to go on being despised or patronised by condescending sighted people. We do not need pity, nor do we need to be reminded that we are vulnerable. We must be treated as equals – and communication is the way we can bring this about.[12]

---

[9] Lennard Bhickel, *Triumph Over Darkness: The Life of Louis Braille* (1988) Allen & Unwin Books, 78–80.

[10] <en.wikipedia.org/wiki/Valentin_Ha%C3%BCy#/media/File:Statue_de_Valentin_Ha%C3%BCy.jpg> (accessed 18 November 2016).

[11] Bhickel, *Triumph Over Darkness*, 56 and 57.

[12] Ibid., 10.

While Braille has revolutionised the lives of millions of blind people across the globe, the Braille Code has not and will not achieve reading equality. The first Braille book in 1873 took two years of effort to create, using hand-pressing to make the raised dots on pages.[13] Even with modern technology, books printed in Braille are expensive and extremely large. The Holy Bible, King James Version 1611, published by the American Bible Society (English Braille Grade 2 version), consists of eighteen volumes and can be purchased used for $630.[14] While Braille has had a transformational impact on enabling the blind to access the written word, the prohibitive cost and the need to transport full Braille books in large suitcases cannot compete with technological advances in terms of cost and ability to transport and store thousands of books in accessible digital formats on a smart phone.

Improved but Limited Access: E-Libraries with E-Books in Disability-Specific Formats

Laws and institutions recognised that persons with print disabilities could not read standard books printed on paper. This gave rise to an exemption in copyright laws that is analysed in Chapter 5 of this monograph. Predominantly, charities that assist the blind have utilised these exemptions to provide persons with print disabilities with a library of books in alternative or accessible formats. Charities, such as the Canadian National Institute for the Blind, the National Library Service for the Blind and Physically Handicapped, the Royal National Institute of Blind People and Vision Australia, have impressive catalogues of books in Braille, large print and audio cassette. Most of these works have been created by volunteers reading books onto tape, as well as scanning, editing and printing books in alternative formats.

Persons with print disabilities can consume books in digital formats using screen readers, such as Non-Visual Desktop Access (NVDA) and Job Access With Speech (JAWS).[15] The emergence of screen-reading software and other adaptive technologies led to the creation of E-Books in disability-specific

---

[13] Ibid., 106–9.

[14] Amazon, *The Holy Bible* (English Braille Grade 2) 18-volume set, King James Version 1611, Containing the Old and New Testaments (translated out of the original tongues and with the former translations diligently compared and revised, American Printing House for the Blind) <www.amazon.com/gp/aw/d/B001RTGoRK/ref=mp_s_a_1_2?qid=1450662614&sr=82&key words=Grade+2+Braille%2C&dpPl=1&dpID=61s21Co2AXL&ref=plSrch&pi=SX200_QL40> (accessed 18 November 2016).

[15] Freedom Scientific, 'Blindness Solutions: Jaws. The World's Most Popular Windows Screen Reader' <www.freedomscientific.com/Products/Blindness/JAWS> (accessed 18 November 2016); Non-Visual Access, 'NVDA Features' <www.nvaccess.org/about/nvda-features/> (accessed 18 November 2016); Paul Harpur and Nicolas Suzor, 'The Paradigm Shift in

formats, such as the DAISY format.[16] Disability-specific formats were created, in part, to enable persons with print disabilities to use their adaptive technology more effectively, and in part to reduce concerns from rights-holders that there would be leakage from the special case of print-disabled readers to the wider population. Formats such as Braille Ready Format (BRF) are only usable by people using specialised devices created for persons with print disabilities. While it is possible to convert a BRF document to a PDF or rich text format (RTF), the conversion will result in disability-specific formatting being converted. The time taken to remove this coding and format it for a sighted person acts as a safeguard against leakage. Even if the book were successfully edited and formatted, the end product would not contain the graphics and appearance of a digital file that was ripped using a multi-feed scanner. Essentially, it is quicker for a sighted person to rip a print book using a multi-feed scanner than to try to convert a BRF file.

While the growth of the mainstream E-Book market is altering existing practices, currently persons with print disabilities lawfully obtain E-Books through one of two means. The first example is where a charity or educational institution provides the person with a print disability with a copy of the book using a copyright exemption (analysed in Chapter 5 of this monograph). The second method is where E-Libraries have been developed, which operate to provide persons with print disabilities with books in accessible formats. There are substantial limitations with the interactions between copyright laws and the exemptions which regard persons with print disabilities as special cases. This chapter, however, will leave the legal analysis to subsequent parts of this monograph, and will now focus on illustrating the problems experienced by persons with print disabilities as a result of the operation of existing legal frameworks.

Delays and Difficulties: Educators and Charities Providing Accessible E-Books under an Exception to Copyright

Research demonstrates that the exemption to copyright that regards persons with print disabilities as a special case is no answer to the book famine. The limitations with the current model can be illustrated by analysing how a student with a print disability obtains access to a textbook in a format they can consume. Students with print disabilities have more support than the

---

Realising the Right to Read: How Ebook Libraries Are Enabling in the University Sector' (2014) 29(10) *Disability and Society* 1658.

[16] George Kerscher and Jennifer Sutton, 'DAISY for All: Publishers' Collaboration Enabling Print Access' (2004) 10 *Information Technology and Disabilities*, 1.

wider print-disabled population, yet even this group is experiencing a book famine in an information-rich educational environment.

The exemption to copyright analysed in Chapter 5 of this monograph has resulted in a cumbersome and inefficient process for securing an accessible version of a textbook for a student with a print disability. Rather than requiring the publisher to provide a digital copy of the textbook, this exemption results in the following process:

1. The student decides what classes they will take and enrols in those classes.
2. The student contacts the professor to obtain a final reading list. This can occur in some institutions in the first week of class.
3. The student contacts the disability support officer for help in obtaining their textbooks in accessible formats. In many situations, the student must first purchase a print copy of the textbook and provide evidence of this purchase.
4. Providing the student has already provided medical evidence attesting to their disability and has a disability access plan, the disability support officer will search a range of databases to determine if the book has already been scanned into an accessible format, and will contact the publisher. If this fails, they will start scanning the book.
5. Finally, the accessible book is edited and provided to the student.[17]

This approach of relying on educational institutions and charities to source accessible copies or convert standard books into alternative formats is simply not achieving reading equality.[18]

The author and Dr Rebecca Loudoun have published primary research on the experiences of university students with print disabilities in Australia.[19] This

[17] Paul Harpur, 'Providing Students with Vision Impairment Print Material in an Accessible Electronic Format: Identifying Barriers in the Current Model' (report, Queensland University of Technology Division of Technology, Information and Learning, QUT Library and Law School, 2010); Pat Renfranz, Sandy Taboada and Jill Weatherd, *Progress and Stalemates: The Complexities of Creating a Textbooks-on-Time System for Blind Students* (July 2008) Braille Monitor <nfb.org//Images/nfb/Publications/bm/bmo8/bmo807/bmo80706.htm> (accessed 18 November 2016).

[18] Guy Whitehouse, James Dearnley and Ian Murray, 'Still "Destined to Be Under-Read"? Access to Books for Visually Impaired Students in UK Higher Education' (2009) 25(3) *Publishing Research Quarterly* 17c; RNIB, *Where's My Book?* (2006) Royal National Institute of Blind People; Nicolas Suzor, Paul Harpur and Dylan Thampapillai, 'Digital Copyright and Disability Discrimination: From Braille Books to Bookshare' (2008) 13(1) *Media and Arts Law Review* 1.

[19] Paul Harpur and Rebecca Loudoun, 'The Barrier of the Written Word: Analysing Universities' Policies to Include Students with Print Disabilities and Calls for Reforms' (2011) 33(2) *Journal of Higher Education Policy and Management* 153.

research involved analysing the websites of all Australian universities to ascertain how they describe their services to students and staff with print disabilities. It involved qualitative and quantitative research with 56.4 per cent of Australia's universities. This research found that 40 per cent of Australian universities indicated that they had no formal policy on assisting students with print disabilities. Whether or not they had a policy, all universities participating in the research indicated that they provided students with print disabilities with support in obtaining textbooks in accessible formats.

The nature of support varied considerably across universities and depended on whether the book was prescribed as mandatory reading or only recommended by the professor to assist with enhancing understanding. All universities provided support to students to obtain their prescribed readings. If the instructional material was only recommended, then 14 per cent of universities said they required the student to manage the process of sourcing accessible versions of that content. To assist students in obtaining recommended readings and for research purposes, 96 per cent of universities would provide assistance in gathering textbooks from library shelves, while only 74 per cent would provide assistance in photocopying textbooks, and only 51 per cent would provide assistance in scanning parts of textbooks into digital formats.

Where universities did provide their students with access to essential or prescribed readings, students with print disabilities were overwhelmingly obtaining the readings late. Only 50 per cent indicated that first-year students with print disabilities were provided with access to prescribed textbooks before the semester started. The majority of students with print disabilities obtained the full set of their readings when 14 per cent, or about 1.9 weeks, of a fourteen-week semester was over. Some students, however, obtained their readings much later. Two universities reported that students with print disabilities did not receive all their essential readings in accessible formats until week five of a twelve-week semester. This means some students with print disabilities were obtaining their material after 42 per cent or more of the semester was already over. In the worst-case scenario, one university reported that they provided a student with the last of their essential readings in week eleven of a thirteen-week semester. Students with print disabilities at this university received the last of their essential readings after 85 per cent of the teaching period was concluded.

While university administrators in this survey operated as if it were acceptable to provide students with print disabilities with their readings late, this was definitely not the opinion of the librarians, equity officers and disability services personnel. These staff members were generally active and worked above and beyond what was required of them. Despite their efforts, they were working against an ableist system which seemingly accepted that students with print disabilities would have a far inferior educational experience than the wider student cohort. Consider for a moment how the university would react if a student cohort was not provided with their readings until 85 per cent of the semester was over, and yet were still expected to complete assessment items throughout the teaching period that drew from the readings not available to students. If this substandard approach were imposed on the wider student cohort, then the professor would likely be placed on review and higher management would become actively involved in ensuring the problems were addressed. The fact that no such effort has been taken to address the book famine experienced by students with print disabilities suggests either ignorance or a world-view that accepts unequal treatment for persons with disabilities.

There are a number of policy steps that universities could take that would help mitigate the impact of the book famine on their students with print disabilities. It can take weeks to source a textbook in an accessible format. If professors finalise their class lists in week one of the teaching period, then this will result in students with print disabilities receiving their textbooks late. Further, universities are major customers of textbooks. Universities can utilise their market power to pressure publishers to be more proactive in providing alternative format books to students with print disabilities. The book famine has existed for a significant period of time and university practices have not altered. It would seem that alternative means need to be found to reverse the book famine experienced by the print-disabled.

E-Libraries for the Print-Disabled

In the first half of the twenty-first century, charities and educational institutions utilised exceptions in copyright to convert standard books into formats that the print-disabled could use. This conversion process generally resulted in a digital copy of the text. While disability organisations would share files between themselves and permit authorised employees to request files, fears of copyright infringement curtailed the creation of E-Libraries that the print-disabled could access directly.[20] A notable exception to this trend was and is Bookshare.[21]

---

[20] Suzor, Harpur and Thampapillai, 'Digital Copyright and Disability Discrimination', 1.
[21] Dylan Thampapillai and Paul Harpur, 'Unlocking the Library: Copyright Access and the Disabled' (2008) 11(3) *Internet Law Bulletin* 14.

Bookshare was developed and is operated by Benetech, a leading Silicon Valley-based non-profit technology company.[22] The Bookshare E-Library originally relied upon volunteers to manually scan and edit books. In addition to volunteers, many universities and colleges upload books they provide to students to increase the E-Library through Bookshare's University Partner Program.[23] Scanning books into digital formats is a slow process. Book rippers can scan up to 500 pages per hour now.[24] Following the scanning process, the file would need to be processed through optical character recognition software and then manually edited. This process was slow and inefficient. In response, Bookshare has focused on avoiding the need to scan and edit books. Bookshare has developed working relationships with the publishing industry, and now has more than 500 partner publishers. These partner publishers provide digital copies of a selection of their works to Bookshare for distribution to people with print disabilities.[25]

Persons with print disabilities use a range of technologies to consume information through non-standard means. Bookshare provides E-Books in a range of these formats to maximise usability:

1. Bookshare Web Reader is a customised reading tool for Bookshare members which reads the content on the computer screen using a synthetic voice. This reader offers all the features of the DAISY format.

2. DAISY (Digital Accessible Information System) is one of the most popular digital book file formats used by the print-disabled. DAISY-formatted books are usable with almost all adaptive technology that reads text, such as screen readers, self-voicing synthetic-voice DAISY players, Braille note-takers, portable self-voicing DAISY Players, and scan-and-read software such as Read:OutLoud – Bookshare Edition, Kurzweil K1000 and K3000, WYNN and OpenBook.

3. BRF (Braille Refreshable Format, also referred to as Braille Ready Format) is a specialised format which is designed to operate with refreshable Braille devices (essentially, a Braille screen where the user reads using touch) and Braille embossers (braille printers).

[22] Bookshare, 'Who We Are' <www.bookshare.org/cms/about> (accessed 18 November 2016).
[23] Bookshare, 'University Partners' <www.bookshare.org/cms/partners/university-partners> (accessed 18 November 2016).
[24] Joshua L Simmons, 'Catwoman or the Kingpin: Potential Reasons Comic Book Publishers Do Not Enforce their Copyrights against Comic Book Infringers' (2010) 33 *The Columbia Journal of Law & the Arts* 267, 278–9.
[25] Bookshare, 'Publishers' <www.bookshare.org/cms/partners/publishers> (accessed 18 November 2016).

4. MP3 (Mpeg audio layer 3) provides audio only with no text. These books are created with a text-to-speech engine and spoken by Kendra, a high-quality synthetic voice from Ivona. Any device that supports MP3 playback is compatible.

5. DAISY Audio is similar to the DAISY option above; however, this option uses MP3 files created with Bookshare's text-to-speech engine that utilises Ivona's Kendra voice. This will work with DAISY Audio-compatible players such as VictorReader Stream and Read2Go.[26]

Not every title is available in each format. The capacity for Bookshare to offer the title in these formats depends on the quality of the file uploaded to Bookshare. For this reason, the Bookshare library search engine enables users to limit the quality of books returned by publisher quality: excellent, good or fair.[27] In addition, not all images and graphs are described in every E-Book. The search engine enables users to limit their search by books that contain no images or that provide descriptions of images.

The size of the Bookshare E-Library is impressive. Bookshare United States and International now have over 370,000 print-disabled members across over seventy countries. Users in the United States can access the full catalogue of over 375,000 titles. Members using Bookshare International have reduced access, as permission to access works depends on permission by publishers.[28]

Country	Number of books available
Argentina	249,000
Australia	186,000
Brazil	250,000
Canada	269,000
Denmark	245,000
France	246,000
Germany	245,000
Ghana	216,000
India	217,000
Kenya	220,000
Republic of Korea	248,000
New Zealand	187,000

(*Continued*)

[26] Bookshare, 'In Which Formats Are the Books Available?' <www.bookshare.org/cms/help-center/which-formats-are-books-available> (accessed 18 November 2016).

[27] Bookshare, 'Advanced Search' <www.bookshare.org/search> (accessed 18 November 2016).

[28] Bookshare, 'Books by Country' <www.bookshare.org/cms/get-started/how-find-books/books-country> (accessed 18 November 2016).

(*Continued*)

Country	Number of books available
Nigeria	221,000
Norway	243,000
Philippines	262,000
Qatar	245,000
South Africa	210,000
United Arab Emirates	245,000
United Kingdom	198,000[29]

A list of the E-Books available, as at January 2016, in a selection of the seventy countries where Bookshare International operates, illustrates the impact the Bookshare initiative has on combatting the book famine.

In addition to the books available on Bookshare International, other disability-specific E-Libraries with smaller collections have developed in Australia, Canada and the United Kingdom, alongside charities' traditional libraries of Braille, large-print and talking books on cassette tapes/CDs. The number of titles, however, cannot match Bookshare International. For example, Vision Australia's E-Library has over 1,000 DAISY-format E-Books, and in the UK, the Royal National Institute of Blind People Overdrive library has just over 20,000 titles.[30] Members of these E-Libraries actively use the services. The Canadian National Institute for the Blind now enables members to download books in digital formats.[31] By the end of 2015, 1,500 of the CNIB's 30,000 library members had downloaded the Direct to Player App to read E-Books.[32] During that year, 32,000 books were downloaded using the Direct to Play Service, which means, on average, each member who had downloaded the Direct to Player App downloaded 21 books over the year. Considering that there are tens of millions of book titles in the world, the list of accessible books in these

[29] Bookshare, 'Books by Country' www.bookshare.org/cms/get-started/how-find-books/books-country (accessed 18 November 2016).

[30] Royal National Institute of Blind People, 'Talking Books by Digital Download' <www.rnib.org.uk/talking-books-digital-download> (accessed 18 November 2016); Vision Australia, 'Books and Resources: Audio Books' <www.visionaustralia.org/living-with-low-vision/library/books-and-resources> (accessed 18 November 2016).

[31] Canadian National Institute for the Blind, 'Opening the Door to Reading for More than Three Million Canadians' (CNIB Library Year in Review, 2010–11, Canadian National Institute for the Blind, 2011), <www.cnib.ca/en/services/library/Documents/CNIB%20Library%20Year%20in%20Review_2010-11_EN.pdf> (accessed 18 November 2016).

[32] Canadian National Institute for the Blind, 'From Dream to Reality: CNIB Library Year in Review 2014–15' (Review, Canadian National Institute for the Blind, 2015), <www.cnib.ca/en/services/library/Documents/Library%20Year%20in%20Review-2014-2015_Eng_Accessible%20version.pdf> (accessed 18 November 2016).

disability-specific E-Libraries, while impressive and valuable, will not reverse the book famine and provide reading equality.

SECTION II PRINT-DISABLED READING IN AN AGE WHERE E-BOOKS ARE THE NORM

The previous section analysed the growth of the written word, and how persons with print disabilities were regarded as exceptions to the norm. During this period of exceptionalism, persons with print disabilities were starved of reading equality. This section analyses how the growth of mainstream E-Books and E-Libraries created the possibility of reading equality. As this new medium of reading expands and starts to replace standard books as the most common books in library catalogues, the digital nature of the books creates the possibility that adaptive technology will enable the print-disabled to access the same information, at the same time, for the same price and at the same quality as the wider public. In other words, the growth of mainstream E-Books and E-Libraries creates the possibility of reversing the book famine and enabling the print-disabled to enjoy reading equality for the first time in human history.

The Potential for Equal Access: E-Books Enter the Mainstream Market

The digital age is transforming how people consume books. While standard books remain a feature of library and personal collections, there is an increasing trend to eschew standard books in favour of E-Books. Around the start of the twenty-first century, universities started exploring the possibilities of purchasing limited numbers of E-Books.[33] The popularity of E-Books has continued to increase. In 2008, E-Book sales were about 0.6 per cent of the US market, in 2010 about 6.4 per cent, and in 2011 about 13.6 per cent.[34] Their comparative cost advantages in purchase and storage are making E-Books especially popular in the educational sector.[35] One major Australian

---

[33] W Abbott and K Kelly, 'Sooner or Later! Have E-books Turned the Page?' (Library Services and IT Services Paper, Bond University, February 2004); D Dillon, 'E-Books: The University of Texas Experience, Part 1' (2001) 19(2) *Library Hi Tech* 113; Ellen Safley, 'Demand for E-Books in an Academic Library' (2006) 45(3–4) *Journal of Library Administration* 445.

[34] Rüdiger Wischenbart et al., *The Global eBook Market* (2013) O'Reilly Media, 9.

[35] Advisory Commission on Accessible Instructional Materials in Postsecondary Education for Students with Disabilities, 'Report' (Educause, 6 December 2011) 22 <www.educause.edu/Resources/ReportoftheAdvisoryCommissiono/242996> (accessed 18 November 2016); Chris Armstrong, Louise Edwards and Ray Lonsdale, 'Virtually There? E-Books in UK Academic Libraries' (2002) 36(4) *Program* 216; Lynn Silipigni Connaway and Timothy J Dickey, 'The Digital Information Seeker: Report of Findings from Selected OCLC, RIN and JISC User Behaviour Projects' (report, OCLC, 15 February 2010) <www.oclc.org/research/themes/user-studies/dis.html> (accessed

university library, in a 2015 purchasing period, acquired twenty-six times more E-Books than print books.[36]

Whether it is for education, work or pleasure, E-Books are cheaper than standard books, and entire E-Libraries can be contained on a smart phone or E-Reader. Whereas print books are only available from the physical library, E-Books can be downloaded while a user is in their office, in a coffee shop, on the bus or while lying in bed. This makes E-Books especially attractive for people who are unable to visit a bricks-and-mortar library to obtain a standard book – due to time restraints, geographic location or disability.[37] E-Books are of course far from perfect for persons with or without disabilities. Some E-Books can be difficult to navigate or make notations on, and some people simply prefer to read paper than a screen.[38]

No Longer Just a Digital Representation of a Print Book: E-Books as a Multimedia Experience

Some E-Books mirror the content and publishing processes of standard paper books. Other E-Books utilise the potential of the digital environment. They may contain audio, images, moving images and video multimedia content, and may alter this content on a rolling basis.[39] This additional content alters the meaning and consumption practices of readers.[40] Instructional materials, for example,

18 November 2016); Pauline Dewan, 'Are Books Becoming Extinct in Academic Libraries?' (2012) 113(1) *New Library World* 27; Barbara Folb, Charles B Wessel and Leslie J Czechowski, 'Clinical and Academic Use of Electronic and Print Books: The Health Sciences Library System E-Book Study at the University of Pittsburgh' (2011) 99(3) *Journal of the Medical Library Association* 218; M Landoni and G Hanlon, 'E-Book Reading Groups: Interacting with E-Books in Public Libraries' (2007) 25(5) *The Electronic Library* 599; Silas Marques de Oliveira, 'E-Textbooks Usage by Students at Andrews University: A Study of Attitudes, Perceptions, and Behaviors' (2012) 33(8) *Library Management* 536; Magdalini Vasileiou, Richard Hartley and Jennifer Rowley, 'An Overview of the E-Book Marketplace' (2009) 33(1) *Online Information Review* 173.

[36] Paul Harpur, 'E-Books and Accessibility' (speech delivered at QUT E-Book Forum, Brisbane, 19 June 2015).

[37] Ranti Junus, 'E-Books and E-Readers for Users with Print Disabilities' (2012) 48(7) *Library Technology Reports* 22; Cathy De Rosa et al., 'Perceptions of Libraries, 2010: Context and Community' (report, OCLC, 2011) <www.oclc.org/content/dam/oclc/reports/2010perceptions/ 2010perceptions_all.pdf> (accessed 18 November 2016).

[38] Princeton University, 'The E-Reader Pilot at Princeton' (report, Princeton University, 2010) <www.princeton.edu/ereaderpilot/eReaderFinalReportLong.pdf> (accessed 18 November 2016).

[39] Michael Lesk, *Understanding Digital Libraries*, 2nd edn (2005) Morgan Kaufmann Publishers, 95 and 107; Randal C Picker, 'Online Markets vs. Traditional Markets: The Mediated Book' (2011) 19(1) *Supreme Court Economic Review* 51, 51.

[40] Peter Shillingsburg, *From Gutenberg to Google: Electronic Representations of Literary Texts* (2006) Cambridge University Press, 47–9.

often use multimedia in E-Books to enhance the learning experience.[41] The inclusion of multimedia content may create challenges for some people with print disabilities.[42] This is not to say that multimedia content is inherently disabling. The inclusion of this medium creates positive educational opportunities for people with print disabilities that are associated with learning disabilities.[43]

When Is an E-Book Accessible and Usable by the Print-Disabled?

This monograph argues that people with print disabilities should be able to access E-Books, E-Libraries and E-Readers on the same basis as the wider population. Equality of access exists when everyone in the community, regardless of their abilities, can consume the same information, at the same time, for the same price and at the same quality. This approach to access combines technical disability accessibility standards and a consideration of practical usability.

Further research, development and implementation of technical disability accessibility standards are critical to promoting internet and E-Book accessibility for persons with the full range of abilities within the community.[44] A number of technical disability accessibility standards have been developed to help determine whether an E-Book is accessible to persons with print disabilities or not. Some of these standards have been developed specifically for a regulatory scheme. An example of this is the National Instructional Materials Access Standard developed for digital files of books uploaded to the National Instructional Materials Access Center, as discussed in Chapter 11

---

[41] Mal Lee and Arthur Winzenried, *Use of Instructional Technology in Schools: Lessons to Be Learned* (2013) Australian Council for Educational Research; Craig Michaels, Fran Pollock Prezant and Kent Jackson, 'Assistive and Instructional Technology for College Students with Disabilities: A National Snapshot of Postsecondary Service Providers' (2002) 17(1) *Journal of Special Education Technology* 5.

[42] Cagatay Goncu and Kim Marriott, 'Creating E-Books with Accessible Graphics Content' (paper presented at Proceedings of the 2015 ACM Symposium on Document Engineering, Switzerland, 8–11 September 2015).

[43] Edward Blackhurst, 'Perspectives on Applications of Technology in the Field of Learning Disabilities' (2005) 28(2) *Learning Disability Quarterly* 175; D L Edyburn, 'Assistive Technology and Mild Disabilities' (2006) 8(4) *Special Education Technology Practice* 18; Michael Kennedy and Donald D Deshler, 'Literacy Instruction, Technology, and Students with Learning Disabilities: Research We Have, Research We Need' (2010) 33(4) *Learning Disability Quarterly* 289; Jacqueline Norman, Belva C Collins and John W Schuster, 'Using an Instructional Package Including Video Technology to Teach Self-Help Skills to Elementary Students with Mental Disabilities' (2001) 16(3) *Journal of Special Education Technology* 5.

[44] Peter Blanck, *E-Quality: The Struggle for Web Accessibility by Persons with Cognitive Disabilities* (2014) Cambridge University Press, ch. 7.

of this monograph. Other standards have been developed with the intention of applying them across the entire industry. The most relevant technical disability accessibility standards to this chapter include:

1. Accessibility Screening Guidelines and Checklist (developed by the DAISY Consortium in collaboration with Tech For All).[45] These disability accessibility guidelines provide clear testing and evaluating criteria to judge reading systems against.

2. Web Content Accessibility Guidelines (WCAG) 2.0.[46] While this monograph is focusing on E-Books, a person with a print disability can only access the E-Book if they can navigate the E-Library. This requires the E-Library platform to be accessible. Persons across a range of impairments, with vision, hearing and cognitive conditions, have reported problems with E-Library websites.[47] All websites, including E-Libraries, should seek to embrace universal design principles. The leading authority on ensuring that persons with disabilities can access websites, and by extension E-Libraries, is the Web Content Accessibility Guidelines. The current version of this at the time of publishing is the WCAG 2.0. These guidelines provide technical details on how to design features which maximise the usability of websites for people with blindness and low vision, deafness and hearing loss, learning disabilities, cognitive limitations, limited movement, speech disabilities, photosensitivity and combinations of these.

3. The EPUB 3.01 Standard.[48] This provides technical guidance on how digital files, including E-Books, can maximise disability access. These standards provide technical guidance on how content should be represented, packaged and encoded. Through technical design and

---

[45] DAISY Consortium and Tech For All, 'Accessibility Screening Methodology Guidelines and Checklist' <daisy.org/accessibility-screening-methodology-guidelines-and-checklist.html> (accessed 18 November 2016).

[46] Web Content Accessibility Guidelines Working Group, 'Web Content Accessibility Guidelines (WCAG) 2.0: W3C Recommendation 11 December 2008' (11 December 2008) <www.w3.org/TR/WCAG20/> (accessed 18 November 2016).

[47] C Hitchcock, 'Digital Content for Individuals with Print Disabilities' in W Preiser and K Smith (eds), *Universal Design Handbook* (2011) McGraw-Hill; William N Myhill et al., 'Distance Education Initiatives and their Early 21st Century Role in the Lives of People with Disabilities' (2007) 8(17) *Focus on Distance Education Developments* 1; Alistair McNaught, Shirley Evans and Simon Ball, 'E-Books and Inclusion: Dream Come True or Nightmare Unending?' in K Miesenberger et al. (eds), *Computers Helping People with Special Needs* (2010) Springer Berlin Heidelberg, 74.

[48] International Digital Publishing Forum, 'EPUB 3 Overview: Recommended Specification' (26 June 2014) <www.idpf.org/epub3/latest/overview> (accessed 18 November 2016).

managing digital layouts, rich media, and interactivity and global typography features, the EPUB Standard embraces universal design.

While these technical disability accessibility standards play an important role, on a more practical level what end users desire is the capacity to consume the E-Book. There are numerous examples of digital spaces complying with accessibility guidelines but being completely unusable.[49]

Equal Access Not Realised: E-Books in the Mainstream Market

To test the extent to which E-Libraries subscribed to by a major university were accessible to persons with print disabilities, the author, along with Dr Nicolas Suzor, developed a practical guide of what is required for meaningful access. The guide was created by focusing on the information that a university student or academic would need to extract from an E-Book.[50] Following discussions with academics and university graduates, the following criteria were developed:

(1) Is the text formatted so that it can be read using a screen reader?
    (a) Can a screen reader read the content of the E-Book? Security settings on some E-Books ensure content cannot be copied, but can also prevent screen readers and other adaptive technologies from enabling persons with print disabilities to consume the content of the E-Book.[51]
    (b) Is line spacing correct or are paragraphs or lines not formatted with hard returns in correct positions?
    (c) Are tables and graphics described in prose?
(2) Is it possible to navigate the E-Book?
    (a) Are contents and index pages available? If yes, do they have links that work?
    (b) Is it possible to search for keywords in the book?
    (c) Is it possible to move to particular pages in the book?

---

[49] A Newell, *Design and the Digital Divide: Insights from 40 Years in Computer Support for Older and Disabled People* (2011) Morgan & Claypool Publishers.

[50] Harpur and Suzor, 'The Paradigm Shift in Realising the Right to Read', 1658; for a similar approach see: Christina Mune and Ann Agee, 'Are E-Books for Everyone? An Evaluation of Academic E-Book Platforms' Accessibility Features' (2016) 28 *Journal of Electronic Resources Librarianship* 3, 172.

[51] George H Kerscher and Jim Fruchterman, 'The Soundproof Book: Exploration of Rights Conflict and Access to Commercial eBooks for People with Disabilities' (2002) 7 *First Monday* 6.

(3) Is the E-Book formatted to enable a user to cite according to leading citation styles?

    (a) Are there page numbers in the E-Book, and do the page numbers of the E-Book correspond to the print version?

    (b) Are the references in footnotes and reference lists accessible?

The study then applied these criteria to a random selection of E-Books on twelve E-Libraries.[52] The study found that some E-Libraries were usable, but some contained irritating barriers. The security settings on some sites required a user to respond to a visual or audio challenge, but these were extremely difficult to complete.

Once the E-Book was opened the most substantial barrier was caused by security settings that entirely prevented adaptive technology from reading the content of the E-Book. On these E-Libraries, the E-Books were entirely inaccessible to people with print disabilities. While not preventing access, the requirement to read the E-Book online page-by-page represented an extreme usability problem. On one E-Library, each page for the E-Book was under 300 words. The user was also required to navigate around approximately 1,000 words of random information to find the button to turn the page and view the footnotes. On this E-Library, two-thirds of the time spent reading was not related to book content.

While some E-Libraries permitted full-text downloads of E-Books, even on these E-Libraries access issues arose. Most E-Books had formatting problems relating to line spacing, paragraph spacing, referencing or issues with headings. Visual representations of information, such as graphs, tables or images, were poorly described or not described in most situations. Overall, the research concluded that the numbers and content of E-Books was helping to combat the book famine, but much more was required to achieve reading equality.

SECTION III CORPORATIONS AS GATE-KEEPERS TO THE BOOK FAMINE

The benefit of the internet is that anyone in the world can publish their work online. Self-publishing and not-for-profit entities publish E-Books and other material online. Despite the existence of various E-publishers, the majority of E-Books used for education, employment and, to a lesser extent, culture are

---

[52] The E-Libraries analysed included: ACLS Humanities E-Book collection, Brill E-Books, Cambridge Books Online, Ebrary, E-Book Library, EbscoHost, Elgar online, Oxford Scholarship Online, Palgrave Macmillan Connect, Sage Knowledge, SpringerLink E-Books and Wiley Online Library.

published by for-profit corporate entities. It is accordingly important to consider what, beyond legal compulsion, would motivate a for-profit corporate entity to publish E-Books in formats that are accessible to the print-disabled. This section will analyse this question by focusing on the motives of corporations. It will also consider the impact of corporate social responsibility.

How Supporting People with Disability Can Be Profitable: Handicapitalism and Increased Markets

Corporations do not have a history of devoting substantial corporate resources to moral causes.[53] Corporations have profited from slavery and colonialism, and have assisted in perpetrating genocide.[54] Overall the corporate form is associated with profit maximisation at the expense of human rights.[55] The shareholder primacy theory of the corporation provides that the primary objective of corporations is to make profits.[56] Under this model, corporations are regarded as legal entities created to generate profits for the shareholders.[57] While the shareholder primacy theory may appear extreme in its pure form, it is arguable that the theory has been gaining increasing support since the 1970s.[58]

Ignoring corporate social responsibility for the moment, is it profitable to take steps to reduce the book famine experienced by persons with disabilities? To answer this question requires a consideration of the potential profits and losses associated with a particular corporation's operations, market and legal requirements. There is growing recognition that persons with disabilities are increasingly economically active and that they represent a market worthy of

---

[53] Daniel Litvin, *Empires of Profit: Commerce, Conquest and Corporate Responsibility* (2003) Texere Publishing, 11.

[54] Edwin Black, *IBM and the Holocaust: The Strategic Alliance between Nazi Germany and America's Most Powerful Corporation* (2001) Crown Books; Anita Ramasastry, 'Corporate Complicity: From Nuremberg to Rangoon – An Examination of Forced Labor Cases and their Impact on the Liability of Multinational Corporations' (2002) 20 *Berkeley Journal of International Law* 91, 93.

[55] Ilias Bantekas, 'Corporate Social Responsibility in International Law' (2004) 22 *Boston University International Law Journal* 309, 309; Milton Friedman, 'The Social Responsibility of Business Is to Increase Profits' in Scott B Rae and Kenman L Wong (eds), *Beyond Integrity: A Judeo-Christian Approach to Business Ethics* (1996) Zondervan, 241–5.

[56] Adolf A Berle, 'For Whom Corporate Managers Are Trustees: A Note' (1932) 45 *Harvard Law Review* 1365, 1367.

[57] Friedman, 'The Social Responsibility of Business'; Lisa M Fairfax, 'The Impact of Stakeholder Rhetoric on Corporate Norms' (2006) 31 *University of Iowa Journal of Corporation Law* 675.

[58] Ronald Chen and Jon Hanson, 'The Illusion of Law: The Legitimating Schemas of Modern Policy and Corporate Law' (2004) 103 *Michigan Law Review* 1, 37.

commercial attention.[59] While persons with disabilities continue to confront considerable discrimination, there are a growing number of persons with impairments who are economically successful. It is not practical to ascertain the impact of so-called 'handicapitalism' in this chapter; it is simply worth noting that the purchasing power of the print-disabled has shifted now that some governors, politicians, professors and leading businessmen have print disabilities.[60] Beyond legal compulsion, arguably the greatest motivation for corporations to ensure disability access to their E-Libraries and E-Books is the corporate social responsibility movement.

Using Corporate Social Responsibility in the Struggle for Reading Equality: Amazon's Kindle Versus Apple's iPhone and iBooks

There is now significant social pressure on corporations to consider their wider impact on human rights and on society at large. What precisely is meant by the term 'corporate social responsibility' is likely to continue to alter as expectations on corporations are negotiated in society. There is, however, significant guidance on some key aspects of the aspirational requirement on corporations to act socially responsibly. Some of the leading authorities on what corporate social responsibility requires can be found in the United Nations Guiding Principles on Business and Human Rights, the OECD Guidelines for Multinational Enterprises, and the International Labour Organization's Tripartite Declaration of Principles Concerning Multinational Enterprises and Social Policy.[61] Complying with these ethical standards requires complying with leading human rights and labour rights conventions. The United Nations Guiding Principles on Business and Human Rights, for example, requires that companies protect, respect and remedy breaches of the *Universal Declaration of Human Rights*, the *International Covenant on Civil and Political Rights*, the *International Covenant on Economic, Social and Cultural Rights* and the core conventions of the International Labour

---

[59] Hershey Friedman, Tomas Lopez-Pumarejo and Linda W Friedman, 'The Largest Minority Group: The Disabled' (2006) University of West Georgia <www.westga.edu/~bquest/2006/dis abled.pdf> (accessed 18 November 2016); Hershey Friedman, Tomas Lopez-Pumarejo and Linda W Friedman, 'Frontiers in Multicultural Marketing: The Disabilities Market' (2007) 32(1) *Journal of International Marketing and Marketing Research* 25; Joshua Harris Prager, 'People with Disabilities Are Next Consumer Niche', *The Wall Street Journal* (online), 15 December 1999.

[60] See, e.g., Wikipedia, 'Blind Politicians' <en.wikipedia.org/wiki/Category:Blind_politicians> (accessed 18 November 2016).

[61] Jan Wouters and Anna-Luise Chané, 'Multinational Corporations in International Law' in Math Noortmann, August Reinisch and Cedric Ryngaert (eds), *Non-State Actors in International Law* (2015) Hart Publishing, 225 and 236.

Organization.[62] Corporations seeking to act socially responsibly are required to consider a large number of factors when conducting their affairs.

A publishing house would be expected to consider its employment practices, labour supply chain, impact on education, the environment and a range of other factors.[63] Ensuring persons with print disabilities can access their E-Libraries and E-Books is just one of many factors. Even within the equality space, there is arguably a hierarchy of attributes.[64] This can result in some attributes, such as gender, having more influential support. Attributes that are 'higher order' may have their interests elevated over interests that are less socially and politically promoted. Even within the disability community, there are impairment hierarchies which elevate the interests of some groups over others.[65] In such circumstances, it is possible that access for persons with print disabilities may not attract significant attention.

There is strong evidence that corporate social responsibility without some form of teeth will not result in significant social improvements.[66] Professor Martha Albertson Fineman has observed that it 'is essential to counter unfettered self-interest. Understood historically as the manifestation of public authority and the ultimate legitimate repository of coercive power, the state is the only realistic contender in that regard.'[67] The general acceptance that there is a need for state regulation can be evidenced by the fact that there are laws, and scholarly and community support for laws regulating the activities of corporate and natural persons. While the need for some interference has wide support, the nature of that support is a hotly contested issue. In the equality space, disputes could arise over who is entitled to protection, the nature of that

---

[62] John Ruggie, 'Protect, Respect and Remedy: A Framework for Business and Human Rights. Report of the Special Representative of the Secretary-General on the Issue of Human Rights and Transnational Corporations and Other Business Enterprises', Human Rights Council, 8th sess., Agenda Item 3, UN Doc. A/HRC/8/5 (7 April 2008) [58].

[63] Harpur and James, 'The Shift in Regulatory Focus', 111; Harpur, 'Clothing Manufacturing Supply Chains', 316.

[64] Government Equalities Office, 'Review of Public Sector Equality Duty: Report of the Independent Steering Group' (Government of the United Kingdom, 6 September 2013) 10, <www.gov.uk/government/groups/review-of-public-sector-equality-duty-steering-group> (accessed 18 November 2016).

[65] Mark Deal, 'Disabled People's Attitudes towards Other Impairment Groups: A Hierarchy of Impairment' (2003) 18(7) *Disability and Society* 897.

[66] Thomas McInerney, 'Putting Regulation before Responsibility: Towards Binding Norms of Corporate Social Responsibility' (2006) 40 *Cornell International Law Journal* 171, 173; Sean D Murphy, 'Essay in Honor of Oscar Schachter: Taking Multinational Corporate Codes of Conduct to the Next Level' (2005) 43 *Columbia Journal of Transnational Law* 389, 433.

[67] Martha Albertson Fineman, 'The Vulnerable Subject: Anchoring Equality in the Human Condition' (2008) 20(1) *Yale Journal of Law and Feminism* 1, 6.

protection (formal or substantive outcomes), or whether the state should curtail property interests at all.

In the absence of legal duties, it is arguable that corporate social responsibility and soft law cannot be relied upon to motivate corporations to promote digital equality.[68] The decision to embrace or ignore disability accessibility is a business choice that is not always favourable to achieving ability equality.[69] The risks of relying on soft law and self-regulation can be illustrated by the contrast between the disability access features on the Amazon and Apple E-Readers. Both Amazon and Apple have almost identical market pressures, limitations and capacity to enable persons with print disabilities to access the written word. Whereas Apple continues to promote equality, however, Amazon has made a conscious decision to prevent persons with print disabilities from full access.

Initially, the Amazon Kindle 2 came with accessibility features activated.[70] The Kindle 2 came with a text-to-speech function that would enable people who could not read standard print to read the content of the E-Books. The American Authors Guild argued that this would place pressure on the audio market and might prevent publishers expanding to cover new titles.[71] Considering the substantial difference between mainstream commercial audio books, with human actors performing and reading the book, often accompanied by sound effects, compared to E-Books in disability-accessible formats that use a text-to-speech function, which has a computerised voice, comparing the two forms of E-Books seems difficult to accept. Although many people who use screen readers purchase audio books when reading fiction, audio books are not available for many titles. The Authors Guild also raised a range of other unsubstantiated arguments. Rather than seeking alternatives, Amazon simply enabled publishing houses to shut the print-disabled out of E-Books by enabling them to turn accessibility features off.[72] This has occurred in a number of situations, and now the Kindle is not accessible for

---

[68] Margot E Kaminskiand and Shlomit Yanisky-Ravid, 'The Marrakesh Treaty for Visually Impaired Persons: Why a Treaty Was Preferable to Soft Law' (2014) 75 *University of Pittsburgh Law Review* 255, 263.

[69] Gerard Goggin and Christopher Newell, 'The Business of Digital Disability' (2007) 23(3) *The Information Society* 159.

[70] Kel Smith, *Digital Outcasts: Moving Technology Forward without Leaving People Behind* (2013) Morgan Kaufmann, ch. 4.

[71] Mary Bertlesman, 'The Fight for Accessible Formats: Technology as a Catalyst for a World Effort to Improve Accessibility Domestically' (2012) 27 *Syracuse Science and Technology Law Reporter* 26, 40.

[72] Paul Harpur, 'From Universal Exclusion to Universal Equality: Regulating Ableism in a Digital Age' (2013) 40(3) *Northern Kentucky Law Review* 529.

the print-disabled.[73] This means the Kindle should not be adopted in educational settings or other spaces where accessibility is a high priority.[74]

Apple, in contrast, has encountered the same arguments from publishing lobbyists. Unlike Amazon, Apple has continued to enable the print-disabled to read E-Books hosted on Apple iBooks.[75] The Apple iPhone comes with its own screen reader and is accessible for persons with print disabilities.[76] The iPhone Voice Over reads the content of the iPhone and will read the content of E-Books downloaded to the user's iBook account. Essentially, Apple responded to the calls to shut the print-disabled out of reading equality by refusing to partake in a digital apartheid. Publishers can decide to host their E-Books on a platform that enables the print-disabled to access those E-Books, or they can decide not to have their E-Books available on one of the world's largest E-Book platforms. Apple's approach to disability access makes it a market leader, and a leading choice to create inclusive digital environments.[77]

CONCLUSION

Equal access to the written word has been a dream for people with print disabilities for centuries. Section 1 of this chapter illustrated how the print-disabled have been unable to participate in the reading revolution throughout history. While the invention of the printing press by Gutenberg in 1450 transformed reading from the province of a very small elite to something accessible by the masses, the print-disabled entirely missed out on this

---

73 Darren Burton, 'An Evaluation of Kindle 2 and Sony Reader Digital Book Players' (2010) 11(1) *American Foundation for the Blind AccessWorld Magazine* <www.afb.org/afbpress/pub.asp?DocID=aw110104> (accessed 18 November 2016).

74 National Federation of the Blind, 'Make Kindle Ebooks Accessible' (2012) <nfb.org/kindle-books> (accessed 18 November 2016); Open Letter from National Federation of the Blind to Vanessa Leung, Carmen Fariña and Victor Calise, 13 August 2015 <nfb.org/proposed-contract-between-new-york-city-department-education-and-amazon-digital-services-inc-o> (accessed 18 November 2016).

75 Chris Danielsen, Anne Taylor and Wesley Majerus, 'Design and Public Policy Considerations for Accessible E-Book Readers' (2011) 18(1) *Interactions* 67; Stephanie L Maatta and Laurie J Bonnici, 'An Evaluation of the Functionality and Accessibility of E-Readers for Individuals with Print Disabilities' (2014) 32(4) *The Electronic Library* 493.

76 Gerard Goggin, 'Adapting the Mobile Phone: The iPhone and its Consumption' (2009) 23(2) *Continuum: Journal of Media & Cultural Studies* 231.

77 Linda Chmiliar and Carrie Anton, 'Building on What We Know: The iPad as an Assistive Technology Tool for Post-Secondary Students with Disabilities' (2015) 3 *Journal on Technology & Persons with Disabilities* 45; Kimberly Maich and Carmen Hall, 'Implementing iPads in the Inclusive Classroom Setting: Intervention in School and Clinic' (2016) 51(3) *Intervention in School and Clinic* 145.

revolution. In 1824, Braille was the first significant step to enabling blind people to access the written word. Since the advent of Braille, adaptive technologies have improved levels of access, but overall, most of the written content in the world is either not readily available, or not available to the print-disabled.

Persons with print disabilities cannot read standard print, but they can read digital books. The growth of E-Books and E-Libraries analysed in Section II demonstrated that the possibility of reading equality is now achievable. Many E-Books and E-Libraries are already reasonably accessible to persons with print disabilities. Section III demonstrated that corporations cannot be relied upon to embrace inclusive design. Although Apple iBooks are accessible and enable persons with print disabilities to read, the Amazon Kindle decided to turn accessibility features off and thus denied the print-disabled the opportunity of reading equality. Advances in technology create the possibility of reversing the book famine, and providing persons with print disabilities with the possibility of enjoying reading equality for the first time in human history. The challenge is to implement strategies to ensure that E-Books and E-Readers are accessible to persons with print disabilities.

2

Access to Information Communication Technologies, Universal Design and the New Disability Human Rights Paradigm Introduced by the *Convention on the Rights of Persons with Disabilities*

INTRODUCTION

Persons with print disabilities cannot read most of the digital and print books in the world and are said to be experiencing a book famine. This monograph argues that persons with print disabilities have a right to access the written word, and that emerging digital technologies provide the best means of redressing the book famine. This chapter will analyse international human rights law to demonstrate that persons with print disabilities have a right to access the written word in digital formats. The primary means of realising this right to read is through using information communication technologies. Information communication technologies include the means to consume E-Books and other digital content.

This chapter analyses how the United Nations *Convention on the Rights of Persons with Disabilities* (*CRPD*) has swept in a new disability human rights paradigm which transforms the rights of persons with disabilities to accessible information communication technologies.[1] This chapter is divided into three sections. The first section analyses how the *CRPD* has introduced a new disability human rights paradigm which transforms how disability is theorised. A number of theoretical models have been employed to explain disability. This chapter will analyse the three leading models used to explain disablement, and will illustrate how the *CRPD* sweeps in a new rights-based disability model. The new disability human rights model rejects the negative aspects of the medical model and advances the social model and critical studies school in order to create a new understanding of how disability should be constructed by law and society.

[1] *Convention on the Rights of Persons with Disabilities* (*CRPD*), opened for signature 30 March 2007, 2515 UNTS 3 (entered into force 3 May 2008).

The second section of this chapter will illustrate how the new disability human rights paradigm enshrines persons with disabilities with the right to read. This section will analyse the rights of persons with disabilities under the human rights frameworks at the time the CRPD was introduced, and contrast this with the new model of access. The right to read can be divided into rights pertaining to what information is available and the medium through which that information is communicated. This monograph analyses how laws can achieve substantive equality of access to information. Accordingly, the issue which is most relevant to this chapter and this monograph is how the CRPD can create a rights framework that will ensure disability-inclusive information communication technologies. Rather than focusing on retrofitting systems to render them accessible, the CRPD promotes an inclusive model that encourages states and non-state actors to adopt universal design principles.

Thirdly, this chapter will analyse how the right to access information communication technologies enables persons with disabilities to exercise their right to read when exercising their rights to education, work, freedom of expression and participation in the cultural life of the community, and recreation. While the analysis of each right illustrates the impact of the CRPD, the analysis of the right to participate in culture, and how disability rights have been elevated over intellectual property rights, demonstrates how far the CRPD has gone in creating a new disability paradigm.

SECTION I THEORISING DISABILITY

The concept of equality in the CRPD was developed after a long political and theoretical journey. Before analysing the text of the CRPD, this chapter will explain the theoretical developments which made the CRPD possible. The notions of able body, disability and impairment have never been settled and remain grounds for considerable disagreement. Irina Metzler observes that 'bodies are never just physical objects, to be described in a neutral, "scientific" way, but are objects whose understanding is determined by the intellectual culture of the day'.[2] For example, the Old Testament in the Christian Bible focused on impairment as a punishment for sin.[3] The New Testament altered this position by providing that in some cases there is a connection between sin and impairment, but in others the existence of impairment was without blame, and existed to provide an opportunity for God to perform a miracle and cure. The concept of disablement has been

---

[2] Irina Metzler, *Disability in Medieval Europe: Thinking about Physical Impairment during the High Middle Ages, c.1100–1400* (2006) Routledge, 38.

[3] Ibid.

understood throughout the ages through a range of theoretical models. Within each period there are a number of conflicting models which influence how society and laws interact with people with abilities that fall outside the notion of normality.

This section will analyse the operation of the three leading models, medical, social and critical disability studies,[4] and then analyse how the CRPD has built on these models to create a new disability human rights paradigm.

Medical Model

One of the most enduring approaches to disability is through the medical model. As the name suggests, the model focuses on the medical aspects of disability.[5] Under this approach, medical professionals create criteria to guide treatment. Part of this process involves labelling people as either able-bodied or disabled.[6] While this categorisation process is essential for identifying where treatment might be provided, this approach results in negative outcomes if it is applied to broader public policies. When applied to public policy, the medicalisation of different abilities as imperfect or lesser marks out people with disabilities for special supervision, interference and oppression. The paternalistic approach of the medical model results in persons with disabilities being outside the social contract which regulates how the state interacts with the wider population.[7]

The construction of different abilities as a problem requiring cure or treatment is associated with eugenics,[8] brutal oppression,[9] policies that regard people with disabilities as requiring charity and pity,[10] and with medical

---

[4] Leanne Dowse, Eileen Baldry and Phillip Snoyman, 'Disability Criminology: Conceptualising the Intersections of Critical Disability Studies and Critical Criminology for People with Mental Health and Cognitive Disabilities in the Criminal Justice System' (2009) 15 *Australian Journal of Human Rights* 29.

[5] Neil Rees, Simon Rice and Dominique Allen, *Australian Anti-Discrimination Law*, 2nd edn (2014) Federation Press, [6.3.2.1].

[6] Dan Goodley, *Dis/Ability Studies: Theorising Disablism and Ableism* (2014) Routledge, 4.

[7] Martha Albertson Fineman, '"Elderly" as Vulnerable: Rethinking the Nature of Individual and Societal Responsibility' (2012) 20(1) *The Elder Law Journal* 101; Martha Albertson Fineman and Anna Grear, 'Equality, Autonomy, and the Vulnerable: Subject in Law and Politics' in Martha Albertson Fineman and Anna Grear (eds), *Vulnerability: Gender in Law, Culture, and Society* (2013) Ashgate, 13.

[8] For an account in the United States see: Willie V Bryan, *The Social Perspectives and Political History of Disabilities and Rehabilitation in the United States* (2010) Charles C Thomas Publishing, 71–2; Marius Turda, *Modernism and Eugenics* (2010) Macmillan, 84–5.

[9] Ravi Malhotra, 'The Politics of the Disability Rights Movements' (2001) 7(3) *New Politics* 65.

[10] Thomas Hammarberg, 'Disability Rights: From Charity to Equality' (2011) 6 *European Human Rights Law Review* 638; Arlene Mayerson and Matthew Diller, 'The Supreme Court's

interventions that often cause minimal medical improvements but substantial harm to the lives of people with disabilities.[11] Nazi Germany took eugenics to the extreme and targeted people with disabilities for special treatment.[12] This special treatment started with the Nazi laws of 1933 which mandated the sterilisation of people with mental and physical disorders.[13] This project was expanded into 'Aktion T4'. Under the Aktion T4 project, carbon monoxide gas was first used to murder people who had disabilities. This was regarded as so successful that six 'euthanasia' killing centres were established in Germany and Austria. Aktion T4 was further expanded to involve medical professionals to select people for extermination, and soldiers who shot down patients in hospitals. Overall, 750,000 people with disabilities were murdered because of their impairment.[14]

Under the medical model approach, the policy focus is upon the personal issue of impairment, rather than attempting to critique the social processes and policies that cause disablement.[15] The limitations of the medical model are highlighted in situations where there is limited or no current means of 'curing' the impairment. Under this model, supporters argue that until medicine can 'cure' them, persons with disabilities are regarded as imperfect specimens who are unable to reach 'their human potential given their insufferable condition[s]'.[16]

Under the medical model, persons with disabilities are not discussed in terms of equality or rights, but rather they are often regarded as people who must be cured or institutionalised. This model often results in the denial of autonomy, robbing people of their privacy, sexuality and humanity.[17] Under

Nearsighted View of the ADA' in Leslie Pickering Francis and Anita Silvers et al. (eds), *Americans with Disabilities: Exploring Implications of the Law for Individuals and Institutions* (2000) Routledge, 124 (courts have reinforced the notion of people with disabilities as objects of pity and charity).

[11] Some medical interventions are defined as 'soul-destroying': Michael Oliver, 'What's So Wonderful About Walking?' (Inaugural Professorial Lecture, University of Greenwich, London, 1993) 16–17, cited in Fiona Campbell, *Frontiers of Ableism* (2009) Palgrave Macmillan, ch. 9.

[12] For an account of the inclusion of persons with disabilities in the Nazi Holocaust see: Kerstin Braun, '"Nothing About Us Without Us": The Legal Disenfranchisement of Voters with Disabilities in Germany and its Compliance with International Human Rights Standards on Disabilities' (2015) 30 *American University International Law Review* 315, 315.

[13] Nicole Rafter, *The Crime of All Crimes: Toward a Criminology of Genocide* (2016) New York University Press, 137–51.

[14] Ibid.

[15] Simi Linton, *Claiming Disability: Knowledge and Identity* (1998) New York University Press, 11.

[16] Kaley Maureen Roosen, 'From Tragedy to "Crip" to Human: The Need for Multiple Understandings of Disability in Psychotherapy' (2009) 1 *Critical Disability Discourse* 1, 2–3.

[17] Tobin Siebers, *Disability Theory* (2008) University of Michigan, 162–6.

the medical model, the cause of this oppression is the 'problem' of impairment, with the impairment being held to define people as 'abnormal, deserving of pity and care'.[18]

Social Model

During the 1980s, a new disability model emerged that focused on promoting equality and the concept of different abilities, rather than focusing on medicalised understandings of impairment.[19] This model is known as the social model. Professor Michael Oliver, one of the leading social model scholars, argues that once impairments are constructed as the cause of disablement, then this arguably reduces the social consciousness about the role society plays in disabling people who fall outside the 'normal' range of abilities.[20] Social model scholars rejected the notion that disability was caused by impairment and focused on the external sources of disablement.[21]

Instead of focusing on ability issues, social model scholars deconstructed disability discrimination to identify the actual causes of disablement.[22] So called 'strong social model' scholars use Marxist critiques to identify how capitalist structures result in people with different abilities being excluded from the means of production, and thus are turned into second-class ability citizens.[23] So-called 'non-radical social model' scholarship also turns the focus away from impairment; however, these scholars employ a non-Marxist critique.[24] To reject the problematising of functional limitations, non-radical social model scholars instead focus on disabling barriers, whether attitudinal, physical or political, without engaging in analysis of the underlying capitalist system.[25]

One limitation with the social model is its emancipatory focus on the structures of disablement. Focusing attention upon the role society has in

---

[18] Rees, Rice and Allen, *Australian Anti-Discrimination Law*, [6.3.2.1].

[19] Samuel Bagenstos, *Law and the Contradictions of the Disability Rights Movement* (2009) Yale University Press, 7–13 (describing 'the endorsement of a social rather than a medical model of disability' as 'the one position that approaches consensus within the movement').

[20] Michael Oliver, *Understanding Disability: From Theory to Practice* (1996) Palgrave Macmillan, 37.

[21] Michael Oliver, *The Politics of Disablement* (1990) Macmillan, 11.

[22] Paul Harpur, 'From Universal Exclusion to Universal Equality: Regulating Ableism in a Digital Age' (2013) 40 *Northern Kentucky Law Review* 529, 535.

[23] Vic Finkelstein, *Attitudes and Disabled People: Issues for Discussion* (1980) World Rehabilitation Fund; Oliver, *The Politics of Disablement*.

[24] Paul Harpur, 'Embracing the New Disability Rights Paradigm: The Importance of the Convention on the Rights of Persons with Disabilities' (2012) 27 *Disability and Society* 1, 1.

[25] Sandra Fredman, *Discrimination Law*, 2nd edn (2011) Oxford University Press, 171–3.

turning impairment into disability empowers people with disability and creates a more homogeneous voice.[26] Many social model scholars, however, have not engaged with the medical aspects of impairment. People who experience pain or discomfort, for example, can feel disabled by their physical state as well as by how society responds to their impairments. The rejection of the impact that medical narratives of disability have in the lives of people with disabilities was a key reason that new models, such as critical disability studies, were developed.[27]

Critical Disability Studies

Critical disability studies have developed 'across, through and with disciplines of the social sciences and humanities'.[28] Similar to social model scholars, the critical disability studies school rejects the notion that the social construct of disability is a problem requiring correction.[29] The key difference between the social model and the critical disability studies school lies in what factors are considered in determining the causes of disablement.

One interpretation of the critical disability studies school focuses on cultural and linguistic critiques. Dr Tom Shakespeare has labelled this group as the cultural disability studies school.[30] Cultural disability scholars examine the category of disability and focus on how representations of different abilities attract socially constructed meaning. For example, Professor Daniel Goodley analyses how disability becomes about discourse, not about abnormality.[31] Representations in society portray people as disabled and undesirable at one end of the spectrum, and as hyper-capable and full economic citizens at the other.[32] Professor Margrit Shildrick explores the attitudes

---

[26] Bradley A Areheart, 'When Disability Isn't "Just Right": The Entrenchment of the Medical Model of Disability and the Goldilocks Dilemma' (2008) 83 *Indiana Law Journal* 181, 186–7.

[27] Ian Hacking, *The Social Construction of What?* (1999) Harvard University Press, 14; Tom Shakespeare, *Disability Rights and Wrongs Revisited*, 2nd edn (2014) Routledge, 60.

[28] Dan Goodley, Bill Hughes and Lennard Davis, 'Introducing Disability and Social Theory' in Dan Goodley, Bill Hughes and Lennard Davis (eds), *Disability and Social Theory: New Developments and Directions* (2012) Palgrave Macmillan, 1.

[29] Tanya Titchkosky and Rod Michalko, 'The Body as the Problem of Individuality: A Phenomenological Disability Studies Approach' in Goodley, Hughes and Davis (eds), *Disability and Social Theory*, 127.

[30] Shakespeare, *Disability Rights and Wrongs Revisited*, 49–55.

[31] Dan Goodley, '"Learning Difficulties": The Social Model of Disability and Impairment: Challenging Epistemologies' (2001) 16(2) *Disability and Society* 207, 209.

[32] Dan Goodley, 'Markets, Cruel Optimism and Civil Society: Producing Dis/ability' in Goodley, *Dis/Ability Studies*, ch. 9.

of non-disabled people and the notion of able-bodiedness,[33] and Dr Fiona Campbell analyses how ableism in society manifests through the projection of 'perfect, species-typical' levels of ability.[34] A person who fails to meet those socially constructed standards of ability is constructed as disabled.

Another focus of critical disability studies is on establishing a relational understanding of disability. Theorists in the relational critical disability studies school argue that the experiences of people with disabilities can only be understood through analysing the interaction between individuals and the environment (including institutional, legal and societal factors). Dr Tom Shakespeare is one of the leading supporters of the relational critical disabilities studies school, arguing for a more 'balanced approach to cure and therapy within disability studies'.[35] This approach accepts that while society is a major factor in the construction of disability, medical factors can have a significant impact on how some people experience their impairments. For example, for a person with a wheelchair, the built environment may play a major role in constructing their disability;[36] however, for a person who has advanced Huntington's disease, their brain deterioration, loss of control over their voluntary movements and pain would be major factors in how they experience disability. Under this model, the concept of disability is recognised as 'so complex, so variable, so contingent, and so situated. It sits at the intersection of biology and society and of agency and structure.'[37] Shakespeare has proposed an interactional model that explains how 'disability is always an interaction between individual and structural factors'.[38] Shakespeare's interactional approach explains that disability is understood by medical, psychological, environmental, economic and political factors.[39] The CRPD embraces this wider understanding of disability and recognises that conceptions of disablement are influenced by both social and medical factors.[40] As will be seen in the next section, this intersectional approach to constructing disability is reflected in the duties that are placed over state signatories by the CRPD.

---

[33] Margrit Shildrick, 'Critical Disability Studies: Rethinking the Conventions for the Age of Postmodernity' in Nicholas Watson, Alan Roulstone and Carol Thomas (eds) *Routledge Handbook of Disability Studies* (2012) Routledge, 30–41.

[34] Campbell, *Frontiers of Ableism*, 5.

[35] Shakespeare, *Disability Rights and Wrongs Revisited*, 153. He refers to this approach as the 'critical realist school'.

[36] Philippa Clarke et al., 'Mobility Disability and the Urban Built Environment' (2008) 168 *American Journal of Epidemiology* 506.

[37] Tom Shakespeare and Nicholas Watson, 'The Social Model of Disability: An Outdated Ideology' (2002) 2 *Research in Social Science and Disability* 9, 28.

[38] Shakespeare, *Disability Rights and Wrongs Revisited*, 74–5.   [39] Ibid., 83.

[40] Harpur, 'Embracing the New Disability Rights Paradigm', 1.

How the Convention on the Rights of Persons with Disabilities
Has Swept in a New Disability Public Policy Paradigm

The medical, social and critical disability studies models are used to explain and justify remedial interventions. The anti-discrimination regimes analysed in Chapters 5, 6 and 7 of this monograph are heavily based upon ideas of equality drawn from the social model. This anti-discrimination approach appears in statutes across the globe.[41] In comparison to the social model, the focus is on respecting people's dignity. The indefeasibility of human rights has limited legislative support. Indeed, this paradigm has only recently been embraced by the United Nations in the CRPD and by states that have ratified the Convention.

The concept of 'equality' adopted in the CRPD can be understood through reflecting on models of disabilities. One of the limitations with the social model was that it ignored the additional needs that may arise with certain impairments.[42] The social model focused on removing physical barriers to inclusion. This resulted in advocacy to enable persons with disabilities to enter buildings through the main entrance using ramps, rather than going around the back to a tradesman's entrance by trash cans. Through enabling persons with disabilities to enter through the front door, the social model has arguably advanced the rights of many persons with disabilities. Physical access, however, will not ensure equality. Persons with disabilities may require medical support to enable them to exercise their rights.[43] The social model targeted environmental barriers, but has not promoted a holistic agenda. The disability human rights paradigm found in the CRPD, in contrast, provides that states are required to regulate for the removal of environmental barriers, as well as

---

[41] Jared D Cantor, 'Note and Comment: Defining Disabled: Exporting the ADA to Europe and the Social Model of Disability' (2009) 24 *Connecticut Journal of International Law* 399.

[42] See for discussion: Michael Ashley Stein and Penelope J S Stein, 'Symposium: Beyond Disability Civil Rights' (2008) 58 *Hastings Law Journal* 1203, 1223.

[43] Examples of some impairments which require continuous medical support are: diabetes mellitus type 1, which requires constant blood glucose testing, injections and the care of an endocrinologist; chronic airway diseases (such as asthma), and autoimmune diseases leading to chronic kidney disease which requires both dialysis and constant drug intervention; and myelomeningocele, for which most individuals will need periodic evaluations by a variety of specialists, including: orthopaedists to monitor growth and the development of bones, muscles and joints; neurosurgeons to perform surgeries at birth and manage complications associated with tethered cord and hydrocephalus; neurologists to treat and evaluate nervous system issues, such as seizure disorders; urologists to address kidney and bladder dysfunction – many will need to manage their urinary systems with a programme of catheterisation, and bowel management programmes aimed at improving elimination are also designed; ophthalmologists to evaluate and treat complications of the eyes; and orthotists to design and customise various types of assistive technology, including braces, crutches, walkers and wheelchairs to aid in mobility.

encourage proactive conduct to enable persons with disabilities to exercise their rights.

Following the trend set by the World Health Organization and the World Bank,[44] the CRPD emphasises the role society has on disabling people.[45] This position is most clearly articulated in the Preamble of the CRPD, where in paragraph (e) the CRPD '[r]ecogniz[es] that disability is an evolving concept and that disability results from the interaction between persons with impairments and attitudinal and environmental barriers that hinders their full and effective participation in society on an equal basis with others'. While similar to social model scholarship, the CRPD Preamble explains that one of the key causes of disablement is barriers in society. Overall it adopts an understanding of disablement that more closely reflects an understanding of disability found in the critical disability studies school.

The CRPD considers a wide range of factors when conceptualising disablement, including health care, habilitation and rehabilitation, poverty and economic exclusion,[46] and the impact of intersecting attributes, such as race, colour, sex, language, religion, political or other opinion, national, ethnic, indigenous or social origin, property, birth, age or other status.[47] The CRPD then takes this wide understanding of the concept of disablement and advances equality through promoting a disability human rights paradigm.[48]

The rights protected in the CRPD are comprehensive.[49] As a sweeping human rights convention, the CRPD posits an extremely broad human rights agenda.[50] The CRPD Preamble builds upon existing human rights conventions, including the *Universal Declaration of Human Rights*, the *International Covenant on Economic, Social and Cultural Rights*, the *International Covenant on Civil and Political Rights*, the *International Convention on the*

---

[44] The World Health Organization and the World Bank adopt a bio-psycho-social model of disability which acknowledges 'the negative aspects of the interaction between an individual (with a health condition) and that individual's contextual factors (environmental and personal factors)'. See World Health Organization and The World Bank, *World Report on Disability* (2011) 3.

[45] Ron McCallum and Hannah Martin, 'The CRPD and Children with Disabilities' (2013) 20 *Australian International Law Journal*, 17.

[46] CRPD, Preamble (m).   [47] Ibid., Preamble (p).

[48] Harpur, 'Embracing the New Disability Rights Paradigm', 1.

[49] Jill Stavert, 'United Nations *Convention on the Rights of Persons with Disabilities*: Possible Implications for Scotland for Persons with Mental Disorder' (2009) 49 *Scottish Human Rights Journal* 2.

[50] Janet E Lord, Deepti S Raja and Peter Blanck, 'Law and People with Disabilities' in Neil J Smelser and Paul B Baltes (eds), *International Encyclopedia of the Social and Behavioral Sciences*, 2nd edn (2015) Elsevier, 497.

Elimination of All Forms of Racial Discrimination, the *Convention on the Elimination of All Forms of Discrimination against Women,* the *Convention against Torture and Other Cruel, Inhuman or Degrading Treatment or Punishment,* the *Convention on the Rights of the Child,* and the *International Convention on the Protection of the Rights of All Migrant Workers and Members of their Families.*[51] While the CRPD can be said to build on these existing United Nations conventions, the CRPD does much more. Whereas previous United Nations human rights conventions applied to people with disabilities indirectly, the CRPD specifically targets the rights of persons with disabilities. For example, the *Universal Declaration on Human Rights* states that 'everyone' is entitled to the rights and freedoms set forth in the declaration.[52] While persons with disabilities fall within the description of 'everyone', it is significant that disabilities are not included in a list of classes in need of protection from human rights violations.[53] These generalist instruments were drafted during a period when persons with disabilities were particularly oppressed and silenced; arguably, the decision to recognise the specific needs of persons with disabilities influenced the drafting of these instruments.[54]

Prior to the CRPD, international law, while recognising the rights of persons with disabilities, viewed people with disabilities as separate but equal.[55] The CRPD approaches the equality of persons with disabilities

---

[51] *Universal Declaration of Human Rights,* GA Res 217A (III), UN GAOR, 3rd sess., 183 plen. mtg, UN Doc. A/810 (10 December 1948); *International Covenant on Civil and Political Rights,* opened for signature 16 December 1966, 999 UNTS 171 (entered into force 23 March 1976); *International Covenant on Economic, Social and Cultural Rights,* opened for signature 19 December 1966, 993 UNTS 3 (entered into force 3 January 1976); *International Convention on the Elimination of All Forms of Racial Discrimination,* opened for signature 21 December 1965, 660 UNTS 195 (entered into force 4 January 1969); *Convention of the Elimination of All Forms of Discrimination against Women,* opened for signature 18 December 1979, 1249 UNTS 13 (entered into force 3 September 1981); *Convention against Torture and Other Cruel, Inhuman or Degrading Treatment or Punishment,* opened for signature 10 December 1984, 1465 UNTS 85 (entered into force 26 June 1987); *Convention on the Rights of the Child,* opened for signature 20 November 1989, 1577 UNTS 3 (entered into force 2 September 1990); *International Convention on the Protection of the Rights of All Migrant Workers and Members of their Families,* opened for signature 18 December 1990, 2220 UNTS 3 (entered into force 1 July 2003).

[52] *Universal Declaration of Human Rights,* art. 2.

[53] The non-exhaustive list of categories requiring such attention include 'race, colour, sex, language, religion, political or other opinion, national or social origin, property, birth or other status'.

[54] Charles D Siegal, 'Fifty Years of Disability Law: The Relevance of the Universal Declaration' (1999) 5 *ILSA Journal of International and Comparative Law* 267, 269.

[55] Gerard Quinn, 'A Short Guide to the United Nations Convention on the Rights of Persons with Disabilities' (2009) 1 *European Yearbook of Disability Law* 89, 89–90.

from a fundamentally different perspective to existing legal models.[56] The CRPD promotes inclusion and equal accessibility in society as a fundamental human right, and rejects the notion that persons with disabilities should have their rights discounted due to differences in ability.[57] Under the human rights paradigm, the notion of ability equality is not a privilege, but a human right that the state must help to realise.[58] The CRPD Preamble focuses on achieving 'Equalization of Opportunities': mainstreaming disability protections for persons requiring intensive support or less support; actively involving persons with disabilities in policy developments; and recognising that action is required to redress past discrimination that has resulted in poverty.[59]

The CRPD then has introductory articles in articles 1 and 2, posits rights of universal application in articles 3–9, posits substantive rights in articles 10–30, develops implementation and monitoring schemes in articles 31–40, and explains how the CRPD should be governed in articles 41–50. The CRPD is a general human rights instrument and accordingly posits rights across the full gamut of human activities. The rights protected by the CRPD include rights to access roads, transport, information technologies and communications;[60] the right to life;[61] the right to protection and safety in situations of risk, including situations of armed conflict, humanitarian emergencies and the occurrence of natural disasters;[62] the right to equal recognition before the law and the support necessary to exercise this right;[63] the right to effective access to justice on an equal basis with others, including accommodations where required;[64] the right to liberty and security of the person;[65] the right to be free from torture or cruel, inhuman or degrading treatment or punishment;[66] the right to be free from exploitation, violence and abuse;[67] the right to respect of physical and mental integrity;[68] rights to liberty of movement, of freedom to choose residence and to a nationality;[69] the right to live in the community, with choices equal to others and to have their state implement effective and appropriate measures to facilitate full enjoyment of this right;[70] the right to personal mobility and to have state-provided support to achieve this end, including

---

[56] Rosemary Kayess and Phillip French, 'Out of Darkness into Light? Introducing the *Convention on the Rights of Persons with Disabilities*' (2008) 8 *Human Rights Law Review* 1.

[57] Anna Lawson, 'Accessibility Obligations in the UN *Convention on the Rights of Persons with Disabilities: Nyusti and Takacs v. Hungary*' (2014) 30(2) *South African Journal on Human Rights* 380.

[58] Arlene S Kanter, *The Development of Disability Rights under International Law: From Charity to Human Rights* (2015) Routledge, 31.

[59] CRPD, Preamble (f), (g), (j), (o), (p), (t) and (v).   [60] Ibid., art. 9.   [61] Ibid., art. 10.

[62] Ibid., art. 11.   [63] Ibid., art. 12.   [64] Ibid., art. 13.   [65] Ibid., art. 14.   [66] Ibid., art. 15.

[67] Ibid., art. 16.   [68] Ibid., art. 17.   [69] Ibid., art. 18.   [70] Ibid., art. 19.

provision of mobility aids and training;[71] the right to freedom of expression and opinion, including the freedom to seek, receive and impart information and ideas on an equal basis with others and through all forms of communication of their choice;[72] the right of privacy, regardless of place of residence or living arrangements;[73] the right to be free from discrimination in all matters relating to marriage, family, parenthood and relationships;[74] the right to education, including lifelong learning and accommodations to exercise this right;[75] the right to the enjoyment of the highest attainable standard of health without discrimination;[76] the right to state-sponsored comprehensive habilitation and rehabilitation services and programmes;[77] the right to work, including rights to non-discriminatory employment, provision of accommodations, state-sponsored support, support for self-employment and further education, and measures to promote the employment of persons with disabilities, return-to-work programmes and to equal remuneration;[78] the right to an adequate standard of living and social protection;[79] the right to participation in political and public life;[80] and the right to participation in cultural life, recreation, leisure and sport.[81]

The human rights agenda of the CRPD substantially transforms how international human rights laws approach people with disabilities.[82] Professors Janet Lord and Michael Stein explain that:

> The CRPD advances social rights in a way that may profoundly affect the development of emergent social rights jurisprudence and advance human rights advocacy. Its comprehensive rights catalogue allows direct invocation of social rights claims, eliminating the need to fit such claims within the framework of more established civil or political rights.[83]

---

[71] Ibid., art. 20.   [72] Ibid., art. 21.   [73] Ibid., art. 22.   [74] Ibid., art. 23.   [75] Ibid., art. 24.
[76] Ibid., art. 25.   [77] Ibid., art. 26.   [78] Ibid., art. 27.   [79] Ibid., art. 28.   [80] Ibid., art. 29.
[81] Ibid., art. 30.
[82] Heiner Bielefeldt, 'New Inspiration for the Human Rights Debate: The *Convention on the Rights of Persons with Disabilities*' (2007) 25(3) *Netherlands Quarterly of Human Rights* 397; Paul Harpur, 'Time to Be Heard: How Advocates Can Use the *Convention on the Rights of Persons with Disabilities* to Drive Change' (2011) 45(3) *Valparaiso University Law Review* 1271; Camilla Parker and Luke Clements, 'The UN *Convention on the Rights of Persons with Disabilities*: A New Right to Independent Living?' (2008) 4 *European Human Rights Law Review* 508; Nell Munro, 'Define Acceptable: How Can We Ensure that Treatment for Mental Disorder in Detention Is Consistent with the UN *Convention on the Rights of Persons with Disabilities*?' (2012) 16(6) *International Journal of Human Rights* 902; Michael Waterstone, 'The Significance of the United Nations *Convention on the Rights of Persons with Disabilities*' (2010) 33 *Loyola International and Comparative Law Review* 1.
[83] Janet E Lord and Michael Ashley Stein, 'Social Rights and the Relational Value of the Rights to Participate in Sport, Recreation, and Play' (2009) 27 *Boston University International Law Journal* 249, 251.

Professor Gerard Quinn heralds the *CRPD* as the Declaration of Independence for persons with disabilities.[84] For the first time in history, persons with disabilities are regarded by international law as full and equal citizens.[85] As an international convention, state signatories are required to comply with the provisions of the *CRPD*, such that the sweeping human rights agenda should drive domestic law and policy reforms. The *CRPD* requires states to take immediate, effective and appropriate measures:

(a) To raise awareness throughout society, including at the family level, regarding persons with disabilities, and to foster respect for the rights and dignity of persons with disabilities;

(b) To combat stereotypes, prejudices and harmful practices relating to persons with disabilities, including those based on sex and age, in all areas of life;

(c) To promote awareness of the capabilities and contributions of persons with disabilities.[86]

Effectively, the *CRPD* requires states to institute positive conduct to promote a sweeping disability rights-based agenda.[87] The interventions are not just limited to changing laws, but include wider community education and the promotion of organisations of persons with disabilities.[88]

SECTION II INTRODUCING THE RIGHT TO READ IN THE *CONVENTION ON THE RIGHTS OF PERSONS WITH DISABILITIES*

The paradigm-shifting nature of the *CRPD* can be illustrated by considering how this Convention has shifted the debate around the right to read of persons with disabilities. This chapter argues that persons with disabilities enjoyed

---

[84] Gerard Quinn, 'Closing: Next Steps – Towards a United Nations Treaty on the Rights of Persons with Disabilities' in Peter Blanck (ed.), *Disability Rights* (2005) Ashgate, 519, 541.

[85] Waterstone, 'The Significance of the UN *CRPD*', 2.   [86] *CRPD*, art. 8.

[87] Eilionóir Flynn, 'Ireland's Compliance with the *Convention on the Rights of Persons with Disabilities*: Towards a Rights-Based Approach for Legal Reform?' (2009) 31(1) *Dublin University Law Journal* 357; Piers Gooding, 'Navigating the "Flashing Amber Lights" of the Right to Legal Capacity in the United Nations *Convention on the Rights of Persons with Disabilities*: Responding to Major Concerns' (2015) 15(1) *Human Rights Law Review* 45; Kelley Johnson, 'The UN *Convention on the Rights of Persons with Disabilities*: A Framework for Ethical and Inclusive Practice?' (2013) 7(3) *Ethics and Social Welfare* 218; Janet Lord, Deepti Samant Raja and Peter Blanck, 'Beyond the Orthodoxy of Rule of Law and Justice Sector Reform: A Framework for Legal Empowerment and Innovation through the *Convention on the Rights of Persons with Disabilities*' (2013) 4 *World Bank Legal Review* 45.

[88] *CRPD*, art. 29.

a limited right to read prior to the CRPD. The continuation of the book famine suggests that, to the extent that this right exists, it has failed to provide meaningful access. The framers of the CRPD arguably recognised the need to protect persons with disabilities' right to access and consume information, and accordingly have facilitated the right to read in the Convention. While the CRPD has been said to restate rights and not create new rights,[89] the introduction of a right to access information communication technologies and a right to access cultural materials in the CRPD arguably represents a significant paradigm shift under international human rights law.

The right to read can be divided into rights pertaining to *how* people read and rights that pertain to *what* people read. In other words, one group of rights focuses on the medium by which information is transferred, and the other group focuses on creating rights to what information should be available. Where information is already in a digital format, then reading equality will be achieved where the E-Book, E-Library and E-Reader are accessible to persons with print disabilities. This chapter will now analyse how the CRPD enshrines a right to digital reading equality.

The Right to Access Using Information Communication Technologies Prior to the Convention on the Rights of Persons with Disabilities

One of the benefits of the CRPD is that it has taken existing human rights and restated them in a way that is more relevant for persons with disabilities. While this is the general position, the CRPD plays a more significant role in promoting the right to accessible information communication technologies. The CRPD has not simply restated an existing human right in a way relevant to persons with disabilities. Rather the CRPD has also clarified the existence of the underlying human right: the right to information communication technologies.

There was no right to disability-accessible information communication technologies prior to the CRPD. Scholars had argued that information rights should entitle all people to the free and unfettered right to access internet content.[90] As will be analysed below in this chapter, with limited exceptions, there was no right to access digital content.

---

[89] Paul Harpur and Richard Bales, 'ADA Amendments Issue: The Positive Impact of the *Convention on the Rights of Persons with Disabilities*: A Case Study on the South Pacific and Lessons from the U.S. Experience' (2010) 37 *Northern Kentucky Law Review* 363; Gerard Quinn, 'The United Nations *Convention on the Rights of Persons with Disabilities*: Toward a New International Politics of Disability' (2009) 15 *Texas Journal on Civil Liberties and Civil Rights* 33.

[90] J Britz et al., 'On Considering the Application of Amartya Sen's Capability Approach to an Information-Based Rights Framework' (2013) 29(2) *Information Development* 106.

There is uncertainty how the right to information communication technologies might operate outside the jurisdiction created by the CRPD. The strongest indication that there is a right pertaining to access different forms of media is sourced in the *Universal Declaration of Human Rights*. Article 19 of the *Universal Declaration of Human Rights* provides that:

> Everyone has the right to freedom of opinion and expression; this right includes freedom to hold opinions without interference and to seek, receive and impart information and ideas through any media and regardless of frontiers.

The *International Covenant on Civil and Political Rights* also reflects the right to receive information where it states that:

> Everyone shall have the right to freedom of expression; this right shall include freedom to seek, receive and impart information and ideas of all kinds, regardless of frontiers, either orally, in writing or in print, in the form of art, or through any other media of his choice.[91]

Scholars have contended that there is a 'reasonable case' that the right to media creates a right to access the internet.[92] There seems to be insufficient certainty, however, to say that the right to the internet – or, more broadly, a right to access information communication technologies – exists at the global level outside limited situations.

The use of information communication technologies enhances the flow of information and thus individuals' capacity to exercise their human rights.[93] As explored below in this chapter, access to information communication technologies is recognised as enabling people with disabilities to exercise a range of human rights, including education, work and freedom of expression. This right is also associated with enabling people without disabilities to exercise their human rights. People in isolated locations, or people who have their freedom of movement reduced, can utilise information communication technologies to identify and exercise their rights.[94] Access to the internet also operates as a vehicle to access new markets and ideas, and is associated with economic development. Indeed, the digital divide between information haves

[91] *International Covenant on Civil and Political Rights*, art. 19(2).

[92] Ivar A Hartmann, 'A Right to Free Internet? On Internet Access and Social Rights' (2013) 13 *Journal of High Technology Law* 297, 302.

[93] Frank La Rue, 'Report of the Special Rapporteur on the Promotion and Protection of the Right to Freedom of Opinion and Expression', UN GAOR, 17th sess., Agenda Item 3, UN Doc. A/HRC/17/27 (16 May 2011) [67] and [78].

[94] Geoffrey A Hoffman, 'In Search of an International Human Right to Receive Information' (2003) 25 *Loyola of Los Angeles International and Comparative Law Review* 165, 165.

and have nots is associated with a large range of civil, economic and social disparities.[95]

Some jurisdictions have recognised the role of the internet in promoting human rights and have introduced restrictions limiting interference with users' access.[96] Recognising the importance of communication technologies, article 1(3)(a) of the European Union's new Framework Directive Article explains that:

> Measures taken by Member States regarding end-users' access to or use of services and applications through electronic communications networks shall respect the fundamental rights and freedoms of natural persons … Any of these measures regarding end-users' access to or use of services and applications through electronic communications networks liable to restrict those fundamental rights or freedoms may only be imposed if they are appropriate, proportionate and necessary within a democratic society, and their implementation shall be subject to adequate procedural safeguards … including effective judicial protection and due process.[97]

Accordingly, even though the right to access information communication technologies does not have universal support by states, there is certainly growing recognition of the importance of this right.

The Convention on the Rights of Persons with Disabilities *Enshrines the Right to Access Information Communication Technologies*

Whether or not a right to information communication technologies exists within the broader international human rights regime, the CRPD has clarified the situation. Article 9 of the CRPD posits access to information communication technologies as a human right, and details state obligations to enable persons with disabilities to exercise this right.[98] The CRPD recognises that the right to access is critical for persons with disabilities to exercise their fundamental rights, including rights to social, economic and cultural equality, health, education, information and communication.[99] The right to access also requires

---

[95] Lennard G Kruger and Angele A Gilroy, 'Broadband Internet Access and the Digital Divide: Federal Assistance Programs' (CRS Report, Congressional Research Service, 17 July 2013).

[96] Brooke Menschel, 'One Web to Unite Us All: Bridging the Digital Divide' (2011) 29 *Cardozo Arts and Entertainment Law Journal* 143, 147.

[97] European Union, Directive 2009/140/EC, Article 1.3a.

[98] CRPD, art. 9. This right of access impacts on various other rights. For example, the right to participate in political public life and the right to vote found in CRPD, art. 29. See for discussion: Ron McCallum, 'Participating in Political and Public Life: A Challenge for We Persons with Sensory Disabilities' (2011) 36(2) *Alternative Law Journal* 80.

[99] CRPD, Preamble (v).

state signatories to 'ensure to persons with disabilities' equal access 'to the physical environment, to transportation, to information and communications, including information and communications technologies and systems'.[100]

Universal Design

To protect the right to access the CRPD adopts a two-pronged regulatory approach. The first prong focuses on rendering communication systems accessible at the design and manufacturing stage through the concept of 'universal design'.[101] Universal design is defined in the CRPD to mean:

> The design of products, environments, programmes and services to be usable by all people, to the greatest extent possible, without the need for adaptation or specialized design. 'Universal design' shall not exclude assistive devices for particular groups of persons with disabilities where this is needed.[102]

The importance of universal design/inclusive design can be evinced by how widely it is referred to in the CRPD. The focus on inclusive design also appears with reference to 'inclusive education',[103] workplaces that are 'open, inclusive and accessible' to persons with disabilities,[104] and ensuring that international development programmes are 'inclusive . . . and accessible'.[105]

A key concept behind universal design is the notion of universal application.[106] Universal application does not seek to satisfy every person's individual preference for consuming information. Achieving universal preference can make design and commercial sense, however this is not a target that is promoted by the CRPD. Universal design focuses on the capacity to use by the majority of people with the majority of abilities. Universal preference focuses on individual preferences (which can alter), whereas universal design focuses on design that enables everyone to use the end product, regardless of their abilities.

Universally designed products should be usable for disabled people.[107] Universal design seeks to ensure that products are usable by the entire community with as little adjustment as possible.[108] Where universal design is adopted,

---

[100] Ibid., art. 9(1).   [101] Ibid., art, 9(2)(h).   [102] Ibid., art. 2.   [103] Ibid., art. 24(1).
[104] Ibid., art. 27(1).   [105] Ibid., art. 32(1)(a).
[106] Lisa Schur, Douglas Kruse and Peter Blanck, *People with Disabilities: Sidelined or Mainstreamed?* (2013) Cambridge University Press, 13.
[107] Richard M Jackson, 'Curriculum Access for Students with Low-Incidence Disabilities: The Promise of Universal Design for Learning' (2005, updated 2011) National Center on Accessing the General Curriculum <aem.cast.org/about/publications/2005/ncac-curriculum-access-low-incidence-udl.html> (accessed 18 November 2016).
[108] Jason Scott Palmer, 'The *Convention on the Rights of Persons with Disabilities*: Will Ratification Lead to a Holistic Approach to Postsecondary Education for Persons with Disabilities?' (2013) 43 *Seton Hall Law Review* 551, 583.

many access barriers are not created in the first place, and thus the need to engage in retrofitting is reduced or eliminated. Universal design, however, does not mean universal access. The definition of 'universal design' in the CRPD acknowledges that inclusive access cannot always be provided. Under universal design, access should be provided 'to the greatest extent possible'.[109] Where universal design cannot be achieved, then the second prong becomes relevant.

Right to Reasonable Accommodation/Adjustments

The second prong to protect the right to access in the CRPD requires states to ensure that 'reasonable accommodations' are made to enable persons with disabilities to obtain access.[110] Reflecting approaches in other international conventions, the CRPD does not provide specifics on what is required to achieve access, but instead explains what parties need to do to enable access.[111] In addition to imposing obligations directly upon the state,[112] the right to receive reasonable accommodations requires non-state actors, such as telecommunication providers, employers, educators and the like, to engage in positive conduct to enable persons with disabilities to obtain access.[113]

In addition to requiring certain groups in society to make reasonable accommodations and adjustments, state actors are required to provide funding for and facilitate the development of assistive technologies.[114] Funding research and development is aimed at increasing the range of technologies that can be utilised to promote equality. Ideally, this funding targets the development of universally designed products as well as disability adaptive technologies. Overall, the duty to accommodate persons with disabilities requires states to strive for substantive equality for persons with disabilities.[115]

[109] *CRPD*, art. 2.
[110] Reasonable accommodation is used in the definition of disability discrimination in *CRPD*, art. 2; to promote equality and non-discrimination in *CRPD*, art. 5(3); to ensure the liberty and security of the person in *CRPD*, art. 14(2); to ensure the right to education in *CRPD* art. 24(2) and (5); and to exercise the right to work in *CRPD* art. 27(1)(i).
[111] Nadina Foggetti, 'E-Accessibility Standards Definition in the UN *Convention on the Rights of Persons with Disabilities*: Current Issues and Future Perspectives' (2012) 18(2) *Computer and Telecommunications Law Review* 56.
[112] Anna Lawson, 'Disability Equality, Reasonable Accommodation and the Avoidance of Ill-Treatment in Places of Detention: The Role of Supranational Monitoring and Inspection Bodies' (2012) 16(6) *International Journal of Human Rights* 845.
[113] Kanter, *The Development of Disability Rights under International Law*, 47.
[114] Johan Borga, Stig Larssona and Per-Olof Östergrena, 'The Right to Assistive Technology: For Whom, for What, and by Whom?' (2011) 26(2) *Disability and Society* 151.
[115] Rebecca Brown and Janet Lord, 'The Role of Reasonable Accommodation in Securing Substantive Equality for Persons with Disabilities: The UN *Convention on the Rights of Persons with Disabilities*' in Marcia H Rioux, Lee Ann Basser and Melinda Jones (eds),

SECTION III ANALYSING HOW THE RIGHT TO READ IMPACTS ON RIGHTS IN THE *CONVENTION ON THE RIGHTS OF PERSONS WITH DISABILITIES*

To clarify how the right to read is operationalised, this chapter will now analyse how the right to read will alter the legal regulation of information flows in education, work and public affairs. Prior to the CRPD there was no clear statement that persons with disabilities were entitled to inclusive educational and work environments.[116] When these rights to inclusive environments are combined with the right of access, this arguably creates a new paradigm that promotes access to information and reading equality.

This section also analyses situations where the CRPD introduces more substantial reforms to how public policy models approach the right to read. The right to information is limited to situations where persons with disabilities seek, receive and impart information and ideas to exercise their freedom of expression and opinion. While the rights of freedom of expression and participation have long been accepted, prior to the CRPD persons with disabilities had limited recognition of their right of access. Finally, this section will analyse how the CRPD operationalises the right to cultural materials. How the CRPD articulates the right to access cultural materials is especially transformational, as it places copyright interests behind the right to access of persons with disabilities.

Operationalising the Right to Access in Promoting Inclusive Education

While states have duties to provide access to instructional materials under anti-discrimination laws, as well as under novel legal regimes,[117] and possibly under state constitutions,[118] prior to the CRPD there was no specific international human rights law that persons with disabilities could rely upon. The lack of clear guidance on what the right to education required from states encouraged some to question the extent of state responsibility in educating people with disabilities.[119]

Critical Perspectives on Human Rights and Disability Law (2011) Martinus Nijhoff Publishers, ch. 10.

[116] Arlene Kanter, Michelle Damiani and Beth Ferri, 'The Right to Inclusive Education under International Law: Following Italy's Lead' (2014) 17(1) *Journal of International Special Needs Education* 21.

[117] See especially discussion in Chapters 8 and 11.

[118] See for example the Supreme Court of Africa, which held in *Minister of Basic Education v. Basic Education for All* (20793/2014) [2015] ZASCA 198 (2 December 2015) that the right to education in article 29 of the South African Constitution creates a requirement that each learner must be provided with a textbook for each subject before commencement of the academic year.

[119] John-Stewart Gordon, 'Is Inclusive Education a Human Right?' (2013) 41 *Journal of Law, Medicine and Ethics* 754.

The *International Covenant on Economic, Social and Cultural Rights* and the *Universal Declaration on Human Rights* recognised that people have a right to education, but did not consider the right of people with disabilities to exercise this right.[120] Indeed, it is telling that people with disabilities did not even feature as a target category worthy of special attention in the *International Covenant on Economic, Social and Cultural Rights*. Article 13 of the *International Covenant on Economic, Social and Cultural Rights* grants everyone a right 'to education' that shall promote 'understanding, tolerance and friendship among all nations and all racial, ethnic or religious groups, and further the activities of the United Nations for the maintenance of peace'.

The United Nations specifically considered the rights of young people with disabilities by adopting the *Convention on the Rights of the Child*.[121] The *Convention on the Rights of the Child* recognises the right of all children to an education.[122] This has been interpreted to apply to children with disabilities.[123] More relevantly for this discussion, the *Convention on the Rights of the Child* requires states to provide assistance, whenever possible, to disabled children and their families.[124] This assistance should 'ensure that the disabled child has effective access to and receives education ... in a manner conducive to the child's achieving the fullest possible social integration and individual development'.[125]

Subsequent to the *Convention on the Rights of the Child*, the Salamanca Statement and Framework for Action on Special Needs Education proclaimed the right of every child to an education in 'regular schools'.[126] Similarly, the *Standard Rules on the Equalization of Opportunities for Persons with Disabilities* encouraged states to educate children with disabilities in mainstream schools.[127]

---

[120] *Universal Declaration of Human Rights*, art. 26; *International Covenant on Economic, Social and Cultural Rights*, art. 23.

[121] Vanessa Torres Hernandez, 'Making Good on the Promise of International Law: The *Convention on the Rights of Persons with Disabilities* and Inclusive Education in China and India' (2008) 17 *Pacific Rim Law and Policy Journal* 497, 502.

[122] *Convention on the Rights of the Child*, art. 28.

[123] Gerard Quinn and Theresia Degener, 'Building Bridges from "Soft Law" to "Hard Law": The Relevance of the United Nations Human Rights Instruments to Disability' in Gerard Quinn and Theresia Degener (eds), *Human Rights and Disability: The Current Use and Future Potential of United Nations Human Rights Instruments in the Context of Disability* (2002) United Nations, 47.

[124] *Convention on the Rights of the Child*, art. 23.   [125] Ibid.

[126] UNESCO and Ministry of Education and Science Spain, *The Salamanca Statement and Framework for Action on Special Needs Education* (1994) UNESCO, iii–iv.

[127] *Standard Rules on the Equalization of Opportunities for Persons with Disabilities*, GA Res 48/96, UN GAOR, 48th sess., Agenda Item 109, UN Doc. A/RES/48/96 (20 December 1993) Rule 6.

The CRPD specifically recognises the rights of persons with disabilities to inclusive lifelong education.[128] At a minimum, the right of inclusive education includes the right not to be segregated and to enjoy the same educational opportunities and support as students without disabilities.[129] The CRPD goes further than this notion of equality. The CRPD explains that this inclusive education system must be 'without discrimination and on the basis of equal opportunity'.[130] Simply providing an inclusive educational experience is not enough. The CRPD explains that the educational experience must be a 'quality' educational experience, with quality being judged against the experiences of students without disabilities.[131]

The notion of what constitutes an inclusive educational environment reflects the principles discussed above on the right to access. Persons with disabilities are granted the right to demand that their education is delivered through 'alternative modes, means and formats of communication'.[132] The right to education in the CRPD is accordingly a powerful right, as it entitles persons with disabilities to be educated and specifies that educational materials must be delivered through accessible modes of communication.

To comply with the right to education in the CRPD, states should first seek to remove all barriers to full and equal education through adopting universal design.[133] In relation to promoting universal design in education, the CRPD explains that, where possible, the education system should not create any environmental barriers to full inclusion.[134] Where barriers to full inclusion are created, the CRPD requires states to ensure that reasonable accommodations are made so that people with disabilities can exercise their right to education.[135] This includes providing the 'support required, within the general education system, to facilitate ... effective education'.[136] Relevantly for the book famine, it is impossible to study without access to instructional materials and, accordingly, article 24 of the CRPD requires that states facilitate access to such materials for students with disabilities.

Article 24 of the CRPD represents a paradigm shift in how states and educators approach students with disabilities. Under existing anti-discrimination laws, analysed primarily in Chapters 6, 7 and 8 of this

---

[128] Ravi Malhotra and Robin F Hansen, 'United Nations *Convention on the Rights of Persons with Disabilities* and its Implications for the Equality Rights of Canadians with Disabilities: The Case of Education' (2011) 29 *Windsor Yearbook of Access to Justice* 73.

[129] Vernor Muñoz, 'The Right to Education of Persons with Disabilities: Report of the Special Rapporteur on the Right to Education', UN GAOR, 4th sess., Agenda Item 2, UN Doc. A/HCR/4/29 (19 February 2007) 6.

[130] *CRPD*, art. 24(1).   [131] Ibid., art. 24(2)(b).   [132] Ibid., art. 24(3)(a).

[133] Palmer, 'Will Ratification Lead to a Holistic Approach to Postsecondary Education?', 556.

[134] *CRPD*, art. 24(2)(d).   [135] Ibid., art. 24(2)(c).   [136] Ibid., art. 24(2)(d).

monograph, duties on educators are generally enlivened once a person with a disability has approached the institution, demonstrated they have a disability and explained the accommodation they require. Article 24 of the *CRPD* adopts a significantly different approach. Under article 24, states and educators are required to proactively seek out and remove environmental barriers by universally designing the educational experience. At a minimum, this would include taking steps to ensure procurement processes do not result in the acquisition of instructional materials that do not embrace inclusive design principles.

Operationalising the Right to Access in Promoting Inclusive Workplaces

The capacity to access and consume digital content is equally important to persons with disabilities when they complete their education and enter the workforce. Prior to the *CRPD*, international human rights laws failed to provide persons with disabilities with any meaningful protection at work. The capacity to exercise the right to work is connected with the capacity to exercise social and economic rights. Simply put, a person without work is unable to participate in the economy.[137] More broadly, Professor Philip Alston claims that if economic rights are not realised, people will be denied many of the rights in the *Universal Declaration of Human Rights*.[138]

The right to work has wide acceptance by states,[139] and under international human rights laws notionally includes persons with disabilities. Despite this formal protection, this right has often not translated into substantive enjoyment of the right to work.[140] The right to work in the *Universal Declaration of Human Rights* provides that:

[137] Rhoda E Howard and Jack Donnelly, 'Human Dignity, Human Rights, and Political Regimes' (1986) 40(3) *American Political Science Review* 817.

[138] Philip Alston, 'Making Economic and Social Rights Count: A Strategy for the Future' (1997) 68(2) *Political Quarterly* 188.

[139] Aleah Borghard, 'Free Trade, Economic Rights, and Displaced Workers: It Works If You Work' (2006) 32 *Brooklyn Journal of International Law* 161, 183.

[140] Jody Hemann, Michael Ashley Stein and Gonzalo Morena, 'Disability, Employment and Inclusion Worldwide' in Jody Hemann, Michael Ashley Stein and Gonzalo Morena (eds), *Disability and Equity at Work* (2014) Oxford University Press, ch. 1; Samuel R Bagenstos, 'Has the *Americans with Disabilities Act* Reduced Employment for People with Disabilities? The Decline in Employment of People with Disabilities: A Policy Puzzle' (2004) 25 *Berkeley Journal of Employment and Labor Law* 527; Paul Dan Goodley and Ghashem Norouzi, 'Enabling Futures for People with Learning Difficulties? Exploring the Employment Realities behind the Policy Rhetoric' in Alan Roulstone and Colin Barnes(eds), *Working Futures* (2005) Policy Press, 219; Nicole B Porter, 'Reasonable Burdens: Resolving the Conflict between Disabled Employees and their "Coworkers"' (2007) 34 *Florida State University Law Review* 313.

Everyone has the right to work, to free choice of employment, to just and favourable conditions of work and to protection against unemployment.[141]

Article 6(1) of the *International Covenant on Economic, Social and Cultural Rights* provides clear support for article 23 of the *Universal Declaration of Human Rights* through the following provision:

> The States Parties to the present covenant recognize the right to work, which includes the right of everyone to the opportunity to gain his living by work which he freely chooses or accepts, and will take appropriate steps to safeguard this right.

The difficulty for persons with disabilities with the rights to work posited in the *Universal Declaration of Human Rights* and the *International Covenant on Economic, Social and Cultural Rights* is that it is unclear precisely what states need to do to discharge these rights. The phrase 'just and favourable conditions of work' could include the right to fair pay,[142] the right to not be unemployed,[143] the right to use work to alleviate poverty,[144] the right to employment for immigrants,[145] and the right to decent work for people with disabilities.[146] The right to work, therefore, could be said to contain a number of sub-rights. The challenge under the pre-*CRPD* human rights regime was defining precisely which sub-rights applied and how all these rights were to be implemented. In the absence of certainty, it was arguably possible to adopt an approach that maximised or minimised the capacity of persons with disabilities to exercise their right to work.

---

[141] Despite being a declaration, the *Universal Declaration of Human Rights* has such wide acceptance by nations that it has been contended that most rights in the *Universal Declaration of Human Rights* constitute customary law. See Scott L Porter, 'The *Universal Declaration of Human Rights*: Does It Have Enough Force of Law to Hold "States" Party to the War in Bosnia–Herzegovina Legally Accountable in the International Court of Justice?' (1995) 3 *Tulsa Journal of Comparative and International law* 141; Penelope Mathew, 'Human Rights' in Sam Blay, Ryszard Piotrowicz and Martin Tsamenyi (eds), *Public International Law: An Australian Perspective*, 2nd edn (2005) Oxford University Press, 268–9.

[142] Sally Cowling, William F Mitchell and Martin J Watts, 'The Right to Work Versus the Right to Income' (2006) 2(1) *International Journal of Environment, Workplace and Employment* 89; Philip Harvey, 'The Right to Work and Basic Income Guarantees: Competing or Complementary Goals?' (2004) 2 *Rutgers Journal of Law and Urban Policy* 4.

[143] John Burgess and William Mitchell, 'Unemployment, Human Rights and a Full Employment Policy in Australia' (1998) 2 *Australian Journal of Human Rights* 76.

[144] Nsongurua J Udombana 'Social Rights Are Human Rights: Actualizing the Rights to Work and Social Security in Africa' (2006) 39 *Cornell International Law Journal* 181.

[145] Borghard, 'Free Trade, Economic Rights, and Displaced Workers', 183.

[146] Arthur O'Reilly, 'The Right to Decent Work of Persons with Disabilities' (Working Paper No. 14, International Labour Organization, 2003).

Prior to the *CRPD*, states could construe a worker with a disability through various understandings, including as defective and in need of cure (medical model), disabled by society generally (social model), or as a full person disabled by internal and external causes (critical disability studies). International instruments provided very little guidance on how to realise this right. Considering the *Universal Declaration of Human Rights* and the *International Covenant on Economic, Social and Cultural Rights* were posited in the 1940s, when the medical model was the governing paradigm, it is not surprising that it took most of the twentieth century to implement workplace disability discrimination laws. It was not until the social model gained traction that states began to take concrete steps to provide workplace protections. In the United States, for example, the *Rehabilitation Act of 1973*[147] and the *Americans with Disabilities Act of 1990*[148] were not enacted until well after the adoption of the international bill of rights.

The uncertainty about what the right to work means for persons with disabilities has been substantially redressed by the *CRPD*. Unlike the earlier human rights conventions, the *CRPD* is a human rights convention that deals specifically with the issues concerning persons with disabilities. Accordingly, article 27 of the *CRPD* provides significant detail on what states must do to ensure that persons with disabilities can enjoy their right to work. Article 27(1) provides that:

1. States Parties recognize the right of persons with disabilities to work, on an equal basis with others; this includes the right to the opportunity to gain a living by work freely chosen or accepted in a labour market and work environment that is open, inclusive and accessible to persons with disabilities. States Parties shall safeguard and promote the realization of the right to work, including for those who acquire a disability during the course of employment, by taking appropriate steps, including through legislation, to, inter alia:
    (a) Prohibit discrimination on the basis of disability with regard to all matters concerning all forms of employment, including conditions of recruitment, hiring and employment, continuance of employment, career advancement and safe and healthy working conditions;
    (b) Protect the rights of persons with disabilities, on an equal basis with others, to just and favourable conditions of work, including equal opportunities and equal remuneration for work of equal value, safe and healthy working conditions, including protection from harassment, and the redress of grievances;

[147] 29 USC § 701–794.   [148] 42 USC §§12101–12117.

(c)   Ensure that persons with disabilities are able to exercise their labour and trade union rights on an equal basis with others;

(d)   Enable persons with disabilities to have effective access to general technical and vocational guidance programmes, placement services and vocational and continuing training;

(e)   Promote employment opportunities and career advancement for persons with disabilities in the labour market, as well as assistance in finding, obtaining, maintaining and returning to employment;

(f)   Promote opportunities for self-employment, entrepreneurship, the development of cooperatives and starting one's own business;

(g)   Employ persons with disabilities in the public sector;

(h)   Promote the employment of persons with disabilities in the private sector through appropriate policies and measures, which may include affirmative action programmes, incentives and other measures;

(i)   Ensure that reasonable accommodation is provided to persons with disabilities in the workplace;

(j)   Promote the acquisition by persons with disabilities of work experience in the open labour market;

(k)   Promote vocational and professional rehabilitation, job retention and return-to-work programmes for persons with disabilities.

Article 27 expressly provides that states have positive and negative obligations to ensure the right to work of persons with disabilities. Article 27, however, does not create a right to access information communication technologies at work. There is an obligation to create work environments that are 'open, inclusive and accessible to persons with disabilities', but this right does not go as far as the right to education in the CRPD. The right to education guarantees people with disabilities that they will be able to access education, and that this will be provided in modes of communication that are accessible. The right to work, in contrast, provides that people with disabilities will be free to seek work and, except for employment in the public service, the CRPD does not guarantee employment.

Rebecca Brown and Janet Lord note that 'affirmative steps must be taken beyond the guarantee of formal legal equality to move toward equality in fact'.[149] The assessment of reasonable accommodations under the CRPD differs substantially from the assessment of reasonable accommodations and adjustments under anti-discrimination laws (discussed later in Chapter 8 of this monograph). The assessment of reasonable accommodations under anti-discrimination laws focuses on what it is reasonable to expect of an employer

---

[149] Brown and Lord, 'The Role of Reasonable Accommodation in Securing Substantive Equality', ch. 10.

to help a worker with a disability. The reasonable accommodation assessment under the CRPD does not ask what it is reasonable to expect from an individual employer. The CRPD imposes the duty on the state to ensure that reasonable accommodations are made for all workers with disabilities in that state. To achieve this end, CRPD article 27(1) explains that 'States Parties shall safeguard and promote the realization of the right to work'. Accordingly, when considering what reasonable accommodations are under article 27, the question is whether it is reasonable to expect the state to ensure that a particular accommodation is made in workplaces. Whereas it might be unreasonable to require some employers to use information communication technologies that are accessible to persons with disabilities, it is far more reasonable to expect the state to mandate that, where possible, all information communication technologies used in workplaces adopt universal design principles. While this would be reasonable to expect from states, the Committee on the Rights of Persons with Disabilities has not made a ruling to this effect. Nevertheless the Committee has noted that in other areas (such as banking) there is a high expectation that services will be fully accessible.[150]

The Committee has ruled that anti-discrimination laws that qualify the employers' duty with a reasonableness test are compliant with the CRPD.[151] In *Jungelin v. Sweden*, a worker was precluded from employment as their employer's computer system was not accessible to persons with disabilities. The Swedish courts held that in the circumstances the employer's refusal to make accommodations was reasonable. The Committee on the Rights of Persons with Disabilities held that the Swedish laws were not in violation of article 27 of the CRPD.[152]

Operationalising the Right of Access by Creating a Right to Information for Freedom of Expression

The right to obtain information on public interest matters and impart this information is regarded as a cornerstone of democracy.[153] Publicity and

---

[150] *Nyusti and Takács v. Hungary*, Communication 1/2010, views adopted by the Committee on the Rights of Persons with Disabilities at its 9th Session, UN Doc. CRPD/C/9/D/1/2010 (21 June 2013).

[151] *Jungelin v. Sweden*, Communication No. 5/2011, views adopted by the Committee on the Rights of Persons with Disabilities at its 12th Session, UN Doc. CRPD/C/12/D/5/2011 (14 November 2014).

[152] Ibid.

[153] James Madison explained in 1822: 'A popular Government, without popular information, or the means of acquiring it, is but a Prologue to a Farce or a Tragedy; or, perhaps both. Knowledge will forever govern ignorance: and a people who mean to be their own Governors, must arm themselves with the power which knowledge gives.' See Gaillard Hunt (ed.), *The Writings of James Madison* (1910) Putnam's Sons, 103.

transparency are means to promote democracy and to combat corruption.[154] People cannot hold political representatives accountable unless citizens are informed and can freely debate public issues.[155] The right of expression can be observed through the rights associated with free speech,[156] to obtain information on public affairs,[157] and to be protected for making public interest disclosures.[158] Accordingly, the right of freedom of expression can be regarded as a core civil and political right.[159]

The right to freedom of expression strongly correlates with the right to information. The right to access information has been linked with the right to express public opinions in many human rights instruments. This link can be observed from the above discussion on the right to access information communication technologies, where article 19 in both the *Universal Declaration of Human Rights* and the *International Covenant on Civil and Political Rights* include the right to impart and receive information in the same clause. The right to access information related to expression of opinion in accessible formats is an area where the *CRPD* imposes significant obligations on states.

The *CRPD* requires states to ensure that political discourse is accessible to persons with disabilities. Article 21 of the *CRPD* requires that member states

> shall take all appropriate measures to ensure that persons with disabilities can exercise the right to freedom of expression and opinion, including the freedom to seek, receive and impart information and ideas on an equal basis with others and through all forms of communication of their choice.

Article 21(1) expressly references the definition of 'communication' in article 2 of the *CRPD*. Article 2 defines communication widely, to include

> languages, display of text, Braille, tactile communication, large print, accessible multimedia as well as written, audio, plain-language, human-reader and

---

[154] Louis Brandeis, *Other People's Money and How the Bankers Use It* (1914) 92.

[155] Paul Finn, 'Public Trust and Public Accountability' (1994) 3 *Griffith Law Review* 224.

[156] See for discussion Michael Curtis, *Free Speech, 'The People's Darling Privilege': Struggles for Freedom of Expression in American History* (2000) Duke University Press.

[157] For a discussion of how the right to information/freedom of information has become a recognised right see Roy Peled and Yoram Rabin, 'The Constitutional Right to Information' (2011) 42 *Columbia Human Rights Law Review* 357.

[158] A J Brown and M Donkin, 'Introduction' in A J Brown (ed.), *Whistleblowing in the Australian Public Sector* (2008) Australian National University E-Press, 11; Paul Latimer and A J Brown, 'Whistleblower Laws: International Best Practice' (2008) 31 *University of New South Wales Law Journal* 766; Sarah Wood Borak, 'The Legacy of "Deep Throat": The Disclosure Process of the Whistleblower Protection Act Amendments of 1994 and the No Fear Act of 2002' (2005) 59 *University of Miami Law Review* 617.

[159] Braun, '"Nothing About Us Without Us"', 319.

augmentative and alternative modes, means and formats of communication, including accessible information and communication technology.

To enable persons with disabilities to exercise their right to freedom of expression and opinion requires:

(a) providing information intended for the general public to persons with disabilities in accessible formats and technologies appropriate to different kinds of disabilities in a timely manner and without additional cost;

(b) accepting and facilitating the use of sign languages, Braille, augmentative and alternative communication, and all other accessible means, modes and formats of communication of their choice by persons with disabilities in official interactions;

(c) urging private entities that provide services to the general public, including through the Internet, to provide information and services in accessible and usable formats for persons with disabilities;

(d) encouraging the mass media, including providers of information through the Internet, to make their services accessible to persons with disabilities.

The considerable impact of article 21 of the *CRPD* is somewhat diluted by its requirement only to '[urge] private entities'[160] and '[encourage] the mass media'[161] to make information and services available in accessible formats. Regardless of these qualifications, article 21 arguably reflects the vital role that accessible public discourse plays in maintaining democracy and highlights the detrimental effect the book famine is having upon persons with disabilities, including their capacity to exercise their right to freedom of expression and opinion.

Operationalising the Right to Access Cultural Materials over Intellectual Property Interests: A Paradigm-Shifting Development

The paradigm shift introduced by the *CRPD* is most apparent when analysing the right of persons with disabilities to exercise their right to participate in cultural life, recreation, leisure and sport. Generally, international human rights laws have strongly supported intellectual property interests such as copyright. The *International Covenant on Economic, Social and Cultural Rights*, for example, recognises that all people have a right to take part in cultural life and to enjoy the benefits of scientific progress and its applications.[162] Under this Convention, the right of people to access scientific, literary or artistic production is limited by a right of individuals 'to benefit from the protection of the moral and material interests resulting from' creating such

---

[160] *CRPD*, art. 21(c).   [161] Ibid., art. 21(d).

[162] *International Covenant on Economic, Social and Cultural Rights*, art. 15(1)(a) and (b).

works. Arguably, article 15 of the *International Covenant on Economic, Social and Cultural Rights* creates a tension between access to artistic, cultural and scientific works and the right of people to restrict access for exploitative purposes. Article 15 illustrates how human rights laws accepted the notion that rights-holders should be entitled to set the terms on which people could exercise their right to access cultural materials.

The CRPD adopts a transformational approach to the interaction between intellectual property and the human rights of persons with disabilities. Article 30 of the CRPD directly addresses the right to participate in culture, recreation and leisure. Article 30(1) entitles persons with disabilities to 'take part on an equal basis with others in cultural life', and requires that member states 'shall take all appropriate measures to ensure that persons with disabilities . . . [e]njoy access to cultural materials in accessible formats'.[163] 'Cultural material' is defined widely in CRPD article 30(1) to include literature, artefacts, radio, screen and television productions, performance and visual arts.[164] The wide concept of 'culture' can be illustrated by analysing scholarship on this right in other conventions. The 2009 General Comment on 'the right to take part in cultural life', issued by the United Nations Committee on Economic, Social and Cultural Rights, provided a very wide definition of 'culture':

> [Culture] encompasses, inter alia ways of life, language, oral and written literature, music and song, non-verbal communication, religion or belief systems, rites and ceremonies, sport and games, methods of production or technology, natural and man-made environment, food, clothing and shelter, the arts, customs and traditions, through which individuals, groups of individuals and communities express their humanity and the meaning they give to their existence, and build their world view representing their encounter with the external forces affecting their lives.[165]

Culture is not static and develops as society and technology change.[166] Anthropologists and cultural studies scholars explain that a society's culture

---

[163] CRPD, art. 30(1).

[164] The concept of cultural material is broadly defined in a range of international agreements. For example: *Convention for the Safeguarding of Intangible Cultural Heritage*, opened for signature 17 October 2003, 2368 UNTS 3 (entered into force 20 April 2006); *Hague Convention for the Protection of Cultural Property in the Event of Armed Conflict*, opened for signature 14 May 1954, 249 UNTS 3511 (entered into force 7 August 1956).

[165] UN Economic and Social Council, Committee on Economic, Social and Cultural Rights, *General Comment No. 21: Right of Everyone to Take Part in Cultural Life (art. 15, para. 1 (a), of the International Covenant on Economic, Social and Cultural Rights)*, UN Doc. E/C.12/G (21 December 2009) 13.

[166] Lea Shaver and Caterina Sganga, 'The Right to Take Part in Cultural Life: On Copyright and Human Rights' (2010) 27 *Wisconsin International Law Journal* 637, 644.

is made up of all human endeavours, including art, music, scholarship, education, work, philosophies, religion, family and social structures.[167] Even if cultural materials are read narrowly, the obligation on states to provide persons with disabilities with access to cultural materials will require significant efforts to achieve the substantive equality envisaged by the *CRPD*.

The duty in the *CRPD* to provide persons with disabilities with access to cultural material can create the situation where copyright interests may be impacted. Providing persons with disabilities with access to artistic works, film, science and books will almost certainly require dealing with copyright-protected materials in ways that the copyright owner may resist. Article 30(3) specifically considers how the potential conflicts between access to culture and intellectual property should be resolved. The article addresses the manner in which member states balance the potential conflict with intellectual property:

> States Parties shall take all appropriate steps, in accordance with international law, to ensure that laws protecting intellectual property rights do not constitute an unreasonable or discriminatory barrier to access by persons with disabilities to cultural materials.

In this way, the *CRPD* continues and further entrenches access to cultural materials as a human right in international law, as first codified in article 15 of the *International Covenant on Economic, Social and Cultural Rights*.

The term 'intellectual property' incorporates a range of laws which restrict the use of information and ideas. These intellectual property laws include copyright, trademarks, patents, industrial design rights, trade dress and trade secrets.[168] The primary legal doctrine that is relevant for this monograph is the law of copyright. Copyright entitles rights-holders, often creators, to restrict the use of information they own the rights in, such as books or computer software programs. Other intellectual property doctrines include patent law, which protects inventions and certain discoveries, trademark law, which protects words and symbols used for identification, trade-secret law, which protects commercially valuable information, and the right of publicity, which protects the profile of certain people in society. Each of these informational goods has their own market and unique characteristics.[169]

---

[167] Clifford Geertz was a key figure in establishing the interpretivist approach to culture. See Clifford Geertz, *The Interpretation of Cultures: Selected Essays* (1973) Basic Books.

[168] William Fisher, 'Theories of Intellectual Property' in Stephen R Munzer (ed.), *New Essays in the Legal and Political Theory of Property* (2001) Cambridge University Press, 168; Brad Sherman and Alain Pottage, 'On the Prehistory of Intellectual Property' in Helena Howe (ed.), *Concepts of Property in Intellectual Property Law* (2013) Cambridge University Press, 11.

[169] Niva Elkin-Koren and Eli M Salzberger, *The Law and Economics of Intellectual Property in the Digital Age* (2013) Routledge, 41.

During the sessions of the Ad Hoc Committee on a Comprehensive and Integral International Convention on the Protection and Promotion of the Rights and Dignity of Persons with Disabilities, the wording of article 30(3) was discussed. During the sixth session, a proposal to replace 'intellectual property rights' with 'copyright' received strong support, but there was no general agreement.[170] Accordingly, the scope of *CRPD* article 30(3) includes the interaction between disability and copyright, but the use of the term 'intellectual property' means that this provision has much wider application.

Article 30 of the *CRPD* imposes a strong positive obligation on member states to ensure that persons with disabilities enjoy access to culture and knowledge on an equal basis, including to material protected by copyright.[171] Article 30, in particular, is an extremely important provision that provides for a potential paradigm shift in the balance between intellectual property and disability rights. For many years, the *Berne Convention* and other related agreements (discussed in Chapter 3) have marked the minimum standard of copyright protection. Copyright industry groups have vehemently opposed suggestions that international treaties should require a maximum limit to the strength of copyright. But this is exactly what the *CRPD* requires. The *CRPD* provides that copyright can exist up to the point at which it creates a conflict with the access of persons with disabilities to cultural material. In effect, this creates a 'ceiling' on international intellectual property law in the context of disability access rights.[172]

CONCLUSION

This chapter has analysed the new disability human rights paradigm introduced by the *CRPD*. The *CRPD* has swept in a new disability rights-based agenda that transforms the right of persons with disabilities to read. This chapter commenced by analysing how the disability human rights paradigm advances theoretical models used to explain disability. The operation of the

---

[170] UN General Assembly, *Report of the Ad Hoc Committee on a Comprehensive and Integral International Convention on the Protection and Promotion of the Rights and Dignity of Persons with Disabilities on its Sixth Session*, 60th sess., UN Doc. A/60/266 (17 August 2005) 139.

[171] Archbishop Silvano Tomasi, the Vatican's permanent observer to UN agencies, has cited both the *CRPD* and Blessed John Paul II's encyclical *Laborem Exercens* to support calls for copyright reforms to address the book famine. See Clare Myers, 'Blind People Are Suffering from "Book Famine", Says Vatican Official', *Catholic Herald* (online), 21 June 2013 <www.catholicherald.co.uk/news/2013/06/21/blind-people-are-suffering-from-book-famine-says-vatican-un-envoy/> (accessed 18 November 2016).

[172] Henning Grosse Ruse-Khan, 'Time for a Paradigm Shift – Exploring Maximum Standards in International Intellectual Property Protection' (2009) 1 *Trade, Law and Development* 56, 62.

medical model, social model, and some of the leading approaches within the critical disability studies school were examined. This chapter then illustrated how the CRPD has introduced a model that advances a holistic human rights and access to information understanding of disability generally in line with the critical disability studies school, in particular the interactional model.

The second section of this chapter analysed how the disability human rights paradigm transforms the right to read of persons with disabilities. This section commenced by analysing the impact of the right to access information communication technologies in the CRPD. The right to control how information is provided in society has the potential to promote the adoption of universal design, and to substantially reduce barriers of disablement in society. Finally, this chapter analysed how this right to access information communication technologies advances the right to read of persons with disabilities when exercising their rights to education, work, and freedom of expression and participation in culture. The significance of the new human rights paradigm was most apparent in this chapter when analysing how article 30(3) of the CRPD shifted the balance between intellectual property interests and the right of persons with disabilities to participate in culture. As will be illustrated in the next three chapters of this monograph, in most situations copyright laws largely trump human rights and access to information. The shifting of the balance between access and copyright in the CRPD to elevate disability access over intellectual property interests is ground-breaking, and reflects the significance of the new disability human rights paradigm.

3

The Weakening of the Exception Paradigm: The World
Intellectual Property Organization Changes Path with
the *Marrakesh Treaty to Facilitate Access to Published
Works for Persons Who Are Blind, Visually Impaired,
or Otherwise Print Disabled*

INTRODUCTION

The United Nations *Convention on the Rights of Persons with Disabilities*
(*CRPD*) has created a new disability politics which has been sweeping the
world.[1] The *CRPD* and the disability human rights paradigm have been
credited with influencing a significant shift in international copyright laws.
The previous chapter analysed the impact of the *CRPD* and introduced the
significance of article 30(3) on altering how international law balances the
human rights of persons with disabilities with the copyright interests of rights-
holders. This chapter continues the analysis of how international developments are transforming the balance between the human rights of persons with
disabilities and information monopolies associated with copyright.

This chapter first argues that international copyright law reluctantly adopts
an exception approach to persons with disabilities. Well over a century before
the United Nations was considering whether persons with disabilities should
enjoy the protection of a specialised human rights convention, the international community had enshrined the notion that copyright interests should
be protected. Later, in 1967, the World Intellectual Property Organization
(WIPO) was formed as a specialised United Nations agency, with the objectives of promoting creative activities by enabling copyright holders to exclusively exploit such works.[2] Copyright protections were extended over all
creative works which restricted the flow of information. The international
copyright system was later amended to tolerate persons with print disabilities

[1] *Convention on the Rights of Persons with Disabilities*, opened for signature 30 March 2007, 2515
UNTS 3 (entered into force 3 May 2008).
[2] *Convention Establishing the World Intellectual Property Organization*, opened for signature
14 July 1967, 828 UNTS 5 (entered into force 26 April 1970), Preamble.

using restricted information by alternate means. The application of these exceptions was extremely limited, and their application in domestic laws will be analysed in Chapters 4 and 5 of this monograph.

The previous chapter analysed how the CRPD has introduced a new paradigm that alters the balance between intellectual property and the rights of persons with disabilities. Following the adoption of the CRPD, disability rights advocates have been successful in lobbying for a further substantial shift in how international copyright approaches persons with print disabilities. This chapter argues that the adoption of the *Treaty to Facilitate Access to Published Works for Persons Who Are Blind, Visually Impaired, or Otherwise Print Disabled (Marrakesh Treaty)* represents a significant shift in how WIPO and international copyright law approach persons with print disabilities.[3] This chapter further argues that the *Marrakesh Treaty* represents a significant step in moving international copyright laws from exceptionalism towards inclusion.

International copyright law generally strikes a balance that favours the right to exploit creative works over the rights of people to exercise their human rights. The *Marrakesh Treaty* is significant as it shifts the balance slightly in favour of persons with disabilities who seek to exercise their human rights. While this shift falls far short of ensuring equality, disability rights advocates were able to secure the adoption of the *Marrakesh Treaty* in the face of sustained and well-organised opposition by extremely powerful groups in society. This chapter will now critically analyse the *Marrakesh Treaty* and consider how it can be used legally and politically to advance the human right to read.

SECTION I COPYRIGHT UNDER THE *BERNE CONVENTION*: FACILITATING THE PERPETUATION OF DISABLING BARRIERS AND CONSTRUCTING DISABILITY ACCESS AS A LIMITED EXCEPTION

Under the *Berne Convention for the Protection of Literary and Artistic Works (Berne Convention)* international copyright law establishes the notion that people who create works or purchase the rights to such works have the exclusive right to exploit how their work is used.[4] This legal power to restrict the use of information is called copyright.

---

[3] *Marrakesh Treaty to Facilitate Access to Published Works for Persons Who Are Blind, Visually Impaired, or Otherwise Print Disabled*, opened for signature 28 June 2013, WIPO Doc. VIP/DC/8 (not yet in force).

[4] *Berne Convention for the Protection of Literary and Artistic Works*, opened for signature 9 September 1886, 1161 UNTS 30 (entered into force 5 December 1887).

Copyright interests are not human rights; rather they are economic interests that exist for a limited purpose.[5] The economic interest referred to as copyright can conflict with the operation of inalienable human rights. Perhaps the most well-known critique of the intellectual property regime surrounds the conflict between rights to make copies of works and rights to health and life. Through restricting access to use of patented drugs, millions of people have had their rights to health and life denied to them.[6] Lobbyists advocating for rights-holders, in this situation primarily pharmaceutical companies, argue that companies will only invest in research if there is the capacity to exercise an exclusive right of exploitation.[7] Critics have observed that the state funds much of the research and that pharmaceutical companies are making billions of dollars while people are unable to access essential health care.[8] The harm caused by the existence of copyright means it is extremely important to analyse the justification for creating a right of exclusive exploitation in the first place.

This section will now analyse how the international copyright regime, established by the *Berne Convention*, limits the right to read of persons with disabilities. First, this section will analyse the policy motives that justify the formation of a regime that distorts the market to create information monop- olies. The second section will analyse how this regime restricts the consump- tion of information by constructing a right to deal exclusively with works. Later concepts of copyright reluctantly recognised that this regime may result in substantial social harm. Accordingly, the *Berne Convention* approach to copyright was slightly modified to tolerate an extremely narrow and tightly regulated exception to the exclusive right of exploitation. This section will also analyse the operation of this exception to the prevailing approach of copyright to prevent unauthorised use of works.

---

[5] United Nations Economic and Social Council, Committee on Economic, Social and Cultural Rights, *General Comment No. 20: Non-Discrimination in Economic, Social and Cultural Rights (art. 2, para. 2, of the International Covenant on Economic, Social and Cultural Rights)*, UN Doc. E/C.12/GC/20 (2 July 2009) 2.

[6] Lawrence Helfer, 'Toward a Human Rights Framework for Intellectual Property' (2007) 40 *UC Davis Law Review* 971, 1017–18; Office of the High Commissioner for Human Rights, *UN Commission on Human Rights Sub-Commission on the Promotion and Protection of Human Rights, Intellectual Property Rights and Human Rights Resolution* 2000/7, 52nd sess., 25th mtg, UN Doc. E/CN.4.Sub.2/Res/2000/7 (17 August 2000), Preamble, [1].

[7] Silvia Salazar, 'Intellectual Property and the Right to Health', WIPO-UNHCR/IP/PNL/98/3 (28 October 1998).

[8] Jamie Crook, 'Balancing Intellectual Property Protection with the Human Right to Health' (2005) 23 *Berkeley Journal of International Law* 524, 525; Ping Xiong, *An International Law Perspective on the Protection of Human Rights in the TRIPS Agreement: An Interpretation of the TRIPS Agreement in Relation to the Right to Health* (2009) Martinus Nijhoff Publishers, 1–7.

What Is the Social Construct Called Copyright?

Copyright has been developed to serve particular social purposes. The application of these different theoretical paradigms can create challenges for regulators attempting to balance economic and rights-based interests.[9] In his seminal work on copyright, Professor William Fisher analyses the four primary theories justifying copyright, being:

1. Utilitarianism
2. Labour theory
3. Personality theory
4. Social planning theory.[10]

1. **Utilitarianism copyright theory** primarily builds on the economic theories of Professor William Landes and Justice Richard Posner.[11] Landes and Posner employ economic efficiency arguments for intellectual propertisation. These scholars argue that, once created and expressed, most intellectual property rights are non-excludable and are easily replicated. The costs associated with replication are substantially cheaper than the costs associated with creation and production. This creates a commercial risk that the creators of intellectual property will not be able to recoup their costs in creating the work unless they retain the exclusive right to exploit their creation. If there is no financial benefit in creating intellectual property, then creators will arguably be deterred from investing in creating new works. This model operates on the basis that creators are not motivated by reasons unrelated to the right to exploit, such as a personal desire to create art, the desire to act altruistically, an attempt to attract prestige, or a desire to obtain or advance a career which does not depend on royalties. To ensure that profit-driven creators are not deterred from creating works, Landes and Posner argue that intellectual property interests must be protected.[12]

2. **Labour copyright theory** builds on the basis of property rights postulated by John Locke.[13] Labour copyright theorists argue that a person creates an

---

[9] Julie Cohen, 'Creativity and Culture in Copyright Theory' (2007) 40 *University of California Davis Law Review* 1151, 1155.

[10] William Fisher, 'Theories of Intellectual Property' in Stephen R Munzer (ed.), *New Essays in the Legal and Political Theory of Property* (2001) Cambridge University Press, 168.

[11] William Landes and Richard Posner, 'An Economic Analysis of Copyright Law' (1989) 18(2) *Journal of Legal Studies* 325.

[12] William Landes and Richard Posner, *The Economic Structure of Intellectual Property Law* (2003) Harvard University Press, 11–36.

[13] John Locke, *Two Treatises of Government* (1970) Cambridge University Press, Second Treatise, section 27.

intellectual property interest when they labour on interests that are either unknown or held in common.[14] According to this theory, without the efforts of the creator, the valuable interest would not have been known or invented.[15] The fruits of the creator's labours are valuable only because they have exerted their labour, and accordingly the creator should have their labour recognised and protected.[16]

3. **Personality copyright theory** refers loosely to the concepts developed by Wilhelm Hegel and Immanuel Kant.[17] Personality theory justifies the existence of copyright on the basis that a person 'must not be alienated from the work that she or he has produced, as that work is an expression of self and to separate it from its creator is to detract from the creator's personhood'.[18] This conclusion is based upon the premise that private property interests are essential for the satisfaction of certain human needs.[19] Under this theory, protecting intellectual property interests is essential, as it protects a creator's will to create, and supports a regulatory framework that encourages innovation.[20]

4. **Social planning copyright theory** focuses on how copyright laws can foster the advancement of a vibrant, democratic, just and attractive culture.[21] Under this model, copyright exists as a limited proprietary interest which is used by the state to achieve wider social objectives.[22] Copyright is only justified where granting exclusive exploitation rights will guide market forces to achieve the intended social objectives. Copyright can assist social planning through two primary interventions.[23] First, copyright can encourage creative production and expression. Second, through maintaining a structure which

---

[14] Peter Drahos, *A Philosophy of Intellectual Property* (1996) Ashgate, 41–72.

[15] Adam D Moore, *Intellectual Property and Information Control: Philosophic Foundations and Contemporary Issues* (2004) Transaction, 103–19.

[16] Justin Hughes, 'The Philosophy of Intellectual Property' (1988) 77 *Georgetown Law Journal* 287, 299–330.

[17] Margaret Jane Radin, *Reinterpreting Property* (1993) University of Chicago Press; Jeremy Waldron, *The Right to Private Property* (1998) Clarendon; Alan Brudner, 'Hegel and the Crisis of Private Law' (1989) 10 *Cardozo Law Review* 949; Edward J Damich, 'The Right of Personality: A Common-Law Basis for the Protection of the Moral Rights of Authors' (1988) 23 *Georgia Law Review* 1, 1.

[18] Alexandra George, *Constructing Intellectual Property* (2012) Cambridge University Press, 343.

[19] Hughes, 'The Philosophy of Intellectual Property', 330–50.

[20] Radin, *Reinterpreting Property*; Waldron, *The Right to Private Property*.

[21] William Fisher, 'Reconstructing the Fair Use Doctrine' (1988) 101 *Harvard Law Review* 1659, 1744–94.

[22] Neil Weinstock Netanel, 'Copyright and a Democratic Civil Society' (1996) 106(2) *Yale Law Journal* 283.

[23] George, *Constructing Intellectual Property*, 347.

protects copyright interests, copyright laws can facilitate the operation of an independent sector for the funding, development and dissemination of works. According to social planning theory, laws should only protect copyright interests where they do not hinder critical discourse or detract from wider social objectives.[24]

Out of these four theoretical perspectives, arguably only the social planning theory includes any noteworthy consideration of the potential conflict between copyright and human rights. The other theories rely upon speculative economic arguments to justify protecting an exclusive right to exploit works. Essentially, the social planning perspective argues that copyright regimes should operate in a way that protects the interests of both the powerful and the vulnerable in society. The other copyright theories essentially argue that protecting the right of exclusive exploitation in itself will result in wider benefits. This provides rights-holders with greater protections, as it reduces pressures to consider the wider implications of maintaining their right of exclusive exploitation.

The Berne Convention: *Limited Access through the Three-Step Test*

With the intention of protecting their own financial interests, in 1878 a group of authors called the Association Littéraire et Artistique Internationale passed five resolutions, which in 1886 became the *Berne Convention*.[25] Throughout the *Berne Convention*'s five revisions, the focus has primarily been on vehicles to increase rights-holders' capacity to exploit their works. As a consequence of this focus, 'the scope of authors' rights has increased markedly'.[26]

From the adoption of the *Berne Convention*, the right of authors was paramount. Creative works are automatically in force upon their creation without being asserted or declared. An author need not 'register' or 'apply for' a copyright in every jurisdiction. The *Berne Convention* provides that authors of works have an exclusive right to reproduce, translate and create derivative works.[27]

The primacy of copyright is reinforced by a sense of crisis in copyright created by the spectre of cheap copying and new communication technologies.[28] This

---

[24] Neil Weinstock Netanel, 'Asserting Copyright's Democratic Principles in the Global Arena' (1998) 51 *Vanderbilt Law Review* 217.

[25] Peter Burger, 'The *Berne Convention*: Its History and its Key Role in the Future' (1998) 3 *Journal of Law and Technology* 1, 5.

[26] Ibid.   [27] *Berne Convention*, art. 9(1).

[28] Julie E. Cohen, 'Pervasively Distributed Copyright Enforcement' (2006) 95 *Georgetown Law Journal* 1.

perceived crisis has resulted in a one-way ratcheting of copyright law towards greater protection[29] and has, to date, arguably inhibited more ambitious action by governments worldwide to address the book famine. The general approach of the *Berne Convention* places no duties on people to make accessible copies, but places restrictions on people trying to make the written word available to those with print disabilities.

In its original manifestation, the *Berne Convention* did not permit any variation of a work without express permission from the rights-holder. The 1967 revision of the *Berne Convention* in Stockholm introduced a new provision in article 9(2) which has become known as the 'Three-Step Test', or 'the Berne Three-Step Test'.[30] The Three-Step Test contains an exception to the general position that a person cannot deal with a work without obtaining permission from the rights-holder.[31] The Three-Step Test constructs non-standard uses of copyright works as exceptions and permits such uses where three factors are met:

(1) there is a 'certain special case' or use;
(2) that does not 'conflict with a normal exploitation of a work'; and
(3) that does not 'unreasonably prejudice the legitimate interests of the author'.

Following its adoption in the Stockholm amendment to the *Berne Convention*, the Three-Step Test has been adopted in every subsequent copyright treaty,[32] most notably in the *Agreement on the Trade-Related Aspects of Intellectual Property Rights*,[33] the *Marrakesh Agreement Establishing the World Trade Organization*,[34] the *WIPO Copyright Treaty of 1996*,[35] and the

---

[29] Jessica Litman, *Digital Copyright* (2006) Prometheus Books, 80; Diane Leenheer Zimmerman, 'Adrift in the Digital Millennium Copyright Act: The Sequel' (2000) 26 *University of Dayton Law Review* 279, 289–90; Rochell Cooper Dreyfuss, 'TRIPS – Round II: Should Users Strike Back?' (2004) 71 *University of Chicago Law Review* 21, 22; Raymond Shih Ray Ku, Jiayang Sun and Yiying Fan, 'Does Copyright Law Promote Creativity? An Empirical Analysis of Copyright's Bounty' (2009) 62 *Vanderbilt Law Review* 1669, 1681.

[30] Christophe Geiger, Daniel Gervais and Martin Senftleben, 'The Three-Step Test Revisited: How to Use the Test's Flexibility in National Copyright Law' (2014) 29 *American University International Law Review* 583, 583.

[31] Bashar H Malkawi, 'A Long "TRIP" Home: How the Berne Convention, TRIPS Agreement, and Other Instruments Complement the International Copyright System' (2013) 35(2) *European Intellectual Property Review* 93, 94.

[32] Aaron Scheinwald, 'Who Could Possibly Be against a Treaty for the Blind?' (2012) 22 *Fordham Intellectual Property, Media and Entertainment Law Journal* 445, 463.

[33] *Marrakesh Agreement Establishing the World Trade Organization*, opened for signature 15 April 1994, 1867 UNTS 3 (entered into force 1 January 1995), Annex 1C (*Agreement on Trade-Related Aspects of Intellectual Property Rights*) art. 1.

[34] *Marrakesh Agreement Establishing the World Trade Organization*.

[35] *WIPO Copyright Treaty*, opened for signature 20 December 1996, WIPO Doc. WO/033/EN (entered into force 6 March 2002) art. 10.

WIPO Performances and Phonograms Treaty of 1996.[36] The Three-Step Test also appears in some free trade agreements which bind Australia,[37] Canada[38] and the United Kingdom,[39] and in almost every United States free trade agreement.[40]

[36] *WIPO Performances and Phonograms Treaty of 1996*, opened for signature 20 December 1996, WIPO Doc. WO/034/EN (entered into force 6 March 2002) art. 16.

[37] The following agreements include the Three-Step Test: *Australia–United States Free Trade Agreement*, Australia–United States, signed 18 May 2004, [2005] ATS 1 (entered into force 1 January 2005) art. 17.4(10); *Japan–Australia Economic Partnership Agreement*, Australia–Japan, signed 8 July 2014, [2015] ATS 2 (entered into force 15 January 2015) art. 16.12(4); *Korea–Australia Free Trade Agreement*, Australia–Korea, signed 8 April 2014, [2014] ATS 43 (entered into force 12 December 2014), art. 13.15(13); *Malaysia–Australia Free Trade Agreement*, Australia–Malaysia, signed 22 May 2012, [2013] ATS 4 (entered into force 1 January 2013) art. 13.12. The Three-Step Test is not included in the intellectual property chapters in the *China–Australia Free Trade Agreement*, Australia–China, signed 17 June 2015, [2015] ATS 15 (entered into force 20 December 2015); or in the *Singapore–Australia Free Trade Agreement*, Australia–Singapore, signed 17 February 2003, [2003] ATS 16 (entered into force 28 July 2003).

[38] The Three-Step Test is included in the *North American Free Trade Agreement*, United States–Mexico–Canada, signed 17 December 1992, 32 ILS 612 (entered into force 1 January 1994) art. 17.05(5). The *Free Trade Agreement between the Government of Canada and the Government of the State of Israel*, Canada–Israel, signed 31 July 1996, CTS 1997/49 (entered into force 1 January 1997) mentions intellectual property in article 9.1; however, there is no mention of the Three-Step Test. No intellectual property chapters appear in the free trade agreements between Canada and Chile, Costa Rica, Columbia, Jordan, Panama or Peru.

[39] A version of the Three-Step Test appears in *Directive 2001/29/EC of the European Parliament and Council* [2001] OJ L 167/10, art. 5(3)(b).

[40] The following agreements includes the Three-Step Test: *United States–Chile Free Trade Agreement*, United States–Chile, signed 6 June 2003, KAV 6375 (entered into force 1 January 2004) art. 17.7(3); *Colombia–United States of America Free Trade Agreement*, Colombia–United States, signed 22 November 2006, KAV (entered into force 15 May 2012) art. 16.7(8); *The Dominican Republic–Central America–United States Free Trade Agreement*, signed 5 August 2004, KAV 7868 (entered into force 1 January 2009) art. 15.4(10); *Panama–United States of America Trade Promotion Agreement*, Panama–United States, signed 28 June 2007, KAV 9546 (entered into force 31 October 2012) art. 15.5(10); *Peru–United States Trade Promotion Agreement*, Peru–United States, signed 12 April 2006, KAV 9736 (entered into force 1 February 2009) art. 16.7(8); *Bahrain–United States of America Free Trade Agreement*, Bahrain–United States, signed 14 September 2004, KAV 7824 (entered into force 1 August 2006) art. 14.4(10); *Jordan–United States Free Trade Agreement*, Jordan–United States, signed 24 October 2000, KAV 5970 (entered into force 17 December 2001) art. 4(16); *Morocco–United States of America Free Trade Agreement*, Morocco–United States, signed 15 June 2004, KAV 7206 (entered into force 1 September 2004) art. 15.5(11); *Oman–United States of America Free Trade Agreement*, Oman–United States, signed 19 January 2006, KAV 8673 (entered into force 1 January 2009) art. 15.4(9); *United States of America–Republic of Korea Free Trade Agreement*, Republic of Korea–United States, signed 4 December 2010, KAV (entered into force 15 March 2012) art. 18.1(11); *United States–Singapore Free Trade Agreement*, United States–Singapore, signed 6 May 2003, KAV 6376 (entered into force 1 January 2004) art. 16.4(10). The *United States of America–Israel Free Trade Agreement*, United States–Israel, signed 22 April 1985, KAV 7204 (entered into force 19 August 1985) does not include the Three-Step Test, but article 14 reaffirms each state's obligations under existing international copyright laws, which includes the Three-Step Test.

Limits and exceptions to broad copyright interests are highly restrained.[41] Reflecting this approach, the Three-Step Test represents a limited exception to the general monopoly of copyright owners. The first step of the cumulative Three-Step Test permits exceptions only 'in certain special cases'.[42] Analogous provisions have been interpreted extremely narrowly, with one judgment explaining the exception is 'a narrow exception – one which makes only a small diminution of the rights in question',[43] and with a panel of legal experts concluding that the exception or limitation 'should be clearly defined and should be narrow in its scope and reach'.[44] Commenting on the first requirement of the Three-Step Test, Andrew Christie and Robin Wright concluded that 'it can be seen that every embodiment of the first step imposes the condition of "narrowness"'.[45] This framework, by permitting only limited and narrowly tailored exceptions to copyright, subjugates any social measures designed to enhance access rights against the interests of copyright holders.[46]

Within the narrow exception in the Berne Three-Step Test there is arguably a significant degree of flexibility that is not widely utilised by states. The Three-Step Test does not clearly prohibit nation states from taking measures such as enabling the establishment of accessible repositories. Small, accessible repositories exist in many countries, discussed further in Chapters 1, 5 and 11 of this monograph, and there is no reason to believe that encouraging the growth of these repositories or establishing new, public ones would contravene obligations under the *Berne Convention*. There is no question that persons with print disabilities constitute a 'special case' under the first limb of the Three-Step Test.[47] This limb of the test requires that the exception is 'clearly defined and

---

[41] See Henning Grosse Ruse-Khan, 'Time for a Paradigm Shift: Exploring Maximum Standards in International Intellectual Property Protection' (2009) 1 *Trade, Law and Development* 56.

[42] *Berne Convention*, art. 9(2).

[43] World Trade Organization, 'Canada – Patent Protection of Pharmaceutical Products', WTO Doc. WT/DS114/R (17 March 2000) [4.37(c)(i)], [7.45] <www.wto.org/english/tratop_e/dispu_e/7428d.pdf> (accessed 18 November 2016).

[44] World Trade Organization, *United States – Section 110(5) of the US Copyright Act*, WTO Doc. WT/DS160/R (15 June 2000) [6.112] <www.wto.org/english/tratop_e/dispu_e/1234da.pdf> (accessed 18 November 2016).

[45] Andrew F Christie and Robin Wright, 'A Comparative Analysis of the Three-Step Tests in International Treaties' (2014) 45(4) *International Review of Intellectual Property and Competition Law* 409, 411.

[46] Ruse-Khan, 'Time for a Paradigm Shift'.

[47] See Martin Senftleben, *Copyright, Limitations, and the Three-Step Test: An Analysis of the Three-Step Test in International and EC Copyright Law* (2004) Kluwer Law International, 139.

narrow in its scope and reach'.[48] Redressing the inequitable levels of access of persons with print disabilities arguably fulfils both these criteria.[49]

The second limb of the Three-Step Test analyses whether the potential use would interfere with the core licensing market of the copyright owner. Here, the test 'refers simply to the ways in which an author might reasonably be expected to exploit [their] work in the normal course of events'.[50] It has been contended that conflict with normal exploitation only occurs where 'the authors are deprived of an actual or potential market of considerable economic and practical importance',[51] which involves substantial gains.[52] Under this approach, the concept of normal exploitation would only extend to the main avenues of exploitation of the work, and not to exploitations that the rights-holder never had any intention of making.[53]

The third step in the Three-Step Test requires balancing any harm caused to authors by the proposed exception against the benefit that it would provide to people with a print disability. Some level of harm will be permissible; the term 'unreasonably prejudice' involves a proportional balancing between the interests of people with disabilities and copyright owners.[54] Similarly, the term 'legitimate interests' implies 'a normative claim calling for protection of interests that are "justifiable" in the sense that they are supported by relevant public policies or other social norms'.[55] The main issue here is whether copyright owners should be compensated for uses of their works by people with disabilities, even if these uses do not fall within their core licensing markets. Under the third step there is room for states to consider whether rights-holders should be entitled to prevent access or to be compensated for the provision of access to persons with print disabilities.[56]

---

[48] Sam Ricketson and Jane C Ginsburg, *International Copyright and Neighbouring Rights: The Berne Convention and Beyond* (2006) Oxford University Press, [13.11].

[49] Ibid. [13.37] (listing exceptions for people with disabilities as an example of 'exceptions that might be justified' under the Berne Three-Step Test).

[50] Sam Ricketson, *The Berne Convention for the Protection of Literary and Artistic Works: 1886–1986* (1987) Centre for Commercial Law Studies, Queen Mary College, Kluwer, 483.

[51] Senftleben, *Copyright, Limitations, and the Three-Step Test*, 193.

[52] Andre Lucas, 'For a Reasonable Interpretation of the Three-Step Test' (2010) 32 *European Intellectual Property Review* 277, 277.

[53] Jonathan Griffiths, 'The "Three-Step Test" in European Copyright Law: Problems and Solutions' (2009) *Intellectual Property Quarterly* 428, 457.

[54] Ricketson and Ginsburg, *International Copyright and Neighbouring Rights*, [13.26].

[55] World Trade Organization, *Canada – Patent Protection of Pharmaceutical Products* [7.69].

[56] See Robin Wright, 'The "Three-Step Test" and the Wider Public Interest: Towards a More Inclusive Interpretation' (2009) 12 *The Journal of World Intellectual Property* 600, 611–12; Martin Senftleben, 'Towards a Horizontal Standard for Limiting Intellectual Property Rights? WTO Panel Reports Shed Light on the Three-Step Test in Copyright Law and

Even if the Three-Step Test were interpreted as widely as possible, this would not resolve the book famine. The task of obtaining and converting millions of books for a small market is a prohibitively expensive and inefficient undertaking. Without a commitment from authors and publishers to provide accessible copies, the burden of converting works into accessible formats would be prohibitive. The Three-Step Test does not expressly permit sharing of works that have been converted into accessible formats within or across jurisdictions. Furthermore, the exemption does not deal with the situation where a work is created digitally but is not released in a format that is accessible to persons with disabilities, or the more concerning situation, where the E-Book is released in an accessible format but access is subsequently blocked.

The *Berne Convention* is focused on protecting the capacity of rights-holders to exploit their interests for their own benefit. The drafters of the *Berne Convention* did not place burdens on those who create inaccessible works. While some authors may self-publish, in many situations the party deciding whether to include disability accessibility features or not is a multinational publishing house. Rather than asking publishers to explain why digital content is not accessible, copyright laws place the burden on those seeking to use the Three-Step Test exception to reduce the disablement caused by works that are not accessible to persons with print disabilities. This creates a situation where the people who are least able to create accessible works, often charities and persons with disabilities, are left to do all the heavy lifting in the struggle to reverse the book famine. At best, the reluctance of nation states to positively address the book famine shows a tendency to err on the side of copyright owners where there is uncertainty. Under the exceptions paradigm, the onus of proof has been on disability advocates, who suggest that laws should deviate from the status quo of strong monopoly rights and market solutions.

Scholars such as Professor James Boyle have argued that using copyright to protect knowledge goods is inefficient and may retard scientific and cultural innovations.[57] The impact of copyright retarding creativity is evinced by the interaction between copyright and persons with print disabilities attempting to access works. The policy reason for copyright existing in the first place is to facilitate the creation of works. It seems ironic that a system that exists to promote the creation of works is the very system that is reducing a large

---

Related Tests in Patent and Trademark Law' (2006) 37 *International Review of Intellectual Property and Competition Law* 407, 434.

[57] James Boyle, 'A Politics of Intellectual Property: Environmentalism for the Net?' (1997) 47 *Duke Law Journal* 87.

percentage of the population's capacity to create works. Based on evidence presented to WIPO, there are hundreds of millions of people who are being disabled by the current copyright system.[58] When works are published in formats that limit the capacity of persons with print disabilities to utilise works, then those persons are not able to use works in the way intended. When persons with print disabilities are unable to obtain access to works, they are arguably inhibited by copyright laws from participation in the creative processes.[59]

The Three-Step Test: The Exception Paradigm in Action

Focusing on accessibility as a limited exception perpetuates the subordination of persons with print disabilities. The exception allows accessible copies to be made on an ad hoc basis, enabling people with disabilities to use adaptive technologies to gain access to individual titles through authorised institutions. Because the creation of accessible copies is still costly and slow, obtaining access remains the exception, rather than the norm. The current exceptions paradigm in copyright law can be said to tolerate limited unauthorised dealings with copyright material to try to reduce inequalities confronting persons with disabilities.

Regulation that approaches the needs of people with disabilities through a lens of tolerance has attracted considerable scholarly critique. Professor Wendy Brown, for example, argues that tolerance is generally used to describe a situation where a divergence is morally repugnant, but endured under sufferance for a greater good.[60] Brown observes that in most professional fields, tolerance is used to describe the existence of an undesirable element. In engineering or statistics, for example, tolerance indicates the point at which an impure factor will create a serious defect. In plant physiology, tolerance describes the point at which a substance will be fatal to life. Tolerance, by definition, 'involves managing the presence of the undesirable, the tasteless, the faulty – even the revolting, repugnant, or vile'.[61] Laws

---

[58] Kaya Koklu, 'The Marrakesh Treaty – Time to End the Book Famine for Visually Impaired Persons Worldwide' (2014) 45(7) *International Review of Intellectual Property and Competition Law* 737, 737; Jingyi Li, 'Reconciling the Enforcement of Copyright with the Upholding of Human Rights: A Consideration of the *Marrakesh Treaty* to Facilitate Access to Published Works for the Blind, Visually Impaired and Print Disabled' (2014) 36(10) *European Intellectual Property Review* 653, 655.

[59] Lea Shaver and Caterina Sganga, 'The Right to Take Part in Cultural Life: On Copyright and Human Rights' (2010) 27 *Wisconsin International Law Journal* 637, 648.

[60] Wendy Brown, *Regulating Aversion: Tolerance in the Age of Identity and Empire* (2006) Princeton University Press, ch. 2.

[61] Ibid.

that promote tolerance focus upon the necessity of coping with difference. Similar to policies based upon the medical model, laws that tolerate difference do not address the infrastructure that creates power imbalances and inequalities.

Disability scholars emphasise the limitations of models that tolerate difference, without addressing the root causes of inequalities.[62] This has led to the emergence of the social model to explain disablement, and ultimately the human rights paradigm and the CRPD. Through focusing on the role society has on causing disablement, it becomes clear that the major problem facing persons with print disabilities in gaining access to print materials for culture, education and employment, is an active societal choice to continue to refuse to provide books in versions accessible to persons with print disabilities. This is especially the case where the technology exists to publish E-Books in formats that are accessible to all readers, regardless of their abilities, at relatively little cost. The example of the accessibility features of Amazon's Kindle E-Book reader analysed in Chapter 1 of this monograph is an excellent case study here. The social model and human rights paradigm highlights that in this situation, a person is not print-disabled because of their low vision or other impairment; the cause of disablement is the decision by Amazon to allow publishers to turn accessibility features off.

The decision by states to permit E-Books, E-Libraries and E-Readers to be developed and distributed without accessibility features arguably disables the world's print-disabled. The technology exists to digitise existing works, and it is even easier to ensure that most works sold now and in the future in electronic form are made accessible. While it might be difficult to render a graphic heavy work, such as a work on architecture or economics, into a fully accessible format, there are no notable overheads in publishing a text-based work, such as law or philosophy, in a format that embraces inclusive design. The fact that states have not yet been willing to take the steps required to ensure adequate levels of access is a failure of political will. The social model and human rights paradigm cast the major barriers to accessibility as socially constructed, and the CRPD requires nation states to take action to combat the book famine.

---

[62] Lee Ann Basser and Melinda Jones, 'The *Disability Discrimination Act 1992* (Cth): A Three-Dimensional Approach to Operationalising Human Rights' (2002) 26 *Melbourne University Law Review* 254, 262; Michael Ashley Stein, Anita Silvers, Bradley Areheart and Leslie Pickering Francis, 'Accommodating Every Body' (2014) 81 *Chicago Law Review* 689.

SECTION II PARADIGM SHIFTS IN INTERNATIONAL COPYRIGHT LAW: THE IMPORT AND IMPACT OF THE *MARRAKESH TREATY*

Developments in the Lead-Up to the Marrakesh Treaty

The international community has recognised for a considerable period of time that the tolerance model to disability access is not providing adequate access. The United Nations Educational, Scientific and Cultural Organization and WIPO recognised in 1982 that persons with a print disability struggled to obtain access to standard books, and they proposed improving the operation of exemption-based access.[63] The Intergovernmental Copyright Committee, in 1985, suggested that resolving the book famine for the print-disabled might require an 'entirely new international instrument'.[64] In 2004, the WIPO Standing Committee on Copyright and Related Rights held informal discussions about forming a specialised access treaty for the print-disabled.[65] These informal discussions evolved in 2008 to formal steps to draft a treaty to improve access for persons with print disabilities in the WIPO Standing Committee on Copyright and Related Rights.[66] A number of different draft conventions were prepared and discussed.[67] Ultimately, the Diplomatic Conference to Conclude a Treaty to Facilitate Access to Published Works by Visually Impaired Persons and Persons with Print Disabilities adopted the *Marrakesh Treaty* on 27 June 2013. The *Marrakesh Treaty* commenced operation three months after twenty eligible parties lodged their instruments of ratification or accession.[68] As fifty-one states signed the *Marrakesh Treaty* before the end of the conference, it was expected that this convention would rapidly reach the required number of accessions and ratifications. Canada became the twentieth state to accede to or ratify the *Marrakesh Treaty* on 30 June 2016, and

---

[63] UNESCO and WIPO, *Application of the Berne Convention for the Protection of Literary and Artistic Property and the Universal Copyright Convention to Material for the Visually and Auditory Handicapped*, UN Doc. UNESCO/WIPO/WGH/I/2 (August 1982).

[64] *The Intergovernmental Copyright Committee of the Universal Copyright Convention, Copyright Problems Raised by the Access by Handicapped Persons to Protected Works*, IGC (1971)/IV/11 (12 March 1985) 25.

[65] Silke von Lewinski, *International Copyright Law and Policy* (2008) Oxford University Press, [22.15].

[66] WIPO, Standing Committee on Copyright and Related Rights, *Draft Agenda*, 17th sess., WIPO Doc. SCCR/17/1 (1 September 2008).

[67] WIPO, Standing Committee on Copyright and Related Rights, *Comparative List of Proposals Related to Copyright Limitations and Exceptions for the Visually Impaired Persons and Other Persons with Print Disabilities*, 22nd sess., WIPO Doc. SCCR/22/8 (16 March 2011) 2.

[68] *Marrakesh Treaty*, art. 18.

accordingly, on 30 September 2016, the *Marrakesh Treaty* commenced operation.[69]

What Does the Marrakesh Treaty *Do?*

The *Marrakesh Treaty* seeks to enhance the right to read of persons with print disabilities by reducing the restrictive operation of copyright.[70] As will be analysed in Chapter 6 of this monograph, who qualifies as disabled can be a contentious issue. The definition of print disability is also a contested social construct (as analysed in Chapter 1 of this monograph). The *Marrakesh Treaty* is significant as it extends protection to all people who have disabilities that impair their capacity to read, and is targeted at benefiting all persons with print disabilities. The Treaty employs a functional definition, which extends protection to people who are blind, those with 'visual impairment[s] or a perceptual or reading disability', and those who are 'unable, through physical disability, to hold or manipulate' reading materials.[71] As noted in Chapter 1 of this monograph, the definition of print disability in the *Marrakesh Treaty* does not extend its operation to some groups of impairments that are recognised as print disabilities.

Reproduction of Accessible Versions

The *Marrakesh Treaty* assists persons with print disabilities through three main vehicles. First, the *Marrakesh Treaty* makes it mandatory for state signatories to adopt copyright exceptions for the non-profit creation and distribution of accessible versions of works for the benefit of persons with print disabilities.[72] This provision requires all signatories to bring their copyright legislation into line with the standard already followed by countries such as Australia, Canada, the United Kingdom and the United States.[73] This is remarkable, as the *Marrakesh Treaty* is one of the rare international instruments that make exceptions to mandate, rather than permit, exceptions to copyright's exclusive rights – thus imposing a ceiling on the strength of copyright interests.

---

[69] World Intellectual Property Organization, 'Marrakesh Notification No. 21: [Marrakesh Treaty] Entry into Force' <www.wipo.int/treaties/en/notifications/marrakesh/treaty_marrakesh_21 .html> (accessed 18 November 2016). As of 28 November 2016, there are twenty-five parties that have acceded to or ratified the *Marrakesh Treaty*: <www.wipo.int/treaties/en/ShowResults .jsp?search_what=N&treaty_id=843> (accessed 28 November 2016).

[70] Li, 'Reconciling the Enforcement of Copyright with the Upholding of Human Rights'.

[71] *Marrakesh Treaty*, art. 3.   [72] Ibid., art. 4.

[73] For a discussion of the exception in these countries see Chapter 5 of this monograph.

Unfortunately, the way in which the *Marrakesh Treaty* permits the creation of accessible works reinforces the charity status of persons with disabilities. The *Marrakesh Treaty* permits persons with print disabilities, someone acting on their behalf or authorised entities to reproduce, distribute and make publicly available accessible-format copies to persons with print disabilities.[74] How the *Marrakesh Treaty* defines who is an authorised entity arguably restricts disability organisations from being non-charitable organisations. To be authorised, an entity must satisfy four elements:

(1) The party converting the work must have 'lawful access' to the copyrighted work.

(2) The conversion of the work must only change what is needed to make the work accessible to the beneficiary.

(3) The convertor may only supply the accessible works to beneficiaries.

(4) This activity must be 'undertaken on a non-profit basis'.[75]

Why is it necessary to prevent for-profit organisations from producing accessible works? Importantly, the power to convert works under article 4(2)(a) is limited to converting works to accessible formats for the benefit of persons with print disabilities.[76] If an entity was permitted to make profits from converting inaccessible works to accessible works, then presumably this would illustrate the commercial viability of providing persons with print disabilities materials in accessible formats. If it was clear that profits could be made from providing accessible versions of the work, then presumably rights-holders could be motivated to stop another entity exploiting their work for profit, by either providing accessible versions or licensing another entity to provide such versions. Providing the state signatory has exercised their rights under article 4(4), the creation of commercial accessible copies would prevent other entities creating copies under the *Marrakesh Treaty*. Article 4(4) operates to empower state signatories to confine article 4 to 'works which, in the particular accessible format, cannot be obtained commercially under reasonable terms for beneficiary persons in that market'.[77] Accordingly, permitting entities to make profits from creating accessible versions could illustrate the potential profitability of exploiting the print-disabled market.

---

[74] *Marrakesh Treaty*, art. 4(2)(a).   [75] Ibid., art. 4(2)(a)(i–iv).   [76] Ibid., art. 4(1)(a).
[77] Ibid., art. 4(4).

Permitting Distribution of Accessible Copies

For decades, disability person organisations have been reporting that copyright laws were hindering and even preventing the international exchange of books and publications in formats accessible to the print-disabled.[78] Considering the cost that is involved in creating an accessible copy, preventing the cross-border sharing of such material has represented a significant barrier to accessing the written word.[79] To create efficiencies and enhance access, the *Marrakesh Treaty* requires signatories to allow lawfully made, accessible copies to be distributed by organisations assisting persons with print disabilities to similar organisations in other signatory countries, or directly to disabled individuals in those countries.[80] The Treaty also requires WIPO to establish information-sharing procedures to enhance cooperation between member states by establishing a voluntary register of institutions assisting persons with print disabilities.[81] These provisions reduce the marked inefficiency of the current system under the Three-Step Test, which requires that institutions in each country digitise their own accessible copies of each work. This also allows economies of scale by enabling institutions in some countries to provide works directly to beneficiaries in other countries. Importantly, this is likely to have a strong positive effect by allowing comparatively well-funded organisations in some countries to support people, particularly in developing countries, who do not have strong institutional support.

While permitting international sharing is an extremely positive development, this aspect of the *Marrakesh Treaty* will not ensure equality. A student of history or politics will read a number of similar works, regardless of their jurisdiction. There are, however, many more works that are specific to each state's creation and internal political developments. A student of law would confront similar difficulties. While theoretical models often cross borders, every jurisdiction has its own body of law related to contracts, criminal law and procedure, equity (including trusts), ethics and professional responsibility, evidence, constitutional law, real property and torts, just to name a few key areas. It can be said, therefore, that the permitting of international file sharing represents a small step in reducing the impact of the book famine.

---

[78] Simonetta Vezzoso, 'The Marrakesh Spirit – A Ghost in Three Steps?' (2014) 45(7) *International Review of Intellectual Property and Competition Law* 796, 807–8.

[79] WIPO, Standing Committee on Copyright and Related Rights, *Study on Copyright Limitations and Exceptions for the Visually Impaired*, 15th sess., WIPO Doc. SCCR/15/7 (20 February 2007) 47.

[80] *Marrakesh Treaty*, arts 5, 6.   [81] Ibid., art. 9.

Exceptions to Anti-Circumvention Schemes

The *Marrakesh Treaty* requires that states introduce exceptions to anti-circumvention schemes (where applicable) to ensure that those schemes '[do] not prevent beneficiary persons from enjoying the limitations and exceptions'[82] that the Treaty provides for. This is particularly important for enabling people with disabilities (or their representatives) to circumvent digital locks (digital rights management, DRM) placed ·on E-Books and other works, so that they can utilise adaptive technologies to access the work.[83] Adaptive technologies, such as screen readers, are software packages that talk to E-Readers to present content in a format that can be consumed by persons with disabilities. Non-Visual Desktop Access, for example, sends a digital request to Adobe Digital Editions to provide access to the content of an E-Book. If the E-Book has security settings, then Adobe Digital Editions responds to Non-Visual Desktop Access that there is no available content. However, if there are no security settings, then Adobe Digital Editions will provide access to the code and text in the E-Book, and Non-Visual Desktop Access will convert the content into a usable audio format that can be consumed by persons with print disabilities. Digital rights management, accordingly, has the capacity to lock persons with print disabilities out of digital libraries.

The Marrakesh Treaty: *Shifting the Debate*

The *Marrakesh Treaty* makes an important contribution to improving access for persons with print disabilities worldwide. While the Three-Step Test enabled states to create exceptions to enable the print-disabled to access written material, existing international copyright laws did not require states to provide access. The *Marrakesh Treaty* alters this situation.[84] Effectively, it requires developing countries to adopt the limited exceptions that some Western jurisdictions have adopted, enabling ad hoc digitisation and other measures to provide access to people with disabilities. While this is a very important development, its terms provide only incremental advancements that will not systematically tackle the book famine. In a best-case scenario, the Treaty will equalise the level of access enjoyed by persons with print

---

[82] Ibid., art. 7.

[83] How copyright laws regulate anti-circumvention schemes will be analysed in Chapter 4 of this
· monograph.

[84] Tshimanga Kongolo, 'Towards an International Legal Instrument on Exceptions and Limitations to Copyright for Visually Impaired Persons/Persons with Print Disabilities – Current International Negotiations' (2012) 34(12) *European Intellectual Property Review* 812.

disabilities around the world up to the level enjoyed by United States residents. As analysed in Chapters 1, 5 and 11 of this monograph, the United States has some of the most effective charities and legal vehicles to enable persons with disabilities to access the written word. This means that, upon ratification by the United States, the *Marrakesh Treaty* will enable access to several hundred thousand English- and Spanish-language books digitised by volunteers and held by Bookshare.org, as well as similar collections by other, smaller institutions. The HathiTrust digital library holds up to 10 million more digital copies of books digitised by Google,[85] which will also be able to be made available.[86] Conceivably, then, the Treaty may enable access to up to 15 per cent of the world's books. This is a significant step forward, but is not, on its own, sufficient to redress the book famine. The *Marrakesh Treaty* does not mandate equal access or a broader right to read.

The *Marrakesh Treaty* will not achieve equality. To achieve equality will require transformational reforms. Dan Pescod, Vice Chair of the Right to Read Campaign, World Blind Union, explains:

> Many said the treaty would never happen. Some said it was not worth pursuing, arguing that in itself it would not end the book famine. I can confirm that it will not end the book famine. The treaty, though a great and important achievement, is just one part of the larger jigsaw puzzle of full accessibility. But we cannot omit a piece of a jigsaw on the grounds that it will not solve the whole puzzle. Without this vital piece – the treaty – the puzzle could never happen.[87]

Expanding on the words of Dan Pescod, the *Marrakesh Treaty* may be one piece of the puzzle, but arguably it is a corner piece which can be used to help guide how the book famine can be converted to a book feast. Ultimately, the *Marrakesh Treaty* continues the tolerance approach, which has not addressed the book famine. The *Marrakesh Treaty* may not solve the book famine, but it does shift the international copyright debate in a way that provides greater recognition of the rights of persons with print disabilities.

---

[85] See HathiTrust, 'Welcome to HathiTrust!' <www.hathitrust.org/about> (accessed 18 November 2016). Note that these books have been scanned, but have not necessarily undergone optical character recognition (OCR) and error checking; significant additional work may be required to make these books accessible.

[86] See *Authors Guild, Inc.* v. *HathiTrust*, 902 F. Supp. 2d 445 (S.D.N.Y., 2012).

[87] Dan Pescod, 'What the Marrakesh Treaty Means for Blind People' (August 2013), *WIPO Magazine* <www.wipo.int/wipo_magazine/en/2013/04/article_0002.html> (accessed 18 November 2016).

Significance of the Marrakesh Treaty *in Shifting Copyright Politics*

The *Marrakesh Treaty* will harmonise copyright disability accessibility norms.[88] Traditionally, the reform efforts at WIPO have favoured strong intellectual property protections for rights-holders rather than flexible user rights.[89] Considering the direction of the historic trend in copyright, the *Marrakesh Treaty* significantly turns the gaze of international copyright law onto enabling persons with print disabilities to have access to works. Shae Fitzpatrick explains that, at a minimum, the norms established in the *Marrakesh Treaty* require that 'persons with print disabilities need copyright exceptions to facilitate access to copyrighted works'.[90] Despite the fact that these new copyright norms fall short of human rights obligations in the CRPD, the widening of the exception paradigm confronted substantial well-funded and positioned resistance.

The debates leading up to the adoption of the *Marrakesh Treaty* in June 2013 illustrated the tension between the limited exceptions paradigm adopted in international copyright law and the disability human rights paradigm adopted in international human rights law. The fact that hundreds of millions of people across the world were experiencing a book famine demonstrated that the current regime was not working. While the perpetuation of the book famine was widely accepted, how to address this problem highlighted substantial divisions, which reflected existing political lines within the copyright movement. There were some disability rights advocates seeking full and substantive equality through promoting open access, while others called for incremental steps that were more likely to be achieved.[91] Then there were commentators who argued that the Three-Step Test provides meaningful access and strikes a fair balance between disability access and copyright protection.[92] Others, such as the American Publishing Association, argued

[88] James Love, 'Comments to the Copyright Office and the USPTO Regarding the WIPO Draft Proposal to Facilitate Access to Copyrighted Works for Persons, Who Are Blind or Have Other Reading Disabilities, in Response to the Federal Register Notice of October 13, 2009', Knowledge Ecology International (2009) <www.copyright.gov/docs/sccr/comments/2009/comments-2/james-love-knowledge-ecology-international.pdf> (accessed 18 November 2016).

[89] Vera Franz, 'Back to Balance: Limitations and Exceptions to Copyright' in Gaelle Krikorian and Amy Kapczynski (eds), *Access to Knowledge in the Age of Intellectual Property* (2010) Zone Books, 516, 518–25.

[90] Shae Fitzpatrick, 'Setting its Sights on the *Marrakesh Treaty*: The U.S. Role in Alleviating the Book Famine for Persons with Print Disabilities' (2014) 37 *Boston College Law School* 139, 147, 162.

[91] Scheinwald, 'Who Could Possibly Be against a Treaty for the Blind?', 469.

[92] Guy Pessach, 'Reciprocal Share-Like Exemptions in Copyright Law' (2008) 30 *Cardozo Law Review* 1245, 1275; Pamela Samuelson, 'The US Digital Agenda at WIPO' (1997) 37 *Virginia Journal of International Law* 369, 404–5; Guido Westkamp, 'The "Three-Step Test" and Copyright

that modifying copyright laws was not the answer to resolving the book famine, and that wider social responses should be adopted that operated within the Three-Step Test.[93]

The *Marrakesh Treaty* attempts to extend the exceptions to infringement that currently exist in developed nations to developing nations, and to reduce some of the duplicative effort that is required under the current scheme by enabling accessible books to be shared across national borders. Nothing in the *Berne Convention* or other international treaties would prevent these measures.[94] The exceptions that already exist for digitising and disseminating copyright works for the benefit of people with disabilities are generally considered to be compliant with the Three-Step Test.[95] For example, Martin Senftleben argues that article 5(3)(b) of the European Copyright Directive (Directive 2001/29/EC of the European Parliament and of the Council of 22 May 2001 on the harmonisation of certain aspects of copyright and related rights in the information society), which allows EU states to create exceptions for non-commercial uses for the benefit of people with a disability, is compliant with the Three-Step Test.[96] Similarly, international copyright law does not require countries to prohibit the unlicensed importation of accessible books.[97] States are free to make changes to domestic law to permit the cross-border flow of accessible books for the print-disabled.[98]

Even though the limited goals of the *Marrakesh Treaty* are compliant with international law, the Treaty was, and remains, opposed by a strong publishing lobby.[99] Copyright owners sought strongly to limit any exception to cases where they were not providing access on commercial terms, reserving their right to enter into the market to serve people with disabilities at a future date.[100] These

Limitations in Europe: European Copyright Law between Approximation and National Decision Making' (2008) 56 *Journal of the Copyright Society of the U.S.A.* 1, 26.

[93] WIPO, Standing Committee on Copyright and Related Rights, *Report*, 13th sess., WIPO Doc. SCCR/13/6 (9 June 2006) 32.

[94] Caterina Sganga, 'Disability, Right to Culture and Copyright: Which Regulatory Option?' (2015) 29(2/3) *International Review of Law Computers and Technology* 88.

[95] See WIPO, *Study on Copyright Limitations and Exceptions for the Visually Impaired*; Ricketson, *The Berne Convention*.

[96] Senftleben, *Copyright, Limitations, and the Three-Step Test*, 259–69.

[97] See Ricketson and Ginsburg, *International Copyright and Neighbouring Rights*, [11.46].

[98] Jane C Ginsburg and June M Besek, 'Comment to US Copyright Office Notice of Inquiry and Request for Comments on the Topic of Facilitating Access to Copyrighted Works for the Blind or Other Persons with Disabilities' (13 November 2009) <www.copyright.gov/docs/sccr/comments/2009/comments-2/ginsburg-besek-columbia-law-school.pdf> (accessed 18 November 2016).

[99] Koklu, 'The *Marrakesh Treaty*'.

[100] For example, see emails from the Publishers Association to the UK Intellectual Property Office, 2013 <www.scribd.com/doc/140886790/Redacted-UK-IP-Office-Pub-Assoc-Emails-digitized-searchable-version> (accessed 18 November 2016); James Love, 'UK IPO Office Releases

arguments usually relied on a form of technological determinism, noting that while persons with print disabilities had been poorly served by the market to date, '[w]ith each passing day, via the Internet and other digital technologies, the blind and visually impaired are being provided with more options, more alternatives and more opportunities'.[101] Just as the market might be about to flourish, copyright owners argued, enhancing exceptions for persons with print disabilities would lead copyright owners to 'have understandable doubts about the wisdom of investing in the production of accessible versions for the market'.[102]

Reserving commercial rights was probably the most important substantive point of opposition to the Treaty, as publishers and their supporters sought to defend the basic proposition that exceptions to copyright should only apply in cases of market failure.[103] The Australian Society of Authors (ASA) went so far as to state that voluntary licensing by Australian authors meant that 'Australian

Emails that Show Close Collaboration with Publishers on WIPO Treaty for the Blind', Knowledge Ecology International (11 May 2013) <keionline.org/node/1719> (accessed 18 November 2016); James Love, 'Disney, Viacom and Other MPAA Members Join Book Publishers to Weaken a Treaty for the Blind', *Huffington Post Politics* (23 April 2013) <www .huffingtonpost.com/james-love/disney-viacom-and-other-m_b_3137653.html> (accessed 18 November 2016); Jim Fruchterman, 'Poisoning the Treaty for the Blind', *Huffington Post Politics* (7 May 2013) <www.huffingtonpost.com/jim-fruchterman/poisoning-the-treaty-for-_b_3 225181.html> (accessed 18 November 2016).

[101] Software and Information Industry Association, Submission to the US Copyright Office, 'Notice of the U.S. Copyright Office and the U.S. Patent and Trademark Office on October 13, 2009 Requesting Comments on the Topic of Facilitating Access to Copyrighted Works for the Blind or Persons with Other Disabilities' (13 November 2009) 2 <www.copyright.gov/docs/sccr/comments/2009/comments-2/keith-kupferschmid-software-in formation-industry-association.pdf> (accessed 18 November 2016); Keith Kupfrerschmid, Software and Information Industry Association Reply, Comments to the US Copyright Office, 'Notice of the U.S. Copyright Office and the U.S. Patent and Trademark Office on October 13, 2009 Requesting Comments on the Topic of Facilitating Access to Copyrighted Works for the Blind or Persons with Other Disabilities' (4 December 2009) 6 <- www.copyright.gov/docs/sccr/comments/2009/reply-2/15-keith-kupferschmid.pdf> (accessed 18 November 2016).

[102] Allan Adler, Association of American Publishers, Inc., Reply Comments to US Copyright Office, 'Notice of Inquiry and Request for Comments on the Topic of Facilitating Access to Copyrighted Works for the Blind or Other Persons with Disabilities' (4 December 2009) 6 <- www.copyright.gov/docs/sccr/comments/2009/reply-2/19-allan-adler.pdf> (accessed 18 November 2016).

[103] Letter from Richard Glenn, Assistant Secretary, Business and Information Law Branch, Australian Attorney-General's Department, to Australian Society of Authors, 27 March 2013 <asauthors.org/files/submissions/signed_glenn_-_loukakis_asa_-_response_to_asa_submis sion_-_wipo_vip_tr....pdf> (accessed 18 November 2016). Gordon and Bahls call the assumption that exceptions should only exist in cases of market failure the 'fared use fallacy'. See Wendy J Gordon and Daniel Bahls, 'The Public's Right to Fair Use: Amending Section 107 to Avoid the Fared Use Fallacy' (2007) 3 *Utah Law Review* 619; see further Wendy J Gordon, 'Fair Use as Market Failure: A Structural and Economic Analysis of the Betamax Case and its Predecessors' (1982) 82 *Columbia Law Review* 1600.

copyright law or publishing practice' was not 'an impediment to access for the visually impaired in this country'.[104] This approach, emphasising market-based solutions, drastically underestimates the extent of the book famine. Even if private efforts are 'well advanced', as the Australian Society of Authors contends,[105] it is indisputable that persons with print disabilities remain very poorly served, in Australia and worldwide, by the private market.

In their efforts to limit the scope of the Treaty, publishers sought treaty language that would threaten to reduce existing exceptions and limit the operation of institutions currently providing accessible copies of works by prohibiting the distribution of works that become commercially available in accessible form.[106] Ultimately, a compromise was reached so that the mandatory exception 'was limited to works which, in the particular accessible format, cannot be obtained commercially under reasonable terms for beneficiary persons in that market'.[107] Importantly, however, no obligation was introduced that would require organisations who assist persons with print disabilities in foreign countries to determine whether accessible works were commercially available in that country before providing them with access.[108]

The other major copyright industries also opposed significant portions of the Treaty. Publishers of audiovisual works, in particular, were successful in limiting its operation to only literary works (books and other texts), related illustrations and audio books. As originally proposed, the Treaty also sought to improve access to films and television broadcasts by enabling audio descriptions and to provide access to deaf people by enhancing subtitling. In 2009, the Obama administration cut these issues out of negotiations, focusing the Treaty on the 'more mature' issues of print disabilities.[109]

The most interesting points of opposition to the Treaty were not those focused on its substantive merits, but the broader concerns about the effect

---

[104] Letter from Angelo Loukakis, Australian Society of Authors, to Norman Bowman, Attorney-General's Department, June 2012 <asauthors.org/files/submissions/submission_to_a-g_june_2012 .pdf> (accessed 18 November 2016).

[105] Ibid.

[106] See Knowledge Ecology International, 'KEI Position on Commercial Availability, Marrakesh Note 5' (17 June 2013) <keionline.org/node/1751> (accessed 18 November 2016); National Federation of the Blind, 'The Petition Supporting WIPO Treaty for the Blind and Print Disabled' <nfb.org/civicrm/petition/sign?sid=2> (accessed 18 November 2016).

[107] *Marrakesh Treaty*, art. 4(4).

[108] Catherine Saez, 'New Draft Text Shows Progress on WIPO Treaty on Books for the Print Disabled', *Intellectual Property Watch* (25 June 2013) <www.ip-watch.org/2013/06/25/new-draft-text-shows-progress-on-wipo-treaty-on-books-for-the-print-disabled/> (accessed 18 November 2016).

[109] KEI Staff, 'Audiovisual Materials in the Classroom and the WIPO Treaty for Copyright Exceptions for Persons with Disabilities', Knowledge Ecology International (8 June 2013) <keionline.org/node/1738> (accessed 18 November 2016).

the Treaty would have on global copyright politics. Publishers of audiovisual works, for example, staunchly opposed the Treaty; the Motion Picture Association of America, which represents Disney and Viacom and other media organisations, has strongly lobbied to further limit the Treaty, even after audiovisual works were excluded from its scope.[110] The copyright industries, broadly defined, have consistently sought to retain the integrity of an international copyright system that creates strong rights and only allows limited exceptions.

Publishing lobby groups expressed particular concern about any provisions that might require states to introduce mandatory exceptions into domestic law.[111] Previously, while states were free to create exceptions to increase access to persons with print disabilities, this process was relatively piecemeal. Most Western countries already have these exceptions, but developing nations do not. In their opposition to the *Marrakesh Treaty*, the United States copyright industries – including the Association of American Publishers, the Independent Film and Television Alliance, the Motion Picture Association of America, the National Music Publishers' Association and the Recording Industry Association of America – did not dispute the justification to include specific exceptions to assist persons with print disabilities. What these bodies most sought was to ensure that any changes to copyright laws were kept narrow and relatively isolated, and would not challenge the global level of deference to rights-holders' interests.

The submission by the United States copyright industries to the United States Copyright Office reinforces their insistence that the piecemeal approach be retained:

> we strongly endorse and support reasonable efforts to increase the practical and functional access of blind and visually impaired persons to works protected by copyright. But among the strategies least likely to advance the goal of increased access by the blind and visually impaired is the path down which the draft treaty points: to begin to dismantle the existing global treaty structure of copyright law, through the adoption of an international instrument at odds with existing, long-standing and well-settled norms.[112]

---

[110] Love, 'Disney, Viacom and other MPAA Members'.

[111] Steven J Metalitz, Submission on behalf of the Association of American Publishers (AAP), the Independent Film and Television Alliance (IFTA), the Motion Picture Association of America (MPAA), the National Music Publishers' Association (NMPA) and the Recording Industry Association of America (RIAA) to the US Copyright Office, 'Notice of Inquiry and Request for Comments on the Topic of Facilitating Access to Copyrighted Works for the Blind or Other Persons with Disabilities' (13 November 2009) www.copyright.gov/docs/sccr/comments/2009/comments-2/steven-j-metalitz-aap-ifta-mpaa-nmpa-riaa.pdf (accessed 18 November 2016).

[112] Ibid., 2.

The 'existing, long-standing and well-settled norms' at question here are those that reinforce the continued dominance of the limited exceptions paradigm, which has largely contributed to the creation and perpetuation of the book famine. The copyright norms which were argued to be maintained permitted only ad hoc digitisation and distribution to redress the inequities in access that persons with print disabilities confront. The United States copyright industries strongly opposed the 'giant step' of the *Marrakesh Treaty* of introducing a mandatory exception to copyright law:

> By <u>requiring</u> the recognition of a specific, detailed exception to copyright protection, the draft treaty would break the mould of every previous treaty instrument that forms part of the long-standing global framework of copyright norms.[113]

Essentially, the United States copyright industries were arguing that the book famine was not sufficiently serious to justify altering international copyright norms.

Copyright industry groups fear any changes that threaten to weaken the basic presumption that any exceptions to the copyright monopoly must be limited and strictly optional. The copyright industries are unable to directly argue against limited exceptions to provide access to persons with print disabilities. The publishing lobby constructs any attempt to require greater access in domestic or international law as an ideological threat. This ideological tension at WIPO is evident in the removal of language in an early draft of the *Marrakesh Treaty* that would have explicitly recognised that member states could meet the requirements of the Treaty through either a new specific exception or through a generic United States-style 'fair use' clause.

As will be analysed in Chapter 5 of this monograph, fair use, as it exists in the United States, provides a flexible approach to enable courts to balance the rights of copyright owners against the social interests in increasing dissemination.[114] Rights-holders have never been particularly comfortable with fair use, and have opposed its introduction into other countries.[115] In large part, this is because fair use has become a proxy for paying more attention to 'user rights'[116] and the social interests in dissemination and access to information that must be balanced against private interests in copyright returns. In a 2006 report that focuses on the copyright interests of developing

---

[113] Ibid., 3.   [114] 17 USC § 107.

[115] For a review of the arguments against fair use, see Australian Law Reform Commission, 'Copyright and the Digital Economy', Report No. 122 (2014) 71–9.

[116] For discussion of the importance of 'user rights' in copyright, see L R Patterson and Stanley W Lindberg, *The Nature of Copyright: A Law of Users' Rights* (1991) University of Georgia Press.

countries, Ruth Okediji concludes that '[t]he important role of limitations and exceptions to copyright's fundamental purpose should become a more central part of the structure and operation of the international copyright system'.[117] An email from the United Kingdom Publishers Association to the United Kingdom Intellectual Property Office refers to Okediji's report and notes: 'Perhaps this helps explain why we are all so concerned about the insertion of fair use into the Treaty text.'[118] While fair use itself is not highly problematic for publishers in the United States context, the implication is that publishers fear measures that may lead to the weakening of the copyright system in other contexts. Opposing such change is crucial from the copyright industries' perspective, particularly since there is growing global concern that current intellectual property laws may reduce innovation[119] and not provide the best outcomes for consumers.[120]

The United States copyright industries representatives explain their fear that the *Marrakesh Treaty* is the thin end of a wedge which threatens the dominance of copyright law:

> viewed in context, the ... treaty appears to many as the not-so-thin edge of a wedge to be driven into the longstanding structure of global copyright norms. It advocates a U-turn in the approach to global copyright norms that would almost certainly not be restricted to the issue of access for the visually impaired, or even for the disabled community generally. Adoption of this proposal would be used to justify its radical approach – mandating in national law exceptions and limitations that reach far beyond what would be even permissible under global norms today – in many other fields of copyright law.[121]

[117] Ruth L Okediji, 'International Copyright System: Limitations, Exceptions and Public Interest Considerations for Developing Countries' (Issue Paper, International Centre for Trade and Sustainable Development, 2006) 34.

[118] See email from the Publishers Association to the UK Intellectual Property Office (5 March 2012), 5 <www.scribd.com/doc/140886790/Redacted-UK-IP-Office-Pub-Assoc-Emails-digitized-searchable-version> (accessed 18 November 2016).

[119] Michele Boldrin and David K Levine, *Against Intellectual Monopoly* (2008) Cambridge University Press, ch. 4; Jorn Sonderholm, 'Ethical Issues Surrounding Intellectual Property Rights' in Annabelle Lever (ed.), *New Frontiers in the Philosophy of Intellectual Property* (2012) Cambridge University Press, ch. 4; Thomas Rogers and Andrew Szamosszegi, 'Fair Use in the U.S. Economy: Economic Contribution of Industries Relying on Fair Use' (report, Computer and Communications Industry Association, 2010); John Houghton and Nicholas Gruen, 'Lateral Economics Report: Exceptional Industries – The Economic Contribution to Australia of Industries Relying on Limitations and Exceptions to Copyright' (Australian Digital Alliance, August 2012).

[120] See Jessica Litman, 'Real Copyright Reform' (2010) 96(1) *Iowa Law Review* 1.

[121] Steven J Metalitz, Submission on behalf of the Association of American Publishers (AAP), the Independent Film and Television Alliance (IFTA), the Motion Picture Association of America (MPAA), the National Music Publishers' Association (NMPA) and the Recording Industry

The United States copyright industries representatives argued that the *Marrakesh Treaty* and its negotiations could set a 'dangerous precedent for other areas of ... [intellectual property] law'.[122] This, then, is the ultimate source of opposition to addressing the book famine at a global level. While the *Marrakesh Treaty* was never intended to interfere with the minimum rights of copyright owners in international law, it was seen as a threat because it challenges the limited exceptions paradigm. This is perhaps seen most clearly in a letter by Business Europe to WIPO, raising fears that the *Marrakesh Treaty*

> is strongly supported by the same group of NGOs and advanced emerging economy countries that pursue a general ... [intellectual property rights]-weakening agenda at WIPO and other international forums. They would rely on the harmful precedent set by its hasty conclusion.[123]

This fear is reinforced by advocates for a major shift in WIPO's approach. Luis Villaroel, who advised Ecuador in the Treaty negotiations, explained, for example, that 'if we change the culture, we will not only be solving the problem for the blind but also for the libraries, for educators, and so on'.[124] Seen in this way, the *Marrakesh Treaty* might be an instance of 'regime-shifting'[125] by those who seek more limits on intellectual property rights. By introducing mandatory limitations in this particular forum, it is possible that this will enhance the relative power of developing countries and human rights advocates in other forums and social contexts.

Association of America (RIAA) to the US Copyright Office, 'Notice of Inquiry and Request for Comments on the Topic of Facilitating Access to Copyrighted Works for the Blind or Other Persons with Disabilities' (13 November 2009) www.copyright.gov/docs/sccr/comments/2009/comments-2/steven-j-metalitz-aap-ifta-mpaa-nmpa-riaa.pdf (accessed 18 November 2016); see also Letter from the Intellectual Property Owners Association to Teresa Stanek Rea, Acting Under Secretary of Commerce for Intellectual Property and Director of the US Patent and Trademark Office (15 April 2013), 1 <keionline.org/sites/default/files/2013.4.15IPO_Letter_WIPO_VIP_Treaty.pdf> (accessed 18 November 2016).

[122] Ibid.

[123] Letter from Markus J Beyrer, Business Europe, to Michel Bainier, Commissioner for Internal Market and Services, European Commission (14 May 2013), 2 <keionline.org/sites/default/files/BusinessEurope_v_Blind_2013-00525-E.pdf> (accessed 18 November 2016).

[124] Luis Villaroel (speech delivered at 'The 2013 *Marrakesh Treaty*: Providing Access to Copyrighted Works for the Blind and Print Disabled', American University, Washington College of Law, 12 September 2013) <www.pijip-impact.org/events/marrakesh/> (accessed 18 November 2016).

[125] See Laurence Helfer, 'Regime Shifting: The TRIPs Agreement and New Dynamics of International Intellectual Property Lawmaking' (2004) 29 *Yale Journal of International Law* 1; Laurence Helfer, 'Regime Shifting in the International Intellectual Property System' (2009) 7 *Perspectives on Politics* 39.

CONCLUSION

Historically, disability rights have been peripheral to copyright law. While copyright did not explicitly develop to exclude people with disabilities, now that the possibility of universal design and full access has become real, current copyright law supports a publishing regime whose practical effect is to deliver wildly discriminatory levels of access. Over the last half-century, action to increase access for people with disabilities by nation states has mainly targeted instances of direct conflict between the interests of copyright owners and the rights of people with disabilities. Where it has become an issue, the focus has been on the modern, liberal task of removing the barriers to digitisation and distribution. The new disability politics that has developed following the CRPD, however, requires more than removing barriers: it requires taking positive action to ensure that people with disabilities have adequate access to educational and cultural resources.

People with a print disability have a fundamental right to access cultural works for their education, work, play and pleasure. Currently, the international copyright regime is restricting the capacity of persons with print disabilities to exercise this right. The dominance of international content industries in global copyright debates has historically confined disability rights to ad hoc limited exceptions to the general copyright monopoly. The CRPD suggests that a paradigm shift is necessary to reframe accessibility debates. By introducing positive obligations on member states to 'take all appropriate measures to ensure that persons with disabilities [can enjoy] access to cultural materials in accessible formats', the CRPD requires a move away from the exception paradigm and ad hoc exceptions to copyright and towards internationally coordinated, large-scale, systematic attempts to reverse the book famine. The *Marrakesh Treaty* reflects a new international consensus which uses limited copyright reforms to promote a human rights objective. Human rights can be promoted and inhibited by the operation of copyright.[126]

The *Marrakesh Treaty* ensures that all signatories will be obliged to introduce a minimum baseline exception that allows persons with print disabilities to receive, make and use accessible copies of works. Importantly, the *Marrakesh Treaty* also allows the cross-border flow of accessible books, laying the groundwork for a globally coordinated approach to pooling accessible books digitised around the world.

---

[126] For an example of a human rights convention that protects copyright see: *Universal Declaration of Human Rights*, GA Res 217A (III), UN GAOR, 3rd sess., 183 plen. mtg, UN Doc. A/810 (10 December 1948), art. 27(2), which provides that 'Everyone has the right to the protection of the moral and material interests resulting from any scientific, literary or artistic production of which he is the author.'

The adoption of the *Marrakesh Treaty* represents a monumental victory for disability rights advocates and those who support the right to read. However, while the *Marrakesh Treaty* has shifted international copyright law towards inclusion, overall the governing copyright paradigm remains one of exceptionalism. While people with print disabilities will be more able to read, the *Marrakesh Treaty* continues to construct such access as an exception. Realisation of the notion of equality as envisaged in the *CRPD* will not be achieved by these small and important steps alone, but by the adoption of a regime that restricts the capacity of people to produce barriers to equality, as opposed to a regime that focuses on restricting people who are trying to obtain access.

4

The Role of Copyright Laws in Restricting Access to Information and Contributing to the Book Famine

INTRODUCTION

The previous two chapters have analysed how international law is altering the balance between copyright interests and disability human rights. The United Nations *Convention on the Rights of Persons with Disabilities* (*CRPD*) focuses on removing barriers to access and elevates access over intellectual property interests.[1] In contrast to the position in the *CRPD*,[2] international copyright laws create barriers to access to enable rights-holders to profit from exclusive exploitation of a work.

Arguably, the international copyright regime is restricting the capacity of persons with disabilities to exercise their right to read. Under the international copyright regime, disability access is regarded as an exception to the norm that is partially tolerated. The *Berne Convention for the Protection of Literary and Artistic Works* established a regime which restricted access to works unless a use was authorised by the rights-holder, or came within the narrow Three-Step Test exception.[3] While the drafters of the international copyright regime may not have intended to create a book famine, the operation of copyright has substantially contributed to the current crisis.

The *Treaty to Facilitate Access to Published Works for Persons Who Are Blind, Visually Impaired, or Otherwise Print Disabled* (*Marrakesh Treaty*) is a small first step in reversing the denial of the right to read. The *Marrakesh Treaty* ensures that all signatories will be obliged to introduce a minimum baseline exception that allows persons with print disabilities to receive, make and use accessible copies of works. Whereas the previous two chapters focused

---

[1] *CRPD*, opened for signature 30 March 2007, 2515 UNTS 3 (entered into force 3 May 2008).
[2] Ibid.
[3] *Berne Convention*, opened for signature 9 September 1886, 1161 UNTS 30 (entered into force 5 December 1887).

on the operation of international law, the next two chapters will focus on how copyright norms are translated into domestic laws in Australia, Canada, the United Kingdom and the United States.

The next two chapters of this monograph argue that copyright regimes focus on restricting the distribution of knowledge and tolerate reading ability differences as a limited exception to the norm. Copyright norms are not intended to prevent persons with print disabilities from exercising their human right to read; from the perspective of copyright this is just an unfortunate consequence.[4] Despite strong criticism and human rights critiques, intellectual property norms have not been significantly weakened to enable the exercising of human rights.[5]

Copyright laws operate on the basis that enabling people to exploit copyright-protected works will encourage the creation of more discoveries and works.[6] Under this model, the ability of persons with print disabilities to obtain access becomes a secondary concern and a tolerated exception to the norm. This chapter will analyse how the recognition and protection of copyright interests reduces the ability of persons with print disabilities to exercise their right to read. The next chapter will analyse the exceptions in copyright which enable limited access to the written word for people with print disabilities.

The starting point with copyright is that access without authorisation from the rights-holder is not permitted. This chapter argues that the restrictions on creating derivative works, combined with the long life of these restrictions, inhibit creativity and the development of disability-accessible markets. This chapter will commence by analysing how copyright laws restrict unauthorised use of works. While Creative Commons licences are a form of copyright that enhances access, most copyrighted works are only usable with the permission of the rights-holder, unless one of the exceptions discussed in the following chapter applies. While digital forms of books are often available, copyright laws enable rights-holders to use code to prevent people using adaptive technology from accessing content. This chapter argues that while some rights-holders are prepared to tolerate difference and provide support, relying upon support from rights-holders will never achieve equality. This is especially

4   Abbe Brown, Shawn H E Harmon and Charlotte Waelde, 'Do You See What I See? Disability, Technology, Law and the Experience of Culture' (2012) 43(8) *International Review of Intellectual Property and Competition Law* 901, 909.
5   Laurence Helfer, 'Toward a Human Rights Framework for Intellectual Property' (2006) 40 *UC Davis Law Review* 971; Lea Shaver, 'The Right to Science and Culture' (2010) *Wisconsin Law Review* 121; Matthew Rimmer, 'Patents for Humanity' (2012) 3(2) *The World Intellectual Property Organization WIPO Journal* 196–221.
6   William M Landes and Richard A Posner, 'An Economic Analysis of Copyright Law' (1989) 18 *Journal of Legal Studies* 325.

the case where many works are so-called orphan works; that is, where rights-holders are not readily identifiable or contactable. Finally, this chapter will consider how the operation of secondary infringement liability operates as a disincentive to reduce the creation of derivative works in formats that are more accessible to persons with disabilities. Overall this chapter concludes that copyright laws have a disabling impact on persons with disabilities who seek to exercise their right to read.

SECTION I WHAT DOES COPYRIGHT PROTECT?

What Are Copyright-Protected Works?

The law constructs copyright interests as intangible property rights. When an author writes a manuscript, they may use a computer to type and digitally store their work. A computer is a chattel that is recognised in the same way as any other personal property.[7] In writing a manuscript, an author may spend thousands of hours planning, researching and writing, incur significant other expenses and spiritually invest in the work through significant artistic and emotional effort.[8] Recognising the property right over the computer on which the work is stored or on the paper on which the work is printed does not protect the true value of a literary work. Copyright is not concerned with physical property that suffers from scarcity, but instead constructs concepts, information and knowledge as goods capable of protection.[9] To protect the creative cost and production costs, the law grants authors an exclusive right to control how their work is exploited.[10] This granting of a right of exclusive exploitation of a work occurs through the law of copyright.[11]

Copyright laws create an intangible property interest in a literary work when it is created.[12] Unlike trademarks and patents, there is no need to register an interest in a work to benefit from copyright laws.[13] A copyright interest is created providing that the work comes within one of the categories recognised

---

[7] See, e.g., *St Albans City and District Council* v. *International Computers Ltd* [1997] FSR 251. A whole computer system is sold as a good, and thus is a personal chattel. See also *Toby Construction Ltd* v. *Computa Bar (Sales) Pty Ltd* (1983) 2 NSWJR 48.

[8] Graeme Harper, *On Creative Writing* (2010) Wiley, ch. 12.

[9] Niva Elkin-Koren and Eli M Salzberger, *The Law and Economics of Intellectual Property in the Digital Age* (2013) Routledge, 44–5.

[10] Landes and Posner, 'An Economic Analysis of Copyright Law', 326.

[11] Alexandra George, *Constructing Intellectual Property* (2013) Cambridge University Press, 146. See generally Kathy Bowrey, Michael Handler and Dianne Nicol, *Australian Intellectual Property: Commentary, Law and Practice* (2010) Oxford University Press.

[12] See generally Peter Knight, *Copyright: The Laws of Australia* (2013) Tomson Reuters.

[13] See generally Bowrey, Handler and Nicol, *Australian Intellectual Property*.

under the relevant copyright acts. Copyright protects a range of categories, including those relating to literary works, musical works, dramatic works, pantomimes and choreographic works, pictorial, graphic and sculptural works, motion pictures and other audiovisual works, sound recordings and architectural works.[14] Standard books and E-Books attract copyright protection under the category of authorial works (literary, dramatic, artistic and musical works).[15]

The drafters of copyright laws have introduced restrictions on how the public uses certain works within the utilitarian objective of encouraging the development of more creative works. Thomas Babington Macaulay commented when creating the *English Copyright Act of 1842* (UK) that copyright was 'a tax on readers for the purpose of giving a bounty to writers'.[16] In return for this limited monopoly over their work, authors 'are encouraged to create works that they would not have produced otherwise'.[17] Accordingly, copyright is designed around objectives of stimulating activity and progress for the intellectual enrichment of the public.[18] This utilitarian goal is achieved by permitting authors to reap the rewards of their creative efforts.[19] In terms of the creation of books, the right to exclusive exploitation is granted to authors 'in return for making a work available to the reading public'.[20] Of course, this utilitarian approach to incentivising the creation of works does not ensure that all the reading public can benefit from a work.

As analysed in Chapter 1, people with print disabilities often do not read books in the same way as the wider public. Copyright laws start from a position that providing access to the wider public is a secondary concern. Copyright laws do not place any requirements on authors to produce their works in any particular format. Instead, copyright law focuses on restricting people from dealing with protected works without permission. The restriction on dealing with a copyright-protected work extends to making adaptations and derivative works.[21]

---

[14]   See for example, 17 USC § 102(a).

[15]   *Copyright Act* 1968 (Cth) s 10; *Copyright Act*, RSC 1985, c C-42, s 5; *Copyright, Designs and Patents Act* 1988 (UK) s 1(1); 17 USC § 102(a)(1).

[16]   Thomas B Macaulay (speech delivered in the House of Commons, London, 5 February 1841) in Thomas Babington Macaulay, *The Life and Works of Lord Macaulay* (1897) Longmans, Green and Co, 201.

[17]   Joshua L Simmons, 'Catwoman or the Kingpin: Potential Reasons Comic Book Publishers Do Not Enforce their Copyrights against Comic Book Infringers' (2010) 33 *The Columbia Journal of Law & the Arts* 267, 269.

[18]   Elkin-Koren and Salzberger, *The Law and Economics of Intellectual Property*, 47–50.

[19]   Pierre N Leval, 'Toward a Fair Use Standard' (1990) 103 *Harvard Law Review* 1105, 1107–8.

[20]   *IceTV Pty Limited* v. *Nine Network Australia Pty Limited* (2009) 239 CLR 458, 471 (French CJ, Crennan and Kiefel JJ).

[21]   *Copyright Act* 1968 (Cth) s 13(2); *Copyright Act*, RSC 1985, c C-42, s 3(1); *Copyright, Designs and Patents Act* 1988 (UK) s 21; 17 USC § 103.

An adaptation or derivative work includes reproducing the work, or a substantial part thereof, in formats including translations, pictorial representations, dramatic works, music or musical arrangement or transcription. The absence of a private copying exception in jurisdictions such as the United Kingdom means that it is unlawful 'to copy music from a CD that one has purchased onto a computer or MP3 player that one has also legitimately purchased'.[22] While the exceptions discussed in the next chapter tolerate dealings with works without permission in special cases, the general position is that copyright does not permit the creation of derivative works.[23]

If a work is not accessible to a person with a disability, then subject to having a person sit and read the book to them, the person with a disability needs to alter the work to a format that is accessible to persons with print disabilities. This could be through a disability-specific option, such as using a digital scanner, or through a mainstream option, such as accessing a derivative copy that is released to the public in an accessible format. A good example of an original work that is not able to be read by people who cannot read paper books, but where there are publicly available derivative works that are accessible in disability-accessible formats, is the Bible. While centuries-old versions of the New King James Bible are not accessible to people who cannot read paper-based books, derivative copies of this work are freely available on various websites in formats that can easily be read using screen readers. Arguably, constraining the secondary derivative works market has a significant disabling impact upon persons who cannot read print books. Copyright protection of derivative works means that there will be a limited lawful market of accessible derivative works, and persons with disabilities will generally need to utilise one of the exceptions to copyright to gain access to the work.

Not Quite Forever: The Legal Fiction of Copyright Does Not Operate in Perpetuity

Copyright laws exist to enable authors to benefit from exploiting their work. To balance the interest in incentivising creation and the public's interest in having unrestricted access to works, copyright laws in Australia, Canada, the United Kingdom and the United States limit the life of copyright restrictions. While copyright interests are not perpetual, there is a strong argument that the

---

[22]   Andrew Gowers, *Gowers Review of Intellectual Property* (report, Government of the United Kingdom, 2006) 62 <www.official-documents.gov.uk/document/other/0118404830/0118404830 .pdf> (accessed 18 November 2016).

[23]   Brown, Harmon and Waelde, 'Do You See What I See?'.

length of the right to exclusive use is disproportionate to the effort in creating the information.

Australia, the United Kingdom and the United States extend the life of copyright the longest out of the jurisdictions analysed. They all provide that copyright which subsists in a literary, dramatic, musical or artistic work will continue to operate until the end of seventy years after the end of the calendar year in which the author of the work died.[24] Canada limits the copyright period to the end of the period of fifty years from the end of the calendar year in which the author dies.[25] A significant difficulty with the length of copyright is determining whether or not copyright continues to restrict use to the work. The United States Copyright Act contains a measure to assist where it is difficult to ascertain precisely when the author of the work has died. Section 302(e) explains that copyright in a work expires either ninety-five years from its first publication or a period of 120 years from the year of its creation, whichever occurs first.

It is arguable that the exceptionally long life of copyright restrictions is not aligned with the objectives of such laws. The argument that authors need a period of exclusive exploitation to benefit from their creation is reasonably sound. The length of copyright restrictions, however, bears no relation to the actual time required for an author to obtain sufficient returns to reward them for their creation. A good example of the disconnect between the length of copyright and the need to incentivise authors is the creation of academic research monographs. Academic authors' creativity and productivity are primarily driven by a desire to retain and advance their university careers. Furthermore, many academics writing research monographs benefit more from incentives from their university than from royalties on their work. Steven Shavell has argued that academics would continue to publish even where they had no capacity to exploit their creative outputs for profits.[26]

---

[24]   *Copyright Act 1968* (Cth) s 33(2); *Copyright, Designs and Patents Act 1988* (UK) s 12(1); 17 USC
§ 302. The *Duration of Copyright and Rights in Performances Regulations 1995* (UK) reg. 5
increased the length of copyright in the *Copyright, Designs and Patents Act 1988* (UK) s 12,
from fifty to seventy years. Australia used to adopt the fifty-year rule similar to Canada, but as
a consequence of signing a free trade agreement with the United States, Australia's laws were
amended to seventy years: Australia–United States Free Trade Agreement, signed
18 May 2004, [2005] ATS 1 (entered into force 1 January 2005) art. 17.4; *US Free Trade
Agreement Implementation Act 2004* (Cth) Schedule 9, s 120; US Free Trade Agreement
Implementation Bill 2004 (Cth), Explanatory Memorandum, <www.austlii.edu.au/cgi-bin/
sinodisp/au/legis/cth/bill_em/uftaib2004373/memo1.html?stem=0&synonyms=0&query=
copyright%20and%20"70%20years> (accessed 18 November 2016), at 533.

[25]   *Copyright Act*, RSC 1985, c C-42, s 6.

[26]   Steven Shavell, 'Should Copyright of Academic Works Be Abolished?' (2010) 2 *Journal of
Legal Analysis* 301, 304.

Even where authors are driven by a desire to exploit their work, it is difficult to accept that those authors would be disincentivised if time periods of over a century from creation were shortened. Not only does it seem unreasonably excessive to restrict access to works for this duration, it is difficult to believe that many authors would alter their creative output if their work was protected for, say, 20 years rather than 120 years. In determining what a reasonable length is, it is important to consider the time periods where authors obtain maximum returns on their investment. Many authors obtain the primary benefits from their works within a few years of completing them. In some disciplines, teaching and research texts are out of date within a few years. Indeed, many university texts are updated on an annual basis. It seems unnecessary to have copyright protections for all works lasting significantly longer than authors' natural lives, and possibly their great-grandchildren's lives.

Despite the arguably excessive long life of copyright protections, the limited life of copyright has enabled many classical works to be made freely available to people with print disabilities and the wider public. Project Gutenberg is a good example of how works that are no longer restricted by copyright are made freely available to the public. As of May 2015, Project Gutenberg offers over 46,000 previously published books in digital formats that are accessible to everyone in the community, including people with print disabilities.[27]

The team at Project Gutenberg can efficiently turn a work that has had its copyright expired into an accessible digital format. Where the life of copyright has expired, it takes approximately 50 hours to use a special scanner to digitise the work, proofread, format and assemble the book for uploading to the site.[28] The scanning and editing are performed by a large number of volunteers who help create and grow this valuable resource. While Project Gutenberg represents a valuable cultural resource, relying on volunteers and the expiration of copyright will not provide access to the majority of books, including those required for education and work, and thus cannot reverse the book famine.

SECTION II OBTAINING ACCESSIBLE COPIES WITHIN THE COPYRIGHT REGIME: LICENCE TO EXPLOIT WORKS

The primary focus of copyright laws is to restrict unauthorised exploitation of works. If a person with a disability is unable to use a work in its current form, then one option is to use the work under the terms of a copyright licence. There are a range of different copyright licences which enable a person with a print

---

[27] Project Gutenberg <www.gutenberg.org/> (accessed 18 November 2016).
[28] Marie Lebert, *Project Gutenberg (1971–2008)* (2008) Project Gutenberg <www.gutenberg.org/cache/epub/27045/pg27045.html> (accessed 18 November 2016).

disability to modify a work without breaching copyright laws. This chapter will now analyse two such licences and consider the limitations of these authorisations on providing persons with print disabilities with meaningful access to works.

Creative Commons Licences and E-Book Disability Access

Creative Commons licences arguably provide persons with print disabilities with the greatest level of access to the written word. Creative Commons licences are a form of copyright licence where the rights-holder grants substantial exploitation rights freely to the public.[29] These licences enable an author to retain copyright in their work while granting the public the right to access their work freely and create derivative works with certain restrictions. There are, broadly, six standardised Creative Commons licences that differ on what rights are retained and granted.[30] As Creative Commons licences amount to a donation to the public good, rights-holders are free to decide what rights to retain and what rights they desire to grant the public. A common form of Creative Commons licence grants the right to exploit a work and create derivative works on the condition that the derivative work is also made available under a Creative Commons licence.[31]

The Creative Commons movement operates on the basis that restricting access to creative works is an inefficient means of facilitating creativity.[32] Creativity is a continuum, with each new creation building, to some extent, on existing works.[33] Creative Commons authors argue that copyright can restrict access to cultural works, inhibit derivative works and inhibit academic freedom.[34] In contrast, Creative Commons licences encourage fairness and promote human development.[35]

---

[29] For further information on Creative Commons licences see generally Lawrence Lessig, *The Future of Ideas* (2001) Random House; see also Creative Commons Australia <creative commons.org.au/> (accessed 18 November 2016).

[30] Tony Simmonds, 'Common Knowledge? The Rise of Creative Commons Licensing' (2010) 10 *Legal Information Management (UK)* 162.

[31] Ashley West, 'Little Victories: Promoting Artistic Progress through the Enforcement of Creative Commons Attribution and Share-Alike Licenses' (2009) 36 *Florida State University Law Review* 903, 906.

[32] Lessig, *The Future of Ideas*, 4.

[33] Wendy J Gordon, 'Toward a Jurisprudence of Benefits: The Norms of Copyright and the Problem of Private Censorship' (1990) 57 *University of Chicago Law Review* 1009, 1030–1.

[34] Severine Dusollier, 'The Master's Tools v. the Master's House: Creative Commons v. Copyright' (2006) 29 *The Columbia Journal of Law & the Arts* 271, 271–2; Niva Elkin-Koren, 'What Contracts Cannot Do: The Limits of Private Ordering in Facilitating a Creative Commons' (2005) 74 *Fordham Law Review* 375, 376–7.

[35] Nicolas Suzor, 'Free-Riding, Cooperation, and "Peaceful Revolutions" in Copyright' (2014) 28(1) *Harvard Journal of Law and Technology* 138, 185.

There is no legal requirement to grant Creative Commons licences to enable persons with print disabilities to access works. There have been limited steps to utilise concepts drawn from the Creative Commons movement to force educational book prices down.[36] The Californian legislature, for example, recognised the impact copyright was having on prescribed educational materials and used mandatory open-source reforms to reduce prices.

Chapter 621 of the Californian open-source reforms facilitates the provision of limited textbooks to students, free of charge in an E-Book format or for a $20 fee in a printed version in a selection of courses.[37] In the selected courses, open-source textbooks are commissioned that are published on a Creative Commons attribution licence, which 'allows others to use, distribute, and create derivative works based upon the digital material while still allowing the authors or creators to receive credit for their efforts'.[38] While the focus of these reforms is keeping textbook prices low, there is no reason that the terms on which the books are commissioned could not include a requirement that they comply with principles of universal design so that they are fully accessible to persons with print disabilities.

The Creative Commons organisation claims that over a billion works are published on the internet using Creative Commons licences.[39] This impressive figure includes works from all categories protected by copyright, as mentioned above. The difficulty is that many titles for culture, education and work are not released under Creative Commons licences.[40] Absent legislative reforms, arguably the Creative Commons movement will only scratch the surface of the millions of works published each year for culture, education, science and work.

One of the primary barriers to the uptake of open-source publishing are institutions and structures in society that encourage authors to limit the exploitation of their works. Academic publishing illustrates the role society has in working against Creative Commons. Academics are told to publish or perish, and universities are not satisfied with just any publications. Academics are required to publish in journals and with publishers that will assist their university in maintaining and improving its ranking in league tables.[41] This

---

[36] Benjamin Grimes, 'Education: Chapter 621: Using Open-Source Textbooks to Lower the Cost of Education' (2013) 44 *McGeorge Law Review* 628.
[37] Cal. Educ. Code § 66409 (enacted by Chapter 621).   [38] Ibid., § 66409(f)(1).
[39] Creative Commons, 'State of the Commons' (2015) <stateof.creativecommons.org/report/> (accessed 18 November 2016).
[40] Michael J Madison, 'The Idea of the Law Review: Scholarship, Prestige and Open Access' (2006) 10 *Lewis and Clark Law Review* 991.
[41] Carel Stolker, *Rethinking the Law School: Education, Research, Outreach and Governance* (2014) Cambridge University Press, 80.

means academics are strongly encouraged to publish with the highest-ranking publishers. As most of the higher-ranking publishers are for-profit commercial publishers, most works are not published under open-source licences. This is despite the fact that publishing open source can provide better educational outcomes. Joseph Miller and Lydia Loren argue that timely open-source and course-specific digital casebooks provide law students with the greatest learning activity at the lowest cost.[42] To date, however, works published under a Creative Commons licence are the exception rather than the norm. It will take a significant shift in publishing practices for this trend to alter and Creative Commons to make a significant contribution to reversing the book famine.

Restricted Licences and E-Book Disability Access

Where a work is published as a standard book or as an E-Book that is not in a format that is accessible for people with print disabilities, one option is to approach the rights-holder to request the publishing house grant a limited licence and/or provide an accessible copy. If the rights-holder grants permission to use the work in a particular way, then it is not an infringement of copyright to use the work in the way authorised.

Research performed by the author and Rebecca Loudoun, which was discussed in more detail in the introduction to this monograph, and follow-up interviews by the author conducted in 2014 and 2015 with university officials providing students with disabilities support, found that most university officials assisting university students with print disabilities approach publishers to obtain copies of textbooks in accessible formats. This research indicated that many publishers are willing to provide universities and students with print disabilities with copies of such books under a restricted licence. The licence attached to the work generally requires that the work only be used by a particular student, not shared with other students with print disabilities, and that the institution and student agree to indemnify the copyright holder for any damage flowing from a breach of this restricted licence.

Some publishers regard providing books in alternative formats as a derivative right from owning a copy of the book. Publishers who adopt this perspective require a student with a print disability to first purchase a copy of the textbook before an accessible copy is provided. If the textbook is a required text for a course, and if all other students in the course purchase the textbook,

---

[42] Joseph Miller and Lydia Loren, 'The Idea of the Casebook: Pedagogy, Prestige, and Trusty Platforms' (2015) 12 *Washington Journal of Law, Technology and Arts* 10.

then financially the students are in a similar position to the rest of the wider student cohort. Of course, the wider student cohort has access to the textbook from the second they leave the bookstore, whereas the student with a print disability needs to wait for the publisher to process their request and provide an accessible copy. Requiring students with print disabilities to purchase books to obtain alternative copies becomes even more unfair where the textbook is being used for research purposes rather than coursework. Students who are writing research assignments do not purchase books for their assignments, but instead utilise library resources.

Publishers that provide students with print disabilities with accessible copies of textbooks do so on a voluntary basis. Laws do not require publishers to provide university students with print disabilities with alternative copies of works. Accordingly, these publishers should be applauded for exceeding their statutory duties. While this service is positive and improves textbook access for many students with print disabilities, such services cannot achieve equality and will not resolve the book famine.

One of the greatest limitations with this approach to obtaining access to the written word is time. The Harpur and Loudoun research found that some publishers were responding quickly to requests from universities, while other publishers were delaying longer than four weeks.[43] Most respondents (49 per cent, or nine respondents) found that publishers would delay between two and four weeks to respond to a request. Owing to delays caused by publishers responding and providing accessible textbooks, 59 per cent, or 13 respondents, indicated that universities started scanning material to avoid delays caused by publishers delaying the provision of accessible textbooks. Most university teaching semesters in this study were thirteen weeks (excluding holidays and exam periods), which means that if the request is provided in week one, then the student may not have their readings until week five of the semester. If the request pertains to a research assignment and the assignment is released in week two or three of semester, then the chance of obtaining material from publishers within a useful time frame is very low.

Who Has the Right to Authorise Use? Problems in Identifying the Rights-Holder

The permission-based approach to copyright restricts access unless it is authorised by law or by the rights-holder. This approach is regarded as more

[43]   Paul Harpur and Rebecca Loudoun, 'The Barrier of the Written Word: Analysing Universities' Policies to Include Students with Print Disabilities and Calls for Reforms' (2011) 33(2) *Journal of Higher Education Policy and Management* 153.

efficient than requiring a rights-holder to discover who is using their works and asking them to compensate them for the use.[44] The permission-first approach to copyright can create inefficiencies where the existence of copyright is uncertain or, if copyright does exist in the work, where there is uncertainty about who holds the copyright in the work. The digital age has enabled information to be communicated in volumes and speeds unimaginable a few years ago. In this digital era, it is possible that users may deal with materials without being aware of their copyright status.[45] The risk of innocent infringement is arguably less of a problem when dealing with E-Books, or derivatives thereof. In most situations, the problem is not identifying that the work is copyrighted, but identifying who holds the copyright in the target work.

A person who is seeking a restricted licence to deal with a book can open the cover and identify who is listed as the copyright holder. Copyright might be held jointly between the publishing house and the author. If the book was published in the last decade then it is possible that the publishing house may continue as a going concern. This does not mean that the publishing house continues to hold the copyright in the work. The author to this monograph coordinates a large course which has, for many years, prescribed a title that was published by CCH Australia Limited, with a new edition each year. Each year the publisher contacted the author to offer inspection copies of the next edition. In 2014 the publisher had not contacted the author. The author was trying to obtain information about the 2015 edition to prescribe it in the course. During the time the author was attempting to contact CCH Australia Limited for the book, it emerged that Oxford University Press had purchased the copyright to twenty-one titles, including the title that the author was seeking information about.[46] It took over a month of effort to ascertain that the title had been sold to Oxford University Press and to find out who was the appropriate person to contact to obtain an inspection copy. This was a situation where the publishing house was extremely keen for the author to be able to make contact with the rights-holder. In a course with between 350 and 400 students run twice a year, with the textbook costing $135 AUD or about $100 USD, clearly

---

44 Ariel Katz, 'Symposium: Orphan Works and Mass Digitization: Obstacles and Opportunities: The Orphans, the Market, and the Copyright Dogma: A Modest Solution for a Grand Problem' (2012) 27 *Berkeley Technology Law Journal* 1285, 1289; Oren Bracha, 'Standing Copyright Law on its Head – The Googlization of Everything and the Many Faces of Property' (2007) 85 *Texas Law Review* 1799, 1827; Antonio Nicita and Giovanni B Ramello, 'Property, Liability and Market Power: The Antitrust Side of Copyright' (2007) 3 *Review of Law and Economics* 767, 775.

45 Jacqueline D Lipton, 'Cyberspace, Exceptionalism, and Innocent Copyright Infringement' (2011) 13 *Vanderbilt Journal of Entertainment and Technology Law* 767.

46 'Oxford University Press Acquires CCH Academic Titles' (2014) Oxford University Press <annualreport.oup.com/academic> (accessed 18 November 2016).

Oxford University Press was keen to have their title prescribed. The time delays could have been even more extensive if there was less incentive to provide the author with an accessible copy.

Authors often retain copyright in the books they write. Arguably, contacting authors can be even more difficult than contacting publishing houses. Independent authors may or may not keep current websites. Academic authors are increasingly employed on short-term contracts, as the university sector is increasingly casualised and project-based.[47] Even for those academics who do enjoy tenure, many move institutions in order to fast-track their career paths. All these factors can make it time-consuming for an individual who is attempting to contact an author to obtain authorisation to deal with a work.

The difficulties identifying and contacting rights-holders are often intensified the older works are. As mentioned earlier in this chapter, copyright restricts dealing with a work for between fifty and seventy years from the death of the author. The length of copyright can create significant difficulties in tracking down who holds copyright in a particular work. For example, did the author sell their copyright interest? Has it been bequeathed in a last will and testament? Or has the existence of the copyright simply been forgotten? Professor William Patry has observed that, for many works, identifying 'the proper rights holder is prohibitively expensive, and often impossible'.[48] Where a work appears to be protected by copyright but without a readily locatable rights-holder, the work is said to be an 'orphan work'.[49]

The number of works that have no readily identifiable rights-holder are significant. The British Library has estimated that 40 per cent of its collection could be described as orphan works, and the Carnegie Mellon University Libraries found that the publishers for 22 per cent of its works could not be contacted.[50] The costs associated with finding the rights-holders of orphan works are prohibitive.[51] A European Union Directorate for Information Society and Media report noted that one project to identify the rights-

---

[47] Jacquelyn Colin Bryson, 'The Consequences for Women in the Academic Profession of the Widespread Use of Fixed-Term Contracts' (2004) 11(2) *Gender, Work and Organization* 187–206; Megan Kimber, 'The Tenured "Core" and the Tenuous "Periphery": The Casualisation of Academic Work in Australian Universities' (2013) 25(1) *Journal of Higher Education Policy and Management* 41.

[48] William Patry, *How to Fix Copyright* (2011) Oxford University Press, 193.

[49] Ryan Andrews, 'Contracting Out of the Orphan Works Problem: How the Google Book Search Settlement Serves as a Private Solution to the Orphan Works Problem and Why It Should Matter to Policy Makers' (2009) 19 *Southern California Interdisciplinary Law Journal* 97, 98.

[50] Bingbin Lu, 'The Orphan Works Copyright Issue: Suggestions for International Response' (2011) 60 *Journal of the Copyright Society of the USA* 255, 256.

[51] Patry, *How to Fix Copyright*, 194.

holders for one million photographs and films had a budget of €625,000, with three people working full-time for three years trying to find who the appropriate rights-holders were.[52] Another project was trying to digitise 1,000 Dutch history books. After five months the rights-holders to only fifty books had been identified.[53]

The orphan works problem is a disabling barrier to people with print disabilities who are attempting to obtain assistance or restricted licences from rights-holders. While there are exceptions that permit copies to be made specifically for persons with disabilities, which are discussed in the next chapter, the existence of the orphan works problem reduces the capacity of the wider public to create derivative works in more accessible formats.[54] Many older works are published in formats that are not readily accessible to persons with disabilities. Older fonts are harder to scan, and E-Books are a reasonably new phenomenon. If a work is orphaned and over a decade old, then there is a high probability that it is not in a format that is readily accessible to persons with print disabilities. As people are unable to obtain permission from the rights-holder to create a derivative work, such as an E-Book, then the number of universally accessible derivative works will decrease. If persons with print disabilities cannot access works in the mainstream market, then they will need to find an alternative means to obtain access to the work.

SECTION III HOW DIGITAL MEASURES CAN REDUCE DISABILITY ACCESS

What Are Technical Protection Measures?

Copyright operates to curtail the free flow of information. Except for limited circumstances, rights-holders are granted the right to control who may use and copy information that is protected by copyright laws. Restricting the exploitation of digital works is especially challenging due to the ease with which such works can be copied and distributed.[55] To restrict how people use digital content, rights-holders or others involved with distributing such works can

---

52   Anna Vuopala, 'Assessment of the Orphan Works Issue and Costs for Rights Clearance' (report, European Commission, 2010) 6.

53   Ibid.

54   Other countries outside this study adopt a more reasonable approach to orphan works. See for example the French *Loi n° 2012-287 du 1er mars 2012* [Law No. 2012-287 of 1 March 2012] (France).

55   Ian Brown, 'The Evolution of Anti-Circumvention Law' (2006) 20(3) *International Review of Law Computers and Technology* 39.

use digital measures, often referred to as digital rights management or technical protection measures to control access.[56]

Ultimately, digital content is code that a software package turns into a video, image, music or E-Book. It is possible to include access restrictions within this code to limit the number of times the content can be viewed, limit the time the file can be viewed, prevent copying or saving of the file, limit what other software packages can interact with the file, and limit when E-Book readers can open the file.[57] In addition to code restricting how files might be read, the E-Book readers can also contain code that restricts how users might interact with content and where accessibility features can operate.

While digital measures can be used to protect copyright interests, they also can be used to restrict lawful access.[58] With the exception of anti-discrimination laws (discussed in Chapters 6, 7 and 8) and the positive and novel duties (discussed in Chapters 9, 10 and 11), laws do not fetter how people design digital content and hardware. This enables anyone who has lawful control over digital content to employ technical protection measures to control access.[59] Accordingly, a person may have a lawful reason to access digital content, but the decision to use digital measures to restrict access may limit or even deny that person the right to access the information.[60]

While digital rights measures can help prevent unauthorised use of a file, they often prevent persons with disabilities from using adaptive technology to access content. Many screen readers translate what is on the computer screen into an audio description. Screen readers generally can only translate text into audio where the text is capable of being copied. If technical measures prevent content from being copied, then this will also prevent persons with print disabilities from using their screen readers. Accordingly, technical measures aimed to limit access can prevent persons with print disabilities from the lawful use of digital files.[61] The operation of technical protection measures is contributing to the book famine by limiting the capacity of persons with

[56] Gwen Hinze, 'Brave New World, Ten Years Later: Reviewing the Impact of Policy Choices in the Implementation of the WIPO Internet Treaties' Technological Protection Measure Provisions' (2006) 57 *Case Western Reserve Law Review* 779.
[57] Carys Craig, 'Digital Locks and the Fate of Fair Dealing in Canada: In Pursuit of "Prescriptive Parallelism"' (2010) 13(4) *The Journal of World Intellectual Property* 503.
[58] Jason Puckett, 'Digital Rights Management as Information Access Barrier' (2010) 34/35 *Progressive Librarian* 11.
[59] Frederick Bowes, 'Accessibility' in William Kasdorf (ed.), *The Columbia Guide to Digital Publishing* (2003) Columbia University Press, 325.
[60] Allen Renear and Dorothy Salo, 'Electronic Books and the Open eBook Publication Structure' in Kasdorf (ed.), *The Columbia Guide to Digital Publishing*, 455.
[61] Elsa Kramer, 'Digital Rights Management: Pitfalls and Possibilities for People with Disabilities' (2007) 10 *Journal of Electronic Publishing*, 1.

print disabilities to read books that are already digital and, but for steps to disable access, would be readable using adaptive technologies.

Restrictions on Circumventing Technical Protection Measures

The computer code that restricts access uses a key to determine whether access should be denied or permitted. Since this key is often the difference between persons with disabilities accessing content or not, it is important to consider how this key can be circumvented. It is possible to use circumvention software to crack the key to enable access.[62] Copyright laws support rights-holders' efforts to maintain information monopolies by prohibiting the circumvention of digital rights measures.[63] The copyright laws in Australia, Canada, the United Kingdom and the United States enable legal action to be taken against people who circumvent digital rights measures.[64]

Copyright laws construct the removal of technical protection measures as a form of theft, and circumvention software tools as programs created and distributed to assist that unlawful act.[65] The copyright laws in Australia, Canada, the United Kingdom and the United States prohibit the creation and distribution of circumvention programs.[66] The prohibition on the creation and distribution of circumvention programs is arguably quite an extreme measure, considering it is possible to insert technical measures over material that does not attract copyright, and that exceptions to circumventing digital rights management apply.

Circumventing Digital Rights Measures to Enable Access for the Print-Disabled: Limited Exception

Copyright laws in Australia, Canada, the United Kingdom and the United States permit the circumvention of technical protection measures to provide access to content for persons with print disabilities. Canadian copyright laws have the most generous exception out of the jurisdictions analysed in this

---

[62] Mark Stamp, *Information Security: Principles and Practice* (2011) Wiley, 460–3.

[63] Alan Dinsmore, 'Why You Should Care about Digital Rights Management' (2003) 3 *AccessWorld Extra* 3.

[64] *Copyright Act 1968* (Cth) s 116AN; *Copyright Act*, RSC 1985, c C-42, s 41.1; *Copyright, Designs and Patents Act 1988* (UK) s 296ZA; *Digital Millennium Copyright Act*, Pub. Law No. 105–304, § 1201(a), 112 Stat 2860.

[65] Bill Herman, 'A Political History of DRM and Related Copyright Debates: 1987–2012' (2012) 14 *Yale Journal of Law and Technology* 162.

[66] *Copyright Act 1968* (Cth) s 116AO; *Copyright Act*, RSC 1985, c C-42, s 41.1(c); *Copyright, Designs and Patents Act 1988* (UK) s 296ZB; *Digital Millennium Copyright Act*, Pub. Law No. 105–304, §§ 1201(a) and (b), 112 Stat 2860.

monograph. In Canada, a person, a person acting at their request or a non-profit organisation is authorised to circumvent a technical protection measure for the purpose of making a work available to a person with a perceptual disability.[67] In addition to permitting the circumvention, Canadian copyright laws permit the creation and distribution of circumvention tools, where they are created and used exclusively to enable persons with perceptual disabilities to circumvent digital rights measures that prevent them using adaptive technology to read content.[68]

United States copyright laws are more restrictive than Canadian laws. The *Digital Millennium Copyright Act*, codified in Chapter 12 of Title 17 of the United States Code, prohibits the circumvention of certain technological measures employed by or on behalf of copyright owners to restrict access to digital works. Section 1201(b) of that Act empowers the Librarian of Congress to exempt certain people from the prohibition against circumventing digital rights measures where the implementation of access control measures diminishes the ability of individuals to use copyrighted works in ways that are not infringements. A range of factors contained in s 1201(a)(1)(C) are balanced to determine if this adverse impact justifies the exemption. These factors include:

(i)   the availability for use of copyrighted works;
(ii)   the availability for use of works for nonprofit archival, preservation, and educational purposes;
(iii) the impact that the prohibition on the circumvention of technological measures applied to copyrighted works has on criticism, comment, news reporting, teaching, scholarship, or research;
(iv)   the effect of circumvention of technological measures on the market for or value of copyrighted works; and
(v)   such other factors as the Librarian considers appropriate.

The rulings narrowly describe the circumstances in which the exemption applies, and each exemption ruling is valid for three years. The Library of Congress Copyright Office holds triennial rule-making processes where draft rulings are released and submissions accepted. To ensure the accuracy of the determinations, every three years the Library of Congress Copyright Office releases draft rules and accepts submissions on the content of exemptions. Groups that seek the granting of an exception must show a substantial adverse impact by preventing the circumvention of technical measures. The proposed exemption class must be properly tailored to address not only the

---

[67]   *Copyright Act*, RSC 1985, c C-42, s 41.16(1).   [68]   Ibid., s 41.12(3).

demonstrated harm, but also to limit the adverse consequences that may result from the exemption.

The Library of Congress first enabled the circumvention of digital protections on some literary works in the third and fourth triennial rule-making proceedings held in 2006 and 2010 respectively.[69] At the time, these exemptions were considered information communication technologies and E-Books were not widely available. Most E-Books during this period were read on personal computers and laptops, and not on specialist E-Readers. In 2006 and 2010, the exemptions applied to '[l]iterary works distributed in ebook format when all existing ebook editions of the work (including digital text editions made available by authorized entities) contain access controls that prevent the enabling either of the book's read-aloud function or of screen readers that render the text into a specialized format'.[70] This rule only permitted digital rights measures to be circumvented on an E-Book if every E-book in the market had technical measures which restricted access for persons with disabilities.

During the 2011 hearings for the 2012 rule, it was observed that the market for E-Books had altered substantially since the rule was first considered in 2003. E-Books were by then far more common and available in many more formats requiring the use of various hardware and software. The Librarian of Congress observed that the

> designated class is not merely a matter of convenience, but is instead intended to enable individuals who are blind or visually impaired to have meaningful access to the same content that individuals without such impairments are able to perceive. As proponents explained, their desire is simply to be able to access lawfully acquired content. In short, the exemption is designed to permit effective access to a rapidly growing array of ebook content by a population that would otherwise go without.[71]

---

[69] Library of Congress Copyright Office, 'Exemption to Prohibition on Circumvention of Copyright Protection Systems for Access Control Technologies: Final Rule' (November 2006) <www.copyright.gov/fedreg/2006/71fr68472.pdf> (accessed 18 November 2016); Library of Congress Copyright Office, 'Exemption to Prohibition on Circumvention of Copyright Protection Systems for Access Control Technologies: Final Rule' (July 2010) <www.copyright.gov/fedreg/2010/75fr43825.pdf> (accessed 18 November 2016).

[70] Library of Congress Copyright Office, 'Final Rule' (November 2006); Library of Congress Copyright Office, 'Final Rule' (July 2010).

[71] Library of Congress Copyright Office, 'Exemption to Prohibition on Circumvention of Copyright Protection Systems for Access Control Technologies: Final Rule' (October 2012) <www.copyright.gov/fedreg/2012/77fr65260.pdf> (accessed 18 November 2016); Library of Congress Copyright Office, 'Exemption to Prohibition on Circumvention of Copyright Protection Systems for Access Control Technologies: Final Rule' (October 2015) <copyright.gov/1201/2015/fedreg-publicinspectionFR.pdf> (accessed 18 November 2016).

Only permitting a person with a disability to circumvent an E-Book that they had purchased if every other E-Book was also inaccessible would require persons with disabilities to purchase several E-Readers, and possibly the same E-Book several times, as the fact that an E-Book contains digital restrictions is often not known until a person attempts to read the E-Book after purchase. The exemption adopted in 2012, and approved and adopted in 2015, provides:

> Literary works, distributed electronically, that are protected by technological measures which either prevent the enabling of read-aloud functionality or interfere with screen readers or other applications or assistive technologies, (i) when a copy of such a work is lawfully obtained by a blind or other person with a disability, as such a person is defined in 17 U.S.C. 121; provided, however, the rights owner is remunerated, as appropriate, for the price of the mainstream copy of the work as made available to the general public through customary channels; or (ii) when such work is a nondramatic literary work, lawfully obtained and used by an authorized entity pursuant to 17 U.S.C. 121.[72]

Therefore, providing that a person with a disability has obtained a licence to use the copyright-protected E-Book, which usually occurs through purchase, then that person is entitled to circumvent any digital rights measures that hinder them using adaptive technology to access content. It is interesting to observe that during the sixth triennial rule-making proceeding in 2015, there was no opposition from publishing associations to renewing the 2012 exemption. The Association of American Publishers, representing book publishers, justified their support of this exemption on the basis that 'the market does not yet offer sufficient accessibility to literary works'.[73]

Although Canada and the United States permit individuals to circumvent technical measures, Australian copyright law only permits parties who hold a statutory licence to convert works into accessible works to circumvent technical measures. The Australian *Copyright Act 1968* (Cth) s 116AN(9) enables a technical measure to be circumvented if it does not infringe the copyright in the work and is prescribed by a regulation. The *Copyright Regulations 1969* (Cth) in Item 3 of Schedule 10A provides that 'the reproduction or communication by an institution assisting persons with a print disability for provision of assistance to those persons of copyright material of a kind, and in the circumstances, mentioned in Division 3 of Part VB of the

---

[72]   Library of Congress Copyright Office, 'Final Rule' (October 2012); Library of Congress Copyright Office, 'Final Rule' (October 2015).

[73]   Library of Congress Copyright Office, 'Final Rule' (October 2015).

Act' is an exception.[74] The operation of Part VB will be analysed in the next chapter. Essentially, entities which come within this exception include educational institutions and charities such as Vision Australia and the Royal Society for the Blind.

The United Kingdom adopts the most restrictive approach to authorising the circumvention of technical measures. Section 296ZE of the *Copyright, Designs and Patents Act 1988* (UK) only authorises circumvention where a person has a lawful right to access the work, and where the application of any effective technological measure to a copyright work other than 'a computer program prevents a person from carrying out a permitted act in relation to that work', but does not apply to 'copyright works made available to the public on agreed contractual terms in such a way that members of the public may access them from a place and at a time individually chosen by them'.[75] As almost all E-Books and information communication technologies are available under contractual terms which enable a person to access the content at a time and place chosen by them, it would seem that the exception under the *Copyright, Designs and Patents Act 1988* (UK) applies in very limited situations.

A person is not authorised to circumvent a technical measure simply because it falls within the restrictive situation prescribed in s 296ZE. Rather than empowering people to circumvent technical measures that restrict persons with print disabilities from using an E-Book on the same terms as persons who do not use adaptive technology, s 296ZE creates a complicated and time-consuming process to compel the person who controls the technical measure to reduce access barriers. Accordingly, s 296ZE requires an aggrieved party 'to issue a notice of complaint to the Secretary of State'.[76] Following lodgement of this complaint and after investigation, 'the Secretary of State may give to the owner of that copyright work or an exclusive licensee such directions as appear to the Secretary of State to be requisite or expedient' to making the content available to the complainant.[77] A direction by the Secretary of State creates a right that a complainant can enforce.[78] It is arguable that s 296ZE creates a convoluted and impractical system which requires a person with a print disability desiring to circumvent a barrier to equality to complain to a government department, wait for that department to make an order, then wait for the party who created the barrier to digital equality to consider and deal with that order. If they fail to comply appro-priately, then a person with a print disability has to commence action to

---

[74]   Australian Law Reform Commission, *Copyright and the Digital Economy*, Report No. 122 (2014) 358.

[75]   *Copyright, Designs and Patents Act 1988* (UK) s 296ZE(2), (9) and (10).

[76]   Ibid., s 296ZE(2).   [77]   Ibid., s 296ZE(3).   [78]   Ibid., s 296ZE(6).

enforce the direction issued by the Secretary of State. This process is expensive and grants extreme deference to copyright interests at the expense of reading equality.

How Copyright Restricts the Distribution of Derivative Works in Digital Formats

Copyright laws provide authors with a limited monopoly by restricting unauthorised uses of works.[79] To achieve this objective, copyright laws require a person who desires to lawfully use a protected work to either obtain express permission from a copyright holder or ensure that their use comes within one of the exceptions to copyright discussed in the next chapter. There is an increasing social trend to disregard copyright laws and distribute works and create derivative copies.[80] When these infringements involve the removal of security measures or scanning hard-copy books, then the distribution of such files increases access for persons with print disabilities to the written word.

The primary infringers who create unauthorised copies are extremely difficult to identify and sanction. Enforcing copyright laws against primary infringers in the digital age has proven almost impossible.[81] A primary infringer can scan a print book or strip the digital rights management off an E-Book and distribute it online through a range of methods. For persons with print disabilities, the increased distribution of information is arguably positive. Rights-holders and their supporters take a very different perspective.

Focusing on Secondary Copyright Infringement to Reduce the Distribution of Derivative Works in Digital Formats

Copyright regulators and rights-holders have turned their enforcement focus away from primary infringements to secondary infringements.[82] There are two primary means of expanding liability through secondary copyright

---

[79] *Copyright Act 1968* (Cth) s 31; *Copyright Act*, RSC 1985, c C-42, s 3; *Copyright, Designs and Patents Act 1988* (UK) s 2; 17 USC § 102 and 106.f.

[80] See, e.g., Australian Attorney-General's Department, 'Online Copyright Infringement' (Discussion Paper, Parliament of Australia, 2014) for acknowledgement of the issue.

[81] Alain Strowel, 'Introduction: Peer-to-Peer File Sharing and Secondary Liability in Copyright Law' in Alain Strowel (ed.), *Peer-to-Peer File Sharing and Secondary Liability in Copyright Law* (2009) Edward Elgar, 1.

[82] Robert Burrell and Kimberlee Weatherall, 'Before the High Court: Providing Services to Copyright Infringers: *Roadshow Films Pty Ltd v. iiNet Ltd*' (2011) 30 *The Sydney Law Review* 801, 802.

infringement.[83] The first is contributory liability, which attributes secondary liability where a person intentionally induces or encourages direct infringement.[84] The second means of attributing liability is through relying on vicarious liability. A party can be vicariously liable where they '[profit] from direct infringement while declining to exercise a right to stop or limit it'.[85]

All the jurisdictions analysed in this book have some form of secondary liability for copyright infringement. Australian copyright legislation has the widest approach to secondary liability. The *Copyright Act 1968* (Cth) s 101 provides that a person is liable for secondary infringement if they knowingly authorise the distribution of material that constitutes primary infringement. A factor in determining if a party authorises the distribution of infringing material through their website or internet service is whether the secondary party 'took any other reasonable steps to prevent or avoid the doing of the act, including whether the person complied with any relevant industry codes of practice'.[86] Potentially, s 101 requires people to take proactive action in seeking out and removing material that infringed copyright. The High Court of Australia, however, has read down the scope of s 101 so that it aligns with the position in Canada, the United Kingdom and the United States.[87]

In *Roadshow Films Pty Ltd* v. *iiNet Ltd,* thirty-four copyright holders commenced proceedings against Australia's then third-largest internet service provider (iiNet), arguing that iiNet had authorised copyright infringement.[88] It was alleged that iiNet authorised the distribution of infringing works by omitting to take proactive action to seek out and remove infringing works. Chief Justice French and Justices Crennan and Kiefel found that iiNet lacked the technical capacity or power to identify and prevent the distribution of infringing materials. The notices it was provided with by rights-holders did not provide sufficient detail to enable iiNet to take action against customers. Justices Gummow and Hayne reached a similar conclusion and found that the only option was for iiNet to respond to allegations of copyright infringement by terminating customers' accounts. This was held to be an

---

[83] Joseph M Eno, 'What Motivates Illegal File Sharing? Empirical and Theoretical Approaches' (2013) 69 *New York University Annual Survey of American Law* 587, 593.

[84] *Metro-Goldwyn-Mayer Studios Inc.* v. *Grokster, Ltd,* 545 US 913, 929–30 (2005).

[85] *Metro-Goldwyn-Mayer Studios Inc.* v. *Grokster, Ltd.*

[86] *Copyright Act 1968* (Cth) s 101(1A)(c).

[87] Rebecca Giblin, 'Australia's High Court Rules on ISP's Liability for User Infringements' (2012) 7(8) *Journal of Intellectual Property Law and Practice* 559.

        ̇012] HCA 16; (2012) 248 CLR 42; see also Daniel MacPherson, 'The Implications of ·dshow v. *iiNet* for Authorisation Liability in Copyright Law' (2013) 35 *Sydney Law v* 467.

unreasonable step. Justices Gummow and Hayne found that it was 'too long a march' from 'indifference' to countenancing or authorisation.

The copyright statutes in Canada, the United Kingdom and the United States only impose secondary infringement liability where there is knowledge of the infringement.[89] Under these regimes, the rights-holder has the duty to identify the primary infringement and provide the secondary party with sufficient information to enable them to identify where a primary infringement has occurred. After all, secondary parties lack basic information about who owns the copyright in a particular work and the terms on which copyright licences may have been granted.[90] This notice does not always need to identify a specific individual, but instead can identify a general class of infringement that is occurring. The courts in the United Kingdom have held that while 'actual knowledge' can only be ascertained by reference to all the circumstances, it is 'not essential to prove actual knowledge of a specific infringement of a specific copyright work by a specific individual'.[91] While reforms have increased obligations on internet service providers in some jurisdictions,[92] overall the onus to identify the primary infringer remains with the rights-holder.

The capacity of rights-holders to identify when primary infringements are occurring and to provide sufficient notice can prove a difficult task. One of the earlier methods of distributing files involved a website being established where primary infringers informed a central database of what files they held. The central server maintained a central indexing database, which facilitated peer-to-peer file transfers. Napster became the most popular site using this method of distributing works.[93] Ultimately, the capacity to identify primary infringers, combined with Napster's knowledge of the infringing material, resulted in Napster being held liable for secondary infringement.[94]

---

[89]   *Copyright Act*, RSC 1985, c C-42, s 42; *Copyright, Designs and Patents Act 1988* (UK) s 97; 17 USC § 512.

[90]   Salil Mehra and Marketa Trimble, 'Computers: Secondary Liability, ISP Immunity, and Incumbent Entrenchment' (2014) 64 *The American Journal of Comparative Law* 685, 689.

[91]   *Twentieth Century Fox Film Corp.* v. *British Telecommunications Plc* [2011] EWHC 1981, [148].

[92]   See for example: *Digital Economy Act 2010* (UK) s 4B, which contains an obligation to provide copyright infringement lists to copyright owners; Benjamin Farrand, 'The Digital Economy Act 2010: A Cause for Celebration, or a Cause for Concern?' (2010) 32(10) *European Intellectual Property Review* 536.

[93]   Jamie Gregorian, 'Grokster, BitTorrent, Copyright Infringement, and Inducement: How Modus Operandi Can Provide a Functional Standard for Future File-Sharing Cases' (2009) 10 *Texas Review of Entertainment and Sports Law* 145, 153.

[94]   *A&M Records, Inc.* v. *Napster, Inc.*, 239 F 3d 1004, 1081, 1022 (9th Cir., 2001).

Methods to Avoid Detection and Prosecution for Secondary Copyright Infringement

To reduce the risk of secondary infringement liability parties have turned to peer-to-peer methods of distributing files.[95] Peer-to-peer systems involve users downloading software which enables them to communicate directly with other users and exchange files. The files are not hosted or controlled by a central server. The United States Supreme Court has analysed whether a party who hosts a peer-to-peer network could be liable for secondary infringement. Grokster was a peer-to-peer network where the majority of files distributed across the network were found to be infringing copyright. In *Metro-Goldwyn-Mayer Studios* v. *Grokster Ltd* the court rejected the argument that Grokster was just a conduit and should not be liable for the files being transferred between users.[96] Grokster was providing a product 'with the object of promoting its use to infringe copyright, as shown by clear expression or other affirmative steps taken to foster infringement.'[97] As there was intent to facilitate the infringement of copyright, Grokster was liable for secondary infringement.[98]

The capacity to identify primary infringements on peer-to-peer networks is increasingly more difficult.[99] To increase security and to reduce the capacity to identify who and what is transferred, a range of tools have been developed.[100] These include proxy and virtual private network (VPN) services. Proxy services, such as TorrentPrivacy and BTGuard, and VPN services create a digital tunnel between an individual user and the internet. The user's internet traffic is encrypted on their computer and then goes through their internet service provider to a remote server. The remote server has the capacity to engage in encrypted communications with the individual. The remote server then anonymises the data stream and filters the data stream through a number of other remote services around the world. The servers which finally

95   Graham Reynolds, 'Case Comment: Pirate Bay on English Bay? BitTorrent File Sharing and Copyright Infringement in the Supreme Court of British Columbia' (2012) 43 *UBC Law Review* 193, 196; Linda Young, 'Online File Sharing: Current Law and Developments in Ireland – Part I' (2013) 31 *Irish Law Times* 209.
96   *MGM Studios, Inc.* v. *Grokster, Ltd*, 545 US 913, 936 (2005).
97   *MGM Studios, Inc.* v. *Grokster, Ltd*, 936–7 (2005).
98   Stacey Dogan, 'Principled Standards vs. Boundless Discretion: A Tale of Two Approaches to Intermediary Trademark Liability Online' (2014) 37 *The Columbia Journal of Law & the Arts* 503, 507.
99   B Bodó, 'Set the Fox to Watch the Geese: Voluntary IP Regimes in Piratical File-Sharing Communities' in M Fredriksson and J Arvanitakis (eds), *Piracy: Leakages from Modernity, Sacramento* (2013) Litwin Books.
100 Mark Hoorebeek, 'eBooks, Libraries and Peer-to-Peer File Sharing' (2003) 52(2) *Australian Library Journal* 163.

communicate with the wider internet have internet protocol addresses from jurisdictions that have laws that protect digital privacy or jurisdictions that enable downloading (for example, some databases only permit people to download to US-based internet protocol addresses). Through these processes, the individual user's digital activities are shielded from detection. This essentially prevents rights-holders and authorities from knowing who is transferring data, and what is being transferred. In these circumstances, it is almost impossible to detect where primary infringements are occurring. While people may wish to secure their activities to hide copyright infringement, there is a wide spectrum of lawful reasons why users may desire to ensure digital privacy.

Breaching Copyright to Share Content: Robin Hoods or Pirates?

The reduced capacity for regulators and rights-holders to prosecute secondary infringement suits is arguably positive news for people with print disabilities. There is a significant proportion of the population who desire to utilise the potential of the internet to share the written word.[101] There are a range of diverse motivations attributed to these so-called (depending on your perspective) pirates or Robin Hoods. Some focus on conserving and promoting culture and knowledge, while others feel copyright has no moral compulsion and are prepared to ignore its restrictions,[102] and others engage in piracy for profit.[103] Regardless of the motives, there is arguably a widely held belief that sharing digital files is morally acceptable.[104]

In addition to the E-Libraries discussed throughout this work, there are now a significant amount of E-Books available freely on the internet.[105] Some of these E-Books are available through E-Libraries which purport to comply with copyright restrictions. Examples of such services include Textbook

---

[101] Martin Zimerman, 'E-books and Piracy: Implications/Issues for Academic Libraries' (2011) 112(1/2) *New Library World* 67.

[102] D Tenen, 'Book Piracy as Peer Preservation' (2014) 11 *Computational Culture* 1.

[103] Sam Castree, 'Cyber-Plagiarism for Sale! The Growing Problem of Blatant Copyright Infringement in Online Digital Media Stores' (2012) 14 *Texas Review of Entertainment and Sports Law* 1.

[104] David Lametti, 'The Virtuous P(eer): Reflections on the Ethics of File Sharing' in Annabelle Lever (ed.), *New Frontiers in the Philosophy of Intellectual Property* (2012) Cambridge University Press, 284.

[105] Melanie Ramdarshan Bold, 'The Best Things in Life Are Free: Can Paid Content Survive in a World Where Content Roams so Freely?' (2011) 9(12) *International Journal of Humanities* 59; Jeffrey Young, 'On the Web, a Textbook Proliferation of Piracy' (2008) 54(44) *Chronicle of Higher Education* 1.

Torrents,[106] TextbookRevolution,[107] and ManyBooks.[108] These E-Libraries that purport to comply with copyright hold thousands of works that are under Creative Commons licences or are apparently not protected by copyright laws. The majority of works used in education and work are within copyright. While such works may appear on these E-Libraries, once a notice has been provided to the E-Library demonstrating that there is an infringement, the work is removed.

While there are services which purport to comply with copyright, there are others that actively ignore copyright laws.[109] The largest shadow library in the world has its history in the dissolved Union of Soviet Socialist Republics (the Soviet Union). Under the iron curtain there was tight censorship and people lacked the resources to access the written word easily. Unauthorised publishing of work was subject to criminal sanction.[110] This situation led to books being authored clandestinely and smuggled into the Soviet Union, and then copied by whatever means possible.[111]

When the Soviet Union disintegrated into fifteen separate nations in 1991, many of the censorship laws were eased. At the same time as this monumental social transformation, the digital age and the internet were providing more efficient means of creating and distributing material. Samizdat publications often consisted of carbon copies of typewritten sheets which were shared between readers. The digital age provided highly efficient means to create and distribute samizdat publications.[112] The global reach of samizdat communities placed their members in conflict with rights-holders who desired to enforce their copyright.[113]

Copyright restrictions were and are regarded by many people in the samizdat underground book distribution movement as a new form of censorship, to be approached as a concept to be resisted.[114] When this approach to censorship

106 Textbook Torrents <archive.is/20150408005653/www.textbooktorrents.com/> (accessed 18 November 2016).

107 'About', TextbookRevolution <textbookrevolution.org/index.php/TextbookRevolution:About> (accessed 18 November 2016).

108 ManyBooks <manybooks.net/> (accessed 18 November 2016).

109 Dennis Tenen and Maxwell Henry Foxman, 'Book Piracy as Peer Preservation' (2014) 4 *Computational Culture* 1.

110 Under articles 70 and 190–1 of the USSR *Criminal Code*.

111 Alice F Yurke, 'Copyright Issues Concerning the Publication of Samizdat Literature in the United States' (1987) 11 *Columbia-VLA Journal of Law & the Arts* 449.

112 Bodó Balázs, 'Eastern Europeans in the Pirate Library' (2015) 1(7) *Visegrad Insight* 98; Maurice Friedberg, Masaji Watanabe and Nobuyuki Nakamoto, 'The Soviet Book Market: Supply and Demand' (1984) 2 *Acta Slavica Iaponica* 177.

113 Joe Karaganis and Bodó Balázs, *Multimedia: Copy Culture, Media Piracy, and Shadow Libraries* (2012) American University Washington College of Law.

114 Ibid.

and copyright was combined with very limited enforcement across the states in the former Soviet Union, it was not surprising that digital samizdat E-Libraries became popular.

Based in Russia, Library Genesis is the largest samizdat shadow library in the world. The library consists of approximately one million non-fiction E-Books, 900,000 fiction E-Books and over 20 million papers from academic journals.[115] An interesting feature of Library Genesis is that it is possible to download the entire collection of works and use them to start a new E-Library. This makes it extremely difficult to shut down the shadow library.[116] The sheer size of Library Genesis leads to the question whether widespread copyright infringement might be the answer to the book famine.

Can Copyright Piracy Resolve the Book Famine?

Under the current international and domestic legal regime, copyright piracy cannot reliably resolve the book famine. This is because copyright infringement remains unlawful and offending sites can be blocked or shut down. In the United Kingdom High Court of Justice, Chancery Division, rights-holders successfully relied on s 97A of the *Copyright, Designs and Patents Act 1988* (UK) to require the internet service providers BT, Virgin Media, Sky, TalkTalk and EE to block access to certain websites that provide access to material that infringes copyright laws.[117] Justice Birss ordered various infringing websites to be blocked, and blocked websites that allowed users to download applications which enabled users to circumvent the blocking order.[118]

Library.NU (previously called EBooksclub), anb.org, gigapedia.com and www.ifile.it were shut down in 2012 by court order.[119] The take-down notice claimed that Library.NU had over 400,000 books on it and that many of these copies violated copyright.[120] Through advertising, donations and sales of premium accounts, shadow libraries returned over 8 million euros per year. A number of publishers commenced proceedings against these shadow

[115] Library Genesis / LibGen – The Meta Library: <sites.google.com/site/themetalibrary/library-genesis> (accessed 18 November 2016).
[116] Devon Weston, 'Catching the Pirates', IPG Blogs (24 July 2014) Independent Publishers Guild <www.ipg.uk.com/?id=3520> (accessed 18 November 2016).
[117] *Twentieth Century Fox Film Corporation and Ors* v. *Sky UK Ltd and Ors* [2015] EWHC 1082.
[118] Ibid., [60]–[62].
[119] Andrew T Forcehimes, 'A Defence of Stealing Ebooks' (2013) 12(34) *Think* 109.
[120] Christopher Kelty, 'The Disappearing Virtual Library' (1 March 2012) Aljazeera (online) <www.aljazeera.com/indepth/opinion/2012/02/2012227143813304790.html> (accessed 18 November 2016).

libraries in the regional Landgericht Munich court in Germany.[121] At the time, these shadow libraries were owned by an Irish entity which ran the library servers through Germany. The libraries transferred their operations to Ukraine and later ran other aspects of the library through Italy and Niue.[122] While the capacity to move digital shadow libraries between jurisdictions outstrips the capacity of legal proceedings to transfer between jurisdictions, the fact remains that copyright violations are unlawful. If copyright is causing undesirable outcomes, then a better solution is to reform the system rather than relying on people to act unlawfully.

Until lawful means to obtain access to the written word are provided, people with print disabilities may consider turning to unlawful means to exercise their right to read. On the one hand, the fact that accessible works that infringe copyright are potentially available can help to address the book famine. On the other hand though, the unlawful distribution of these works can motivate rights-holders to find new vehicles to restrict the distribution of their works. Some of the measures adopted by rights-holders may hurt users who are unable or unwilling to break the law to obtain access to works. Whether or not the secondary infringement market can help combat the book famine, relying on unlawful acts to achieve a social end is an undesirable and unsustainable policy option.

Illegality is not the only reason that shadow digital libraries cannot resolve the book famine. Currently, the number of E-Books available on shadow digital libraries is inadequate to enable people with print disabilities to exercise their right to read on an equal basis as others. While the number of

---

[121]   These proceedings are unreported, but their filing references in the regional Landgericht Munich court include: 7 O 28506/11: Walter de Gruyter GmbH and Co. KG./. Ivanova/Nunez/DF Hosting Ltd; 7 O 29035/11: Informa UK Limited./. Ivanova/Nunez/DF Hosting Ltd; 7 O 29036/11: The McGraw-Hill Companies Inc./. Ivanova/Nunez/DF Hosting Ltd; 7 O 29037/11: John Wiley and Sons Inc./. Ivanova/Nunez/DF Hosting Ltd; 7 O 29038/11: Verlag C.H. Beck OHG./. Ivanova/Nunez/DF Hosting Ltd; 7 O 29047/11: Elsevier Inc./. Ivanova/Nunez/DF Hosting Ltd; 7 O 29048/11: Springer Verlag GmbH./. Ivanova/Nunez/DF Hosting Ltd; 21 O 29039/11: Oxford University Press Inc./. Ivanova/Nunez/DF Hosting Ltd; 21 O 29040/11: Cambridge University Press./. Ivanova/Nunez/DF Hosting Ltd; 21 O 29041/11: Cengage Learning Inc./. Ivanova/Nunez/DF Hosting Ltd; 21 O 29042/11: Pearson Education Inc./. Ivanova/Nunez/DF Hosting Ltd; 33 O 29043/11: HarperCollins Publishers./. Ivanova/Nunez/DF Hosting Ltd; 33 O 29044/11: Hogrefe Verlag GmbH and Co. KG./. Ivanova/Nunez/DF Hosting Ltd; 37 O 29046/11: The Chancellor, Masters and Scholars of the University of Oxford./. Ivanova/Nunez/DF Hosting Ltd; 37 O 29034/11: Pearson Education Limited./. Ivanova/Nunez/DF Hosting Ltd; 37 O 29045/11: Macmillan Publishers Ltd./. Ivanova/Nunez/DF Hosting Ltd; 37 O 29033/11: Georg Thieme Verlag KG./. Ivanova/Nunez/DF Hosting Ltd.

[122]   Lausen Rechtsanwälte, 'Anlage zur Pressemitteilung in der Sache Verlage./. library.nu und ifile.it: Sachverhaltsdarstellung' <boersenverein.de/sixcms/media.php/976/15-02-_library%20nu.pdf> (accessed 1 July 2016).

E-Books is impressive, there are over a hundred million works published, and more are published every day. If a person desires to download a book which was a finalist or winner of the Nobel Prize for Literature, then it is very likely that that user will have little difficulty in finding a copyright-infringing copy of this work online. If a user was, however, seeking a more obscure work, then the capacity to find such a work is reduced. In May 2015, the author searched on Library Genesis for 'jurisprudence' and returned 101 titles. The author was seeking a particular text for which he had permission from the author to download and open it if he could find it online. This particular book, which was a prescribed text in several university courses, was not available on Library Genesis at that point. Nevertheless, a number of other texts on Library Genesis would have been helpful if the author was not after a specific text to read a particular academic's argument. Not all areas are as well served. The author also performed a search for '*Convention on the Rights of Persons with Disabilities*', which returned no hits. Arguably, pirated databases provide a helpful resource, but they will not resolve the book famine.

CONCLUSION

This chapter has analysed the operation of the restrictive and permission-based paradigms in Australian, Canadian, British and American copyright laws. This chapter has argued that the recognition and protection of copyright interests reduces the ability of persons with print disabilities to exercise their right to read. Copyright laws recognise authors' rights to exclusive exploitation of their created works for up to seventy years exceeding the life of the author. If a person desires to use a work restricted by copyright, the prima facie position is that the user must obtain authorisation from the rights-holder. While Creative Commons licences enable the wider public to exploit their work without seeking permission directly from the rights-holders, most restricted works require a user to make contact with the rights-holder to obtain permission. While many publishers are willing to help persons with print disabilities obtain access to books and E-Books, time delays and complications in contacting rights-holders mean this approach cannot provide equality of access to the written word. While there is an increase in E-Books and other content in digital formats, the use of technical protection measures, coupled with legal and practical difficulties in unlocking such works, means that the book famine is being prolonged unnecessarily. Orphan works, in particular, create difficulties for people contacting the rights-holder as, by definition, the rights-holders of such works are not readily identifiable or contactable.

Copyright laws seek to restrict how people use copyright-protected works. Problems with enforcing such laws against primary infringers have resulted in action being taken against secondary infringers. Secondary infringement seeks to hold liable for infringing copyright people who conduct, inter alia, E-Libraries. Attempts to hold secondary infringers liable for copyright breaches have been substantially hindered by advances in technologies, as well as the international nature of the internet. Despite the growth in E-Libraries that distribute copyright-restricted works without authorisation (and which provide a valuable service in combatting the book famine), such activities are unlawful in many jurisdictions and it is against good public policy to rely on such activities to achieve the social goal of equality.

In an age where digital technologies have reduced the costs of reproduction and distribution to virtually zero, copyright laws seek to create scarcity in a post-scarcity world. The operation of copyright laws is a major factor contributing to the scarcity of E-Books. Copyright laws empower rights-holders to act as gatekeepers who can restrict access to material and determine how that access occurs. Copyright laws, however, have failed to stop the growth of significant markets in the unauthorised distribution of primary and derivative works. Despite the existence of shadow libraries, and the operation of the exceptions intended to provide access that are analysed in the next chapter, it could be argued that the current approach to copyright neither sufficiently protects rights-holders' genuine interests, nor enables persons with print disabilities to exercise their right to read.

5

Exceptions to Rights-Holders' Exclusivity Provides Limited Relief from the Disabling Impact of Copyright

INTRODUCTION

Copyright operates on the basis that it is in the public interest to restrict the free flow of information. There are, however, situations where the benefits of enabling access outweigh the public benefit in restricting access to works. Copyright accordingly grants a limited monopoly of exploitation which is subject to reasonable and beneficial secondary uses.[1] The authorising of secondary uses, without rights-holders' permission, overrides the control that rights-holders seek.[2] This chapter will analyse doctrines which modify the principle in copyright that rights-holders should enjoy the exclusive right to exploit works from fifty to seventy years after the death of creators.

The first exception analysed in this chapter is the exception that regards persons with print disabilities as a special case under the Three-Step Test. This long-standing statutory licence has been utilised primarily by charities for the blind to convert standard books into alternative formats, such as Braille, large print and talking books. The statutory licence has operated for a considerable period of time to enable persons with print disabilities to have some access to the written word. Secondly, this chapter will use the experiences of the Google Books and HathiTrust E-Book libraries as case studies to illustrate the limited nature of the exceptions to copyright. This chapter will introduce these E-Libraries, and then analyse the legal framework which permits and restricts their operation.

Finally, this chapter will analyse the operation of the fair dealing and fair use doctrines. The fair dealing doctrine in Australia, Canada and the United

---

[1] Neil Weinstock Netanel, 'Copyright and a Democratic Civil Society' (1996) 106 *Yale Law Journal* 283, 285.

[2] Johnathan Mukai, 'Joint Ventures and the Online Distribution of Digital Content' (2005) 20(1) *Berkeley Technology Law Journal* 781, 783.

Kingdom has a substantially different scope to the equivalent fair use doctrine in the United States. Accordingly, this chapter will analyse the fair dealing and fair use doctrines separately. This chapter argues that the operation of the statutory licence for the print-disabled, as well as fair dealing and fair use exemptions, can increase the availability of books for the print-disabled; however, the level of access will still leave persons with print disabilities without access to the majority of books in the world.

SECTION I THE RIGHT TO CONVERT WORKS INTO AN ACCESSIBLE FORMAT: A STATUTORY LICENCE THAT TOLERATES LIMITED UNAUTHORISED USE TO ASSIST THE PRINT-DISABLED

This section will analyse an exception to copyright which permits the making of derivative works to enable persons with print disabilities to read otherwise inaccessible content. While this exception operates in Australia, Canada, the United Kingdom and the United States, it is important to note that the copyright laws in many other jurisdictions do not provide such vehicles to enable the print-disabled to access copyright-restricted content.[3] The dissemination of knowledge in society is largely dependent on rights-holders authorising the use of copyright-protected works. The problem for minority groups in society is that if the market does not provide access in formats that are accessible to all users then, subject to an exception, copyright laws prevent the creation of accessible derivative works and thus effectively block access to knowledge.

Historically the market has not disseminated knowledge in formats that the print-disabled could read. When the Three-Step Test was adopted in 1967, there were essentially no commercially available formats that were accessible to the print-disabled: large print was rarely published; audible books were technically possible, but were prohibitively expensive; and it would take over a quarter of a century for digitised books to become a possibility. To enable persons with print disabilities to gain access to a few published works, copyright laws introduced exceptions which provided that it was not an infringement of copyright for disability charities to undertake the laborious and expensive task of brailling or creating a raised print version of a copyright-

---

[3] Jingyi Li, 'Copyright Exemptions to Facilitate Access to Published Works for the Print Disabled: The Gap between National Laws and the Standards Required by the *Marrakesh Treaty*' (2014) 45(7) *International Review of Intellectual Property and Competition Law* 740; Jhonny Antonio Pabón Cadavid, 'Copyright Exceptions and Affirmative Actions for Visually Impaired Persons' (2015) 10(6) *Journal of Intellectual Property Law and Practice* 407.

restricted work without first obtaining permission from the rights-holder.[4] This process has arguably become more challenging, with national austerity measures reducing funding for equality interventions, as well as reductions in donations to disability causes.[5]

Australia, Canada, the United Kingdom and the United States have all introduced statutory licences, which authorise derivative copies of books to be made in formats that persons with print disabilities can access.[6] These exceptions have enabled charities, such as the American Printing House for the Blind, Books for the Blind, the Braille Institute of America, the Canadian Federation of the Blind, the Canadian National Institute for the Blind, the Cardiff Institute for the Blind, the National Braille Association, the National Federation of the Blind, the National Library for the Blind, the Royal National Institute of Blind People, Vision Australia and the Washington Talking Book and Braille Library, to create thousands of Braille and embossed books. Of course, during the same period, commercial publishers have published hundreds of millions of books, so the capacity of this statutory licence to resolve the book famine in the past has been highly doubtful.[7] There are now greater scanning techniques and many books are currently being distributed in digital versions. Perhaps now this statutory licence may provide persons with print disabilities with greater access to the written word. This section will analyse how this exception operates in Australia, Canada, the United Kingdom and the United States, to understand the capacity of this exception to resolve the book famine.

Persons with Print Disabilities as Special Cases

People with print disabilities qualify as special cases for the Three-Step Test. Domestic laws reflect this situation and now include all persons with print disabilities in the statutory licences. This was not always the case, however. Even though, by definition, all persons with print disabilities cannot read print books, some copyright laws have only provided support to certain categories of impairment. Until recently, the United Kingdom outlined the narrowest definition of who qualifies as print-disabled.

---

[4] David Nimmer, *Nimmer on Copyright* (2013) LexisNexis, [8.07B], [8.13E] (describing accommodations for disability in US copyright statutes).
[5] Stelios Charitakis, 'Austerity Measures in Greece and the Rights of Persons with Disabilities' (2013) 2(2) *Cyprus Human Rights Law Review* 271; Bob Hepple, *Equality*, 2nd edn (2014) Hart Publishing, 174.
[6] *Copyright Act 1968* (Cth) Part VB, Division 3; *Copyright Act*, RSC 1985, c C-42, s 32; *Copyright, Designs, and Patents Act 1988* (UK) ss 31, 1B; 17 USC § 121.
[7] Dilan Thampapillai and Paul Harpur, 'Unlocking the Library: Copyright Access and the Disabled' (2008) 11(3) *Internet Law Bulletin* 14.

In the United Kingdom, the *Copyright and Rights in Performances (Disability) Regulations 2014* (UK) modified ss 31A and 31B of the *Copyright, Designs and Patents Act 1988* (UK). Prior to these amendments, the exception in the United Kingdom only applied to people with visual impairments. This meant people with other print disabilities were not able to utilise this exception to obtain access to information which had been denied to them since s 31A was originally introduced in 2002.[8]

Following the 2014 amendments, the *Copyright, Designs and Patents Act 1988* (UK) defines disability widely. If a person with a print disability is seeking to convert the work themselves, then s 31A requires the person with a print disability to be prevented by their disability 'from enjoying the work to the same degree as a person who does not have that disability'. The *Copyright, Designs and Patents Act 1988* (UK) imposes fewer restrictions when a derivative work is being created by an authorised body. In this situation, s 31B simply requires the derivative work be created for 'disabled persons'.

The United States has adopted the widest approach to defining who is print-disabled and thus a special case for the Three-Step Test. In the United States, most impairments that reduce a person's capacity to read standard print enliven rights under the so-called 'Chafee Amendment'.[9] The *Copyright Act of 1976* (USA) § 121, otherwise known as the Chafee Amendment, under subsection (a) authorises the reproduction and distribution of a previously published, non-dramatic literary work, in a specialised format, exclusively for use by blind or other persons with disabilities, by an authorised entity.

Australia and Canada specify the types of impairments that can be regarded as print-disabled. Australia uses the term 'print disabilities', whereas Canada labels the category 'perceptual disability'.[10] These terms are substantively the same. The statutes both define print-disabled and perceptual disability to include the following three situations:

(a) severe or total impairment of sight or hearing or the inability to focus or move one's eyes,

(b) the inability to hold or manipulate a book;

(c) an impairment relating to comprehension.[11]

---

[8]   Section 31A was inserted into the *Copyright, Designs and Patents Act 1988* (UK) by the *Copyright (Visually Impaired Persons) Act 2002* (UK).

[9]   Mary Bertlesman, 'The Fight for Accessible Formats: Technology as a Catalyst for a World Effort to Improve Accessibility Domestically' (2012) 27 *Syracuse Journal of Science and Technology Law Reporter* 26, 36–7.

[10]   *Copyright Act 1968* (Cth) ss 135ZN, 135ZP; *Copyright Act*, RSC 1985, c C-42, s 32(1)(8).

[11]   *Copyright Act 1968* (Cth) s 10; *Copyright Act*, RSC 1985, c C-42, s 2.

It is interesting to note that the definitions of print disabilities in copyright laws are more expansive than those adopted in the *Marrakesh Treaty* discussed in Chapters 1 and 3 of this monograph.

There has been limited recognition of the barriers confronting people experiencing comprehension impairments.[12] The recognition of people with non-sensory impairments as being print-disabled has been a long struggle. While the United Nations *Convention on the Rights of Persons with Disabilities* (CRPD) does not create a general right to easy-to-read formats, the Convention does require signage on buildings to be in an 'easy to read' format,[13] and voting papers for public office to be 'easy to understand'.[14] The struggle for recognition of people with comprehension-related impairments has only recently attracted the attention of web accessibility guidelines. Whereas web accessibility guidelines that explain what is required to provide access for persons with sensory impairments are well-established, those for people with comprehension disabilities, such as cognitive disabilities, are only now emerging.[15] Thus the easy-to-read campaign is only now resulting in changes on the ground. The express inclusion of comprehension disabilities as print disabilities in copyright laws represents a significant victory for disability rights advocates, and hopefully will contribute to greater recognition for people with all print disabilities.

Who Can Do the Converting?

The Three-Step Test requires special case exemptions to avoid unreasonably prejudicing the legitimate interests of the rights-holders. The capacity of rights-holders to control who exploits their works is regarded as a legitimate interest. Reflecting this approach, all copyright regimes tightly control who may create derivative works for the exclusive use of persons with print disabilities. The people who are empowered to utilise this exemption in Australia are limited to 'institutions assisting persons with a print disability';[16] in the

---

[12]   Janos Fiala-Butora, Michael Ashley Stein and Janet E. Lord, 'The Democratic Life of the Union: Toward Equal Voting Participation' (2014) 55 *Harvard International Law Journal* 71, 96; Ann Marie Rakowski, 'Just Who Do You Think You're Talking to? The Mandate for Effective Notice to Food Stamp Recipients with Mental Disabilities' (2004) 37 *The Columbia Journal of Law and Social Problems* 485, 501.

[13]   CRPD, opened for signature 30 March 2007, 2515 UNTS 3 (entered into force 3 May 2008) art. 9(2)(d).

[14]   CRPD, art. 29(a)(i).

[15]   Peter Blanck, *E-Quality: The Struggle for Web Accessibility by Persons with Cognitive Disabilities* (2014) Cambridge University Press, ch. 7.

[16]   *Copyright Act 1968* (Cth) s 135ZN.

United Kingdom, authorised bodies;[17] in the United States, authorised entities;[18] and in Canada, bodies not conducted for profit.[19] These entities are generally defined to include educational institutions and not-for-profit organisations.[20] In the United States, the exemption is extended to include any governmental agency 'that has a primary mission to provide specialized services relating to training, education, or adaptive reading or information access needs of blind or other persons with disabilities'.[21]

The exemptions in Canada and the United Kingdom also extend to persons with print disabilities who act independently. Both these jurisdictions permit persons with print disabilities to create derivative works personally, or to request another person to create the derivative works on their behalf.[22] Permitting a person who lawfully possesses a work to make a derivative work for their personal use would not seem to make any practical difference. Even if the creation of such a derivative work were unlawful, it would seem unlikely that a rights-holder would detect the breach and that there would be any benefit in pursuing a person who made a personal copy for their own use. Authorising a person with a print disability to request another to create the derivative work on their behalf arguably empowers the person with a disability to request friends, family or even for-profit entities to help with creating accessible derivative works. While it is possible for for-profit entities to become involved in creating derivative works under the statutory licence, the existence of well-established disability charities that perform such conversions in Canada and the United Kingdom, combined with the restrictions on seeking profits for creating such works in the United Kingdom,[23] are likely to result in the marketplace for creating disability-accessible works under the statutory licence remaining the province of charities.

Without these statutory licences, persons with print disabilities and entities supporting them would need to contact rights-holders and obtain a limited licence before they could start creating accessible derivative works.[24] While this exemption has substantially reduced the barriers to the written word, this exemption falls a long way short of achieving equality. In addition to the barrier of actually creating the derivative work, the exemption contains

[17] *Copyright, Designs and Patents Act 1988* (UK) s 31B.   [18] 17 USC § 121.

[19] *Copyright Act*, RSC 1985, c C-42, s 32.

[20] *Copyright, Designs and Patents Act 1988* (UK) s 6F(6).   [21] 17 USC § 121(d).

[22] *Copyright Act*, RSC 1985, c C-42, s 32(1); *Copyright, Designs and Patents Act 1988* (UK) s 31a(2).

[23] *Copyright, Designs and Patents Act 1988* (UK) s 31A. See *Copyright, Designs and Patents Act 1988* (UK) s 31A(3) which provides that 'If a person makes an accessible copy under this section on behalf of a disabled person and charges the disabled person for it, the sum charged must not exceed the cost of making and supplying the copy.'

[24] Bertlesman, 'The Fight for Accessible Formats', 36–7.

restrictions and can only be utilised if procedural requirements are satisfied. This chapter will now analyse how the exemption operates in Australia, Canada, the United Kingdom and the United States.

Conflict: Which Works Come within the Statutory Licences?

The exemption for the print-disabled does not apply to all copyright-restricted works. All jurisdictions take steps to comply with the requirements in the Three-Step Test with respect to ensuring that the operation of the exemption does not conflict with the normal exploitation of the work, and that the operation of the exemption does not unreasonably prejudice the legitimate interests of the rights-holder. While all jurisdictions take steps to protect rights-holders, the measures adopted in the different copyright regimes differ markedly.

The Australian, Canadian and United Kingdom regimes provide more protection to rights-holders than the equivalent laws in the United States. In Australia, Canada and the United Kingdom, a person making an accessible derivative work is required first to ascertain whether there is an existing commercially available copy.[25] This requirement has been inserted to prevent the print-disabled exemption from being used to create derivative works where derivative works are already commercially available at prices deemed reasonable.

Lawmakers have essentially determined that persons with print disabilities should not be enabled to make derivative works without the permission of rights-holders where derivative copies already exist.[26] The principle behind this is that persons with print disabilities should not get access to information for free where the wider public needs to pay rights-holders to obtain access. Of course, if the wider public accesses information through a public library or a library associated with an educational institution or employer, and such libraries have purchased access to information that is not in an accessible format, then this creates the situation where the wider public can access information for free, but the person with a print disability might be required to pay to obtain access to the information. Considering the hundreds of millions of works held in libraries across the globe that exist in formats that are not accessible to persons with print disabilities, it is reasonable to assume that libraries will continue to hold works that are not accessible to all their

---

[25] *Copyright Act 1968* (Cth) s 135ZP(4)–(6); *Copyright Act*, RSC 1985, c C-42, s 32(3); *Copyright, Designs and Patents Act 1988* (UK) s 31B(2)(f).

[26] Australian Law Reform Commission, *Copyright and the Digital Economy*, Report No. 122 (2014) 35.

members. While anti-discrimination laws, analysed in Chapters 6 to 11 of this monograph, may assist persons with a disability, it is arguably a curious position for copyright to require people with print disabilities to pay to obtain access to information in situations where the wider public has access for free.

The Australian copyright regime partially ignores the issue of access when requiring the search for commercial copies. In Australia, the statutory licence cannot be used to create Braille or large-print derivative works if Braille or large-print books are commercially available in a reasonable time.[27] While this enables rights-holders to protect their interests and avoid conflicts, the statutory licence is not available to create digital disability-accessible derivative works if an electronic version of the work already exists.[28]

Whereas Braille and large-print commercial works are innately accessible, it is possible for electronic versions of a work to be in formats that are not accessible to persons with print disabilities. Indeed, in the previous chapter, the capacity to remove digital protections that prevent access was analysed. If an electronic version of the work exists, and if that work is entirely inaccessible to a person with a print disability, then the Australian position is that no accessible work can be created under the statutory licence. As a consequence, the statutory licence cannot be used to convert a digital file that is not accessible to persons with print disabilities into a digital file that is accessible.

The Canadian and United Kingdom copyright regimes avoid the absurd outcome affecting Australian electronic versions of works. In Canada and the United Kingdom, the statutory licences do not apply only where the derivative digital works are accessible to persons with print disabilities.[29] The United Kingdom goes further and only prevents the creation of accessible derivative works if the existing commercial copy is of the same kind as the one proposed to be created. This means that a person creating an accessible derivative work in DAISY (Digital Accessible Information System) format or Braille Ready Format would only need to search for commercial copies in those formats.

The United States statutory licence is easier to satisfy than the equivalent exceptions in Australia, Canada and the United Kingdom. Unlike in these countries, a person seeking to use the statutory licence in the United States does not need to take any steps to determine if there are commercially available versions of the work.[30] The statutory licence was introduced in the United States Copyright Act when the Chafee Amendment was enacted in

---

[27] *Copyright Act 1968* (Cth) s 135ZP(4), (5).   [28] *Copyright Act 1968* (Cth) s 135ZP(6A).

[29] *Copyright Act*, RSC 1985, c C-42, s 32(3); *Copyright, Designs and Patents Act 1988* (UK) s 31B(2)(f).

[30] 17 USC § 121.

1996.[31] When the Chafee Amendment was enacted, there were limited works in formats that the print-disabled could access. For example, some works were published in large print and there were some audible books available on cassette tapes. As analysed in Chapter 1 of this monograph, the numbers of accessible works commercially available have significantly increased since 1996. Regardless of this fact, the statutory licence in the United States prioritises low-cost access for people with print disabilities over the interests of rights-holders to obtain profits from this cohort.

Are there Restrictions on Dealing with Derivative Works Created under the Statutory Licence?

Copyright laws in Australia, Canada, the United Kingdom and the United States permit authorised entities to provide derivative works they have created to other institutions that serve the print-disabled.[32] The statutory licence exists to assist persons with print disabilities and, providing the end user is a person with a print disability, then the statutory licence protects the transferring of accessible works between authorised entities. The Vision Australia library collection, for example, has been obtained through creating accessible derivative works under a statutory licence, exchanging talking books with other disability charities, purchasing talking books from publishers and obtaining a licence to share the files with members.[33]

The capacity for authorised entities to share derivative works created under statutory licences internationally is more complicated. Some jurisdictions have questionable reputations for positing copyright laws and enforcing laws which are on the books.[34] Rights-holders in Australia, Canada, the United Kingdom and the United States may not desire that disability-accessible derivative digital versions of their works are transferred to such countries. Most copyright regimes are silent on whether or not derivative works created under the statutory licence can be transferred to people with print disabilities in other countries. The regimes do permit distribution of derivative works to persons with print disabilities; however, there is no indication if that person

---

[31]   Alison Lingane and Jim Fruchterman, 'The Chafee Amendment: Improving Access to Information' (2003) 9(1) *Information Technology and Disabilities Journal* 1.

[32]   *Copyright Act 1968* (Cth) s 135ZP(1); *Copyright Act*, RSC 1985, c C-42, s 32(1); *Copyright, Designs and Patents Act 1988* (UK) ss 31A and 31B(2); 17 USC § 121(1).

[33]   Vision Australia, 'Books and Resources: Audio Books' < www.visionaustralia.org/living-with-low-vision/library/books-and-resources> (accessed 18 November 2016).

[34]   Donald Marron and David G Steel, 'Which Countries Protect Intellectual Property? The Case of Software Piracy' (2000) 38(2) *Economic Inquiry* 159.

must be in the country where the derivative work was created under the statutory licence.

Even though it might be possible to transfer files internationally under the statutory licence, in general, authorised entities are reluctant to share files between nations. This was one of the reasons the World Blind Union and other rights advocates fought to have the capacity to share files internationally enshrined in the *Treaty to Facilitate Access to Published Works for Persons Who Are Blind, Visually Impaired, or Otherwise Print Disabled (Marrakesh Treaty)*.[35]

Anecdotal evidence suggests that authorised entities who have created works under statutory licences only normally share works internationally with the permission of rights-holders. This is the approach adopted by the giant disability E-Book charity Bookshare. Bookshare, with 349,027 titles, is the largest collection of online accessible books for the print-disabled in the world.[36] Bookshare is based in the United States and provides users with partial access in fifty countries, including Australia, Canada and the United Kingdom, as well as a number of countries with less robust regulatory approaches to copyright, such as Argentina, China, India, Liberia, Malawi and Mauritius.[37] While Bookshare utilises the statutory licence in the Chafee Amendment to create and distribute books within the United States, with the exception of Canada (which has special status), Bookshare relies on publishers granting permission for books that are made available to international members.[38]

Unlike the other jurisdictions, the Canadian *Copyright Act* expressly authorises the transfer of derivative works created under the statutory licence to other countries. The Canadian *Copyright Act* provides that it is not an infringement of copyright for a non-profit organisation acting for the benefit of persons with a print disability to make a copy of a work, in a format specially designed for persons with a print disability, and to send the copy to a non-profit organisation in another country for use by persons with print disabilities in that country.[39] For some curious reason, the capacity to send works internationally

[35]   *Marrakesh Treaty* opened for signature 28 June 2013, WIPO Doc. VIP/DC/8 (not yet in force); see the discussion of the *Marrakesh Treaty* in Chapter 3 of this monograph.

[36]   Bookshare, An Accessible Online Library for People with Print Disabilities <www.bookshare .org/cms> (accessed 18 November 2016).

[37]   Bookshare, 'Bookshare without Borders' <www.bookshare.org/cms/help-center/bookshare-without-borders> (accessed 18 November 2016).

[38]   Bookshare, 'Copyright Information' <www.bookshare.org/cms/legal/copyright-information> (accessed 18 November 2016).

[39]   *Copyright Act*, RSC 1985, c C-42, s 32.01(1).

from Canada is not extended to transmitting large-print books, and does not allow for a cinematographic work to be sent outside Canada.[40]

Has the Statutory Licence Enabled Google Books or the HathiTrust to Continue their E-Libraries?

When the statutory licences were first used, persons with print disabilities were provided primarily with Braille and large-print books. The growth of the digital age has created the possibility of authorised entities engaging in mass digitisation of works. As will be analysed in Sections II and III of this chapter, Google Books and the HathiTrust engaged in mass digitisation and have massive E-Book libraries. While Google Books is not an authorised entity, the HathiTrust is an educational body that has long had acceptance as an entity that is able to utilise the statutory licence. The HathiTrust, however, substantially altered how universities operated with the statutory licence. Normally, a student with a print disability would approach their university, which would create a derivative work. The HathiTrust turned this approach on its head and went out and created an E-Library of books that were accessible for persons with print disabilities. The Authors Guild and other publishers objected to the move from the responsive approach to proactively creating a universal library.

In *Authors Guild, Inc.* v. *HathiTrust* the plaintiffs argued that the mass digitisation breached copyright laws and that HathiTrust should be ordered to destroy its content.[41] The National Federation of the Blind intervened and argued that HathiTrust enabled persons with blindness and low vision 'to read digital books independently through screen access software that allows text to be conveyed audibly or tactilely to print-disabled readers'.[42] Whereas persons with print disabilities used to rely on extremely slow scanning processes and massive delays, the HathiTrust substantially moved the print-disabled towards equality of access to the written word.

The United States District Court for the Southern District of New York considered the public benefit to the print-disabled in permitting the HathiTrust to continue and concluded that the community 'would be better served by allowing the use than by preventing it'.[43] The court concluded that this mass digitisation benefited persons with print disabilities, and providing the HathiTrust used existing channels within the universities to restrict access to persons with print disabilities, then the HathiTrust fell within the Chafee

---

[40] *Copyright Act*, RSC 1985, c C-42, s 32.01(2).
[41] *Authors Guild, Inc. et al.* v. *HathiTrust et al.* (S.D.N.Y., No. 11 Civ. 6351, 10 October 2012).
[42] Ibid., slip op. 2.   [43] Ibid., slip op. 14.

Amendment.[44] The judgment in *Authors Guild, Inc.* v. *HathiTrust* promotes increased information access for persons with disabilities and helps to reduce the barriers to reading equality.[45]

The greatest restriction to the global reach of the HathiTrust E-Library is copyright. HathiTrust can provide unlimited access across the world to approximately 4.8 million works that are in the public domain.[46] The HathiTrust E-Library restricts access to users outside the United States to copyright-restricted works, in accordance with the copyright restrictions associated with the work.[47] This means that a user in a partner institution outside the United States, such as the University of Queensland in Australia, will be unable to access most works that are not in the public domain. Further, many E-Books are only fully accessible when the user is based at the institution which holds the hard copy of a work.[48]

Unfortunately, the mass digitisation project that provided the HathiTrust with books was largely being led by Google, which could not benefit from the Chafee Amendment. As a consequence, the continuation of the mass digitisation project relied on Google Books being able to continue to scan copyrighted works. As will be seen below, Google's capacity to continue scanning has been substantially curtailed; thus the extent of the mass digitisation project has been substantially reduced and the number of books that are being made available to persons with print disabilities through the HathiTrust is not increasing and is becoming dated.

Statutory licences were introduced with the initial intent of assisting charities for the blind to provide limited access to the written word. These statutory licence exemptions were not intended to create an equal society by removing barriers to the written word. The fact that HathiTrust can operate under the statutory licence represents a significant move towards reducing the impact of the book famine. The HathiTrust, however, lacks the resources to create and maintain a true universal E-Library. Some partner institutions will continue to digitise works; however, the rate of digitisation is unlikely to match the rate of publishing new works each year. Google had the resources to create

---

[44]   Ibid., slip op. 15.

[45]   Joshua L Friedman and Gary C Norman, 'The Norman/Friedman Principle: Equal Rights to Information and Technology Access' (2012) 18 *Texas Journal on Civil Liberties and Civil Rights* 47, 156.

[46]   HathiTrust Digital Library, *Update on April Activities* (14 May 2015) <www.hathitrust.org/up dates_april2015> (accessed 18 November 2015).

[47]   HathiTrust Digital Library, 'Help – Using the Digital Library' www.hathitrust.org/help_digit al_library (accessed 18 November 2016).

[48]   James Aaron, 'The *Authors Guild* v. *HathiTrust*: A Way Forward for Digital Access to Neglected Works in Libraries' (2012) 16 *Lewis and Clark Law Review* 1317, 1318.

a universal library and was on the way to achieving this target. Whether the Google Books project can provide an answer to the book famine depends on whether Google Books can operate under the fair dealing and fair use exemptions. This chapter will analyse next the extent to which copyright laws permit unauthorised use of information on the basis of fairness.

SECTION II THE EMERGENCE OF THE LARGEST LAWFUL COMMERCIAL E-BOOK LIBRARY COLLECTIONS IN THE WORLD: GOOGLE BOOKS AND HATHITRUST

The Google Books Mass Digitisation Project

The concept for the Google Books mass digitisation project was formed in 1996, when Google's co-founders, Sergey Brin and Larry Page, were working on a graduate student project supported by the Stanford Digital Library Technologies Project.[49] Their project analysed how the mass digitisation of books could enable web crawlers to provide new ways of interacting with information. In 2002, a team at Google started analysing how every book in the world could be digitised. Using the scanners of the day, it took about forty minutes to scan a 300-page book. At this time, the University of Michigan estimated that its digitisation effort would take about a thousand years to scan their 7 million works.[50] Google became determined to develop new scanning technology to speed up this process. In 2003, Google developed new nondestructive scanning techniques and advanced optical character recognition software. With this technology, the Google Print project was launched.[51]

In 2004, Google reached an agreement with the Bodleian Library at the University of Oxford to digitise the library's one million eighteenth-century works not restricted by copyright laws.[52] Later in 2004, the Google Print Library Project was launched, with the support of Harvard University, the University of Michigan, the New York Public Library, Oxford University and Stanford University. Under the Google Print Library Project, Google undertook to perform mass digitisation of the 15 million works owned by these institutions. In 2005, the Google Print project expanded to accept partners from Belgium, France, Germany, Italy, the Netherlands, Spain and

---

[49] Google, 'Google Books History' <www.google.com/googlebooks/about/history.html> (accessed 18 November 2016).
[50] Ibid.
[51] Edward Wyatt, 'Googling Literature: The Debate Goes Public', *New York Times* (online), 19 November 2005 <www.nytimes.com/2005/11/19/books/googling-literature-the-debate-goes-public.html?_r=0>.
[52] Google, *Google Books History* <www.google.com.au/googlE-Books/about/history.html>.

Switzerland. In 2005, the Google Print project was branded the Google Books project.

Google joined the effort to preserve cultural heritage by digitising works.[53] The Google Books project has joined other mass digitisation projects. Before Google was even formed, other digitisation projects were attempting to protect information for posterity and provide access. Projects such as JSTOR, Project Muse and the Internet Archive utilise digitisation technologies to preserve the scholarly record and to advance scholarship and teaching.[54] Individual libraries also utilise digitisation to preserve their collections from damage.[55] The most notable differences between other mass digitisation projects and the Google Books project, however, are in terms of size and profits.

In 2004, Google launched Google Print, which enjoyed the support of publishers including Blackwell, Cambridge University Press, University of Chicago Press, Houghton Mifflin, Hyperion, McGraw-Hill, Oxford University Press, Pearson, Penguin, Perseus, Princeton University Press, Springer, Taylor and Francis, Thomson Delmar and Warner Books.[56] The support from the publishing fraternity became strained as Google Print became the Google Books project, which began to deal with copyright-protected works in ways which focused more on enabling access to information than respecting rights-holders' copyright interests. In particular, the Google Print Library Project began creating derivative digital copies of copyright books without first seeking or obtaining permission from rights-holders.[57] While Google retained relationships with rights-holders and used its partner programme to obtain limited and full access to works,[58] copyright infringement litigation was commenced against Google, inter alia, in Europe and the United States, by rights-holders and publishing associations.[59] The extent to which Google was held to have breached copyright will be analysed below in this chapter.

[53]　Matthew Rimmer, *Digital Copyright and the Consumer Revolution: Hands Off my iPod* (2007) Edward Elgar, 230–3.

[54]　William C Dougherty, 'The Google Books Project: Will it Make Libraries Obsolete?' (2010) 36(1) *The Journal of Academic Librarianship* 86.

[55]　Elizabeth Leggett, *Digitization and Digital Archiving: A Practical Guide for Librarians* (2014) Rowman and Littlefield Publishers, ch. 3.

[56]　Google, *Google Books History* <www.google.com.au/googlE-Books/about/history.html>.

[57]　Jonathan Band, 'The Long and Winding Road to the Google Books Settlement' (2010) 9 *John Marshall Review of Intellectual Property* 227, 227.

[58]　Google Books, *Promote Your Books On Google—for Free* <books.google.com/intl/en/googlE-Books/partners/tour.html>.

[59]　Thomas Wilhelm, 'Google Book Search: Fair Use or Fairly Useful Infringement?' (2006) 33(1) *Rutgers Computer and Technology Law Journal* 107.

Using the Google Books E-Library

Google Books has become the largest E-Book library in the world.[60] By 2011 Google had digitised over 15 million works.[61] In 2013, the United States District Court for the Southern District of New York accepted that Google had scanned over 20 million works at the time of the court hearing as part of the Library Project.[62]

The digitisation of millions of works in itself will not reverse the book famine. After all, publishing houses already hold digital copies of all their titles published, stretching back decades. What is required to reverse the book famine is equal access to the written word for persons with and without print disabilities. The problem for Google Books is how it can balance copyright restrictions with providing users with access to the millions of books it has digitised.

The Google Books project has opened up access to a level that may conflict with copyright laws that seek to restrict unauthorised information sharing. Whereas other E-Book libraries restrict access and require users to read books on certain devices, Google Books adopts an open-access model.[63] The Google Books platform employs a double-sided market framework.[64] Under this approach, Google Books attracts as many users as possible and then sells targeted advertising and information on its users to generate revenue. Google uses algorithmic methods to process simple and advanced searches to enable users to search the millions of titles in the Google Books E-Library.

Google provides users with varying levels of access to information about books. The Google Books platform provides an 'About this book' page. This level of access provides the information that could be found in a library catalogue. At the lowest level of access, this page provides basic bibliographic data like title, author, publication date, length and subject.[65] This page also includes links directing you to bookstores where the book can be purchased and to libraries where the book can be borrowed. For some books, this catalogue entry includes contents pages and key words in the book.

---

[60] ParisTech Review, 'Which Economic Model for Digital Books?' (2011) <www.paristechreview .com/2011/10/06/economic-model-digital-books/> (accessed 18 November 2016).

[61] Google Books, 'Search the World's Most Comprehensive Index of Full-Text Books' <books .google.com/> (accessed 18 November 2016).

[62] *The Authors Guild, Inc. and Betty Miles, Joseph Goulden, and Jim Bouton, on behalf of themselves and all others similarly situated* v. *Google Inc.*, 954 F Supp 2d 282 (S.D.N.Y., 2013).

[63] Francoise Benhamou, 'Fair Use and Fair Competition for Digitized Cultural Goods: The Case of E-Books' (2015) 39(2) *Journal of Cultural Economics* 123.

[64] Jean Charles Rochet and Jean Tirole, 'Platform Competition in Two-Sided Markets' (2003) 1(4) *Journal of the European Economic Association* 990.

[65] Google, *What You'll See When You Search on Google Books* <books.google.com/intl/en/ googlE-Books/library/screenshots.html>.

If the book is available in snippet view, in addition to the information mentioned in the previous paragraph, an entry will include a few sentences around the search terms to give context to where and how the terms are used in the book. Snippet view provides potential customers with sufficient information to conclude whether the work is worth purchasing, so that they can read more than a few disconnected sentences of the work. Rights-holders argued that snippet view breached copyright, which led to the litigation discussed later in this chapter.

The higher levels of access require the agreement of rights-holders, and only apply to works not restricted by copyright. The limited preview option relies on rights-holders granting Google permission to enable users to read a number of pages of a book. Where Google is not restricted by copyright laws, then the book is available in full view. The full view enables a user to read any page in the book, and for some works, to download the entire book to the user's computer. Essentially, the Google Books digital library represents a new stage in how people consume information.[66]

Google Enabling the HathiTrust E-Library

The HathiTrust is a not-for-profit trust controlled by a collective of university libraries across the globe.[67] The HathiTrust has over a hundred individual university and university groups as partner libraries.[68] This list includes highly prestigious institutions, including all the Ivy League universities and other highly ranked United States universities, including Boston University, Duke University, Emory University, Massachusetts Institute of Technology, New York University, Syracuse University and the University of California, to name a few; Canadian universities including McGill University and the University of British Columbia; the University of Queensland, Australia, and Universidad Complutense de Madrid, Spain. The HathiTrust operates the HathiTrust universal library, which enables staff and students associated with partner libraries to search and download digital copies of works.[69]

---

[66]   Beverly A Berneman, 'Putting the Google Book Settlement in Perspective: Will Looking for a Book Ever Be the Same Again?' in E Leonard Rubin, Katherine C Spelman and I Fred Koenigsberg (eds), *Understanding Copyright Law* (2009) Practising Law Institute, 291–3.

[67]   Jeremy York, 'Building a Future by Preserving our Past: The Preservation Infrastructure of HathiTrust Digital Library' (7 June 2010) HathiTrust Digital Library <www.hathitrust.org/documents/hathitrust-ifla-201008.pdf> (accessed 18 November 2016).

[68]   HathiTrust, 'Partnership Community' <www.hathitrust.org/community> (accessed 18 November 2016).

[69]   HathiTrust, 'Collections' <babel.hathitrust.org/cgi/mb?colltype=updated> (accessed 18 November 2016).

The Google Books mass digitisation project consists of two vastly different activities. The commercial activity has developed into an extremely profitable operation. The other activity has grown out of Google's relationships with libraries. In return for access to millions of hard-copy books from partner libraries, Google has provided the results of the mass digitisation project to the HathiTrust.[70]

Using primarily the Google Books digitisation project, the HathiTrust E-Library held, at the end of 2014, over 13 million E-Books.[71] As the Google Books digitisation process is slowed down due to the legal difficulties discussed below, the flow of new titles to this universal library has diminished considerably. Rather than benefiting from a mass digitisation project funded by Google, HathiTrust now needs to rely on members scanning and uploading books when it is legally and economically possible.

SECTION III THE GOOGLE BOOKS SETTLEMENT AND ITS REJECTION

The Google Books mass digitisation project included over 5 million works that were not covered by copyright, and included works where rights-holders had granted permission. The digitisation of such works complied with copyright laws and was not contested. The project, however, included millions of works that were regulated by copyright laws. Google had announced that it would borrow 30 million works from participating libraries and that it intended to scan 25 million works that were protected by copyright.[72] Google argued that exceptions to copyright (which are discussed below in this chapter) permitted Google to make derivative digital copies of works.[73] Rights-holders disagreed and filed suit in 2005.[74]

In 2009, the plaintiffs and Google reached an amended settlement.[75] As the litigation was a class action, it would bind all people within the class, whether

---

[70] Barry Sookman, 'The Google Book Project: Is it Fair Use?' (2014) 61 *Journal of the Copyright Society USA* 485.

[71] HathiTrust, '2014 Year in Review' (2 February 2015) <www.hathitrust.org/updates_review2014> (accessed 18 November 2016).

[72] *The Authors Guild* v. *Google Inc.* (S.D.N.Y., No. 05-CV-8136, 22 March 2011).

[73] Jonathan Band, 'Symposium: Collective Management of Copyright: Solution or Sacrifice? The Book Rights Registry in the Google Book Settlement' (2011) 34 *The Columbia Journal of Law & the Arts* 671, 671.

[74] Class Action Complaint, *Author's Guild* v. *Google Inc.* (S.D.N.Y., No. 05-CV-8136, 20 September 2005); Wilhelm, 'Google Book Search', 108.

[75] Amended Settlement Agreement, *Authors Guild, Inc.* v. *Google Inc.*, 93 USPQ 2d 1159 (S.D.N.Y., 2009).

they were involved in the litigation or not.[76] On 18 February 2010, the Southern District of New York held a fairness hearing to determine whether the Google Books settlement should be rejected or certified. On 22 March 2011, Judge Chin rejected the terms of the settlement agreement.[77] The settlement purported to bind a class involving millions of rights-holders to a very ambitious settlement arrangement. It was significant that 6,800 members of this class expressed their desire to reject this settlement, and that a significant percentage of the class were not directly involved in expressing their views to the court.[78]

The version of the Google Books settlement considered in *The Authors Guild* v. *Google Inc.* included details on how authors would be compensated for the use of their work. A book registry was funded by a $45 million payment by Google and ongoing payments by Google from its advertising revenue, institutional subscriptions and consumer sales.[79] The book registry would distribute a flat fee to every rights-holder that registered with the registry. The amount of money each rights-holder would obtain would be between $60 and $300 USD. The precise amount would depend on how many rights-holders contacted the registry to obtain remuneration for the use of their work.[80] Rights-holders would then receive compensation based on a complicated formula of how often their work was viewed and downloaded.

The Amended Settlement Agreement included terms which substantially altered how copyright laws operated. If the Google Books settlement had been approved, it would essentially have required millions of rights-holders to decide to opt out of the Google Books project, or they would have been deemed to have opted in. The Google Books settlement gave rights-holders that held copyright in the 25 million works involved in the project in Australia, Canada, the United Kingdom and the United States until 28 January 2010 to opt out of the project. Requiring rights-holders to take action to avoid having their works exploited is the opposite approach to how international and domestic copyright laws are structured. As mentioned in the previous two chapters, copyright requires people who desire to deal with a work to identify and approach the appropriate rights-holder and obtain permission before dealing with the work. The court held that it was not appropriate to use a settlement agreement to establish a system where a rights-holder could only prevent their copyright being exploited against their will if they asked the party who was exploiting their work without authorisation to stop.

---

[76] Federal Rules of Civil Procedure § 23.
[77] *The Authors Guild* v. *Google Inc.* (S.D.N.Y., No. 05-CV-8136, 22 March 2011) slip op. 227.
[78] *The Authors Guild* v. *Google Inc.*, 770 F Supp 2d 666, 676 (S.D.N.Y., 2011).
[79] Ibid., art. 4.5.   [80] Ibid., art. 1.75.

The court held that fundamentally changing the structure of copyright for millions of rights-holders could only be achieved by Congress.[81]

The Google Books settlement was also criticised on the basis that it would provide Google with an unfair advantage as it was the only defendant that could benefit from the book registry.[82] In addition, Google would likely obtain a competitive advantage as many rights-holders may not be aware of the Google Books settlement, or even aware that they held copyright in an orphan work. Of course, if a rights-holder is not aware that they hold an interest in an orphan work, then it is arguably in the public interest to avoid a creative work 'rotting away in "the bowels of a few great libraries," providing value to no one'.[83] Regardless of this public benefit, as discussed in Chapter 4 of this monograph, copyright operates on the basis that rights-holders, even those who are impossible to find or unaware that they are rights-holders, must be approached and must grant permission prior to dealing with a work they have rights in.

The Google Books settlement provided persons with print disabilities with significant hope. It would have enabled persons with print disabilities to benefit from the largest digitisation project ever attempted. Instead of scanning books themselves or attempting to source accessible copies, persons with print disabilities, theoretically, would have been able to access tens of millions of accessible E-Books at the click of a button. Arguably,

> the technology revolution creates the possibility to increase universal design and to enable people with print disabilities to access material without having to scan and convert material. Sadly the full potential of these technological advancements are often not fully realized due to legal and policy reasons. The . . . settlement represents a positive move to embrace universal design and harness the potential of technological advancements to reduce barriers to people with print disabilities succeeding in their education and professions.[84]

The Google Books settlement may have helped to resolve the book famine, but the operation of copyright laws prevented this possibility from being realised. With the rejection of the Google Books settlement, the parties returned to the litigation process. The continuing operation of Google

---

[81] *The Authors Guild* v. *Google Inc.*, 770 F Supp 2d 666, 677–78 (S.D.N.Y., 2011); Pamela Samuelson, 'The Google Book Settlement as Copyright Reform' (2011) *Wisconsin Law Review* 477, 479.

[82] Band, 'Symposium', 680–1.

[83] Robert Kirk Walker, 'Negotiating the Unknown: A Compulsory Licensing Solution to the Orphan Works Problem' (2014) 35 *Cardozo Law Review* 983.

[84] Paul Harpur, 'Opening the Book: An Academic's Perspective on NFB's Settlement with Google' (March 2009) *Braille Monitor* (National Federation of the Blind) <www.nfb.org/images/nfb/Publications/bm/bm09/bm0903/bm090310.htm> (accessed 18 November 2016).

Books and the HathiTrust thus depended on the below exceptions to copyright.

SECTION IV FAIRNESS IN COPYRIGHT AS AN ENABLER

The number of copyright-restricted works in the world far outstrips the capacity of persons with print disabilities to reverse the book famine using disability-specific exemptions. Rather than relying on persons with disabilities to work within a disabling society, is it possible to create a society that enables all members of the community to access the written word? One option to resolve the book famine would be to remove the ultimate cause of the disablement: the existence of information in inaccessible formats. It is beyond disability groups to reverse the book famine. It is not, however, beyond corporate actors such as Google to create universal libraries that store works in formats that can be accessed by the print-disabled. This section will analyse whether the fair dealing and fair use exemptions in copyright support the creation and operation of a universal library.

Copyright laws recognise that there are situations where it is fair not to restrict the use of information. The notion of fairness has been introduced into copyright regimes through the fair dealing and fair use doctrines. Both the fair dealing and fair use doctrines provide that information is not restricted from being used in circumstances that satisfy statutory tests of fairness. If one of these doctrines applies in a particular situation, then copyright laws do not restrict the use of information. Some jurisdictions, such as Australia, Canada and the United Kingdom, adopt fair dealing doctrines which specify a 'range of specifically enumerated, statutorily permitted uses, such as research or news reporting'.[85] The United States, in contrast, has embraced the fair use doctrine, which is not limited to particularised situations, but instead focuses on the fairness of a use.[86] Within this wider application, the fair use doctrine is an open norm doctrine with a broad, flexible application.[87] Due to the differences between the fair dealing and fair use doctrines, this section will analyse the operation of these two doctrines separately below.

---

[85] Richard Peltz, 'Global Warming Trend? The Creeping Indulgence of Fair Use in International Copyright Law' (2009) 17 *Texas Intellectual Property Law Journal* 267, 274.

[86] Michelle Connelly, 'The Role of the E-Book in the Library System: A Comparative Analysis of U.S. Fair Use and U.K. Fair Dealing in the E-Lending Universe' (2014) 22 *Cardozo Journal of International and Comparative Law* 561, 563.

[87] Tyler G Newby, 'Note: What's Fair Here Is Not Fair Everywhere: Does the American Fair Use Doctrine Violate International Copyright Law?' (1999) 51 *Stanford Law Review* 1633, 1642.

The Operation of the Fair Dealing Doctrine for Education in Australia, Canada and the United Kingdom

The copyright laws in Australia, Canada and the United Kingdom provide that the issue of fairness is only a consideration in particular situations. The fair dealing doctrine applies in situations which include advancing culture, such as fair dealings for the purpose of criticism, review, parody or satire,[88] those which enable journalistic activities,[89] and those that enable the provision of professional advice.[90] This section analyses the extent to which the fair dealing doctrine supports the creation and operation of universally accessible E-Libraries. As a substantial number of libraries are connected with education, whether it be K-12, tertiary, professional or otherwise, fair dealing for educational purposes is the most relevant use.

Australia, Canada and the United Kingdom all provide that copyright restrictions do not hinder unauthorised fair dealings with works for educational purposes in limited circumstances.[91] To come within this doctrine, the unauthorised dealing can be engaged in by a student for their own educational use or by an educational provider for the benefit of their students.[92] The statutory regimes then describe what constitutes fairness by reference to various criteria. The most relevant consideration to determine whether a dealing is fair is the potential commercial harm to the rights-holder.

The deference shown in copyright laws to the actual or potential commercial interests of the rights-holders substantially weakens the capacity of the fair dealing doctrine to achieve its potential of improving the sharing of information for educational purposes. Unlike Canada and the United Kingdom, the Australian *Copyright Act 1968* (Cth) includes commercial availability as only one factor in determining whether a dealing can be regarded as fair. To determine whether the whole or a part of the work constitutes a fair dealing in Australia requires considering a range of factors, including:

(a) the purpose and character of the dealing;
(b) the nature of the work or adaptation;

---

88   *Copyright Act 1968* (Cth) ss 41, 41A; *Copyright Act*, RSC 1985, c C-42, s 29.1; *Copyright, Designs and Patents Act 1988* (UK) s 30.

89   *Copyright Act 1968* (Cth) s 42; *Copyright Act*, RSC 1985, c C-42, s 29.2; *Copyright, Designs and Patents Act 1988* (UK) s 30.

90   *Copyright Act 1968* (Cth) s 43.

91   *Copyright Act 1968* (Cth) s 40; *Copyright Act*, RSC 1985, c C-42, s 29; *Copyright, Designs and Patents Act 1988* (UK) ss 29–36.

92   *Copyright Act 1968* (Cth) s 40; *Copyright Act*, RSC 1985, c C-42, s 29; *Copyright, Designs and Patents Act 1988* (UK) ss 29–36.

(c)   the possibility of obtaining the work or adaptation within a reasonable time at an ordinary commercial price;

(d)   the effect of the dealing upon the potential market for, or value of, the work or adaptation; and

(e)   in a case where part only of the work or adaptation is reproduced – the amount and substantiality of the part copied taken in relation to the whole work or adaptation.[93]

Although Australia, Canada and the United Kingdom all consider the commercial impact of the unauthorised dealing, the Canadian copyright regime constructs competition as the only issue to be considered when determining if a dealing is fair.

In Canada, a dealing with a work for educational purposes is fair unless the work is commercially available as defined in the statute.[94] The Canadian *Copyright Act* defines 'commercially available' to mean, 'in relation to a work or other subject-matter, ... available on the Canadian market within a reasonable time and for a reasonable price and may be located with reasonable effort'.[95] Overall, the Canadian Supreme Court has adopted a liberal approach to the fair dealing doctrine.[96]

The test for commercial availability asks whether the derivative work can be substituted for the copyright-protected work, and whether it negatively impacts on the commercial market of the protected work.[97] The courts have paid particular attention to the risk of competition when determining whether a dealing is 'fair'.[98] If the derivative work would not commercially compete with the copyrighted work, then courts in Canada are likely to find that the dealing is fair. In *Society of Composers, Authors and Music Publishers of Canada* v. *Bell Canada*, the court found that excerpts of music did not infringe the copyright in such music, in part because the previews increased sales of the works.[99] A dealing that increased sales in a work could not be said to be in competition.

Whereas both Australia and Canada require a consideration of the market for a work, the United Kingdom regime goes further than the other regimes to

---

[93] *Copyright Act 1968* (Cth) s 40(2).   [94] *Copyright Act*, RSC 1985, c C-42, s 29.4(1), (3).

[95] *Copyright Act*, RSC 1985, c C-42, s 2(a).

[96] Melissa de Zwart, 'Fairness and Balance: Lessons from Canada for the Proposed Australian Law of Fair Use' (2014) 24 *Australian Intellectual Property Journal* 129; see *Alberta (Education)* v. *Canadian Copyright Licensing Agency (Access Copyright)* [2012] SCR 37.

[97] Kevin Siu, 'Technological Neutrality: Toward Copyright Convergence in the Digital Age' (2013) 71 *University of Toronto Faculty of Law Review* 76.

[98] *CCH Canadian Ltd* v. *Law Society of Upper Canada*, [2004] 1 SCR 339; [2004] SCR 13 [59].

[99] *Society of Composers, Authors and Music Publishers of Canada* v. *Bell Canada* [2012] SCR 36, [48].

protect the commercial interests of rights-holders. The *Copyright, Designs and Patents Act 1988* (UK) provides that a fair dealing for educational purposes is only fair where the total amount copied in a three-month period does not exceed more than 1 per cent of the protected work.[100] Even if the copying is less than 1 per cent, the copying cannot be fair unless there are no licences available to commercially copy the work, and the person copying the work should have reasonably known of such licences.[101]

In the United Kingdom, courts have adopted three questions which need to be analysed to determine if a use satisfies the commercial competition test:

1. Is there actual competition between the unauthorised and actual exploitation of the work?
2. Is the work already in the public domain?
3. Proportionality – What portion of the protected work is being used?[102]

The growth of E-Books means that the probability that any derivative use of a work will compete with the right-holders' exploitation is increased. It would be difficult to envisage many situations where the digitisation of works would not actually or potentially compete with the interests of rights-holders. It is almost certain that any mass digitisation in the United Kingdom would be deemed unfair. In addition to the limitations imposed by the 1 per cent rule, there is a potentiality of licensing the proposed use. It would seem that a rights-holder could offer prohibitively expensive licences to create derivative works, and thus the existence of those licences would go towards deeming any use of the work unfair. It would seem that copyright would regard the creation of any E-Library as falling outside the fair dealing doctrine in Australia, Canada and in the United Kingdom.

Fair Use Doctrine in the United States

The United States' fair use doctrine represents a considerable encumbrance upon information monopolies created by copyright. If a use satisfies the fair use doctrine, then copyright will not prevent that use from occurring. Section 107 of the *Copyright Act 1976* provides a non-exhaustive list of examples where the fair use doctrine might apply. These situations include 'criticism, comment, news reporting, teaching (including multiple copies for classroom use), scholarship, or research'.[103] Section 107 then explains that

---

[100] *Copyright, Designs and Patents Act 1988* (UK) s 36(2).   [101] Ibid., s 36(3).
[102] *Ashdown v. Telegraph Group* [2001] EWCA (Civ) 1142, [2002] ch. 149.
[103] 17 USC § 107.

the factors to be considered shall include –

(1) the purpose and character of the use, including whether such use is of a commercial nature or is for nonprofit educational purposes;
(2) the nature of the copyrighted work;
(3) the amount and substantiality of the portion used in relation to the copyrighted work as a whole; and
(4) the effect of the use upon the potential market for or value of the copyrighted work.

The fair use doctrine analysis involves an 'equitable rule of reason', in which courts balance the interests of the rights-holders to an information monopoly, against the public interest in using information.[104]

Courts have adopted a range of approaches to determine how to balance these competing factors.[105] Professor Barton Beebe has analysed judgments concerning the fair use doctrine between 1978 and 2011.[106] Beebe concluded that there was not one factor that would predict whether a use was fair. Professor Neil Weinstock Netanel concluded that the capacity to understand the factors that cause a use to be fair and unfair are 'hopelessly unpredictable',[107] and Professor David Nimmer has concluded that the notion that there is a decisive factor is 'a fairy tale'.[108]

Dr Charlie Penrod argues, despite the difficulties in applying the fair use doctrine, that it is reasonable to conclude that the impact on the commercial exploitation of the work is the leading factor in determining if a use is fair or unfair.[109] The United States Supreme Court in *Campbell* v. *Acuff-Rose* explained that the 'four statutory factors [may not] be treated in isolation, one from another. All are to be explored, and the results weighed together, in light of the purposes of copyright.'[110] Even though all factors need to be considered, arguably the effect of the use upon the potential market for or value of the copyrighted work is 'undoubtedly the single most important

---

[104] *Sony Corp. of America* v. *Universal City Studios, Inc.*, 464 US 417, 454–5 and n.40 (1984); Meghan McSkimming, 'Google Books and YouTube: Preserving Fair Use on the World's Leading Internet Video Community' (2012) 42 *Seton Hall Law Review* 1745, 1750–1.

[105] Matthew Sag, 'Predicting Fair Use' (2012) 73 *Ohio State Law Journal* 47.

[106] Barton Beebe, 'An Empirical Study of U.S. Copyright Fair Use Opinions: 1978–2005' (2008) 156 *University of Pennsylvania Law Review* 549.

[107] Neil Weinstock Netanel, 'Making Sense of Fair Use' (2011) 15 *Lewis and Clark Law Review* 715, 716.

[108] David Nimmer, '"Fairest of Them All" and other Fairy Tales of Fair Use' (2003) 66 *Law and Contemporary Problems* 263, 287.

[109] Charlie Penrod, 'Restoring the Balancing Test: A Better Approach to Fair Use in Copyright' (2014) 14 *Chicago-Kent Journal of Intellectual Property* 107, 115.

[110] *Campbell* v. *Acuff-Rose Music, Inc.*, 510 US 569, 578 (1994).

element of fair use'.[111] In framing what constitutes competition, courts have analysed what is the actual and real market for the work.

To determine if there is competition, courts use the market substitution test.[112] Under this approach, the United States Supreme Court has held that the 'market for potential derivative uses includes only those that creators of original works would in general develop or license others to develop'.[113] This test asks if the use would 'materially impair the marketability of the work'.[114] Arguably, Congress recognised that new technologies would alter how the fair use doctrine was applied and thus left the fair use doctrine open for judicial interpretation.[115] Applying fair use to digital environments requires consideration of the capacity to transfer data, and how profits are made in this space.[116] It could be argued that if the publisher has not exploited the market for disability-accessible E-Books, then there would be no competition if derivative works were created that were targeted at the print disability community. This use of the fair use doctrine, however, would not notably advance the position of people with print disabilities beyond the benefits of the Chafee Amendment discussed above.

The fair use doctrine can do much more, however, and could potentially permit the creation of a universal library and the mass digitisation of works. If universal E-Libraries stored their works in formats that could be accessed by the print-disabled, then such libraries could significantly reduce the impact of the book famine. Whether the mass digitisation of works can be permitted under the fair use doctrine was one issue that courts needed to determine when considering if the Google Books project came within the fair use doctrine.

Is the Google Books Mass Digitisation of Works a Fair Use?

The application of the fair use doctrine to the Google Books project has the potential to transform how copyright restrictions interact with the digital age. In the *Authors Guild, Inc.* v. *Google, Inc.* case, Judge Chin of the United States District Court for the Southern District of New York determined that the Google Books Project satisfied the fair use doctrine.[117] Rather than analysing every use, Judge Chin adopted a holistic approach which focused on Google

[111]   Beebe, 'An Empirical Study of U.S. Copyright Fair Use Opinions', 616.
[112]   *Sony Corp. of America* v. *Universal City Studios, Inc.*, 464 US 417, 450 (1984).
[113]   *Campbell* v. *Acuff-Rose Music, Inc.*, 510 US 569, 592 (1994).
[114]   Sookman, 'The Google Book Project', 505.
[115]   Edward Lee, 'Technological Fair Use'. (2010) 83 *Southern California Law Review* 797, 801.
[116]   McSkimming, 'Google Books and YouTube', 1752.
[117]   *The Authors Guild, Inc.* v. *Google, Inc.* (S.D.N.Y., No. 05-CV-8136, 14 November 2013).

Books' major activities. Recall that the Google Books project involved two primary activities. The first activity involved digitising copies of books on behalf of libraries, and the second involved digitising copies of books to be used as part of Google's commercial operations. This involved data analytics and searches to enable the public to read snippets of books on pages where Google sold advertising space.

The mass digitising of library books on behalf of libraries was constructed by the court as a service relationship. Judge Chin held that Google's project of scanning books on behalf of libraries and providing those libraries with digital copies of digitised books was a fair use:

> Even assuming plaintiffs have demonstrated a prima facie case of copyright infringement, Google's actions constitute fair use here as well. Google provides the libraries with the technological means to make digital copies of books that they already own. The purpose of the library copies is to advance the libraries' lawful uses of the digitised books consistent with the copyright law. The libraries then use these digital copies in transformative ways. They create their own full-text searchable indices of books, maintain copies for purposes of preservation, and make copies available to print-disabled individuals, expanding access for them in unprecedented ways. Google's actions in providing the libraries with the ability to engage in activities that advance the arts and sciences constitute fair use.[118]

Many libraries across the United States have mass digitisation projects to preserve their works and to improve indexing and catalogue searches. Essentially, Google was assisting the libraries to perform their primary functions. Google benefited from this project by obtaining improved access to millions of works. If Google had not entered into this arrangement with the libraries, then Google could still have accessed many of these works by having agents and employees borrow books from libraries, and gaining their permission for Google to scan them. Google's agreement with the libraries enabled Google to obtain access in a much more efficient manner.

The Google Print Library Project contained a significant not-for-profit component. The Google Books project, and more particularly its snippet view, is a for-profit activity and of a different character from the Library Project. The snippet view was and remains an integral component of the Google Books experience. The quality of the information available to users encourages them to use Google Books, which in turn enables Google to obtain

---

[118]   *The Authors Guild, Inc.* v. *Google, Inc.* (S.D.N.Y., No. 05-CV-8136, 14 November 2013) slip op. 10.

revenue from advertising. The court needed to determine whether this snippet view satisfied the fair use doctrine.

The snippet view did not transform the work and create something new. Generally, where there is no transformational aspect, the commercial nature of the use means the use is more likely to be held not to amount to a fair use.[119] While the absence of a transformational use usually means the commercial nature of the use weighs against a finding of fair use, Judge Chin concluded that the fact that the use was commercial was not determinative: 'even assuming Google's principal motivation is profit, the fact is that Google Books serves several important educational purposes'.[120]

Judge Chin found that rights-holders did not evince sufficient evidence to support their claims that the Google Books snippet view reduced their capacity to exploit works. Judge Chin also found that where Google Books was only showing a snippet of the book, while linking it to the capacity to purchase the book, then this would possibly increase sales. Rather than hurting rights-holders' commercial interests, the capacity to identify works and determine their relevance would allow users to discover authors. Where books were found to be relevant this would have a positive impact on sales. Judge Chin found 'there can be no doubt but that Google Books improves books sales'.[121] Furthermore, the snippet view provided users with a few lines of text which did not amount to a partial or total market substitution.

The fair use doctrine operates to fulfil copyright's very purpose: to promote the progress of science and useful arts.[122] Judge Chin reflected on the overriding purpose of copyright protection and focused on the 'overall social benefits of the project'.[123] Judge Chin accepted that Google Books has become an 'essential research tool, as it helps librarians identify and find research sources, it makes the process of interlibrary lending more efficient, and it facilitates finding and checking citations'.[124] Judge Chin also accepted that Google Books has become an important research tool because it is 'integrated

[119] *Campbell* v. *Acuff-Rose Music, Inc.*, 510 US 569, 578, 580 (1994) 580; *Video Pipeline, Inc.* v. *Buena Vista Home Entm't, Inc.*, 342 F 3d 191 (3rd Cir., 2003).

[120] *The Authors Guild, Inc.* v. *Google, Inc.* (S.D.N.Y., No. 05-CV-8136, 14 November 2013) slip op. 8.

[121] *The Authors Guild, Inc.* v. *Google, Inc.* (S.D.N.Y., No. 05-CV-8136, 14 November 2013) slip op. 9–10.

[122] *United States Constitution* art. 1, § 8, cl 8; *Campbell* v. *Acuff-Rose Music, Inc.*, 510 US 569, 575 (1994); *Cariou* v. *Prince*, 714 F 3d 694, 705 (2nd Cir., 2013).

[123] Sookman, 'The Google Book Project', 507.

[124] *The Authors Guild, Inc.* v. *Google, Inc.* (S.D.N.Y., No. 05-CV-8136, 14 November 2013) slip op. 10.

into the educational system'.[125] Google Books also enables researchers to perform primary data mining and provides improved access to books to people who have limited access to high-quality universities.[126] In relation to addressing the book famine for the world's print-disabled, Judge Chin accepted that:

> Google Books provides print-disabled individuals with the potential to search for books and read them in a format that is compatible with text enlargement software, text-to-speech screen access software, and Braille devices. Digitization facilitates the conversion of books to audio and tactile formats, increasing access for individuals with disabilities.[127]

Judge Chin balanced the social benefits flowing from the Google Book project in education, research, disability access and to rights-holders against the absence of any significant harm to rights-holders' interests, and concluded that the Google Book project came within the fair use doctrine.

The Authors Guild appealed Judge Chin's judgment to the Second Circuit Court of Appeals. The Second Circuit unanimously rejected infringement claims from the Authors Guild and several individual writers, holding that the project provides a public service without violating copyright laws.[128]

CONCLUSION

Copyright restricts how people can access information and makes cultural, educational, professional and scholarly works more difficult to obtain. Exceptions to copyright exist because lawmakers have recognised that the information monopoly created by copyright can have undesirable outcomes. This chapter used the Google Books and HathiTrust E-Libraries to illustrate how technology and corporate will exists to create massive E-Libraries, with tens of millions of books. If such E-Libraries were accessible and full-text, then they would have the capacity to address the book famine significantly. The potential of such universal E-Libraries has been stymied, however, by the operation of copyright laws.

---

[125] *The Authors Guild, Inc. v. Google, Inc.* (S.D.N.Y., No. 05-CV-8136, 14 November 2013) slip op. 11.

[126] *The Authors Guild, Inc. v. Google, Inc.* (S.D.N.Y., No. 05-CV-8136, 14 November 2013) slip op. 11 and 12.

[127] *The Authors Guild, Inc. v. Google, Inc.* (S.D.N.Y., No. 05-CV-8136, 14 November 2013) slip op. 12, citing a letter from Marc Maurer, President of the National Federation of the Blind, to J Michael McMahon, Office of the Clerk, 19 January 2010.

[128] *Authors Guild v. Google Inc* (2nd Cir., Civ. No. 13-4829, 16 October 2015).

While modifications to the primacy of copyright can reduce the disabling impact of copyright restrictions, they cannot address the book famine. This chapter has argued that the statutory licence for the print-disabled, and the fair dealing and fair use doctrines have a limited capacity to address the restrictions in copyright that contribute to the book famine. In limited situations, copyright laws recognise that limiting persons with print disabilities from exercising their right to read is not always in the public interest. Thus the statutory licence was introduced. The statutory licence has existed for decades and has been the primary exemption used to enable the print-disabled to access the written word. This exemption has made a positive impact, but it has not and will not address the book famine.

The statutory licence, arguably, was not intended to create information equality. Statutory licences are constructed as charitable interventions and not as interventions which seek equality. Interventions to further certain purposes are regarded as charitable acts. The purposes that justify the exceptions to copyright are purposes that are commonly accepted as falling within the ambit of charitable purposes, i.e. assisting the disabled and advancing education.[129] A charitable act is one that provides a sufficient public benefit.[130] Charitable interventions are generally mitigating interventions which do not seek to remove the causes of inequalities in society. For example, the creation of a soup kitchen is a charitable act, but this measure does not address the wider factors that create poverty in a capitalist system. Similar to the operation of charitable interventions, the exceptions to copyright analysed in this chapter seek only to mitigate some of the worst inequalities that flow from restricting access to information. The interventions do not attempt to disturb the fundamental causes of the information disparity between those with and without print disabilities.

The fair dealing and fair use doctrines do not exist primarily to assist the print-disabled to gain access to the written word. The fair dealing and fair use doctrines exist to help reduce the unfairness created by information monopolies. If the fair dealing and fair use doctrines can facilitate the creation of a universal E-Library that is accessible to the print-disabled, then these doctrines would have had a significant impact on addressing the book famine. The fair use doctrine, however, has not enabled the largest E-Library in the

---

[129] Since the *Statute of Charitable Uses 1601* (UK), education and 'relief of the aged, impotent and poor people' have been regarded as charitable purposes (see the Preamble).

[130] Debra Morris, 'Public Benefit: The Long and Winding Road to Reforming the Public Benefit Test for Charity: A Worthwhile Trip or "Is Your Journey Really Necessary?"' in Myles McGregor-Lowndes and Kerry O'Halloran (eds), *Modernising Charity Law: Recent Developments and Future Directions* (2010) Edward Elgar, 103.

world, Google Books, to provide full access to the millions of works that it has digitised. The fair use doctrine has improved access to information, but it has not addressed the book famine. Copyright laws exist to restrict how information is used in society. A by-product of these restrictions is that millions of people are restricted from accessing the written word.

6

Anti-Discrimination Laws Help Protect Persons with Disabilities against Digital Disablement, but Who Qualifies for Protection?

INTRODUCTION

The United Nations human rights regime adopted after World War II and early anti-discrimination laws did not expressly extend protection to persons with disabilities. The long struggle by disability advocates resulted in people with disabilities receiving protection under a variety of specific and omnibus anti-discrimination regimes and, most recently, under the *United Nations Convention on the Rights of Persons with Disabilities* (CRPD).[1] One of the challenges in extending regulatory protection to persons with disabilities is determining who qualifies for protection. If human rights and anti-discrimination laws fail to extend coverage to many persons with disabilities, then ipso facto many people with disabilities will not have their rights protected by such laws. Falling outside regulatory protection can have devastating consequences for people who are experiencing oppression, such as digital disablement. As will be seen in the remainder of this monograph, anti-discrimination laws are one of the primary regulatory vehicles to combat digital disablement. It is accordingly critical to determine who is included and excluded from this legal protection. This chapter will analyse this threshold question through critically analysing the theoretical and legal challenges associated with drawing a line between able and disabled; between enjoying the temporary able-bodied state and the disabled state; and between no protection and benefiting from civil rights protection.

Analysing the line between temporary able-bodiedness and disabled is more than an academic exercise. Tens of millions of Americans with disabilities did not qualify for protection under the *Americans with Disabilities Act of 1990* (*ADA*) for almost a decade of its operation.[2] Following a string of United States

---

[1] CRPD, opened for signature 30 March 2007, 2515 UNTS 3 (entered into force 3 May 2008).
[2] 42 USC §§12101–12117.

Supreme Court judgments, from 1999 many people who were diagnosed medically as disabled were not qualified as disabled under the ADA. In a trilogy of judgments, commonly referred to as the 'Sutton Trilogy', the United States Supreme Court found that people with disabilities who successfully mitigated the functional limitations of their impairments through the use of medication, prosthetics, auxiliary devices, diet and exercise were not substantially limited in one or more major life activities, and thus could not qualify as disabled under the impairment prong in the ADA definition of disability.[3] The United States Supreme court held in *Sutton v. United Air Lines* that two pilots who were vision-impaired (severe myopia) were not qualified as disabled as they mitigated their impairment by wearing glasses.[4] In *Murphy v. United Parcel Service*, a mechanic who had high blood pressure was held not to be disabled as he took medication to control his impairment;[5] and in *Albertson's, Inc. v. Kirkingburg*, a truck driver with a vision impairment (monocular vision) was held not to be disabled as he developed strategies to successfully gauge depth and drive safely.[6] The impact of these three United States Supreme Court judgments devastated the capacity of Americans with disabilities to utilise the ADA. It resulted in people being held by lower courts not to have qualifying disabilities who were medically diagnosed with conditions, including muscular dystrophy, diabetes, heart disease and depression.[7] This meant many people with medically diagnosed print disabilities were excluded from the very protection that was introduced to protect them. The distortion of the legal definition of disability was only corrected when the ADA *Amendments Act of 2008* commenced operation.[8]

The ADA *Amendments Act of 2008*, and other disability discrimination statutes, have arguably had a limited impact on understandings of disability

---

[3] Jill C Anderson, 'Just Semantics: The Lost Readings of the Americans with Disabilities Act' (2008) 117 *Yale Law Journal* 992.

[4] *Sutton v. United Air Lines, Inc.*, 527 US 471, 488–9 (1999).

[5] *Murphy v. United Parcel Service, Inc.*, 527 US 516, 521 (1999).

[6] *Albertson's, Inc. v. Kirkingburg*, 527 US 555, 565–6 (1999).

[7] Lawrence D Rosenthal, 'Can't Stomach the *Americans with Disabilities Act*? How the Federal Courts Have Gutted Disability Discrimination Legislation in Cases Involving Individuals with Gastrointestinal Disorders and Other Hidden Illnesses' (2004) 53 *Catholic University Law Review* 449.

[8] Stacy A Hickox, 'The Underwhelming Impact of the *Americans with Disabilities Act Amendments Act*' (2011) 40 *University of Baltimore Law Review* 419; Beth Ribet, 'Naming Prison Rape as Disablement: A Critical Analysis of the *Prison Litigation Reform Act*, the *Americans with Disabilities Act*, and the Imperatives of Survivor-Oriented Advocacy' (2010) 17 *Virginia Journal of Social Policy and the Law* 281; Nancy J Sandoval, 'Disabled Yet Disqualified: Is It "Unreasonable" to Demand Accommodations for Employees with Depression under the *Americans with Disabilities Act*?' (2014) 17 *Chapman Law Review* 687.

in the judiciary and society.[9] There is arguably a strong anti-preference and formalist following in the community and on the bench.[10] Accordingly, how society, the *CRPD* and anti-discrimination laws construct able and disabled requires continued scholarly vigilance, lest people who seek to deny persons with disabilities equality gain control over what it means to be qualified as disabled.

This chapter will start by introducing the anti-discrimination regimes in Australia, Canada, the United Kingdom and the United States. This first section will illustrate that anti-discrimination laws were introduced as remedial statutes and were intended to be read widely. Secondly, this chapter will consider the theoretical challenges associated with drawing the line between temporary able-bodied and disabled. This analysis will highlight the contested and complicated terrain which is the line between the able-bodied and disabled. Finally, this chapter will analyse how international and domestic laws draw the line between temporary able-bodiedness and disability. The *CRPD* and anti-discrimination laws adopt different negotiated understandings of what it means to be disabled. This section will compare and contrast the definition of disability in the *CRPD* with those in domestic anti-discrimination statutes in Australia, Canada, the United Kingdom and the United States. The significant variations in extending protection illustrate the difficulty in how laws define disability. The critique in this chapter will highlight the complications and risks in distinguishing between able and disabled.

SECTION I INTRODUCING ANTI-DISCRIMINATION LAWS

United States

The United States has developed a civil rights anti-discrimination model that has been adopted around the world.[11] The primary operative statutes in the United

---

[9]   Nicole B Porter, 'Special Treatment Stigma after the ADA Amendments Act' (research paper, University of Toledo, 20 January 2015).

[10] Cheryl L Anderson, 'What Is "Because of the Disability" under the *Americans with Disabilities Act*? Reasonable Accommodation, Causation, and the Windfall Doctrine' (2006) 27 *Berkeley Journal of Employment and Labor Law* 323, 327; Ruth Colker, 'The *Americans with Disabilities Act*: A Windfall for Defendants' (1999) 34 *Harvard Civil Rights–Civil Liberties Law Review* 99, 100. ('[D]efendants prevail in more than ninety-three percent of reported *ADA* employment discrimination cases decided on the merits at the trial court level. Of those cases that are appealed, defendants prevail in eighty-four percent of reported cases. These results are worse than results found in comparable areas of the law; only prisoner rights cases fare as poorly.')

[11] Thomas F Burke and Jeb Barnes, 'The Civil Rights Template and the *Americans with Disabilities Act*: A Socio-Legal Perspective on the Promise and Limits of Individual Rights' (research paper, Social Science Research Network, 26 January 2015); Theresia Degener and

States are the *Rehabilitation Act of 1973*[12] and the recently amended ADA.[13] The *Rehabilitation Act of 1973* is limited to federal agencies and contractors. In contrast to the *Rehabilitation Act of 1973*, the ADA has a broad mandate, inter alia: 'to provide a clear and comprehensive national mandate for the elimination of discrimination against individuals with disabilities'.[14] Professor Arlene Kanter notes that the ADA was never intended to achieve equality, but had a more limited purpose of reducing discrimination in certain situations to reduce the reliance of persons with disabilities on welfare.[15] A range of factors, including legalistic interpretation, broad defences and limited damages, has hindered the capacity of the ADA to achieve its limited social change objectives.

Australia

Australia has had some form of anti-discrimination statutes on the books for over thirty years, which culminated in the passage of the first federal protection in the *Disability Discrimination Act 1992* (Cth).[16] Similar to the ADA, Australia's *Disability Discrimination Act 1992* (Cth) was amended in 2009 to reverse judicial hostility to equality that resulted in the statute being read down and distorted.[17] An interesting difference in the reading down of disability discrimination laws between Australia and the United States is that in Australia the definition of disability has always been read widely. Australian courts read down the operation of anti-discrimination laws through a range of other technical steps in the application of the prohibitions against discrimination analysed below.

United Kingdom

The United Kingdom first enacted disability anti-discrimination laws in the *Disability Discrimination Act 1995* (UK). Following recent reviews, anti-

Gerard Quinn, 'A Survey of International, Comparative and Regional Disability Law Reform' in Mary Lou Breslin and Sylvia Yee (eds), *Disability Rights Law and Policy: International and National Perspectives* (2002) Transnational, 122–4; Neil Rees, Simon Rice and Dominique Allen, *Australian Anti-Discrimination Law*, 2nd edn (2014) Federation Press, [2.2].

[12]   29 USC § 701–794.   [13]   42 USC §§12101–12117.   [14]   42 USC § 12101(b) (2012).

[15]   Arlene S Kanter, 'The *Americans with Disabilities Act* at 25 Years: Lessons to Learn from the Convention on the Rights of People with Disabilities' (2015) 63 *Drake Law Review* 819, 822.

[16]   Andrew Frazer, 'Anti-Discrimination Law at Mid-Life Crisis' (2011) 24(1) *Australian Journal of Labour Law* 75.

[17]   Paul Harpur, 'The *Convention on the Rights of Persons with Disabilities* and Australian Anti-Discrimination Laws: What Happened to the Legal Protections for People Using Guide or Assistance Dogs?' (2010) 29(1) *University of Tasmania Law Review* 49; Belinda Smith, 'Fair and Equal in the World of Work: Two Significant Federal Developments in Discrimination Law' (2010) 23(3) *Australian Journal of Labour Law* 199.

discrimination statutes in the United Kingdom have been harmonised in the *Equality Act 2010* (UK). The *Equality Act 2010* (UK) has replaced a number of legislative regimes covering gender, race, disability, religion or belief, sexual orientation and age, being the *Disability Discrimination Act 1995* (UK), the *Equal Pay Act 1970* (UK), the *Race Relations Act 1976* (UK) and the *Sex Discrimination Act 1975* (UK).

Canada

The Canadian approach to promoting social inclusion has some similarities and some significant differences from the other jurisdictions discussed in this chapter.[18] Similar to Australia, the United Kingdom and the United States, Canada has federal and provincial anti-discrimination laws. The federal *Canadian Human Rights Act* creates disability discrimination duties over businesses and activities regulated by federal laws. The parties so regulated include banks, airlines and airports, phone companies and the federal government.[19] Parties who are not regulated by the *Canadian Human Rights Act* will attract non-discrimination duties under provincial laws.

Bounding the Discussion: Focus on Federal Disability Discrimination Law

The discussion in this chapter and the remainder of this monograph will, inter alia, analyse the operation of anti-discrimination and equality laws. For the purpose of bounding this analysis, the primary focus will be on the federal or national laws. Analyses of constitutional, administrative, province/state laws or city/municipality ordinances will only occur where it will significantly advance the analysis. To facilitate further research and advocacy, a list of state and provincial laws with their relevant human rights commissions/tribunals appears as an appendix to this monograph.

---

[18] See for discussion Michael Prince, 'What About a Disability Rights Act for Canada? Practices and Lessons from America, Australia, and the United Kingdom' (2010) 3(2) *Canadian Public Policy/Analyse de Politiques* 199.

[19] Laura Barnett, Julia Nicol and Julian Walker, 'An Examination of the Duty to Accommodate in the Canadian Human Rights Context' (background paper, Library of Parliament (Canada), 2012) <www.lop.parl.gc.ca/content/lop/researchpublications/2012–01-e.pdf> (accessed 18 November 2016).

SECTION II REPRESENTATIONS OF DIFFERENCE: HOW DOES SOCIETY DRAW THE LINE BETWEEN TEMPORARY ABLE-BODIED AND DISABLED?

Vulnerability, Ability and Difference as Disability

'Vulnerability is inherent in the human condition', but when does the vulnerable subject become entitled to protection from laws and institutions?[20] Laws and institutions that promote ability equality generally use the definition of disability to determine who is entitled to protection, and who receives protection and support from laws, society and the state.[21] Society gains its understandings of disability through various competing cultural, legal, medical, religious and other social representations.[22] When analysing the criteria between temporary able-bodiedness and disability, a key question is who has the 'authority' to create this criterion? The models that explain how society approaches different abilities in Chapter 2 are used here to help explain how the criteria that are used to segment society on ability lines are developed.

The medical industry has often managed to take control over the process of categorising a person as able or disabled. The medical industry obviously has a role in treating impairments. Through segmenting society into currently healthy, potentially needing treatment, and needing immediate treatment, the medical industry can determine where members of their industry can ply their trade. Essentially, the medical industry constructs the notion of human health as a trigger to turn a person with a certain set of abilities into a customer for medical treatment.

The financial benefits gained through expanding the concept of imperfection has led some to question whether the medical industry has ulterior motives behind expanding the definition of disability.[23] The medical industry profits

---

[20] Martha Albertson Fineman, 'Equality, Autonomy, and the Vulnerable Subject in Law and Politics' in Martha Albertson Fineman and Anna Grear (eds), *Vulnerability: Gender in Law, Culture, and Society* (2013) Ashgate, 13; see also Martha Albertson Fineman, 'The Vulnerable Subject' (2008) 20 *Ycle Journal of Law and Feminism* 1; Martha Albertson Fineman, 'The Vulnerable Subject and the Responsive State' (2010) 60 *Emory Law Journal* 251; Martha Albertson Fineman 'Beyond Identities: The Limits of an Antidiscrimination Approach to Equality' (2012) 92 *Boston University Law Review* 1713.

[21] Ani B Satz, 'Disability, Vulnerability, and the Limits of Antidiscrimination' (2008) 83 *Washington Law Review* 513; Carol Woodhams and Susan Corby, 'Defining Disability in Theory and Practice: A Critique of the *British Disability Discrimination Act 1995*' (2003) 32(2) *Journal of Social Policy* 159.

[22] Arie Rimmerman, *Social Inclusion of People with Disabilities: National and International Perspectives* (2012) Cambridge University Press, 9–32.

[23] Allan V Horwitz and Jerome C Wakefield, *All We Have to Fear: Psychiatry's Transformation of Natural Anxieties into Mental Disorders* (2012) Oxford University Press; Robert Whitaker,

from disability. A pharmaceutical company, for example, can increase profits in line with its capacity to have more of its medication used in treatment. Nevertheless, while medical corporations have a strong profit focus, there seems little doubt that the medical industry has a voice in promoting public health.

The medical industry creates criteria to decide what health response is appropriate in a situation. These criteria determine when an individual requires medication, treatment, an operation, or is impaired but not capable of help. Problems arise when the medical industry seeks to apply its definitions of normal and abnormal for application outside its limited scope of practice. The divergent interests of the medical industry and those interested in the rights of persons with disabilities have limited the capacity of these groups to work together.[24]

While biological factors do play a role in how people with impairments experience disability, the notion of disablement only exists when society labels certain abilities as different. Differences in ability do not make disability. Differences in ability are simply a form of diversity in society: some people are tall, some short; some wear glasses, some use guide dogs; some are charismatic, others socially awkward; some use steps, some use ramps. Through flawed assessments and by ignoring the broader causes of disablement, medical assessments, unnecessary treatment and public policies that focused on cure rather than realisation of human rights have caused significant harm to people with different abilities.[25]

As analysed in Chapter 2 of this monograph, the social model has recognised the role society has in creating disablement and turns the focus of analyses away from the abilities of the individual and towards the barriers in society that turn impairment into disability. Accordingly, social model scholars argue that laws and institutions in society that cause disablement should be removed. A challenge for social model scholars is how laws can help persons with disabilities without formulating criteria to judge who requires regulatory protection.

Minority Group and Universalist Approach to Disability

The question of how disability should be defined played out in the debates surrounding the formulation of the ADA in 1990. Professor Samuel Bagenstos

---

Anatomy of an Epidemic: Magic Bullets, Psychiatric Drugs, and the Astonishing Rise of Mental Illness in America (2010) Crown Publishing Group.

[24] Gillian Bricher, 'Disabled People, Health Professionals and the Social Model of Disability: Can There Be a Research Relationship?' (2000) 15(5) *Disability and Society* 781.

[25] D Goodley, *Self-Advocacy in the Lives of People with Learning Difficulties* (2000) Open University Press, 42; Bill Hughes, 'Disability and the Body' in John Swain (ed.), *Disabling Barriers, Enabling Environments* (2004) Sage Publications, ch. 9.

observed that social model scholars were divided on whether civil rights laws should adopt either a minority group or universalist approach.[26] Some disability scholars noted that identification of an oppressed group had enabled ethnic and racially oppressed groups in society to better advocate for their rights.[27] The minority group approach constructs persons with disabilities as an oppressed group who are, when compared to other segments of society, disadvantaged by their membership of this group.[28] A key aspect of the minority group approach is formulating criteria to determine who qualifies for protection. This approach reflects the way in which disability persons groups have and continue to arrange themselves by reference to disability advocacy, such as the World Blind Union. While various movements have emerged that include various people with disabilities, being categorised as having a disability remains a barrier to entry.[29]

The reliance on defining disability is regarded as a limitation with the minority group approach. Persons with disabilities are an oppressed group with limited power in society. Civil rights interventions seek to redress this disadvantage by altering the conduct of more powerful groups. It is foreseeable that powerful groups in society may seek to reduce their regulatory burden by lobbying to have the definition of disability read down. If the definition of disability does not capture all persons with disabilities, then this runs the risk of excluding people who need support and protection from such help and protection. Professor Arlene Kanter observes that '[a]lthough the minority group model seeks to provide greater political legitimacy to people with disabilities through their minority status, it also runs the risk of reinforcing the dichotomy between a "deserving" and an "undeserving" person with a disability'.[30] Despite the risks inherent in the minority group approach, is it possible to advocate for the rights of a segment in society without defining who is in that segment?

A universalist approach to addressing ability inequalities avoids the need to adopt biological factors to determine who is able and disabled. The social

---

[26] Samuel R Bagenstos, *Law and the Contradictions of the Disability Rights Movement* (2009) Yale University Press, 20–1.

[27] Harlan Hahn, 'Towards a Politics of Disability: Definitions, Disciplines and Policies' (1985) 22(4) *The Social Science Journal* 87, 94.

[28] Arlene S Kanter, *The Development of Disability Rights under International Law: From Charity to Human Rights* (2015) Routledge, 47.

[29] See for example the Paralympics Movement and the extent to which it integrates different disabilities: Ian Brittain, *The Paralympic Games Explained* (2010) Routledge; David Howe, *The Cultural Politics of the Paralympic Movement: Through an Anthropological Lens* (2008) Routledge.

[30] Kanter, *The Development of Disability Rights under International Law*, 47–8.

model identifies that barriers in society turn different abilities into disabilities. Universalists focus attention on removing barriers to ability equality. The universalist approach argues that civil rights protection should be provided to everyone regardless of their abilities, history, wealth or other status.[31] The universalist approach argues that society should incorporate everyone as far as possible, and civil rights should be able to be enforced by anyone who has had their rights infringed. Many human rights and civil rights regimes adopt universalist approaches when prohibiting discrimination based upon sex or race. Under such laws, a man or woman, an Aboriginal, African, Anglo-Saxon or Asian all have their rights protected. Obviously, some groups require substantially more help due to historic injustices.[32]

Persons with disabilities who support a minority group approach are generally reluctant to have the definition of disability broadened. Professor Elizabeth Emens explains the attitudinal risks that can flow if the definition of disability is broadened: '[a]s the class of those who count as disabled grows, a legal buffer is removed between "nondisabled" and "disabled," in ways that may increase the existential anxiety of the nondisabled and result in empathy failures'.[33] In other words, if the percentage of population who is qualified as disabled is substantially increased, then the economic and political resources to help people qualifying as disabled will be spread thin. This could result in people who have more established categories of disabilities ending up with reduced support. If all older persons with impairments began utilising disability anti-discrimination protection and support, then this would result in an increased demand. If demand for support increases without a proportionate increase in the supply of services, then this would result in other people with impairments receiving reduced protection. The universalist approach to protecting disability civil rights would involve substantial social change around identity politics and to social institutions. Considering the pressure against the universalist approach, it is not surprising that the minority group approach emerged dominant. This outcome means that the issue of how to draw the line between able and disabled remains heavily influenced by medical factors.

---

[31] Bagenstos, *Law and the Contradictions of the Disability Rights Movement*, 20–1.

[32] Mike Oliver, 'If I Had a Hammer: The Social Model in Action' in Swain (ed.), *Disabling Barriers, Enabling Environments*, ch. 1; Susan Schweik, *The Ugly Laws: Disability in Public* (2009) New York University Press.

[33] Elizabeth F Emens, 'Evolutions in Antidiscrimination Law in Europe and North America: Disabling Attitudes: U.S. Disability Law and the ADA Amendments Act' (2012) 60 *The American Journal of Comparative Law* 205, 206.

The Line between Able and Disabled in Action: Old Age and Disability

Disability rights scholars, lawmakers and lobbyists for the medical industry may formulate a definition to segment society into able and disabled, but how are such definitions received in society? How the wider community defines differences in ability is important in understanding how disability should be constructed.[34] The critical disability studies schools provide a critique which seeks to change how society constructs temporary able-bodiedness and disability. How are representations of different abilities valued and negotiated? Who is normal and who is abnormal? A cultural disability studies analysis provides a powerful vehicle to illustrate the difficulties inherent in distinguishing between able and disabled.

The difficulties in drawing a line between able and disabled are highlighted by analysing the interaction between old age and disability. Able-bodiedness is a temporary state in the majority of the human life cycle. While many in society have their abilities substantially reduced during their life by accident, disease or other events, a significant proportion of the population proceeds through most of their lives without such experiences. The majority of people in the Western world go through the following ability stages in the human life cycle. First, people are completely dependent as babies. People then become less dependent as they become children. The level of abilities then starts to peak through middle age, where the deterioration of abilities commences. From middle age, people enter old age and deep old age, where abilities are often reduced. As will be seen, while laws and institutions can define a person's abilities as able or disabled, how society constructs this line is far more complicated.[35]

When is the reduction in abilities during the twilight stages of the human life cycle constructed as simply ability diversity, and when are those reductions in abilities categorised as disabilities? International and domestic laws provide definitions by which the line between 'old age' and 'old age with a disability' can be drawn.[36] Anecdotally, many older persons resist the label of 'disability'.

---

[34]   Sarah Allred, 'Syndrome or Difference: A Critical Review of Medical Conceptualisations of Asperger's Syndrome' (2011) 26(7) *Disability and Society* 343.

[35]   Stephanie Tierney, 'A Reluctance to Be Defined "Disabled": How Can the Social Model of Disability Enhance Understanding of Anorexia?' (2001) 16(5) *Disability and Society* 749.

[36]   Paul Harpur, 'Old Age Is Not Just Impairment: The *Convention on the Rights of Persons with Disabilities* and the Need for a Convention on Older Persons' (2015) 37 *University of Pennsylvania Journal of International Law* 3; Arlene S Kanter, 'The United Nations *Convention on the Rights of Persons with Disabilities* and its Implications for the Rights of Elderly People under International Law' (2009) 25(3) *Georgia State University Law Review* 527.

For older persons, the attracting of the label 'disabled' can have substantial consequences. The transformation from able to disabled moves the individual from insider to outsider status in society.

Being labelled as 'disabled' can have substantial legal and cultural consequences for an individual. This can create legal complications pertaining to capacity. The individual will likely find their capacity to manage their own medical, economic, personal and sexual affairs reduced.[37] There are also pressures pertaining to self-worth. There is a significant trend in Western society to fear the consequences of growing old.[38] Older people can be regarded as expensive and a burden on younger generations. This perceived burden of an aging population is constructed as an inter-generational economic time bomb.[39] As a result of this existential anxiety, people are encouraged by society to do all in their power to keep their body as youthful as possible for as long as possible. Under this young-is-beautiful model, people are encouraged to regard the signs of aging as inherently undesirable.[40] Older people are encouraged to eschew thinking or acting elderly, as to be old is equated with a reduction of abilities and rights.[41]

Many in the community will formulate their own criteria to explain aging and its consequences.[42] Medical diagnoses may label an older person's reduction in eyesight as legal blindness and a disability. The older person and their family may disregard the label of disability and construct their abilities as

[37] Dale Bagshaw et al., 'Financial Abuse of Older People by Family Members: Views and Experiences of Older Australians and their Family Members' (2013) 66(1) *Australian Social Work* 86; Suzanne Doyle, 'The Notion of Consent to Sexual Activity for Persons with Mental Disabilities' (2010) 31(2) *Liverpool Law Review* 111; Michael Perlin and Alison Lynch, *Sexuality, Disability, and the Law: Beyond the Last Frontier?* (2016) Springer 53; Shih-Ning Then, 'Evolution and Innovation in Guardianship Laws Assisted Decision-Making' (2012) 35(1) *Sydney Law Review* 133; Cheryl Tilse et al., 'Managing Older People's Money: Assisted and Substitute Decision Making in Residential Aged-Care' (2011) 31 *Ageing and Society* 93; Penelope Weller, *New Law and Ethics in Mental Health Advance Directives: The Convention on the Rights of Persons with Disabilities and the Right to Choose* (2013) Routledge, 38.

[38] Bryan Appleyard, 'A Life Worth Living? Quality of Life in Older Age' in Paul Cann and Malcolm Dean (eds), *Unequal Ageing: The Untold Story of Exclusion in Old Age* (2009) The Policy Press, 123.

[39] Donald L Venneberg and Barbara Welss Eversole, *The Boomer Retirement Time Bomb: How Companies Can Avoid the Fallout from the Coming Skills Shortage* (2010) ABC-CLIO.

[40] B Bytheway, *Ageism* (1995) Open University Press; Maurice Charney, *Wrinkled Deep in Time: Aging in Shakespeare* (2009) Columbia University Press.

[41] John Braithwaite, Toni Makkai and Valerie Braithwaite, *Regulating Aged Care: Ritualism and the New Pyramid* (2007) Edward Elgar, 3.

[42] Peter Blanck, 'Disability and Aging: Historical and Contemporary Views' in Richard L Wiener and Steven L Willborn (eds), *Disability and Aging Discrimination: Perspectives in Law and Psychology* (2011) Springer-Verlag.

simply poor eyesight associated with old age. Social model scholars would understand the reduction of eyesight as simply an aspect of diversity, and identify barriers in society as the true cause of disablement. When creating legal definitions of disability, lawmakers arguably adopt a compromised approach. These legal definitions in turn create discourse about the correct means to draw the line between temporary able-bodied and disabled. While there is wide support for the notion that persons with disabilities require legal support, how to draw the line between what is able and disabled remains a highly contested space which complicates the responses of lawmakers and decision makers.

SECTION III HOW DO LAWS DETERMINE WHEN A PERSON IS SUFFICIENTLY DISABLED TO QUALIFY FOR PROTECTION?

Where the previous section engaged with a theoretical critique, this section will adopt a positivist approach to compare and contrast the definitions of disability in the CRPD with the anti-discrimination laws in Australia, Canada, the United Kingdom and the United States.[43] This section will explore how anti-discrimination laws that protect persons with disabilities and the CRPD largely embrace the minority-based approach. The CRPD, for example, contains some universal obligations on state signatories (universalist approach), while also constructing most of the rights and obligations by reference to persons with disabilities (minority group approach).

How the CRPD Defines Disability

The debates in the working groups leading up to the drafting of the CRPD illustrate the challenges in defining disability. During the discussions of the Ad Hoc Committee on a Comprehensive and Integral International Convention on the Protection and Promotion of the Rights and Dignity of Persons with Disabilities Working Group in 2004, a draft convention was presented.[44] This draft convention was amended and ultimately became the CRPD.

---

[43] Michael K Addo, *The Legal Nature of International Human Rights* (2010) Brill, 24–59.
[44] Ad Hoc Committee on a Comprehensive and Integral International Convention on the Protection and Promotion of the Rights and Dignity of Persons with Disabilities, *Report of the Working Group to the Ad Hoc Committee*, UN GAOR, UN Doc. A/AC.265/2004/WG.1 (27 January 2004).

The draft convention presented in 2004 proposed that key definitions should appear in article 3. At this stage of the development of the CRPD, the draft convention had twenty-five articles. Ultimately, the CRPD ended up with fifty articles. The draft convention identified that a definition of disability was required and proposed that this definition should appear in a definition article. While there was disagreement in the working group as to where the definition should be, there was reasonable consensus on what the definition should contain:

> Many members of the Working Group emphasised that a convention should protect the rights of all persons with disabilities (i.e. all different types of disabilities) and suggested that the term 'disability' should be defined broadly. Some members were of the view that no definition of 'disability' should be included in the convention, given the complexity of disability and the risk of limiting the ambit of the convention. Other delegations pointed to existing definitions used in the international context including the World Health Organisation's International Classification of Functioning, Disability and Health (ICF). There was general agreement that if a definition was included, it should be one that reflects the social model of disability, rather than the medical model.[45]

The debate around how a disability should be categorised continued to generate significant disagreement in the drafting process. The Seventh Ad Hoc Meeting was devoted almost exclusively to considering the different means of defining disability.[46]

Ultimately, the definition of disability was substantially reduced from a detailed definition to a general statement about what constituted a disability. This watered-down statement was moved from the definition article in the Convention to the Preamble and introductory provision in article 1. The Preamble emphasises the social nature of disability, where it provides in paragraph (e) that

> disability is an evolving concept and that disability results from the interaction between persons with impairments and attitudinal and environmental barriers that hinders their full and effective participation in society on an equal basis with others.

The CRPD then contains a non-exhaustive definition of disability in article 1:

[45] Ibid.
[46] Arlene S Kanter, 'The Promise and Challenge of the United Nations *Convention on the Rights of Persons with Disabilities*' (2007) 34 *Syracuse Journal of International Law and Commerce* 287, 289.

Persons with disabilities include those who have long-term physical, mental, intellectual or sensory impairments which in interaction with various barriers may hinder their full and effective participation in society on an equal basis with others.[47]

Five points arise from the definition of 'disability' in the CRPD. First, it is important to understand the difference between open and closed definitions, and the approaches adopted in the CRPD and in domestic anti-discrimination laws. It is then necessary to consider the three tests posited in article 1 of the CRPD. These tests include the duration test, the impairment test and the barrier test. Finally, it is necessary to consider how the definitions of disabilities manage mitigation of the impact of disabilities. To illustrate the complexity, variation and the ever-present risk of excluding people with disabilities from disability discrimination protections, this section will now compare and contrast the definition of disability in the CRPD with the definitions in the Australian, Canadian, United Kingdom and United States anti-discrimination statutes.

Closed and Open Definitions

The definition of disability is used in the CRPD and the anti-discrimination statutes in Australia, Canada, the United Kingdom and the United States to determine whether a range of abilities qualify as a disability for legislative protection. The grounds on which discrimination is prohibited can be articulated through either open or closed approaches. Closed definitions clearly define the scope of the protection, and exclude the possibility of any significant expansion. Most anti-discrimination regimes adopt a closed list of grounds that are protected.[48] For example, the omnibus *Equality Act 2010* (UK) provides a list of protected characteristics.[49] While it is possible to interpret a ground widely to expand the protection,[50] under a closed definition it is not possible to introduce new grounds.

---

[47] CRPD, art. 1.   [48] Malcolm Sergeant, *Discrimination and the Law* (2013) Routledge.

[49] *Equality Act 2010* (UK) ss 4–12.

[50] For an example of how disability can be read widely to include people who are overweight see: Lauren E Jones, 'The Framing of Fat: Narratives of Health and Disability in Fat Discrimination Litigation' (2012) 87 *New York University Law Review* 1996 (analysing how arguments about health, disability and fat are used through the lens of employment discrimination cases); see also the Australian State of Victoria Civil Administrative Tribunal judgment for an example of where pregnancy associated with morning sickness has been regarded as a temporary disability: *Bevilacqua v. Telco Business Solutions (Watergardens) PL (Human Rights)* [2015] VCAT 269.

Considering the open drafting of the definition of disability in the *CRPD*, the inclusion of the hindering test may provide a vehicle to extend the understanding of disability. The *CRPD* enables other forms of ability difference to be defined as a disability. A person with a short-term or medium-term disability is currently not included within the scope of the definition of disability in the *CRPD*. If, however, a shorter-term disability substantially reduced a person's participation in society, then it is possible that the open-ended nature of the definition might result in this impairment being classified as a disability.

An open definition creates a non-exhaustive category which includes the possibility of expanding the scope of the definition.[51] Open approaches to defining protected groups have been adopted by reference to open-ended concepts such as 'human dignity'.[52] While open-ended definitions can be difficult to clearly determine, define and thus apply,[53] there is a history of such definitions appearing in international human rights instruments. For example, the *Universal Declaration of Human Rights* adopts an open approach to defining who is protected by that declaration: '[e]veryone is entitled to all the rights and freedoms set forth in this Declaration, without distinction of any kind, such as race, colour, sex, language, religion, political or other opinion, national or social origin, property, birth or other status'.[54] The *CRPD* adopts an open approach to defining disability. The *CRPD* explains that the definition 'includes' people who satisfy all the other aspects of the definition. The use of the term 'includes' renders this definition non-exhaustive, open and capable of expansion. This enables state parties to expand the concept of disablement in their domestic laws where impairments may have limited international recognition.

The mere fact that the word 'includes' is used does not always mean a definition is open. The *Canadian Human Rights Act*, for example, defines the standard types of impairment and then explains that this definition includes 'disfigurement and previous or existing dependence on alcohol or a drug'.[55] While the *CRPD* leaves open the scope of the definition, the use of

---

[51] Dagmar Schiek, 'Organizing EU Equality Law around the Nodes of "Race", Gender and Disability' in Dagmar Schiek and Anna Lawson (eds), *European Union Non-Discrimination Law and Intersectionality* (2011) Ashgate.

[52] *Law* v. *Canada (Minister of Employment and Immigration)* [1999] 1 SCR 497.

[53] This places significant lawmaking power in the hands of judges: Lawrence M Solan, *The Language of Statutes: Laws and their Interpretation* (2010) The University of Chicago Press, 50.

[54] *Universal Declaration of Human Rights*, GA Res 217A (III), UN GAOR, 3rd sess., 183 plen. mtg, UN Doc. A/810 (10 December 1948) Article 2.

[55] *Canadian Human Rights Act*, RSC 1985, c H-6, s 25. See for application: *Desrosiers* v. *Canada Post Corp* [2003] CarsweiiNat 2810 (Canadian Human Rights Tribunal).

'includes' in the Canadian statute does not create an open definition; rather it extends a closed definition to include two more forms of impairment that are not always regarded as impairments qualifying for protection.[56]

The anti-discrimination statutes in Australia, the United Kingdom and the United States adopt closed approaches to defining disability. The Australian statute explains that disability 'means' a person who has one of an extensive list of impairments (including mental, physical, disease, disfigurement, disorder and genetic predisposition).[57] Similarly, in the United Kingdom a person will be held to have 'a disability if' they satisfy the requirements of a closed list of factors.[58]

Following the *ADA Amendments Act of 2008*, the approach to defining disability has substantially broadened in the United States.[59] The *ADA Amendments Act of 2008* codified a rule of interpretation requiring that the definition of 'disability' be construed in favour of broad coverage of individuals under the ADA, to the maximum extent permitted by the terms of the ADA.[60] Despite being expanded, the definition of disability in the ADA remains a largely closed definition.[61]

If a person does not meet the qualifying test for disability, then that person will be held not to have a disability for the relevant statutes in Australia, Canada, the United Kingdom and the United States. Whether these jurisdictions should adopt more open definitions of disability should be weighed against the regulatory uncertainty associated with open definitions. The merits and risks associated with open and closed approaches to regulating equality primarily arise when considering the prohibition against discrimination. As will be analysed in Chapter 10, Canada adopts an open

---

[56] Simon Flacks, 'Deviant Disabilities: The Exclusion of Drug and Alcohol Addiction from the Equality Act 2010' (2012) *Social and Legal Studies* 1; Neil Browne and Nancy Kubasek, 'Alcohol and Obesity Law in Canada, the United Kingdom, and Australia' (2013) 21 *Cardozo Journal of International and Comparative Law* 653, 662–3.

[57] *Disability Discrimination Act 1992* (Cth) s 4(a)–(j).

[58] *Equality Act 2010* (UK) s 6(1); see for discussion Tamara Hervey and Philip Rostant, '"All About that Bass"? Is Non-Ideal-Weight Discrimination Unlawful in the UK?' (2016) 79(1) *Modern Law Review* 248.

[59] Kevin Barry, 'Toward Universalism: What the ADA *Amendments Act of 2008* Can and Can't Do for Disability Rights' (2010) 31 *Berkeley Journal of Employment and Labor Law* 203, 222; Chai R Feldblum et al.. 'The ADA *Amendments Act of 2008*' (2008) 13 *Texas Journal on Civil Liberties & Civil Rights* 187, 218–34.

[60] 42 USC § 12102(4)(A). The ADA *Amendments Act of 2008* explained: 'the question of whether an individual's impairment is a disability under the ADA should not demand extensive analysis'.

[61] 42 USC § 12102 provides the definition of disability. Sub-section (2) defines major life activities openly by providing that 'major life activity also includes the operation of a major bodily function, including but not limited to … '.

approach to prohibiting discrimination, whereas Australia, the United Kingdom and the United States adopt more closed approaches. As divergence in domestic legislation provides more scope for critical analysis, the issue of closed versus open approaches in Canada will be left for the discussion in Chapter 10.

The Duration Test

How long does a person need to experience impairment before that impairment qualifies as a disability? This question is answered very differently across different statutory regimes. Australia and Canada do not contain any duration tests to determine if a person is disabled or not. The statute in Australia extends protection to any impairment that 'presently exists, . . . previously existed but no longer exists, . . . may exist in the future (including because of a genetic predisposition to that disability) . . . or is imputed to a person'.[62] The Canadian statute also does not limit protection by reference to duration where it extends protection to 'any previous or existing impairments'.[63] Other regimes operate on the basis that a reduction in abilities is not a sufficient impediment to qualify as a disability unless that impairment is long-term.

The CRPD, the United Kingdom and the United States limit the definition of disability to long-term impairments.[64] The CRPD does not explain when an impairment is of sufficient duration to qualify as 'long-term'. The duration test in the CRPD suggests that short-term and medium-term impairments do not qualify as disabilities. Even if impairment is experienced over a long period of time, does the reduction in abilities need to be continuous? This is especially relevant with intermittent impairments, which are impairments where the person repeatedly suffers a reduction in abilities for a short period of time when they experience an episode, but collectively these episodes of reduced abilities might last for a significant period of time and have a significant impact on the life of the individual in question.

Unlike the CRPD, the *Equality Act 2010* (UK) does define when impairment is long-term. This statute explains that a long-term impairment is one that has lasted twelve months, is likely to last at least twelve months, or is likely to last for the rest of the life of the person affected.[65] If there is sufficient

---

[62] *Disability Discrimination Act 1992* (Cth) s 4(h)–(k).
[63] *Canadian Human Rights Act*, RSC 1985, c H-6, s 10.
[64] CRPD, art. 1; *Equality Act 2010* (UK) s 6(1)(b).
[65] *The Equality Act 2010* (UK) Schedule 1, Para. 2(1).

uncertainty whether or not an impairment will be experienced for this period of time, then the *Equality Act 2010* (UK) provides that this impairment does not count as a disability.[66]

The duration test only applies to certain forms of discrimination in the United States. In the United States an impairment will satisfy the 'impairment' and 'record' prongs of the ADA if it is experienced for any duration, even if it 'is episodic or in remission'.[67] If the person is filing suit under the 'regarded as' prong, then the person must be expected to have or actually have experienced impairment for longer than six months.[68]

Limiting the definition of disability to long-term impairments arguably turns the legislative attention away from the barriers created in society and grants potentially speculative medical diagnoses significant weight in determining who should have their rights protected or not. Society plays a role in disabling people with impairments. Should it matter whether impairment is experienced for six months or six years? For a person experiencing a sudden reduction of abilities, short- and medium-term reductions in ability can be devastating. For example, an impairment which left a person unable to be fully functional for more than a few hours at a time over a four-month period will substantially impact on that individual. If a person was a student, they would have missed a semester, and if the person was working then, providing the impairment is not work-related, their employer could have dismissed them.[69] It is unclear if that employee would receive protection under the *CRPD*, and that person would not have received protection under the *Equality Act 2010* (UK). While there are grounds for limiting what duty holders should need to do to assist people with short- and medium-term impairments, arguably this limitation should be contained in the duty provisions through a test of reasonableness, and not in the definition for who qualifies for protection.

---

[66] Anna Lawson, 'Disability and Employment in the Equality Act 2010: Opportunities Seized, Lost and Generated' (2011) 40(4) *Industrial Law Journal* 359, 363–4.

[67] 42 USC § 12102(4)(D).　　[68] 42 USC § 12102(3).

[69] Australia has some of the most robust employment protections in the world. While employers are restricted from dismissing workers who have acquired a work-related impairment for twelve months by workers' compensation laws (such as the *Workers Compensation and Rehabilitation Act 2003* (Qld) s 232B), it is much easier to dismiss employees who have acquired injuries outside the work environment. The *Fair Work Act 2009* (Cth) s 352 prohibits employers from dismissing employees who are temporarily absent from work. The *Fair Work Regulations 2009* (Cth) Reg 3.01 defines temporary absences to be ones that are shorter than three months in duration in a single period or, if there are a number of shorter absences, where collectively those absences do not total an absence of three months. See for discussion Andrew Stewart, *Stewart's Guide to Employment Law* (2015) Federation Press, ch. 14.

The Impairment Question

The impairment test is the area which focuses on assessing the extent of an individual's abilities. Even though the impairment test draws from medical notions of abnormality, it is not simply a medical diagnosis. The CRPD and anti-discrimination laws explain that certain types of impairments qualify as disabilities. These instruments, however, do not include a closed and technical definition, which would require a medical diagnosis.[70]

The CRPD and all the statutes regard physical and mental impairments as qualifying as disabilities.[71] The CRPD extends the definition to include sensory impairments, whereas Australia extends the definition to include a wide range of impairments. All jurisdictions have held blindness and other severe print disabilities to constitute disabilities.

The adoption of broad terms to define impairments involved an intentional decision to leave the categories open to judicial application.[72] While medical professionals will often be needed to help determine the nature of a person's impairment, the primary role of deciding whether a level of ability qualifies for the statute falls to a decision maker; in most jurisdictions a judicial officer, either on first instance or on appeal. Accordingly, it can be said that the CRPD and anti-discrimination statutes do not cede control over the definition of disability to the medical industry.

It is worth noting that medical practitioners are empowered to determine levels of ability for other areas of law. For example, laws and practices in most jurisdictions still enable persons with mental disabilities to be forcibly detained, forced to receive treatment or even be sterilised.[73] Medical

---

[70] See for example: *McNicol* v. *Balfour Beatty* [2002] IRLR 71 where the Court of Appeal stated that the term 'impairment' should have its 'ordinary and natural meaning'.

[71] *CRPD*, art. 1; *Disability Discrimination Act 1992* (Cth) s 4(a)–(j); 42 USC § 12102(1); *Equality Act 2010* (UK) s 6(1)(a).

[72] Lee Ann Basser and Melinda Jones, 'The Disability Discrimination Act 1992 (Cth): A Three-Dimensional Approach to Operationalising Human Rights' (2002) 26 *Melbourne University Law Review* 254, 261. Commenting on the definition of 'disability' in the *Disability Discrimination Act 1992* (Cth), Basser and Jones wrote: 'the definition ... was specifically drafted in response to the experience of State anti-discrimination laws, where problems had arisen because of the interpretation of strict definitional criteria, which focused on impairment and medical categorisations'.

[73] Kwame Akuffo, 'The Involuntary Detention of Persons with Mental Disorder in England and Wales: A Human Rights Critique' (2004) 27(2) *International Journal of Law and Psychiatry* 109; Gary Chaimowitz, 'The Criminalization of People with Mental Illness' (2012) 57(2) *Canadian Journal of Psychiatry* 1; Michael Coffey and Emrys Jenkins, '"Power and Control: Forensic Community Mental Health Nurses" Perceptions of Team-Working, Legal Sanction and Compliance' (2002) 9(5) *Journal of Psychiatric and Mental Health Nursing* 521; Joel Godfredson et al., 'Police Perceptions of their Encounters with Individuals Experiencing Mental Illness: A Victorian Survey' (2011) 44(2) *Australian and New Zealand*

practitioners also have key roles in a range of less controversial areas of law. The role of medical practitioners in such areas can be illustrated by considering the impact lack of eyesight has as a trigger for various regulatory outcomes. In this context, medical practitioners are empowered to make a determination based upon the Snellen Scale for the purposes of calculating workers' compensation entitlements;[74] to determine whether a person is entitled to hold a motor vehicle driving licence;[75] to hold a heavy vehicle driving licence;[76] as a safety requirement on certain workplace activities;[77] and to determine a person's social security entitlements.[78]

The Interaction Test

The CRPD's express recognition of the role barriers in society play in disabling people with impairments reflects the social model. The fact that the CRPD definition of disability reflects the social model, insofar as it includes the role society plays in disabling people with impairments, is widely applauded.[79] From a disability rights perspective, recognising the role society has in creating

Journal of Criminology 180; Robert Miller, 'The Criminalisation of the Mentally Ill: Does Dangerousness Take Precedence over Need for Treatment?' (1993) 3(4) *Criminal Behaviour and Mental Health* 241–50; Michael Perlin, *The Hidden Prejudice: Mental Disability on Trial* (2000) American Psychological Association; Michael Perlin, 'Things Have Changed: Looking at Non-Institutional Mental Disability Law through the Sanism Filter' (2003) 19 *New York Law School Journal of Human Rights* 165.

74 Australia: Victoria's *Transport Accident Regulations 2007* (Vic) reg. 5. Canada: *Permanent Impairments (Universal Bodily Injury Compensation) Regulation*, Man Reg 41/94, reg. 2.2; *Regulation Respecting Permanent Impairments*, CQLR c A-25, r 2; Saskatchewan's Table 4.1 *Personal Injury Benefits Regulations*, RRS, c A-35, reg. 3.

75 Canada: *Highway Traffic Act*, RSO 1990, c H8; *Drivers' Licences*, O Reg 340/94, reg. 17. United Kingdom: *The Motor Vehicles (Driving Licences) Regulations 1999* (UK) s 73(11); *The Motor Vehicles (Taxi Drivers' Licences) (Amendment) Regulations (Northern Ireland) 2012 No. 7* (UK). United States: 49 CFR § 391.41(10)

76 Charlotte O'Brien, 'Driving Down Disability Equality?' (2014) 21(4) *Maastricht Journal of European and Comparative Law* 723 (discussing the European Court of Justice ruling in *Glatzel v. Freistaat Bayern*, which focused on whether the requirement under the Charter of Fundamental Rights of the European Union 2000 arts 20, 21 and 26 might be breached by requiring certain visual acuity standards to hold heavy goods driving licences).

77 30 CFR § 49.7 – Physical requirements for mine rescue team.

78 Australia: *Social Security and Veterans' Affairs Legislation Amendment (Family and Other Measures) Act 1997* (Cth) Schedule 16. Canada: Quebec's reg. 1.1, *Regulation Respecting the Allowance for Handicapped Children*, 2000 GOQ 2, 13.

79 For example Rachel Heather Hinckley, 'Evading Promises: The Promise of Equality under U.S. Disability Law and How the United Nations *Convention on the Rights of Persons with Disabilities* Can Help' (2010) 39 *Journal of International and Comparative Law* 185, 201; Paul Harpur and Richard Bales, 'ADA Amendments Issue: The Positive Impact of the *Convention on the Rights of Persons with Disabilities*: A Case Study on the South Pacific and Lessons from the U.S. Experience' (2010) 37 *Northern Kentucky Law Review* 363;

disability is a very positive move. This recognition assists in fixing legal attention on the role society has in disabling people with impairments. While focusing on the role society has in disabling people is positive, perhaps including this recognition in the threshold definition may not have been ideal. The definition of disability can be used to read down the operation of remedial interventions. The United States Supreme Court decisions in the Sutton Trilogy, mentioned in the introduction to this chapter, illustrate how the definition of disability can be read down despite legislative intent. Even though the CRPD is intended to be read widely, it is possible that the linking of impairment to barriers could be used to reduce the scope of where qualifying disabilities will exist. To qualify as having a disability under the CRPD, a person may demonstrate that their impairment interacts with barriers. In most cases, the barrier that hinders participation would be the direct or indirect discriminatory conduct or the adverse treatment or impact that would found a cause of action. The question addressed here is whether connecting impairment and barriers in the definition may give grounds to read down the scope of the definition.

The CRPD does not define the term 'barrier', but does use this term in six places. The context where the term 'barrier' is used can give an indication of what the drafters intended this term to mean. The Preamble and the first two articles of the CRPD are introductory, with the articles of universal application appearing in articles 3–9; those addressing substantive rights in articles 10–30; those establishing implementation and monitoring schemes in 31–40; and articles 41–50 setting forth rules governing the operation of the CRPD. Excluding references to 'barrier' in the definition of disability, the term 'barrier' appears twice in the Preamble and once each in the articles of universal design, those containing substantive rights, and those establishing implementation and monitoring schemes.

Preambles are used under a purposive approach to statutory interpretation to help understand operative provisions.[80] The *Vienna Convention on the Law of Treaties* explains that treaties 'shall be interpreted in good faith in accordance with the ordinary meaning to be given to the terms of the treaty in their

Rosemary Kayes and Phillip French, 'Out of Darkness into Light? Introducing the *Convention on the Rights of Persons with Disabilities*' (2008) 8(1) *Human Rights Law Review* 1; Kanter, *The Development of Disability Rights under International Law*, 8 and 9; Janet E Lord and Michael Ashley Stein, 'Social Rights and the Relational Value of the Rights to Participate in Sport, Recreation, and Play' (2009) 27 *Boston University International Law Journal* 249, 253; Ron McCullum, 'The United Nations Convention on the Rights of Persons with Disabilities: Some Reflections' (research paper no. 10/3, University of Sydney, Faculty of Law, 2010) <ssrn .com/abstract=1563883> (accessed 18 November 2016).

[80] Solan, *The Language of Statutes*, 142–6.

context and in the light of its object and purpose'.[81] The *CRPD* Preamble provides a wide definition of what constitute barriers. Subsection (e) of the Preamble amounts to a restatement of the non-radical social model: '[r]ecognizing that disability is an evolving concept and that disability results from the interaction between persons with impairments and attitudinal and environmental barriers that hinder their full and effective participation in society on an equal basis with others'. Subsection (k) of the Preamble similarly regards 'barriers' as anything that hinders persons with disabilities' full and equal participation as equal members of society. While these provisions suggest that 'barriers' should be understood broadly, preambles only influence the interpretation of operative provisions and have little impact where the operative provision is clear.[82]

The universal right to accessibility explains that states have a duty to, inter alia, identify and remove 'obstacles and barriers to accessibility'.[83] A lawyer attempting to read down this right could argue that the use of the conjunction 'and' indicates that this provision creates two classes which have a degree of mutual exclusivity. Under this argument, not all obstacles would be barriers and not all barriers would be described as obstacles. This argument would be unlikely to have any significant impact, however, as dictionary meanings of both 'obstacle' and 'barrier' refer to virtually the same concept.[84]

The reference to 'barrier' in the substantive right appears when referring to the potential conflict between intellectual property interests and the right to participate in cultural life, recreation, leisure and sport discussed earlier in this monograph in Chapter 2. The use of 'barrier' in this provision arguably reinforces the notion that barriers can be intangible legal constructs, such as intellectual property interests. The final provision that refers to barriers does so in the context of states' obligations to gather statistics and data.[85] Article 31(2) requires states to collect and use data and 'identify and address the barriers faced by persons with disabilities in exercising their rights'. 'Barrier' here is used in a broad context in a way that reflects a social model understanding of barriers in society.

---

[81] *Vienna Convention on the Law of Treaties*, opened for signature 23 May 1969, 1155 UNTS 331 (entered into force 27 January 1980) art. 31(1).

[82] *Attorney-General* v. *Prince Ernest Augustus of Hanover* [1957] AC 436 (holding that a preamble of a statute could be used to resolve ambiguities within the body of an Act, however it could not be used to restrict or extend an otherwise plain meaning).

[83] *CRPD*, art. 9(1).

[84] See for examples the definitions provided in the Cambridge University *Cambridge Dictionary* <dictionary.cambridge.org/> (accessed 18 November 2016).

[85] *CRPD*, art. 31.

The term 'barrier' is used in the CRPD to explain aspects of society which disable people with impairments. Where an individual has had their rights violated, there will almost certainly be a barrier associated with this breach. If a person with a disability does not establish that a barrier hinders their full and effective participation in society on an equal basis with others, then this is not fatal to their assertion. The inclusive drafting of the disability definition has already been noted. In addition to this, the definition of disability explains that a barrier 'may' hinder a person with an impairment. The use of the verb 'may' means this is a discretionary requirement. The shall/may rule explains that the use of shall or must means a requirement must be met, while the use of the term 'may' means compliance is not required for the provision to be satisfied.[86]

While the linking of impairments and barriers in the CRPD will not create any notable difficulties, from an ideological perspective it may not be appropriate to require a person with a disability to carry the onus of proving that there is a link, and therefore that their disability qualifies for protection. The CRPD is not a domestic anti-discrimination statute where individual complainants regularly file suit. Under the optional protocol, individuals can bring complaints to the Committee on the Rights of Persons with Disabilities.[87] In most situations the CRPD is primarily targeted at requiring states to enable persons with disabilities to exercise their rights. One way that persons with disabilities are protected is through removing barriers in society. Linking disability to barriers in society in the definition of disability in the CRPD arguably reinforces the role society has in disabling people with different abilities, and helps draw attention to the need to create more inclusive societies.

Domestic anti-discrimination laws adopt different approaches to linking impairment with life activities. The Australian and Canadian anti-discrimination statutes do not include any need to link an impairment with barriers or lack of capacity in life activities. While some form of loss is essential to proving discrimination or adversity, this harm is arguably not necessary to establish the existence of a disability. The necessity to prove a connection could create the curious position where a person in a wheelchair or without any eyesight would be required by law to prove that their impairment hindered them in fulfilling life activities to be qualified as having a disability.

---

[86] *Hands Teaching Hosp. and Clinics, Inc. v. Sidky*, 936 So 2d 715, 721 (Fla 4th D Ct App., 2006).

[87] Optional Protocol to the *Convention on the Rights of Persons with Disabilities*, opened for signature 30 March 2007, 2515 UNTS 3 (entered into force 3 May 2008) art. 3. See for discussion of the Optional Protocol: Michael Ashley Stein and Janet E Lord, 'Monitoring the Convention on the Rights of Persons with Disabilities: Innovations, Lost Opportunities, and Future Potential' (2010) 32(3) *Human Rights Quarterly* 691.

Arguably, the question whether an impairment has hindered a person with a disability should be made when determining if they have suffered harm, and not at the threshold question of whether they have a disability. In a statute related to anti-discrimination laws, the federal *Canadian Employment Equity Act 1995* provides a good example of how laws should not require plaintiffs to establish a link between impairment and disadvantage to prove they have a disability. The *Canadian Employment Equity Act 1995* provides that a person is held to have a disability if they have a 'long-term or recurring physical, mental, sensory, psychiatric or learning impairment' and who:

(a) consider themselves to be disadvantaged in employment by reason of that impairment, or
(b) believe that an employer or potential employer is likely to consider them to be disadvantaged in employment by reason of that impairment.[88]

Unfortunately, however, some regimes confuse the definition of disability with the impact on life activities.

The experiences of the United Kingdom and United States illustrate the potential complications that can flow from linking impairments and life activities. In the United Kingdom a person is only disabled if 'the impairment has a substantial and long-term adverse effect on [a person's] ability to carry out normal day-to-day activities'.[89] The United States is similar, where under the 'impairment' prong a person is qualified as disabled where their impairment 'substantially limits one or more major life activities of such individual'.[90] Normal daily activities, and their link to adversity, are now read widely in the United Kingdom and United States.[91]

If an Impairment Can Be Mitigated, Is It Still a Disability?

There is a difference between mitigating a disability and curing a disability. A disability is mitigated if a person uses glasses to improve their eyesight. A disability is cured if corrective surgery alters a person's ability to see without any corrective aids. Mitigating circumstances are immaterial when determining whether a person comes within the definition of disability in the *CRPD* in Australia, Canada, the United Kingdom and the United States. The *CRPD* and Australia's statute are silent on the issue of mitigation. Whether a person can or cannot mitigate their impairment is not relevant to whether or not they have an impairment. The *Canadian Human Rights*

---

[88] *Employment Equity Act 1995* (Canada) s 3(j).   [89] *Equality Act 2010* (UK) s 6(1)(b).
[90] 42 USC § 12102(1)(a).   [91] Sergeant, *Discrimination and the Law*, 61.

Act is generally silent on mitigation; however, interestingly, it does include some arguably self-induced impairments as disabilities.[92] The United Kingdom and the United States statutes expressly exclude the impact of mitigating circumstances. In the United Kingdom, an 'impairment is to be treated as having a substantial adverse effect on the ability of the person concerned to carry out normal day-to-day activities if measures are being taken to treat or correct it, and but for that, it would be likely to have that effect'.[93]

Similar to determining adverse impact, as mentioned earlier in the introduction to this chapter, the United States Supreme Court has a history of perverting the effect of the ADA by excluding disabilities where a person could mitigate the impact of their impairment on their life. Prior to the *ADA Amendments Act of 2008*, the impact of mitigating circumstances significantly reduced the scope of the impairment prong. The United States Supreme Court in *Toyota Manufacturing, Kentucky, Inc.* v. *Williams* narrowed the concept of substantial limitation, while retaining its emphasis on the impact of the impairment on the individual.[94] The United States Supreme Court focused on 'the effect of that impairment on the life of the individual', rather than on the nature of the impairment.[95] The court found that a 'demanding standard' should be applied to determine whether or not a person was disabled.[96] Disability was determined by reference to medical assessments, and how the individual was actually limited in their life activities. Professor Elizabeth Emens explained that the inclusion of mitigating factors in the definition of disability meant that 'plaintiffs who have mitigated their disabilities [were] considered in their mitigated state; thus, a person who has successfully mitigated was excluded from protection under the statute'.[97] The *ADA Amendments Act of 2008* corrected this position so that plaintiffs are now to be considered without regard to the ameliorating effects of any mitigating measures (other than ordinary eye glasses or contact lenses).[98]

---

[92] *Canadian Human Rights Act*, RSC 1985, c H-6, s 25 extends the definition of disability to include a previous or existing dependence on alcohol or a drug.

[93] *Equality Act 2010* (UK) schedule 1, s 6.

[94] *Toyota Motor Mfg., Ky., Inc.* v. *Williams*, 534 US 184, 198 (2002).

[95] Hickox, 'The Underwhelming Impact of the *Americans with Disabilities Act Amendments Act*', 433.

[96] *Toyota Motor Mfg., Ky.* v. *Williams*, 534 US 184 (2002).

[97] Emens, 'Evolutions in Antidiscrimination Law in Europe and North America, 212.

[98] 42 USC § 12102(4)(E); Michael Ashley Stein et al., 'Accommodating Every Body' (2014) 82 *Chicago Law Review* 689, 716.

CONCLUSION

This chapter has analysed the difficulty in creating and applying criteria to distinguish between able and disabled. As laws have largely embraced a minority group approach to remedial intervention, drawing the line between able and disabled is critical. A key issue is who should draft these criteria. The process of identifying people with disabilities as an oppressed group involves identifying who was and is causing this oppression. People interested in the rights of persons with disabilities sought to wrestle control over the definition of disability from their oppressors and those who sought to profit from the disability industry. The role society played in turning impairments into disabilities was emphasised and new approaches to defining ability difference emerged. However, despite the emergence of more inclusive approaches to disability, there remains significant disagreement within society on when the label of disability should be affixed to a person.

One of the benefits of the CRPD is that it specifically extends protection to persons with disabilities. The CRPD requires states to protect the rights of persons with disabilities and to introduce laws to reduce their digital disablement. Anti-discrimination laws are the primary domestic regulatory vehicle used to reduce social exclusion. Anti-discrimination laws are remedial statutes which seek to reduce inequalities experienced by certain groups in society.[99] To directly benefit from group-based legislative protection, a person is required to come within a protected group. These groups are generally bounded by reference to prescribed aspects referred to as protected attributes or characteristics. The *Equality Act 2010* (UK), for example, protects people against discrimination based on the characteristics of age,[100] disability,[101] gender reassignment,[102] marriage and civil partnership,[103] race,[104] religion or belief,[105] sex and sexual orientation.[106] While people without attributes may experience incidental benefits from a more inclusive society,[107] these benefits are not enforceable and do not include the direct benefits flowing from anti-discrimination laws. Accordingly, drawing a line between able and disabled is more than an academic exercise; it is the threshold test to determine if a person can benefit from legal protections or not.

---

[99] Beth Gaze, 'Context and Interpretation in Anti-Discrimination Law' (2002) 26 *Melbourne University Law Review* 325; John Hasnas, 'Equal Opportunity, Affirmative Action, and the Anti-Discrimination Principle: The Philosophical Basis for the Legal Prohibition of Discrimination' (2002) 71 *Fordham Law Review* 423.

[100] *Equality Act 2010* (UK) s 5.   [101] Ibid., s 6.   [102] Ibid., s 7.   [103] Ibid., s 8.

[104] Ibid., s 9.   [105] Ibid., s 10.   [106] Ibid., ss 11 and 12.

[107] Diana Lawrence-Brown, 'Differentiated Instruction: Inclusive Strategies for Standards-Based Learning that Benefit the Whole Class' (2004) 32(3) *American Secondary Education* 34.

7

Causing Digital Disablement Is Not a Trigger for Regulation by Anti-Discrimination Laws: Ignoring Capacity in Favour of Prescribed Relationships

INTRODUCTION

The human rights paradigm evinced in the United Nations *Convention on the Rights of Persons with Disabilities* (CRPD) explains that laws should seek to remove barriers to an inclusive society as far as reasonably possible.[1] These barriers are explained through the social model as the institutions and structures in society which create and perpetuate disability. The CRPD recognises the role society has in creating disability and seeks to remove the causes of disablement through positing a rights regime. To promote an inclusive society the CRPD explains that laws and policies should require parties who can impact on disablement to take reasonable steps to promote equality. A key element of this process is determining who should be regulated by laws and policies that promote social inclusion.

This chapter argues that anti-discrimination laws are failing to regulate situations that impact on the digital disablement of persons with print impairments. In order to promote digital equality, regulatory interventions must target those parties who have the capacity to significantly influence levels of digital disablement in the community. As anti-discrimination laws are one of the primary vehicles to promote an inclusive society, it is critical for these laws to impose duties on parties who have the capacity to impact on digital disablement.

Anti-discrimination laws do not create general obligations to reduce discrimination in society. Instead, anti-discrimination laws identify a range of relationships as triggers for intervention, and require parties in those relationships to reduce, subject to a range of technical exceptions, discrimination based on a person's disability. The trigger for attracting obligations not to

[1] CRPD, opened for signature 30 March 2007, 2515 UNTS 3 (entered into force 3 May 2008).

discriminate is actual or potential contact with persons with a protected attribute; in this case a person with a disability. If a person is not in a relationship regulated by anti-discrimination laws, then that person has no duty arising from anti-discrimination laws to avoid, or even consider, when asking how their actions may have a discriminatory impact. Excluding classes of people from legislative equality duties creates the possibility that the law may fail to regulate parties who can have a significant impact on the causes of disablement.

Before analysing whether anti-discrimination laws adequately regulate the right to read digital content, it is first important to consider the parties who impact on the capacity of persons with print disabilities to read the digital content on E-Books, E-Libraries and E-Readers. In Chapter 1 this book analysed the range of parties who impact on digital disablement related to E-Books. Broadly, the parties who can impact on the capacity of persons with print disabilities to read content-books can be segmented into groups associated with:

1. Authorship of the manuscript – Whether or not the author employs graphics or visual displays in presenting text impacts on disability accessibility.
2. Copyright holders – Whether or not copyright holders restrict the manuscript from being published in accessible formats impacts on disability access.
3. Publishing of the manuscript – Whether or not digital rights management settings prevent adaptive technology from effectively working, or whether graphics are labelled into an E-Book, impacts on disability accessibility.
4. E-Book libraries – Whether or not the library interface complies with web accessibility guidelines impacts on disability accessibility.
5. Design and manufacture of E-Reader hardware devices – Whether or not devices include disability accessibility features or enable adaptive technology to be installed impacts on disability accessibility.
6. If the person with a disability sources the E-Book through another entity, such as an educational institution, employer or public library, the approach of that other entity to the right to read impacts on disability accessibility.

Where classes of people are exempted from anti-discrimination laws, then arguably lawmakers have determined that people in that class either lack the capacity to reduce the digital disablement of people with impairments, or that it is unreasonable to expect them to avoid engaging in discriminatory conduct.

If laws fail to regulate people who impact on equality then essentially this is a route of no accommodation. The route of no accommodation permits parties with power to act in their own interests and disregard how their conduct might exclude some people from full and equal participation in society.[2] If people who have a material impact on social inclusion are not subject to anti-discrimination laws, and if other regulatory interventions fail to achieve meaningful levels of digital inclusion, then this is arguably a regulatory position which does not advance the human rights paradigm posited in the *CRPD*.

SECTION I THE RELATIONSHIPS SELECTED FOR REGULATION: THE ADOPTION OF A LIMITED SOCIAL MODEL APPROACH

Disability Anti-Discrimination Laws and the Social Model

Many authors have claimed that the *Americans with Disability Act of 1990* (ADA) reflects a social model approach to combatting the disablement of people with impairments.[3] Katharina Heyer, for example, talks of the *ADA's* 'association with a social model of disability',[4] and Professor Carol Rasnic talks of the *ADA* being grounded on the social model.[5] Other scholars have recognised that, even though the *ADA* was strongly influenced by the social model, it had substantial flaws. Professor Matthew Diller explained that even though the social model tenets strongly influenced the drafting of the *ADA*, there remained considerable concern that a hostile judiciary would read down the scope of the statute.[6] Regardless of its flaws, when the *ADA's* regulatory model was exported around the world, the notion that this regulatory approach reflected the social model was widely adopted.[7]

---

[2] Madam Justice Beverley McLachlin, 'Reasonable Accommodation in a Multicultural Society' (speech delivered at Canadian Bar Association Continuing Legal Education Committee and the National Constitutional and Human Rights Section, Alberta, 7 April 1995) 1; Belinda Smith and Dominique Allen, 'Whose Fault Is It? Asking the Right Question to Address Discrimination' (2012) 37(1) *Alternative Law Journal* 31.

[3] Jared D Cantor, 'Note and Comment: Defining Disabled: Exporting the ADA to Europe and the Social Model of Disability' (2009) 24 *Connecticut Journal of International Law* 399.

[4] Katharina C Heyer, 'The ADA on the Road: Disability Rights in Germany' (2002) 27 *Law & Social Inquiry* 723, 735–8.

[5] Carol D Rasnic, 'The ADA: A Model for Europe with "Sharper Teeth?"' (2004) 11 *ILSA Journal of International and Comparative Law* 105, 111.

[6] Matthew Diller, 'Judicial Backlash, the ADA, and the Civil Rights Model' (2000) 21 *Berkeley Journal of Employment and Labor Law* 19, 51–2.

[7] Lee Ann Basser and Melinda Jones, 'The *Disability Discrimination Act 1992* (Cth): A Three-Dimensional Approach to Operationalising Human Rights' (2002) 26 *Melbourne*

A Weak Social Model Approach

While it is true to say that the social model influenced the drafters of the ADA, it is arguably not accurate to say that the ADA embraces the social model. This chapter argues that anti-discrimination laws which follow an ADA regulatory model adopt a weak social model approach to reducing inequalities in society.

The social model analyses how barriers in society turn impairment into disabilities. A regulatory approach which embraced the social model would accordingly target all the causes of disablement in society and require those who control these disabling barriers to take steps to promote inclusion. As analysed in Chapter 2 of this monograph, the strong social model and non-radical social model both focus on the causes of disablement in society. A strong social model approach would incorporate radical elements of this model, and would entail substantial reforms to how capitalist structures turn impairments into disabilities. The non-radical social model continues the emancipatory focus of the strong social model without incorporating a Marxist critique. Disability anti-discrimination laws do not embrace the strong or non-radical social models.

Anti-discrimination laws do not target many of the causes of disablement in society. At best, anti-discrimination laws adopt a weak social model approach, which places duties on parties in a limited selection of situations, while leaving a range of other parties who create barriers to equality free from regulatory attention. This approach is weak, as it substantially limits the number of barriers in society that are targeted and, once targeting those barriers, substantially limits what needs to be done to promote equality. The strong social model calls for major reforms to society. The non-radical social model seeks more incremental reforms that are still substantial. The weak social model essentially leaves most disabling barriers in society without regulatory attention.

The objectives of the ADA illustrate that the statute was not seeking to achieve substantive equality or remove all of the causes of disablement. The ADA provides that:

(8) the Nation's proper goals regarding individuals with disabilities are to assure equality of opportunity, full participation, independent living, and economic self-sufficiency for such individuals; and

University Law Review 254; Elizabeth Dickson, 'Understanding Disability: An Analysis of the Influence of the Social Model of Disability in the Drafting of the *Anti-Discrimination Act 1991* (Qld) and in its Interpretation and Application' (2003) 8(1) *Australia and New Zealand Journal of Law and Education* 47.

(9) the continuing existence of unfair and unnecessary discrimination and prejudice denies people with disabilities the opportunity to compete on an equal basis and to pursue those opportunities for which our free society is justifiably famous, and costs the United States billions of dollars.[8]

The policy motives behind the ADA reflected a mix of economic and charitable perspectives. Professor Elizabeth Emens explains the thinking behind the lawmakers who drafted the ADA:

The ADA had impressive bipartisan support, but it seems likely that those who voted for it had rather different reasons for doing so: combine a few who understand disability as a civil rights issue, with those who see it through the lens of pity, with those economically minded folks who see it as a way to get people off of welfare and onto the tax rolls, and you get the ADA.[9]

Professor Samuel Bagenstos has analysed the strong economic and welfare arguments behind the success of the ADA.[10] Bagenstos argues that advocates for the ADA argued that it made economic sense to make minor modifications to employment practices so that large numbers of people with disabilities could move from dependence on state and charitable support to working and contributing to the economy. While this focus may have ensured the successful passage of the ADA, it arguably drew attention away from the problem of finding vehicles to ensure all disabling barriers in society are not created in the first place. This chapter will argue that the approach adopted in disability anti-discrimination laws reflects a weak social model approach, and fails to regulate key parties who are causing disablement in society.

SECTION II REGULATING BY DEFINED RELATIONSHIPS

Anti-Discrimination Laws Attributing Fault in Defined Relationships

All disability discrimination interventions struggle with the problem of how to promote equality.[11] Anti-discrimination laws generally focus more on attributing

---

[8] *Americans with Disabilities Act of 1990* (ADA), Sec. 2(a) (8) and (9).

[9] Elizabeth F Emens, 'Evolutions in Antidiscrimination Law in Europe and North America: Disabling Attitudes: U.S. Disability Law and the ADA Amendments Act' (2012) 60 *The American Journal of Comparative Law* 205, 206.

[10] Samuel R Bagenstos, 'The *Americans with Disabilities Act* as Welfare Reform' (2003) 44 *William and Mary Law Review* 921, 927.

[11] Hugh Collins, 'Discrimination, Equality and Social Inclusion' (2003) 66(1) *The Modern Law Review* 16.

fault rather than focusing on removing inequalities in society.[12] The fault model creates statutory duties on people in prescribed situations, and then analyses whether or not those parties have discharged their duties. One problem with this approach is that laws can fail to regulate all the parties who have the capability to address the causes of social exclusion. While the fault versus capability discussion involves a range of other issues, this chapter will focus exclusively on how the anti-discrimination laws in Australia, Canada, the United Kingdom and the United States fail to regulate all the key stakeholders who have the capability to reduce the digital disablement of persons with print impairments.

The anti-discrimination regimes in Australia, the United Kingdom and the United States prohibit discrimination in defined relationships. This means that people who do not fall within a prescribed relationship can lawfully engage in discrimination. To determine if it is reasonable or unreasonable to expect a person to take steps to promote social inclusion is only asked by the law once the threshold question is answered. This means that even if it is commercially viable and reasonable to expect a party to make an adjustment to promote digital inclusion, if that party does not attract anti-discrimination duties then the law does not require that party to take any steps to promote equality.

Relationships Regulated by Anti-Discrimination Laws in the United States

By enacting the ADA, the United States was the first jurisdiction to introduce a comprehensive disability discrimination regime. The ADA is divided into five chapters known as titles. Title I prohibits discrimination in the employment context;[13] Title II pertains to discrimination by public entities;[14] Title III covers various types and services of private entities in commerce (engaged in 'places of public accommodation' and 'commercial facilities');[15] Title IV mandates the availability of telecommunications devices and relay services for persons with hearing impairments;[16] and Title V contains miscellaneous provisions to assist in the interpretation and enforcement of Titles I–IV.[17]

Relationships Regulated by Anti-Discrimination Laws in Australia, Canada and the United Kingdom

Even though the Australian, Canadian and United Kingdom regimes drew heavily from United States civil rights laws when developing their

---

[12] Sandra Fredman, 'Changing the Norm: Positive Duties in Equal Treatment Legislation' (2005) 12 *Maastricht Journal of European and Comparative Law* 369.

[13] 42 USC §§12111–12117.   [14] 42 USC §§12131–12150.   [15] 42 USC §§12181–12189.

[16] 42 USC § 225.   [17] 42 USC §§12201–12213.

anti-discrimination regimes, there are significant differences between how the laws are structured. The *Disability Discrimination Act 1992* (Cth), *Canadian Human Rights Act* and the *Equality Act 2010* (UK) contain anti-discrimination duties which regulate a prescribed range of relationships. The relationships regulated in the Australian, Canadian and United Kingdom regimes, but for limited circumstances, centre on parties who may have direct contact with persons with disabilities. The relationships that attract regulation in Australia, Canada and the United Kingdom include employers for potential and actual employees,[18] educators for students,[19] principles for contractors,[20] providers of goods and services for customers,[21] operators of public premises for visitors,[22] and managers of sporting activities for participants.[23]

The *Canadian Human Rights Act* regulates those parties for which the Federal Canadian Parliament has the power to enact laws to govern under s 91 of the *Federal Canadian Constitution Act 1867* (Canada). Courts have determined that the prohibition against discrimination under the *Canadian Human Rights Act* includes a range of public federal institutions, and private institutions under federal jurisdiction, such as banks and financial institutions, airlines, telecommunication companies and interprovincial transportation companies.[24] The relationships which fall outside the coverage of the *Canadian Human Rights Act* are regulated by the provincial human rights codes referred to above. The fact that the Canadian regime does not specifically name who is bound has enabled courts to expand who is regulated by human rights codes. In *Fontaine* v. *Canadian Pacific Ltd* the Court of Appeal determined that a railway had duties towards the employee of a sub-contractor.[25] Under the Canadian approach, the relationship of the parties is not as critical as the equivalent laws in Australia, the United Kingdom and the United States.

There is wide support for the fact that disability anti-discrimination laws have helped reduce overt forms of discrimination.[26] At a minimum, disability

---

[18] *Disability Discrimination Act 1992* (Cth) s 15; *Canadian Human Rights Act*, RSC 1985, c H-6, ss 7 and 8; *Equality Act 2010* (UK) s 39.

[19] *Disability Discrimination Act 1992* (Cth) s 22; *Equality Act 2010* s 88.

[20] *Disability Discrimination Act 1992* (Cth) s 17; *Equality Act 2010* (UK) s 41.

[21] *Disability Discrimination Act 1992* (Cth) s 24; *Canadian Human Rights Act*, RSC 1985, c H-6, s 5; *Equality Act 2010* (UK) s 29.

[22] *Disability Discrimination Act 1992* (Cth) ss 23 and 25; *Canadian Human Rights Act*, RSC 1985, c H-6, ss 5 and 6; *Equality Act 2010* (UK) ss 35–37.

[23] *Disability Discrimination Act 1992* (Cth) s 28; *Equality Act 2010* (UK) ss 29 and 195.

[24] Marni Tolensky and Stephen Lavender, *The 2014–2015 Annotated Canadian Human Rights Act* (2015) Thomson Reuters Canada, 2.

[25] *Fontaine* v. *Canadian Pacific Ltd* (1989) 29 CCEL 192.

[26] Note, however, that resistance to disability civil rights has reduced the impact of the ADA: Linda Hamilton Krieger, *Backlash against the ADA: Reinterpreting Disability Rights* (2003),

anti-discrimination laws empower aggrieved parties to seek redress against people who breach anti-discrimination duties. The problem is that many of the parties who contribute to digital disablement do not attract duties under anti-discrimination laws. While educators, employers, retailers and the like contribute to digital disablement by purchasing access to E-Book libraries with disability access barriers, in most situations the parties who have direct contact with a person with a print disability have limited power to promote universal design. As will be discussed in Chapter 11 in respect of the National Instructional Materials Access Center, it is possible to use anti-discrimination laws to motivate educators to pressure E-Book publishers to provide disability accessibility in limited situations. Beyond the limited situation where an existing duty holder has the legal duty and practical capacity to ensure universal design, anti-discrimination laws have limited application in online environments.

SECTION III E-BOOK LIBRARIES AS ONLINE RELATIONSHIPS THAT ATTRACT ANTI-DISCRIMINATION DUTIES IN AUSTRALIA AND THE UNITED KINGDOM

E-Book publishers control how E-Books and library platforms are designed. A person with a print disability only has access to E-Books where they can navigate the E-Library and use the E-Books hosted on that library platform. This chapter will now analyse the extent to which anti-discrimination laws extend their operation to E-Book libraries and the E-Books on those platforms. In many situations, people with print disabilities will not have a direct contract with E-Book libraries. The fact that educators, employers and public libraries are the paying customers of the E-Libraries impacts on the legal and negotiating position of persons with disabilities. This chapter will analyse the law as if the person with a print disability has privity of contract with the E-Library.

E-Libraries are essentially websites. In Australia, Canada and the United Kingdom it appears reasonably settled that operators of websites do attract some anti-discrimination duties. Website accessibility in Canada has developed recently through the *Canadian Charter of Rights and Freedoms*, which will be analysed in detail in Chapter 10.[27] Canadian law will be analysed in its own chapter due to the significantly different way in which the duty is structured.

University of Michigan Press; Samuel R Bagenstos, 'The *Americans with Disabilities Act* as Risk Regulation' (2001) 101(6) *Columbia Law Review* 1479.

[27] The *Canadian Charter of Rights and Freedoms* appears in Part 1 of the *Constitution Act 1982* (Canada), being Schedule B to the *Canada Act 1982* (UK).

Regulating Digital Spaces and E-Libraries in Australia

Australia was one of the first jurisdictions to have a judicial determination that anti-discrimination laws applied to websites. Even though s 24 of the *Disability Discrimination Act 1992* (Cth) does not mention the provision of digital goods and services, Australian law provides that goods and services applies to both physical and non-physical provision of goods and services. The allegation of discrimination in *Maguire v. Sydney Organising Committee for the Olympic Games* (*Maguire*) concerned claims that the Olympic Games ticketing system was inaccessible to persons with vision impairments who used screen readers.[28] The then Human Rights and Equal Opportunity Commission held that it did not impose an unjustifiable hardship to require the website to be rendered accessible for people with disabilities. Thus the website was deemed unlawful and was required to be altered.

The *Maguire* decision by the then Human Rights and Equal Opportunity Commission, now the Australian Human Rights Commission, was by an administrative tribunal and not a judicial court, and thus the precedent value of this decision is limited. There has not been subsequent judicial acceptance of the *Maguire* judgment in Australia. Scholars, however, have operated on the basis that the ratio decidendi in the *Maguire* decision is settled law in Australia.[29] The Australian Human Rights Commission has provided guidance on how the *Disability Discrimination Act 1992* applies to internet-based relationships. The Australian Human Rights Commission can release guidelines to reduce the instances of discrimination in the community.[30] While these guidelines have no legal force, they can assist in understanding what the *Disability Discrimination Act 1992* requires of parties.

[28] (2001) *EOC* 93; *Maguire v. Sydney Organising Committee for the Olympic Games* [1999] HREOCA 26: <www.austlii.edu.au/au/cases/cth/HREOCA/1999/26.html> (accessed 18 November 2016).

[29] For example: Andrew Arch and Oliver K Burmeister, 'Australian Experiences with Accessibility Policies post the Sydney Olympic Games' (2003) 9(2) *Information Technology and Disabilities*; Basser and Jones, 'The *Disability Discrimination Act 1992* (Cth)'; Simon Darcy, 'Disability, Access, and Inclusion in the Event Industry: A Call for Inclusive Event Research' (2012) 16(3) *Event Management* 259; Catherine Easton, 'Revisiting the Law on Website Accessibility in the Light of the *UK's Equality Act 2010* and the United Nations *Convention on the Rights of Persons with Disabilities*' (2012) 20 *International Journal of Law and Information Technology* 1; Catherine Easton, 'An Examination of the Internet's Development as a Disabling Environment in the Context of the Social Model of Disability and Anti-Discrimination Legislation' (2013) 12(1) *Universal Access in the Information Society* 105; Gerard Goggin and Christopher Newell, 'Disabled E-Nation: Telecommunications, Disability, and National Policy' (2004) 22(4) *Prometheus* 411; Andrea Slane, 'Review Article: Democracy, Social Space, and the Internet' (2007) 57 *University of Toronto Law Journal* 81; Cynthia Waddell, 'Overview of Law and Guidelines' in Jim Thatcher et al. (eds), *Constructing Accessible Web Sites* (2002) Apress, 32.

[30] *Disability Discrimination Act 1992* (Cth) s 67(1)(k).

The Australian Human Rights Commission 'World Wide Web Access: Disability Discrimination Act Advisory Notes' version 4.1 (2014) explains at clause 2.2:

> The provision of information and online services through the web is a service covered by the *DDA*. Equal access for people with a disability in this area is required by the *DDA* where it can reasonably be provided. This requirement applies to any individual or organisation developing a website or other web resource in Australia, or placing or maintaining a web resource on an Australian server. This includes web pages and other resources developed or maintained for purposes related to employment, education, provision of services including professional services, banking, insurance or financial services, entertainment or recreation, telecommunications services, public transport services, or government services, sale or rental of real estate, sport, activities of voluntary associations, or administration of Commonwealth laws and programs. [. . .]
>
> In addition to these specific areas, provision of any other information or other goods, services or facilities through the internet is in itself a service, and as such, discrimination in the provision of this service is covered by the *DDA*.[31]

Accordingly, despite the lack of judicial attention, it appears well-settled in Australia that the parties who provide goods and services via the internet, including E-Libraries, are regulated by Australian anti-discrimination laws.

Regulating Digital Spaces and E-Libraries in the United Kingdom

The United Kingdom is the jurisdiction with the clearest legislative position on the coverage of anti-discrimination laws over digital spaces. Under the now repealed *Disability Discrimination Act 1995* (UK), businesses had an obligation to ensure equality and non-discrimination to 'access . . . and use of means of communication'.[32] When the *Equality Act 2010* replaced the *Disability Discrimination Act 1995* (UK), it expanded this duty, and now deems any person that is concerned with the 'provision of an information society service' as an 'information society service provider'.[33] This creates duties under the *Equality Act 2010* as a service provider.[34]

---

[31] Australian Human Rights Commission, 'World Wide Web Access: Disability Discrimination Act Advisory Notes' (2014) <www.humanrights.gov.au/disability_rights/standards/www_3/www_3 .html> (accessed 18 November 2016).

[32] *Disability Discrimination Act 1995* (UK) ch. 50, s 19.

[33] *Equality Act 2010* (UK) s 206, schedule 25.

[34] See discussion below in relation to *Equality Act 2010* (UK) s 29.

The agency charged with enforcing the *Equality Act 2010*, the Equality and Human Rights Commission,[35] explains the scope of this duty:

> If you provide services through a website – such as online shopping, direct marketing or advertising – you are known as an Information Society Service Provider (ISSP). This applies whether you have a one-page website which you maintain yourself or a very sophisticated website maintained by a professional web design company and covers anything in between.[36]

Schedule 25 of the *Equality Act 2010* extends the definition of 'Information Society Service Provider' to include any commercial website or internet-based provider that is based in Europe and has commercial relationships involving the United Kingdom. This duty, however, does not extend to internet service providers who only act as a conduit for the transmission of information.

SECTION IV UNCERTAIN COVERAGE OVER E-BOOKS AND E-LIBRARIES: CIRCUIT SPLIT IN THE UNITED STATES

United States Courts Read Down Title III: The Focus on Physical Structures

Whether or not anti-discrimination laws regulate websites in the United States is uncertain. Even though this issue has attracted substantial litigation, the uncertainty appears to have grown with the number of judgments. The *ADA* does not explain the extent to which it extends to online goods and services. Not long after the enactment of the *ADA*, Professor Peter Blanck argued that this statute granted persons with disabilities full and equal opportunities to use emerging information technologies.[37] Unfortunately, *ADA* jurisprudence has had varied application over information communication technologies. Digital activities that are conducted by local, state and federal agencies, such as websites, are required by Title 1 of the *ADA* and the *Rehabilitation Act of 1975* to be accessible. The situation is far more complicated with respect to privately owned and run websites.

---

[35] The *Equality Act 2006* (UK) merged the Commission for Racial Equality, the Disability Rights Commission and the Equal Opportunities Commission to form the Equality and Human Rights Commission. For a critical discussion of this process see Bob Hepple, *Equality* (2011) Hart Publishing, 145–9. The *Equality Act 2010* (UK) schedule 26 amended the *Equality Act 2006* (UK). Both the 2006 and 2010 statutes remain operative.

[36] Equality and Human Rights Commission (UK), 'Guidance for Service Providers about their Rights under the *Equality Act*' (Equality and Human Rights Commission, 2010) 56.

[37] Peter Blanck, *Communications Technology for Everyone: Implications for the Classroom and Beyond* (1994) Northwestern University.

ADA Titles III and IV are relevant to digital spaces operated by private entities. Title III focuses on access to public accommodations, and Title IV presents guidelines to ensure that people with disabilities enjoy full and equal access to telecommunications. Title III is most relevant to websites and other digital communication technologies. Title III explains that '[n]o individual shall be discriminated against on the basis of disability in the full and equal enjoyment of the goods, services, facilities, privileges, advantages, or accommodations of any place of public accommodation by any person who owns, leases (or leases to), or operates a place of public accommodation'. The question that has attracted substantial litigation in the United States is whether public accommodations extend to digital spaces.

The ADA explains that public accommodations are defined to include facilities 'operated by a private entity whose operations affect commerce' and come within one of twelve categories of entities that qualify as places of public accommodation.[38] These places include hotels, restaurants, convention centres, grocery stores, laundromats, libraries, parks, zoos, places of recreation or entertainment, schools, homeless shelters, gymnasiums and golf courses.[39]

While the ADA provides an extensive list of places of public accommodation, the Act is silent on the issue of digital environments. Guidance at the time of the enactment of the ADA indicates that this list should be read to keep pace with changes in technology: 'the Committee intends that the types of accommodation and services provided to individuals with disabilities, under all of the titles of this bill, should keep pace with the rapidly changing technology of the times'.[40] Although the Department of Justice has the power to release rules with respect to the application of the ADA to digital environments, the promulgation of such rules has continually been delayed and has most recently been delayed until 2018.[41]

To date, the United States Supreme Court has not considered the interaction between digital technologies and the ADA. While the United States Supreme Court has not considered the impact of the ADA in digital spaces, it has considered the operation of other laws in such environments. For example, the United States Supreme Court has considered how search warrants operate in digital spaces and held that warrants are required to search cell phones.[42] The United States Supreme Court unanimously held in *Riley*

---

[38]   42 USC § 12181(7).   [39]   Ibid.
[40]   House Education Committee Report, H R Rep 101–485 (II) (1990) 108.
[41]   Law Office of Lainey Feingold, 'Fall 2015 Update: More Delay for DOJ Web Regulations' <lflegal .com/2015/11/doj-fall-2015/> (accessed 18 November 2016).
[42]   *Riley* v. *California*, 134 S Ct 2473 (2014).

v. *California* that the Fourth Amendment does not, without a warrant, permit law enforcement officials to search a suspect's digital information on a cellphone without a warrant. The court recognised the need for the law to adapt to the digital age, noting that 'many of the more than 90% of American adults who own a cellphone keep on their person a digital record of nearly every aspect of their lives – from the mundane to the intimate'.[43] The United States Supreme Court in *Riley* v. *California* clearly recognised that the capacity to operate in the digital environment is essential to engaging in many aspects of life in the twenty-first century.[44] Arguably, it is therefore important that such activities are not only protected from government interference, but are also protected from discriminatory conduct carried out by government and private actors.

In the absence of clear United States Supreme Court or statutory guidance, courts have interpreted the relevance of Title III to digital spaces through one of three approaches: the purposive, nexus and physicalist approaches. The *ADA* is federal law and disputes are heard in the United States District Courts. The United States Circuit Courts have appellate jurisdiction over the United States District Courts. There are twelve different United States Circuit Court jurisdictions, covering geographic areas of the United States. Circuit Courts only bind the United States District Courts within their geographical jurisdiction. This means there can be a circuit split on how to approach a legal issue. How the *ADA* applies to digital spaces is one area where there is a circuit split. This chapter will now analyse how the varying Circuit Courts apply the purposive, nexus and physicalist approaches.

Purposive Approach

The purposive approach to Title III looks to the purposes of the Statute and Title. This approach recognises that trade and commerce take place in many of the examples provided in Title III. It would be difficult to find a hotel, restaurant, convention centre, travel service, museum, library or office of an accountant or lawyer in the United States that does not have a website and social media presence. Many grocery stores are partially or fully online.

---

[43] *Riley* v. *California*, 134 S Ct 2473, 2490 (2014).

[44] Federico Fabbrini, 'Human Rights in the Digital Age: The European Court of Justice Ruling in the Data Retention Case and its Lessons for Privacy and Surveillance in the United States' (2015) 28 *Harvard Human Rights Journal* 65; Adam Lamparello, 'The Internet Is the New Marketplace of Ideas: Why *Riley* v. *California* Supports Net Neutrality' (2015) 25 *DePaul Journal of Art, Technology & Intellectual Property Law* 267; Shlomit Yanisky-Ravid, 'To Read or Not to Read: Privacy within Social Networks, the Entitlement of Employees to a Virtual "Private Zone," and the Balloon Theory' (2014) 64 *American University Law Review* 53.

Entertainment is increasingly moving from the physical space to the digital environment. While most schools that offer external or distance education have a strong link with a bricks-and-mortar facility,[45] the growth of massive online open courses is challenging this model.[46]

Early Title III cases from the First, Second and Seventh Circuits found that a connection with a physical space was not required to maintain a suit under Title III.[47] Many of these early cases concerned the impact of insurance policies. The Seventh Circuit found that it was not essential to identify a physical location to pursue a Title III claim for an insurance policy that treated people with AIDS differently than people with other medical conditions.[48] The First Circuit in *Carparts Distribution Ctr., Inc. v. Auto. Wholesaler's Ass'n of New Eng., Inc.* reached the same conclusion on an insurance policy that discriminated between AIDS and other conditions.[49] The court in *Carparts* concluded that

> It would be irrational to conclude that persons who enter an office to purchase services are protected by the ADA, but persons who purchase the same services over the telephone or by mail are not. Congress could not have intended such an absurd result.[50]

In *Palozzi* v. *Allstate Life Ins. Co.*, a Second Circuit Court further explained that there was no need to connect the discriminatory decision with a physical space.[51] Whether the discriminatory underwriting decisions were made in an insurance office or outside, the discriminatory outcome of the decision is the same. The court has noted that it was Congress's intent to impugn discriminatory acts, and that to limit this protection to conduct engaged in in a physical space would confound the intent of the statute.

---

[45] See, e.g., Bieke Schreurs (ed.), *Reviewing the Virtual Campus Phenomenon: The Rise of Large Scale e-Learning Initiatives Worldwide* (Re.ViCa Project, European Commission, 2011), which states that the majority of online learning courses have evolved from traditional, paper-based universities.

[46] See, e.g., Open Universities Australia, which offers online courses without a physical campus. 'About Us' (2015) Open Universities Australia <www.open.edu.au/about-us/> (accessed 18 November 2016).

[47] The First Circuit's jurisdiction includes the districts of Maine, Massachusetts, New Hampshire, Puerto Rico and Rhode Island; the Second Circuit's jurisdiction includes the
, districts of Connecticut, New York and Vermont; the Seventh Circuit's jurisdiction includes the Central District of Illinois, Northern District of Illinois, Southern District of Illinois, Northern District of Indiana, Southern District of Indiana, Eastern District of Wisconsin and the Western District of Wisconsin.

[48] *Doe* v. *Mut. of Omaha Ins. Co.*, 179 F 3d 557, 559 (7th Cir., 1999).

[49] *Carparts Distribution Ctr., Inc.* v. *Auto. Wholesaler's Ass'n of New Eng., Inc.*, 37 F 3d 12, 19 (1st Cir., 1994) (*Carparts*).

[50] Ibid.   [51] *Palozzi* v. *Allstate Life Ins. Co.*, 198 F 3d 28, 33 (2nd Cir., 2000).

Recent Second Circuit judgments have continued to apply the ADA to the internet. In the *National Federation of the Blind* v. *Scribd, Inc.*, the plaintiffs alleged that Scribd was not meeting its obligations under Title III of the ADA.[52] This case is significant as it was the first Second Circuit Court to consider the operation of the ADA over a defendant that operated no physical space open to the public, but nevertheless provided goods or services to the public. Scribd is a digital library that operates reading subscription services on its website and on mobile applications. Plaintiffs alleged that Scribd's website and mobile applications were not accessible to blind users. This denied blind users the opportunity to pay a monthly subscription to access over 40 million titles, including E-Books, academic papers, legal filings and other documents uploaded by users. Scribd moved to dismiss the case on the basis that Title III did not apply to website operators whose goods or services are not made available at a physical location open to the public. The United States District Court for the District of Vermont observed that existing Second Circuit Title III jurisprudence could be extended to a company's refusal to sell a disabled person its merchandise on the internet and, by extension, imposing barriers that essentially have the same effect: 'Otherwise, a company could freely refuse to sell its goods or services to a disabled person as long as it did so online rather than within the confines of a physical office or store.'[53] The court found that to require an online accommodation to be linked to a physical accommodation to obtain ADA coverage 'would lead to absurd results'.[54] The court noted that 'the Internet plays such a critical role in the personal and professional lives of Americans, excluding disabled persons from access to covered entities that use it as their principal means of reaching the public would defeat the purpose of this important civil rights legislation'.[55] In dismissing Scribd's application to dismiss, the court sent a strong message that within the Second Circuit's jurisdiction, Title III applies to E-Libraries and the content in such libraries.

The extent of the circuit split on how Title III should apply to digital spaces is illustrated by litigation against Netflix. Netflix is a large online provider of video programming. Plaintiffs in two cases argued that Netflix provided insufficient accommodation to deaf subscribers and a lack of adequate support tools for deaf persons. Within the Ninth Circuit,[56] the United States District Court for the Northern District of California in *Cullen* v. *Netflix, Inc.* found in

---

[52] *National Federation of the Blind* v. *Scribd, Inc.* (D Vt, No. 2:14-cv-162, 19 March 2015).
[53] Ibid., 13.   [54] Ibid., 17.   [55] Ibid., 25–26.
[56] The Ninth Circuit's jurisdiction includes the District of Alaska, District of Arizona, Central District of California, Eastern District of California, Northern District of California, Southern District of California and District of Guam.

2013 that the digital space occupied by Netflix did not constitute a public space for Title III.[57] In contrast to the *Cullen v. Netflix, Inc.* judgment discussed in the next section, the First Circuit's United States District Court for the District of Massachusetts found in 2012 that an action against Netflix could be maintained under Title III.[58]

The court in *National Association of the Deaf, et al., v. Netflix, Inc.* followed the binding First Circuit ruling in *Carparts*. The court in *National Association of the Deaf, et al., v. Netflix, Inc.* felt that extending Title III's coverage to digital spaces was a natural progression of the statute:

> the fact that the ADA does not include web-based services as a specific example of a public accommodation is irrelevant. First, while such web-based services did not exist when the ADA was passed in 1990 and, thus, could not have been explicitly included in the Act, the legislative history of the ADA makes clear that Congress intended the ADA to adapt to changes in technology.[59]

The court also accepted that Netflix came within the general categories in Title III. The court noted that the website qualifies as a 'service establishment' as it provides customers with the ability to stream video programming over the internet; a 'place of exhibition or entertainment' as customers can view movies, television programming and other content; and a 'rental establishment' as customers can rent video programming.[60] Before the court issued its final ruling on this matter, Netflix agreed to a consent decree.[61] This decree involved Netflix agreeing to provide closed captioning for all of its video content. The judgment in *National Association of the Deaf, et al., v. Netflix, Inc.* was significant as it was the first case to recognise that substantial commercial activities are connected with physical space, and that Title III should reflect this trend in society.

Nexus Approach

While it is rare for courts to accept that entirely online spaces come within Title III, most circuits accept that digital spaces come within that title where

[57] *Cullen v. Netflix, Inc.*, 880 F Supp 2d 1017 (ED Cal, 2012).

[58] *National Association of the Deaf, et al., v. Netflix, Inc.*, 869 F Supp 2d 196 (D. Mass., 2012); 26 Am. Disabilities Cas. (BNA) 1091f.

[59] *National Association of the Deaf, et al., v. Netflix, Inc.* (D. Mass., No. 3:11-cv-30168, 2012) 200–201.

[60] 42 USC § 12181(7).

[61] See the Consent Decree made in *National Association of the Deaf, et al., v. Netflix, Inc.* (D. Mass., No. 3:11-cv-30168, 2012) <dredf.org/captioning/netflix-consent-decree-10-10-12.pdf> (accessed 18 November 2016).

there is a sufficient nexus between the service provided by a place of public accommodation and the website.[62] One of the first cases to apply the nexus test was the Eleventh Circuit's[63] United States District Court for the Southern District of Florida in *Access Now, Inc. v. Sw. Airlines Co.*[64] The Court considered whether an airline's online ticketing website was a place of public accommodation. The Eleventh Circuit Court observed that Title III was plain and not ambiguous,[65] and that 'the plain and unambiguous language of the statute and relevant regulations does not include Internet websites among the [twelve specifically enumerated categories defining] "places of public accommodation"'.[66] As websites are not expressly mentioned in the ADA or regulations, for a website to be a 'place of public accommodation' the court held there must be a connection with a 'physical, concrete structure'.[67] Under the nexus approach, purely non-physical establishments could not be places of public accommodation.[68]

If a person has their access to a physical space impeded or denied by a digital space, then under the nexus test the digital space comes within Title III. An Eleventh Circuit Court has found a person can be impeded from accessing a physical space where the person would have been extremely unlikely to gain access to the physical space even if there was no discrimination. In *Rendon v. Valleycrest Prods., Ltd* the physical space was the studios of *Who Wants to Be a Millionaire?*[69] To gain access to this physical space, members of the public were invited to participate in online contests using a standard audio telephone. As people with hearing impairments were unable to use standard telephones, the discrimination in the digital space denied them the possibility of gaining access to the physical studios of the competition. As a consequence, there was held to be a sufficient nexus with a physical space to have the digital activity regulated by the ADA.

The Eleventh Circuit judgment in *Rendon v. Valleycrest Prods., Ltd* was not followed in a subsequent United States Court of Appeal for the Ninth Circuit judgment in *Stern v. Sony Corporation of America.*[70] In *Stern v. Sony Corporation of America* the Ninth Circuit held that Sony online computer

---

[62] Richard E Moberly, 'The *Americans with Disabilities Act* in Cyberspace: Applying the "Nexus" Approach to Private Internet Websites' (2004) 55 *Mercer Law Review* 963, 1315.

[63] The Eleventh Circuit's jurisdiction includes Middle District of Alabama, Northern District of Alabama, Southern District of Alabama, Middle District of Florida, Northern District of Florida, Southern District of Florida, Middle District of Georgia, Northern District of Georgia and Southern District of Georgia.

[64] *Access Now, Inc. v. Sw. Airlines Co.*, 227 F Supp 2d 1312 (SD Fla, 2002).   [65] Ibid., 1317.

[66] Ibid., 1318.   [67] Ibid., 1318.   [68] Ibid., 1319.

[69] *Rendon v. Valleycrest Prods., Ltd.*, 294 F 3d 1279, 1283 (11th Cir., 2002).

[70] *Stern v. Sony Corporation of America; Sony Computer Entertainment America, Inc.; Sony Online Entertainment, LLC*, 459 Fed Appx 609 (9th Cir., 2011).

games were not sufficiently connected with a physical location, where success on those games was used to determine if a person could attend gaming conventions held in physical locations.[71]

One of the leading cases on the Title III nexus test is the judgment of the United States District Court for the Northern District of California in the *National Federation of the Blind* v. *Target Corp.*[72] The retail chain Target used websites as an integral component of its physical retail stores. Unfortunately, the online retail stores were not accessible for persons who were blind who used screen readers. The National Federation of the Blind and others filed suit against Target for breaching Title III. In response, Target Corporation filed a motion to dismiss the claims on the basis there was an insufficient nexus. Target argued that its inaccessible website did not limit the ability of persons with disabilities to physically access their stores, and therefore was not in breach of the *ADA*.

The Ninth Circuit Court held that according to the nexus approach, a website of a place of public accommodation must accommodate persons with disabilities.[73] The court advised that the *ADA* entitled people with disabilities to access 'the services of a place of public accommodation, not services in a place of public accommodation'.[74] As a result, a website need not deny physical access to a building. A website that forms part of the service of a place of a public accommodation is required by the *ADA* to be accessible.[75]

Arguably, the nexus test unnecessarily complicates and limits what digital spaces are covered by Title III.[76] Kenneth Kronstadt has argued that '[t]he legislative history behind the *ADA*'s enactment supports the view that Congress did not intend to limit Title III's reach to only those entities that are physically accessible for the purchase of goods and services'.[77] The nexus approach has the absurd outcome where a retail store like Target attracts duties under Title III while purely online commercial operations, such as 'amazon.com or buy.com would not need to make any accommodations

[71] Ibid., 610–611.

[72] *National Federation of the Blind* v. *Target Corp.*, 452 F Supp 2d 946 (ND Cal, 2006).

[73] Ibid., 956.   [74] Ibid., 953.   [75] Ibid., 956.

[76] Arana DuPree, 'Recent Development: Websites as "Places of Public Accommodation": Amending the *Americans with Disabilities Act* in the Wake of *National Federation of the Blind* v. *Target Corporation*' (2007) 8(2) *North Carolina Journal of Law and Technology* 273, 282; Michael Goldfarb, 'Comment, *Access Now, Inc.* v. *Southwest Airlines Co.* – Using the "Nexus" Approach to Determine Whether a Website Should Be Governed by the *Americans with Disabilities Act*' (2005) 79 *St. John's Law Review* 1313, 1331.

[77] Kenneth Kronstadt, 'Note: Looking behind the Curtain: Applying Title III of the *Americans with Disabilities Act* to the Businesses behind Commercial Websites' (2007) 81 *Southern California Law Review* 111, 133.

because they have no facilities deemed places of public accommodation'.[78] Nikki Kessling illustrates the absurd outcome of the nexus test using a hypothetical example:

> Jill is profoundly visually impaired but otherwise self-sufficient. Because she cannot operate a car or navigate a busy city on foot without assistance, shopping for groceries (or anything else) is a difficult task. Jill's city has four stores. Store A has a physical storefront only. Store B has a physical storefront as well as a website; shoppers can buy items via the store or the website. Store C has a physical storefront and a website, but regularly offers special 'online-only' deals that apply only to website purchases. Store D has no physical storefront at all; a website is its sole method of selling its goods to the public.[79]

The nexus test means that only the portions of the store that directly relate to a physical store attract duties under the ADA. This means that if businesses structure their websites to avoid linking them to their physical stores, then they will avoid duties under the ADA to ensure that their websites are accessible.

The limitations with the nexus approach can be illustrated by the Ninth Circuit case of *Young v. Facebook, Inc.*[80] Young argued that Facebook was subject to Title III. The court held that Facebook was not subject to Title III as it operated entirely in cyberspace.[81] Young's amended complaint drew from circuits that had accepted the nexus approach to Title III. Since Facebook gift cards could be purchased in physical stores, Young claimed that her inability to access the Facebook website meant there was a sufficient nexus between the digital and physical spaces. The court rejected this attempt and held that it was bound by Ninth Circuit judgments which had not adopted the nexus approach.[82] Nevertheless, even though the court in Young did not adopt the nexus approach, it did apply the facts to the nexus test in finding that Facebook did not own, lease or operate any physical stores. As Facebook does not own, lease or operate any physical spaces, there is no physical space to which a digital space can be linked.[83] As a consequence, the Court found that Title III had no application to Facebook.

The nexus approach to Title III creates the possibility that companies will create separate corporate entities to structure their operations to confound the

---

[78] Ibid., 130.

[79] Nikki D Kessling, 'Why the Target "Nexus Test" Leaves Disabled Americans Disconnected: A Better Approach to Determine Whether Private Commercial Websites are "Places of Public Accommodation"' (2008) 45 *Houston Law Review* 991, 992.

[80] *Young v. Facebook, Inc.*, 790 F Supp 2d 1110, 1115 (ND Cal., 2011).   [81] Ibid.

[82] *Ky Minh Pham v. Hickman*, 262 Fed Appx 35, 39 (9th Cir., 2007) ('in the absence of Supreme Court law, [a district court] is bound to follow Ninth Circuit precedent').

[83] *Young v. Facebook, Inc.*, 790 F Supp 2d 1110 (ND Cal., 2011).

intent behind the ADA. The Redbox litigation in the Ninth Circuit is an example of how a business might be structured in a way that avoids Title III regulation.[84] Redbox Retail owns and operates almost fifty thousand self-service DVD rental kiosks across the United States. There is a separate online DVD rental operation called Redbox Instant. Both of the Redbox operations held a very small range of DVDs that included close captioning. Without close captioning, people without hearing have reduced capacity to enjoy the DVD watching experience.[85]

Jancik, described in the judgment as 'an individual who is deaf', filed suit against both of the Redbox operations under the ADA, California's *Unruh Act*,[86] California's *Disabled Persons Act*,[87] California's *Consumer Legal Remedies Act*,[88] California's *False Advertising Law*[89] and California's *Unfair Competition Law*.[90] The court found that Redbox's bricks-and-mortar retail operations were places of public accommodation and subject to Title III.[91] The extension of Title III over Redbox's digital activities was more problem-atic. Citing *Hart* v. *Massanari*, the Court observed that it was bound by Ninth Circuit precedent: '[a] district judge may not respectfully (or disrespectfully) disagree with his learned colleagues on his own court of appeals who have ruled on a controlling legal issue'.[92] Citing the Weyer judgment, which is discussed below,[93] the Ninth Circuit Court held that Redbox's purely online presence was not a place of public accommodation.[94] The court in *Redbox*, however, was content to accept that websites could be places of public accommodation if the nexus test applied.

Jancik argued that there was a sufficient nexus between the Redbox Instant website and his experiences at the physical Redbox retail kiosks. Jancik argued that similar to *National Federation of the Blind* v. *Target Corp*,[95] the Redbox

---

[84] *Francis Jancik v. Redbox Automated Retail, LLC, et al.* (D Cal., No. SACV 13-1387-Doc., 14 May 2014).
[85] Raja Kushalnagar, 'Who Owns Captioning?' in Michael Stein and Jonathan Lazar (eds), *Frontiers in Human Rights: Disability Rights, Law, and Technology Accessibility* (forthcoming) University of Pennsylvania Press.
[86] Codified as Cal. Civ. Code § 51[5](6). The *Unruh Act* is named for its author, Jesse M Unruh.
[87] Cal. Civ. Code §§ 54 et seq.   [88] Cal. Bus. and Prof. Code §§ 1750 et seq.
[89] Cal. Bus. and Prof. Code §§ 17500 et seq.   [90] Cal. Bus. and Prof. Code §§ 17200 et seq.
[91] *Francis Jancik v. Redbox Automated Retail, LLC, et al.* (D Cal., No. SACV 13-1387-Doc., 14 May 2014) slip op. 8.
[92] *Hart* v. *Massanari*, 266 F 3d 1155, 1170 (9th Cir., 2001).
[93] *Weyer* v. *Twentieth Century Fox Film Corp.*, 198 F 3d 1104, 1114 (9th Cir., 2000).
[94] *Francis Jancik v. Redbox Automated Retail, LLC, et al.* (D Cal., No. SACV 13-1387-Doc., 14 May 2014) slip op. 22.
[95] *National Federation of the Blind* v. *Target Corp.*, 452 F Supp 3d 946, 955 (ND Cal., 2006) ('heavily integrated with the brick and mortar stores and operate[d] in many ways as a gateway to the store').

website was heavily integrated with the physical store and acted as a gateway to the store. The Court was prepared to adopt the nexus approach to Title III; however, it held that the Redbox kiosk and website were not sufficiently integrated or linked to satisfy the nexus test.[96] Even though the Redbox group of companies used a common branding and were closely aligned, the fact that they were separate legal entities was a factor which reduced Jancik's capacity to prove that the digital and physical spaces were integrated.

Arguably, the need to find a nexus between a physical location and a website unnecessarily limits the scope of the *ADA*. The nexus test goes against the bright line rule adopted by the United States Department of Justice.[97] The bright line rule adopted by the Department of Justice provides that the *ADA* applies to the internet and to websites. This approach recognises that significant business is performed on the internet. As persons with disabilities are less mobile than the wider community, this renders internet access even more critical. Limiting the *ADA* to websites that have a nexus with a physical shop substantially limits the operation of this remedial statute. If anti-discrimination law does not regulate parties who create barriers to inclusion, then it is likely that market forces will fail to pressure such parties to adopt inclusive design.[98] The failure to regulate all website designers and operators has reduced the capacity of persons with disabilities to enjoy equal access to digital environments such as E-Books and E-Libraries.

Physicalist Approach

Similar to the purposive approach, early judgments following the physicalist approach to Title III focused on whether non-physical aspects of discrimin-atory insurance policies came within Title III. Courts from the First, Second and Seventh Circuits held that limiting the statute to physical spaces would confound the statute. In contrast, early judgments in the Third, Sixth and Ninth Circuits narrowed the coverage of the *ADA*.[99] Early Third, Sixth and

---

[96] *Francis Jancik v. Redbox Automated Retail, LLC, et al.* (D Cal., No. SACV 13-1387-Doc., 14 May 2014) slip op. 23.

[97] See generally 'Brief of United States as Amicus Curiae in Support of Appellant' in *Hooks v. OKBridge, Inc.* (5th Cir., No. 99-50891, 30 June 2000). See for discussion: Ryan Campbell Richards, 'Current Issues in Public Policy: Reconciling the *Americans with Disabilities Act* and Commercial Websites: A Feasible Solution?' (2010) 7 *Rutgers Journal of Law and Public Policy* 520, 544–5.

[98] Robin Paul Malloy, 'Inclusive Design Concerns the Inclusion by Design: Accessible Housing and Mobility' (2009) 60 *Hastings Law Journal* 699 (analysing the lack of inclusive design standards in single-family residential housing).

[99] The Third Circuit's jurisdiction includes the District of New Jersey, Eastern District of Pennsylvania, Middle District of Pennsylvania and Western District of Pennsylvania; the

Ninth Circuit judgments adopted physicalist approaches to Title III and held that the ADA did not extend to digital spaces.

The Ninth Circuit judgment in *Weyer* v. *Twentieth Century Fox Film* (*Weyer*) is arguably the leading physicalist approach judgment.[100] *Weyer* concerned an employer-arranged insurance policy. The policy distinguished between people with physical and mental disabilities and provided the latter with reduced benefits. It was argued that this distinction was unlawful under, inter alia, Title III. The Court found that public accommodations are only 'actual, physical places where goods and services are open to the public'.[101] Accordingly, an insurance company administering an employer-provided disability policy was held not to be a 'place of public accommodation' under Title III.

A Third Circuit judgment in *Ford* v. *Schering-Plough Corp.* (*Ford*), and a Sixth Circuit judgment in *Parker* v. *Metro. Life Ins. Co.* (*Parker*), reached similar conclusions as the Court in *Weyer*.[102] Both *Ford* and *Parker* involved employer insurance plans which discriminated between people with different impairments. In both *Ford* and *Parker*, the Courts held that public accommodations did not prevent employer health insurance policies from providing employees with a disability plan that discriminated between employees with physical and mental disabilities. The Courts reached these conclusions by explaining that a benefit plan offered by an employer is not a good offered by a place of public accommodation. A public accommodation is a physical place, and the fact that the agreements were offered and accepted in a physical space was not persuasive.

The physicalist courts have read down the scope of the ADA to technological developments. In *Stoutenborough* v. *Nat'l Football League, Inc.*, a Sixth Circuit Court found that television programmes were not public accommodations related to places of recreation or entertainment.[103] Accordingly, a televised broadcast of a football game did not involve an accommodation at a physical facility and thus could not be a public accommodation. This meant the court was not asked to consider whether or not it was reasonable for the defendant to promote social inclusion in the way requested by the plaintiff.

Sixth Circuit's jurisdiction includes the Western District of Kentucky, Eastern District of Michigan, Western District of Michigan, Northern District of Ohio, Southern District of Ohio, Eastern District of Tennessee, Middle District of Tennessee and the Western District of Tennessee.

[100] *Weyer*, 198 F 3d 1104, 1114 (9th Cir., 2000).   [101] Ibid.
[102] *Ford* v. *Schering-Plough Corp.*, 145 F 3d 601, 612–614 (3rd Cir., 1998); *Parker* v. *Metro. Life Ins. Co.*, 121 F 3d 1006, 1010–1013 (6th Cir., 1997).
[103] *Stoutenborough* v. *Nat'l Football League, Inc.*, 59 F 3d 580, 583 (6th Cir., 1995).

The physicalist approach has been applied to the entirely non-physical realm of the internet. The Ninth Circuit case of *Young* v. *Facebook* has already been considered above. Even though the court stated that it rejected the nexus approach, the court in *Young* v. *Facebook* still considered whether the facts would have satisfied the nexus test.

Another Ninth Circuit Court has applied that the physicalist approach to hold Title III does not apply to websites. In *Earll* v. *eBay*, Earll filed a putative class action against eBay, asserting that eBay's seller verification system was inaccessible to the deaf. Earll had filed suit in March 2010 in the Western District of Missouri, which is within the United States Court of Appeals for the Eighth Circuit. At the time of this case there had been no cases concerning websites in the Eighth Circuit.

In January 2011, eBay successfully moved to have the case transferred to the Ninth Circuit's Northern District of California.[104] In contrast to the Eighth Circuit, the Ninth Circuit has a number of authorities adopting the physicalist and nexus approaches, neither of which would provide support for a Title III claim over an entirely non-physical public accommodation. The Ninth Circuit Court cited *Weyer*,[105] and held that 'under controlling Ninth Circuit authority, "places of public accommodation" under the ADA are limited to actual physical spaces. ... Thus, eBay is correct in arguing that the ADA cannot afford a remedy to Earll in this case.'[106] The *Earll* v. *eBay* judgment was appealed and a decision was handed down on 1 April 2015. Earll's appeal was dismissed on the basis that eBay's services are not connected to a physical space.[107]

A clear example of the split between the physicalist and purposive approaches to digital spaces is the Title III litigation against Netflix. Earlier in this chapter the National Federation for the Deaf's litigation against Netflix was analysed. Whereas the First Circuit in *National Association of the Deaf, et al.*, v. *Netflix* found that the digital facilities offered by Netflix were public accommodations, the Ninth Circuit judgment in *Cullen* v. *Netflix* reached the opposite conclusion.[108]

There are three obvious differences between the Cullen and National Federation of the Deaf cases against Netflix. Even though the Ninth Circuit case in *Target* is one of the most ground-breaking Title III website cases, the First Circuit has a longer history in recognising non-physical spaces as public

[104] *Earll* v. *eBay, Inc.*, 764 F Supp 2d 1148 (WD Mo, 2011).
[105] *Weyer* v. *Twentieth Century Fox Film Corp.*, 198 F 3d 1104, 1114 (9th Cir., 2000).
[106] *Earll* v. *eBay, Inc.*, 764 F Supp 2d 1148, 6 (WD Mo, 2011).
[107] *Earll* v. *eBay, Inc.* (9th Cir., No. 13-15134, 1 April 2015).
[108] *Cullen* v. *Netflix* (ND Cal., No. 5:11-cv-01199-EJD, 13 July 2012).

accommodation. Another significant difference is who filed suit. The Cullen litigation was filed as a putative class action initiated by an individual. The First Circuit suit, in contrast, involved a number of leading disability person organisations, including the leading national deaf organisation, the National Federation of the Deaf, and the Western Massachusetts Association of the Deaf and Hearing Impaired, along with an individual litigant. Major disability organisations are representative of their members, tens of thousands in the case of the National Federation of the Deaf, and often have more resources than individuals. It is possible that courts are more willing to accept arguments raised by lawyers representing major disability person organisations than individual plaintiffs. Thirdly, the First Circuit case had reached a settlement over some of the barriers to inclusion that Cullen was raising in the Ninth Circuit. While the merits of the case should not be considered in determining if there was a public accommodation, this may have influenced the court's reasoning.

In *Cullen* v. *Netflix*, Cullen argued that Netflix's website violated Title III of the *ADA*,[109] the California *Unfair Competition Law*,[110] the California *False Advertising Law*,[111] the California *Consumer Legal Remedies Act*,[112] the California *Unruh Civil Rights Act*[113] and the California *Disabled Persons Act*.[114] Following the filing of the original complaint in March 2011, Cullen filed amended complaints in April and September 2011. The second amended complaint in September 2011 dropped the argument under Title III. Regardless of this fact, the Ninth Circuit took the opportunity to note that 'websites are not places of public accommodation'.[115]

It could be argued that the physicalist approach is divorced from the intent of the *ADA* and how public affairs are conducted in the twenty-first century. It has been argued that the distinction between entirely online and partially online is inappropriate in a world where more businesses are fully online. In Chapter 1 of this monograph it was noted that there are increasing numbers of E-Libraries and E-Books, that many libraries do not purchase hard copies of books, and that increasing numbers of titles are never turned into paper copies. Most of the above litigation has observed that the *ADA* was enacted in 1990 and that this was around the birth of the internet. Congress revisited the *ADA* when it enacted the *ADA Amendments Act of 2008*. It is unfortunate that Congress did not take the opportunity to clarify the extent to which Title III applies to digital activities.

---

[109] 42 USC §§ 12181 et seq.   [110] Cal. Bus. and Prof. Code §§ 17200 et seq.
[111] Ibid., §§ 17500 et seq.   [112] Ibid., §§ 1750 et seq.   [113] Cal. Civ. Code §§ 51 et seq.
[114] Ibid., §§ 54 et seq.   [115] *Cullen* v. *Netflix* (ND Cal., No. 5:11-cv-01199-EJD, 13 July 2012).

CONCLUSION

This chapter has analysed the threshold question of what parties are covered by anti-discrimination laws. Arguably, anti-discrimination laws should extend their operation over all parties who contribute to the digital disablement of people with disabilities. There are thousands of E-Libraries and tens of millions of E-Books. Whether it is reasonable to expect that all digital books are accessible to people with print disabilities requires a consideration of what is reasonable.[116] The issue of what anti-discrimination duties require of duty holders is analysed in the next chapter. Arguably, anti-discrimination laws should cast the regulatory net as wide as possible so that the reasonableness balancing test can be applied to all parties that contribute to the digital disablement of persons with print disabilities. Failing to include major stake-holders in the regulatory framework means that many parties who could readily and cheaply improve access have no legal obligation to even consider digital equality.

This chapter has illustrated that the coverage of anti-discrimination statutes over purely online spaces is mixed, at best. The situation in Canada will be analysed later in Chapter 10 due to its substantially different regulatory approach. This chapter has analysed how Australian, United Kingdom and United States courts and laws extend the coverage of disability discrimination protection to digital environments. There is one first instance judgment in Australia indicating that websites are covered by Australian anti-discrimination laws. The situation in the United Kingdom is clear, with the *Equality Act 2010* (UK) expressly extending to online spaces. The coverage of the ADA over digital environments depends on whether a court embraces the purposive, nexus or physicalist approach.

Ultimately, the human rights paradigm and the *CRPD* require states to ensure that anti-discrimination laws combat digital exclusion where it is not prohibitive to do so. While it might be unreasonable to require some digital environments to be inclusive, it is very reasonable to expect a certain level of accessibility from other spaces. This chapter has argued that the issue of reasonableness can only be assessed once the relevant civil rights statute covers an activity, and accordingly all jurisdictions should ensure that their disability discrimination statutes cover purely digital spaces.

---

[116] Robert Huffaker, 'Enforcing eAccessibility: Is the Current Legal Framework Adequate?' (2015) 29(2/3) *International Review of Law, Computers & Technology* 207.

8

The Prohibition against Discrimination: Regulating for Equality through Retrofitting Inaccessible Systems

INTRODUCTION

This chapter will analyse the extent to which the prohibition against discrimination found in anti-discrimination laws can enable persons with print disabilities to exercise their right to read. This chapter argues that the prohibition against discrimination in Australia, the United Kingdom and the United States will not significantly reverse the book famine for persons with print disabilities. The legislative interventions amount to an imperfect and partial solution to the existence of significant inequalities.

The prohibition against discrimination requires limited positive conduct from duty holders; however, these interventions do not deal with the underlying causes of digital disablement. The prohibition against discrimination analysed in this chapter does not seek to ensure that reading rights can be realised; rather these duties attempt to reduce some of the more extreme forms of discrimination. This limited duty only arises in situations where the person with a print disability satisfies the threshold questions analysed in Chapters 6 and 7. Where the prohibition does operate, the duty not to discriminate is cast in narrow and technical terms and omits to address the causes of digital disablement.

The statutory regimes in Australia, the United Kingdom and the United States bifurcate the prohibition against discrimination into two closed categories. In Australia and the United Kingdom, the categories are referred to as direct and indirect discrimination,[1] and in the United States, the categories are referred to as disparate treatment and disparate impact.[2] As will be analysed

---

[1] *Disability Discrimination Act 1992* (Cth) s 5; *Equality Act 2010* (UK) s 13. See the United States Supreme Court three-step, burden-shifting framework for proving disparate treatment: *McDonnell Douglas Corp. v. Green*, 411 US 792, 802 (1973).

[2] Noah Zatz, 'Managing the Macaw: Third-Party Harassers, Accommodation, and the Disaggregation of Discriminatory Intent' (2009) 109 *Columbia Law Review* 1357, 1368

below, the first form of discrimination is intentional and based upon a person's attributes. Section I illustrates that this category of discrimination has limited relevance to digital disablement and combatting the book famine. The second category prohibits facially neutral practices which have a discriminatory impact. This secondary category is more relevant to advancing digital equality and will be analysed in Sections II through to V below.

SECTION I INTRODUCTION TO THE BIFURCATED APPROACH TO PROHIBITING DISCRIMINATION

The Disparate Treatment Doctrine

A discriminator engages in direct discrimination or disparate treatment where the discriminator is found to have intentionally treated or proposed to treat a person less favourably because that person has a disability.[3] This requires a comparison between the treatment received by a person with a disability, and the treatment they would have received if they were not disabled.[4] To establish direct discrimination in Australia and the United Kingdom, plaintiffs need to compare their treatment against an actual or a hypothetical comparator.[5] This has created significant difficulties for complainants seeking to establish different treatment in Australia and the United Kingdom.[6] United States courts have been comparatively more hostile to plaintiffs than courts in Australia and the United Kingdom. The comparator test in the United States is limited to an actual comparator who is almost the twin of the plaintiff to prove the existence of disparate treatment.[7]

Presuming the person with a print disability can surmount the comparator test, direct discrimination and adverse treatment provisions will improve access to digital book content in formats accessible to persons with print disabilities. Unlike other protected attributes, the disability attribute includes

---

(describing the bifurcation of discrimination into disparate treatment and disparate impact theories as being 'embedded in the structure of the *ADA*).

[3] *Disability Discrimination Act 1992* (Cth) s 6; *Equality Act 2010* (UK) ss 13 and 19.

[4] Bonnie Poitras Tucker, '*Disability Discrimination Act*: Ensuring Rights of Australians with Disabilities, Particularly Hearing Impairments' (1995) 21(1) *Monash University Law Review* 15.

[5] Bob Hepple, *Equality*, 2nd edn (2014) Hart Publishing, 64–5.

[6] Claire Darwin, 'Case Comment: Disability Discrimination – Whether Pupil Disabled' (2013) 14(4) *Education Law Journal* 298; Belinda Smith, 'From *Wardley* to *Purvis* – How Far Has Australian Anti-Discrimination Law Come in 30 Years?' (2008) 21(1) *Australian Journal of Labour Law* 3.

[7] Suzanne B Goldberg, 'Discrimination by Comparison' (2011) 120 *Yale Law Journal* 728; Charles A Sullivan, 'The Phoenix from the Ash: Proving Discrimination by Comparators' (2009) 60(2) *Alabama Law Review* 191.

a limited positive duty on duty holders.[8] This limited positive duty requires duty holders to take reasonable efforts to render standard books and digital content accessible to persons with disabilities.[9] This duty on parties to make alterations in the United States and in the *Convention on the Rights of Persons with Disabilities (CRPD)* is described as 'reasonable accommodation',[10] and in Australia and the United Kingdom as 'reasonable adjustments'.[11]

Reasonable accommodations and adjustments involve making alterations to environments to enable persons with disabilities to operate.[12] Dr Carrie Griffin Basas eloquently argues that reasonable accommodations under the ADA are at the centre of the integration of people with disabilities into the mainstream work environment.[13] Professor Bob Hepple explains that there are three broad categories of reasonable adjustments.[14] The first category concerns changing how things are done. This might involve providing sign language interpreters. The second category focuses on changes in the built environment, such as the installation of ramps. The third category concerns the duty holder providing auxiliary aids, such as installing screen readers on computers.

The factors that will result in an adjustment being held to be unreasonable are broadly similar in Australia, the United Kingdom and the United States.[15] These factors include the cost of the adjustments when compared to the resources of the duty holder, the impact of the adjustment on the duty holder, and the position and relationship of the place where the adjustment is to be

---

[8] Brian Doyle, 'Enabling Legislation or Dissembling Law? The *Disability Discrimination Act 1995*' (1997) 60(1) *Modern Law Review* 64.

[9] 42 USC § 12112(b)(5). For a more complete description of what constitutes discrimination under the ADA, see § 12112 in its entirety. *Equality Act 2010* (UK) s 21(1)–(2).

[10] See 42 USC § 12112(b)(5) See CRPD art. 27(1)(i) for the use of this term with respect to the right to work; CRPD, opened for signature 30 March 2007, 2515 UNTS 3 (entered into force 3 May 2008).

[11] *Disability Discrimination Act 1992* (Cth) ss 4, 5(2), 6(2) and 21A(1); *Equality Act 2010* (UK) s 39(5).

[12] Deborah Foster, 'Legal Obligation or Personal Lottery? Employee Experiences of Disability and the Negotiation of Adjustments in the Public Sector Workplace' (2007) 21(1) *Work, Employment and Society* 67; Anna Lawson, 'Reasonable Accommodation and Accessibility Obligations: Towards a More Unified European Approach?' (2011) 11 *European Anti-Discrimination Law Review* 11.

[13] Carrie Griffin Basas, 'Back Rooms, Board Rooms: Reasonable Accommodation and Resistance under the ADA' (2008) 28 *Berkeley Journal of Employment and Labor Law* 59.

[14] Hepple, *Equality*, 94–5.

[15] Although US courts adopt a more narrow view of when an accommodation is linked to a disability. See for discussion: Cheryl L Anderson, 'What Is "Because of the Disability" under the *Americans with Disabilities Act*? Reasonable Accommodation, Causation, and the Windfall Doctrine' (2006) 27(2) *Berkeley Journal of Employment and Labor Law* 323 (analysing how a number of courts have required reasonable accommodations to be linked to narrowly identified aspects of a person's disability. Anderson concludes that US courts have used causation requirements to avoid evaluations on the merits of accommodations claims).

made.[16] Professor Mark Weber has observed that, significantly, the reasonable accommodation test 'is not a cost–benefit comparison, but rather a cost–total budget comparison'.[17] Weber analyses the authoritative sources concerning the ADA accommodation requirement and concludes that reasonable accommodation and undue hardship are two sides of the same coin. The statutory duty is accommodation up to the limit of hardship, and reasonable accommodation should not be a separate hurdle for claimants to surmount.

In an employment scenario, in one case a reasonable accommodation could be over 10 per cent of the employee's annual wage, and in another case it might be below this figure.[18] As a consequence, determining if an accommodation or adjustment is reasonable or unreasonable needs to be assessed on a case-by-case basis. William D Goren explains that courts have been 'all over the place' as to the burden of proof in accommodation cases because reasonable accommodation does not constitute an undue hardship, but undue hardship is an affirmative defence.[19]

United States laws require entities to adopt the most appropriate ways to offer their services and programmes.[20] Peter Blanck explains that this requires entities 'to make reasonable modifications and accommodations to practices and policies, unless they fundamentally change or unreasonably burden the way the services are provided'.[21] Most courts and commentators accept that reasonableness will be established once an individual with a disability demonstrates that the requested accommodation works.[22] The onus then flips to the duty holder to prove that the reasonable accommodation creates an undue hardship for ADA Title I or an undue burden for Titles II and III.[23]

Despite the potential for substantial change, courts have a history of limiting the duty to make reasonable accommodations and adjustments, and of

---

[16] 42 USC § 12111(10)(B); *Disability Discrimination Act 1992* (Cth) s 4. *Equality Act 2010* (UK) s 20 defines the duty to make reasonable adjustments by reference to Schedule 8.

[17] Mark C Weber, 'Unreasonable Accommodation and Due Hardship' (2010) 62 *Florida Law Review* 1119, 1136.

[18] Ibid. For a discussion of the 10 per cent figure see: House Committee on the Judiciary, HR Rep No. 101–485(III) (1990) 41.

[19] William D Goren, *Understanding the Americans with Disabilities Act*, 3rd edn (2010) American Bar Association, 29.

[20] See 28 CFR § 35.130(d) (2010).

[21] Peter Blanck, *Equality: The Struggle for Web Accessibility by Persons with Cognitive Disabilities* (2014) Cambridge University Press, 52.

[22] Erin Grewe, 'Justice May Be Blind, but there Is No Justice for the Visually Disabled: A Guide to the Administration of a Format-Neutral Bar Examination' (2012) 21 *Temple Political and Civil Rights Law Review* 543, 550–1.

[23] For an example of the balancing of financial burdens see *Tucker* v. *Tenn.*, 539 F 3d 526, 533 (6th Cir., 2008).

construing these duties narrowly.[24] When balancing the competing factors, courts focus upon the cost of the adjustment to the duty holder, rather than on the benefit to the individual with a disability or to the community at large.[25] Christopher Brown argues that failing to consider the positive externalities of an adjustment distorts the assessment.[26] Brown argues that courts should adopt a net social benefit model, which assesses all the costs and benefits associated with an adjustment.[27] This approach means that duty holders are not burdened with high adjustment costs where the benefit to an individual is moderate. Focusing on the impact on a single individual substantially reduces the capacity of the reasonable accommodation and adjustment models to reduce the existence of disabling barriers in society.

The duty to make reasonable accommodations and adjustments requires duty holders to take steps to ensure that persons with print disabilities can access certain written content that is relevant to the particular relationship. The prescribed relationship which requires the most from duty holders under domestic and international law is the educator/student relationship.[28] *Argenyi v. Creighton University* is an example of the operation of the duty on educators to provide educational materials in disability-accessible

---

[24] Mark Bell, 'Mental Health at Work and the Duty to Make Reasonable Adjustments' (2015) 44(2) *Industrial Law Journal* 194, 201–2; Anna Lawson, *Disability and Equality Law in Britain: The Role of Reasonable Adjustments* (2008) Hart Publishing, 259.

[25] The United States Supreme Court in *US Airways, Inc. v. Barnett*, 535 US 391, 400–01, 406 (2002) held that an adjustment that cost the duty holder nothing was unreasonable if it interfered with the seniority rights of other employees. See also Elizabeth F Emens, 'Integrating Accommodation' (2008) 156(4) *University of Pennsylvania Law Review* 839 (drawing attention to the many ways accommodations for workers with disabilities yield benefits for third parties in workplaces); Michael Ashley Stein, 'The Law and Economics of Disability Accommodations' (2003) 53 *Duke Law Journal* 79 (analysing how to economically conceptualise disability-related accommodation costs).

[26] Christopher B Brown, 'Incorporating Third-Party Benefits into the Cost–Benefit Calculus of Reasonable Adjustment' (2011) 18 *Virginia Journal of Social Policy and the Law* 319, 320 (providing a theoretical roadmap as to how courts could incorporate third-party benefits into their cost–benefit analysis).

[27] Ibid., 341.

[28] G De Beco, 'The Right to Inclusive Education According to Article 24 of the UN *Convention on the Rights of Persons with Disabilities*: Background, Requirements and (Remaining) Questions' (2014) 32(3) *Netherlands Quarterly of Human Rights* 263; Bob Hepple, 'The European Legacy of *Brown v. Board of Education*' (2006) 3 *University of Illinois Law Review* 605; Philippa Moran, 'No Learner Left Behind: Is New Zealand Meeting its Obligations under Article 24 of the United Nations *Convention on the Rights of Persons with Disabilities*?' (2014) 1 *Public Interest Law Journal of New Zealand* 1; Payel Rai Chowdhury, 'The Right to Inclusive Education of Persons with Disabilities: The Policy and Practice Implications' (2011) 12(2) *Asia-Pacific Journal on Human Rights and the Law* 1; Tamara Walsh, 'Negligence and Special Needs Education: The Case for Recognising a Duty to Provide Special Education Services in Australian Schools' (2015) 18(1) *Education Law Journal* 32.

formats.[29] *Argenyi* v. *Creighton University* involved a medical student who was deaf. In his first year of study, Argenyi had requested Communication Access Real-Time Transcription, which would provide a real-time text display of spoken words in lectures and workshops. Creighton University refused Argenyi's request and only offered him note-taking services. Note-taking services involves the university paying a fellow student to share their notes with the student with a disability after class. As a consequence, Argenyi paid for Communication Access Real-Time Transcription and an interpreter himself. In his second year of study, Argenyi was not only refused accommodations, but he was denied the right to pay for his own interpreter. Argenyi argued he had been discriminated against and the Eighth Circuit agreed. The Eighth Circuit held, inter alia, that ADA Title III required Creighton University to provide Argenyi with the necessary accommodations and services to complete the course.[30] This required Creighton University to provide Argenyi with the meaningful opportunity to access education.[31] When the matter was remanded to the trial court, it was found that Creighton University had discriminated against Argenyi for not providing accommodations that were reasonable.[32] Duty holders are expected to take positive conduct to facilitate access to educational materials, and most certainly cannot block a student from funding their own minor changes to how they consume educational content.

Professors Anna Lawson, Lisa Waddington and Aart Hendriks have argued that the existence of a duty to make reasonable adjustments and accommodations will assist in reducing the impact of disabling barriers in society; however, these duties do not challenge and affect underlying discriminatory policies and practices.[33] The inability of the reasonable accommodation and adjustment duties to effect wider structural change is illustrated by the impact of these duties on addressing the book famine. While the requirement to make reasonable adjustments and accommodations will help reduce the impact of the book famine, this duty does not aim to, nor achieve, reading equality. The duties of reasonable accommodation and adjustment do not target the underlying causes of reading disablement. Employers, libraries and, most commonly, educators, can help people with print disabilities convert books

---

[29] *Argenyi* v. *Creighton University*, 703 F 3d 441 (8th Cir., 2013), rehearing and rehearing en banc denied (5 March 2013).

[30] Ibid. (citing 42 USC § 12182(b)(2)(A)(ii); 34 CFR § 104.44(d)(1) (2000).   [31] Ibid., 448–9.

[32] Ibid. See also the Verdict Form in the case, dated 4 September 2013.

[33] Lawson, *Disability and Equality Law in Britain*, 17; Lisa Waddington and Aart Hendriks, 'The Expanding Concept of Employment Discrimination in Europe: From Direct and Indirect Discrimination to Reasonable Accommodation Discrimination' (2002) 18(3) *International Journal of Comparative Labour Law and Industrial Relations* 403.

into accessible formats; however, these duty holders have little or no capacity to affect the publication of books in formats that exclude persons with print disabilities at the point this duty is enlivened. Even if duty holders had the capacity to promote inclusive practices if involving themselves when books are created, the reasonable adjustment and accommodation model generally only requires duty holders to consider accessibility once a person with a disability has presented to them. The aims of such interventions are limited. S Day and G Brodsky argue that '[i]n short, accommodation is assimilationist. Its goal is to try to make "different" people fit into existing systems'.[34] Retrofitting an inaccessible world will not achieve the same results as creating an inclusive world from the outset. Arguably, the best option for combatting the book famine is to prevent the creation of discriminatory practices. The removal of such practices is the objective of the disparate impact doctrine analysed next in this chapter.

Introducing the Disparate Impact Doctrine

People with print disabilities are disabled when books are not published in digital formats, or when E-Books are published in formats that do not follow disability accessibility guidelines. The creation of facially neutral systems, which through indifference or ignorance have a discriminatory impact, are the type of inequality that the disparate impact doctrine was developed to combat.

The concept of disparate impact theory was first judicially articulated by the United States Supreme Court in *Griggs* v. *Duke Power Company* (*Griggs*).[35] *Griggs* concerned the operation of a promotion policy adopted by the Duke Power Company. Duke Power Company enabled workers to transfer from the low-paying departments provided they had either a high school diploma or could achieve satisfactory scores on general intelligence tests. At this particular time in history, white Americans were almost three times more likely than African Americans to complete a high school certificate in the relevant geographical region. Out of those people who sat the general intelligence tests, 58 per cent of white Americans achieved satisfactory results, while only 6 per cent of African Americans achieved the same level. When African

---

[34] Shelagh Day and Gwen Brodsky, 'The Duty to Accommodate: Who Will Benefit?' (1996) 75 *Canadian Bar Review* 433, 447–57.

[35] 401 US 424 (1971). Prior to Griggs, US agencies had already developed disparate impact standards under Titles VI and VII of the *Civil Rights Act*. For discussion see Olatunde C A Johnson, 'The Agency Roots of Disparate Impact' (2014) 49 *Harvard Civil Rights–Civil Liberties Law Review* 125, 131.

American workers sued for discrimination, the matter ended up before the United States Supreme Court. Burger CJ provided the majority opinion for the United States Supreme Court:

> The objective of Congress in the enactment of Title VII is plain from the language of the statute. It was to achieve equality of employment opportunities and remove barriers that have operated in the past to favour an identifiable group of white employees over other employees. Under the Act, practices, procedures, or tests neutral on their face, and even neutral in terms of intent, cannot be maintained if they operate to 'freeze' the status quo of prior discriminatory employment practices. ... What is required by Congress is the removal of artificial, arbitrary, and unnecessary barriers to employment when the barriers operate invidiously to discriminate on the basis of racial or other impermissible classification. ... The Act proscribes not only overt discrimination but also practices that are fair in form, but discriminatory in operation. The touchstone is business necessity. If an employment practice which operates to exclude Negroes cannot be shown to be related to job performance, the practice is prohibited. On the record before us, neither the high school completion requirement nor the general intelligence test is shown to bear a demonstrable relationship to successful performance of the jobs for which it was used. Both were adopted, as the Court of Appeals noted, without meaningful study of their relationship to job-performance ability.[36]

The United States Supreme Court in *Griggs* established the doctrine that, both intentionally and unintentionally, equal treatment can be unlawful if it has a disparate exclusionary impact on a group of people who share a protected attribute.

The Theory behind the Disparate Impact Doctrine

Before considering how disparate impact operates, it is helpful to consider what this prohibition is seeking to achieve. Despite its longevity, the potential of the disparate impact doctrine remains misunderstood[37] and 'under-theorized'.[38] Professor Richard Primus explains that there are, broadly, two motives behind the development of the disparate impact doctrine.[39] The first

---

[36] 401 US 424, 429–436 (1971).
[37] Michael Selmi, 'Theorizing Systemic Disparate Treatment Law: After *Wal-Mart v. Dukes*' (2011) 32 *Berkeley Journal of Employment and Labor Law* 477, 478.
[38] Tristin K Green, 'The Future of Systemic Disparate Treatment Law' (2011) 32 *Berkeley Journal of Employment and Labor Law* 395, 418.
[39] Richard A Primus, 'Equal Protection and Disparate Impact: Round Three' (2003) 117 *Harvard Law Review* 494, 498–9.

approach constructs disparate impact as an 'evidentiary device aimed at ferreting out present discriminatory states of mind, while others see it as concerned with the lingering structural consequences of discrimination practiced in the past'.[40] These different strands turn the focus of the intervention in different ways. One approach focuses on fault while the other focuses on effects.[41] Perhaps more importantly, these different approaches dictate the outcomes of the intervention. This results in competing visions of equal achievement theory and an equal treatment theory.[42]

Unlike disparate treatment or direct discrimination, in a disparate impact or indirect discrimination suit the intent of the defendant is immaterial. The fact that a person can unintentionally discriminate has attracted criticism from the inception of this doctrine.[43] Michael Gold, Paul Moreno and John Skrentny have argued that the absence of intent in the disparate impact doctrine has moved away from the intent of Title VII of the *Civil Rights Act* to prevent unequal treatment and to make certain decisions colour-blind.[44] Ericka Kelsaw and Michael Selmi have argued that courts are more willing to find that disparate treatment has occurred than to find that a defendant has unintentionally engaged in a disparate impact.[45] Professor Amy Wax contends that the doctrine of disparate impact is uncertain and should either be modified or abolished.[46] Despite the controversy and reservations,[47] the

---

[40] Ibid.

[41] Pamela L Perry, 'Two Faces of Disparate Impact Discrimination' (1991) 59 *Fordham Law Review* 523, 526.

[42] Robert Belton, 'The Dismantling of the Griggs Disparate Impact Theory and the Future of Title VII: The Need for a Third Reconstruction' (1990) 8(2) *Yale Law and Policy Review* 223, 224–5.

[43] Susan D Carle, 'A Social Movement History of Title VII Disparate Impact Analysis' (2011) 63 *Florida Law Review* 251, 255; Joseph A Seiner, 'Disentangling Disparate Impact and Disparate Treatment: Adapting the Canadian Approach' (2006) 25 *Yale Law and Policy Review* 95, 98–104; Charles A Sullivan, 'The World Turned Upside Down? Disparate Impact Claims by White Males' (2004) 98 *Northwestern University Law Review* 1505, 1513–24.

[44] Michael Evan Gold, 'Griggs' Folly: An Essay on the Theory, Problems, and Origin of the Adverse Impact Definition of Employment Discrimination and a Recommendation for Reform' (1985) 7 *Industrial Law Journal* 429, 491–500; Paul D Moreno, *From Direct Action to Affirmative Action: Fair Employment Law and Policy in America 1933–1972* (1999) LSU Press, 1–2; John David Skrentny, *The Ironies of Affirmative Action: Politics, Culture and Justice in America* (1996) University of Chicago Press, 120–1, 127–31.

[45] Ericka Kelsaw, 'Help Wanted: 23.5 Million Unemployed Americans Need Not Apply' (2013) 34(1) *Berkeley Journal of Employment and Labor Law* 1, 19; Michael Selmi, 'Was the Disparate Impact Theory a Mistake?' (2006) 53 *UCLA Law Review* 701, 734.

[46] Amy L Wax, 'Disparate Impact Realism' (2011) 53 *William and Mary Law Review* 621, 624–5.

[47] For a discussion of recent United States Supreme Court judgments that have shaken the standing of the disparate impact doctrine (including *Ricci* v. *DeStefano*, 557 US 557, 580–1 (2009) and *Alexander* v. *Sandoval*, 532 US 275, 282 (2001)) see Johnson, 'The Agency Roots of Disparate Impact'.

United States Supreme Court[48] and Congress have supported the operation of the doctrine of disparate impact.[49] The doctrine of disparate impact has spread across the globe. This chapter will now analyse the capacity of the disparate impact doctrine to reduce the impact of the book famine in Australia, the United Kingdom and the United States.

The Four Elements of the Disparate Impact Doctrine

The judgment by the United States Supreme Court in *Griggs* is perhaps the most transformational judgment in anti-discrimination law yet.[50] The doctrine of disparate impact established in *Griggs* was subsequently adopted in anti-discrimination statutes across the globe, including in Australia and the United Kingdom.[51] While there are significant differences between the operation of the doctrine across jurisdictions, there are four core requirements to proving a suit of indirect discrimination or disparate impact:[52]

1. Equal treatment. The defendant must impose a requirement, condition, policy or practice on the plaintiff.
2. Impact of the requirement or condition. The treatment impacts on the plaintiff's group less favourably than people without the prescribed attribute.
3. There must be unfavourable treatment that is detrimental.
4. The disparate impact cannot be justified. The discriminatory treatment is lawful where it is reasonable or would impose an unjustifiable hardship.

[48] Most notably in *Wards Cove Packing Co., Inc.* v. *Atonio*, 490 US 642 (1989), where the court required plaintiffs to articulate the specific employment practice they were seeking to impugn. Congress has now largely overturned many of the principles in the Wards Cove judgment. See Keith R Fentonmiller, 'The Continuing Validity of Disparate Impact Analysis for Federal-Sector Age Discrimination Claims' (1998) 47 *American University Law Review* 1071, 1119.

[49] Disparate impact is codified in the United States. See *Civil Rights Act of 1991*, Pub L No. 102–166, 105 Stat 1071 (codified at 42 USC § 2000e-2(k)(1)).

[50] Selmi, 'Was the Disparate Impact Theory a Mistake?', 701. Selmi states that '[t]he disparate impact theory long has been viewed as one of the most important and controversial developments in antidiscrimination law'.

[51] Rosemary C Hunter and Elaine W Shoben, 'Disparate Impact Discrimination: American Oddity or Internationally Accepted Concept?' (1998) 19 *Berkeley Journal of Employment and Labor Law* 108, 108; Neil Rees, Simon Rice and Dominique Allen, *Australian Anti-Discrimination Law*, 2nd edn (2014) Federation Press, [4.3.9]. The Equal Employment Opportunity Commission first published the concept of disparate treatment in guidelines under the *Civil Rights Act of 1964*, Pub L No. 88–352, 78 Stat 241. See Primus, 'Equal Protection and Disparate Impact', 506.

[52] Sandra Fredman, *Discrimination Law*, 2nd edn (2011) Oxford University Press, 177; Rees, Rice and Allen, *Australian Anti-Discrimination Law*, [4.3.16].

The remainder of this chapter will analyse the four core elements of the disparate impact doctrine to assess the extent to which it can help combat digital inequality and the book famine.

SECTION II THE IMPOSITION OF EQUAL TREATMENT

The disparate impact doctrine regulates certain practices that arise in the prescribed relationships analysed in Chapter 7. Within those relationships, disparate impact and indirect discrimination are only actionable where a specific practice can be identified. Once this practice can be identified, it is possible to analyse whether this practice is unlawful using the tests analysed in subsequent sections of this chapter. This section will analyse what practices Australian, United Kingdom and United States anti-discrimination laws are prepared to impugn under indirect discrimination and disparate impact provisions.

Before analysing what practices anti-discrimination laws will impugn, it is first critical to consider what practices, within the prescribed relationships, contribute to the book famine for persons with print disabilities. Chapter 1 of this monograph identified the key causes of the book famine. The leading causes include that standard print books are not made available in digital formats, and that when books are digitised they are not published in formats that are accessible for persons with print disabilities. Chapter 7 of this monograph identified that not all parties who impact on the book famine attract duties under anti-discrimination laws. Anti-discrimination duties use prescribed relationships to create duties which fail to regulate all the parties who contribute to the book famine. Within these relationships, educators and employers may adopt practices which require students and workers with print disabilities to operate using standard print books, or may otherwise decline to acquire books in accessible digital formats. This chapter will now consider if any of these practices are regulated by the disparate impact provisions found in anti-discrimination laws in Australia, the United Kingdom or the United States.

Practices under the Disparate Impact Doctrine in the United Kingdom and United States

The first requirement under the disparate impact doctrine will be satisfied if a duty holder engages in treatment that has a facially neutral impact. As will be analysed below, this requirement in the United Kingdom and the United States creates minimal difficulties for plaintiffs arguing that a practice exists. Creating an educational, employment or commercial environment where people were required to read standard print or inaccessible digital material would constitute a practice in both the United Kingdom and the United States. Whether that practice is discriminatory or unreasonable is assessed under subsequent tests.

In *Raytheon Co. v. Hernandez*, the United States Supreme Court found that discrimination under the *ADA* included disparate impact.[53] The first element for disparate impact will exist where a duty holder uses 'practices that are facially neutral in their treatment of different groups', but that in fact have an adverse impact on a protected class without business justification.[54] As analysed in Chapter 7, parties who create digital environments which require certain abilities to navigate them have been held in some circuits to be subject to the *ADA* and disparate impact doctrine. In the employment relationship, the *Civil Rights Act of 1991* adopts a wide concept of which practices are capable of violating the disparate impact doctrine.[55] Practices within the law school university setting that come within the disparate impact doctrine include the activities in which students must participate in the law school classroom,[56] requirements that students read material in particular formats for law school,[57] how law school performs examinations,[58] how the American Bar Association performs its examinations, and law schools' practices in providing their students with support to prepare for those exams.[59]

Initially, when importing the disparate impact doctrine from the United States, United Kingdom anti-discrimination laws limited the practices that

---

[53] 540 US 44 (2003).   [54] *Teamsters* v. *United States*, 431 US 324, 335 (1977).

[55] Pub L No. 102–166, 105 Stat 1071 (codified as amended in ss 2, 16, 29 of Title 42 of the US Code (2012)).

[56] Susan Johanne Adams, 'Leveling the Floor: Classroom Accommodations for Law Students with Disabilities' (1998) 48 *Journal of Legal Ethics* 273; Simon Ball and Helen James, 'Making Law Teaching Accessible and Inclusive' (2009) 3 *Journal of Information, Law and Technology* 3; Robin Boyle, 'Law Students with Attention Deficit Disorder: How to Reach Them, How to Teach Them' (2006) 39 *John Marshall Law Review* 349; Suzanne E Rowe, 'Reasonable Accommodations for Unreasonable Requests: The *Americans with Disabilities Act* in Legal Writing Courses' (2006) 12 *Journal of Legal Writing* 3; Douglas K Rush and Suzanne J Schmitz, 'Universal Instructional Design: Engaging the Whole Class' (2009) 19 *Widener Law Review* 183.

[57] Leah M Christensen, 'Legal Reading and Success in Law School: The Reading Strategies of Law Students with Attention Deficit Disorder (ADD)' (2010) 12(2) *The Scholar* 173; Meredith George and Wendy Newby, 'Inclusive Instruction: Blurring Diversity and Disability in Law School Classrooms through Universal Design' (2008) 69(3) *University of Pittsburgh Law Review* 475.

[58] Ali A Aalaei, 'The *Americans with Disabilities Act* and Law School Accommodations: Test Modifications Despite Anonymity' (2007) 40 *Suffolk University Law Review* 419; Suzanne E Rowe, 'Learning Disabilities and the *Americans with Disabilities Act*: The Conundrum of Dyslexia and Time' (2009) 15 *The Journal of the Legal Writing Institute* 167.

[59] Denise Riebe, 'A Bar Review for Law Schools Getting Students on Board to Pass their Bar Exams' (2007) 45 *Brandeis Law Journal* 269.

were regulated by indirect discrimination provisions. Following European Union directives, the equal treatment requirement in the United Kingdom has been expanded to cover more forms of treatment.[60] Prior to the *Equality Act 2010* (UK), United Kingdom anti-discrimination statutes required the imposition of requirements or conditions. This formulation was interpreted to exclude informal practices and flexible policies.[61] Section 19(1) of the *Equality Act* now adopts an expansive approach, providing for a 'provision, criterion or practice' formulation. There is no doubt that this new formulation captures provision of material used in education, and would extend to designing and using digital environments which reduce usability for persons with disabilities.[62]

The High Court of Australia Reads Down the Situations Where Defendants Are Said to Adopt a Practice for the Doctrine of Disparate Impact

The notion of what practices are capable of being impugned in the United Kingdom and the United States arguably reflects the intent of the disparate impact doctrine. In contrast to this position, the approach adopted in Australia arguably distorts the objective of the disparate impact doctrine by reducing what is regarded as a practice. As will be seen in the paragraphs below, the High Court of Australia has held that a defendant would not be imposing a practice if they followed the minimum standard required by a legislative regime. For persons with print disabilities, this interpretation essentially means that if a duty holder adopts a strategy of only providing students, workers or customers (depending on the prescribed relationship) with books in accessible formats using the statutory licence scheme discussed in Chapter 5, then that duty holder will likely be held to have complied with the other law and not to have adopted any practice that can be impugned under anti-discrimination laws.[63]

Even if students, workers and customers are capable of demonstrating that they have suffered significant harm, and that it would be relatively easy for the duty holder to avoid this harm, that plaintiff only has a remedy under Australian anti-discrimination law for indirect discrimination where the duty

---

[60] *Equality Act 2010* (UK) s 19(1).

[61] *Perera v. Civil Service Commission (No 2)* [1983] IRLR 166.

[62] Catherine Easton, 'Revisiting the Law on Website Accessibility in the Light of the UK's *Equality Act 2010* and the United Nations *Convention on the Rights of Persons with Disabilities*' (2012) 20 *International Journal of Law and Information* 1; Hepple, *Equality*, 96–7.

[63] Paul Harpur, 'Ensuring Equality in Education: How Australian Laws Are Leaving Students with Print Disabilities Behind' (2010) 15(1) *Media and Arts Law Review* 70.

holder is held to have imposed a condition or requirement.[64] The High Court of Australia reached a curious approach to the imposition of conditions and requirements in *New South Wales* v. *Amery*.[65] The practice which was alleged to amount to indirect discrimination in *New South Wales* v. *Amery* flowed from the alleged discriminatory pay differences between male and female teachers. The *Teaching Services Act 1980* (NSW) divided teachers into permanent and casual teachers. When the New South Wales Crown Employment (Teachers and Related Employees) Salaries and Contributions Award was made under the *Industrial Relations Act 1991* (NSW), the award posited a five-level scale for casual teachers and a thirteen-level scale for permanent teachers. The increments between these pay scales differed substantially. Significantly, the top of the casual teacher scale was the equivalent to level eight on the permanent teacher scale. This meant that permanent teachers had substantially more earning potential than casual teachers.

The discriminatory outcome to the facially neutral pay scales was alleged to arise due to the disproportionately high number of female teachers who were casual due to their family responsibilities. It emerged that, even though both male and female teachers were performing substantially the same work, a large number of female teachers were being paid less than their male counterparts because the female teachers were forced to work as casuals due to their family responsibilities.

Industrial relations awards in Australia operate as a safety net below which employees protected by the award cannot be remunerated.[66] There is nothing in awards which prevents employers from deciding to pay their employees more than the minimum rate of pay. Indeed, it is common for employers to pay over award rates in order to attract and retain employees. In *New South Wales* v. *Amery*, the female teachers argued that the education department's decision to pay all teachers at the lowest possible rate of pay meant that the department was imposing a policy which had a discriminatory outcome.

The majority of the High Court of Australia held that the education department was not imposing a condition by deciding not to pay over the award to ensure pay equity:

> The distinction between permanent and non-permanent teachers in the Education Teaching Service is a feature of the structure of the workforce employed in that Service. That structure was not adopted by decision or practice of the Department. It was imposed by the Teaching Services Act. The pay scales set by the Award and the practice, adopted by the Department,

[64] *Disability Discrimination Act 1992* (Cth) s 6(1).   [65] (2006) 230 CLR 174.
[66] Andrew Stewart, *Stewart's Guide to Employment Law*, 5th edn (2015) Federation Press, ch. 7.

of not extending to its supply casual teaching staff over-award payments were an incident of the management of that structure.[67]

In effect, the majority of the High Court of Australia held that because there was a statutory scheme, the decision by the education department to simply follow that scheme meant that the statutory scheme, not the education department, imposed the condition. The fact that the education department decided not to adopt a policy to ensure a non-discriminatory outcome was immaterial. As a consequence, the female teachers were prevented from impugning the department's payment practices under indirect discrimination provisions.

The *New South Wales* v. *Amery* judgment means that a duty holder's decision to adopt a practice to scan print material internally under the statutory licence in the *Copyright Act 1968* (Cth) Part VB Div 3 will not be imposing a practice that is readily impugned. Where the inequality flows from the operation of the statutory licence scheme itself, then the decision of the duty holder to follow the scheme was not imposed by the defendant. The fact that the defendant decided not to adopt more effective measures to achieve equality, such as approaching publishers for a limited licence or purchasing accessible E-Books, is immaterial under this highly technical and narrow reading of when conditions and requirements are adopted by defendants.

SECTION III IMPACT OF THE REQUIREMENT OR CONDITION: THE TREATMENT IMPACTS ON THE PLAINTIFF'S GROUP LESS FAVOURABLY THAN PEOPLE WITHOUT THE PRESCRIBED ATTRIBUTE

Disparate impact and indirect discrimination involve a comparison between how groups of people are impacted by practices. Comparing groups of people requires first determining the boundaries of the groups, and secondly, what percentage of a group needs to suffer detriment for it to be said that the group suffers sufficient detriment to enliven a remedy. As will be illustrated below, persons with print disabilities combatting the book famine will confront substantially more difficulties in satisfying the second of the two requirements.

Statistics and other sociological methods can be utilised to help determine where discrimination against a group has occurred.[68] The requirement for

---

[67] *New South Wales* v. *Amery* (2006) 230 CLR 174, 199 (Gummow, Hayne and Crennan JJ).

[68] Linda Hamilton Krieger, 'The Content of our Categories: A Cognitive Bias Approach to Discrimination and Equal Employment Opportunity' (1995) 47(6) *Stanford Law Review* 1161; European Commission, Directorate-General for Employment and Social Affairs, 'Comparative Study on the Collection of Data to Measure the Extent and Impact of

numeric and statistical evidence in Australia, the United Kingdom and the United States introduces a range of problems specific to the interpretation of statistics.[69] While courts will sometimes employ judicial notice and accept that a group has experienced different treatment without requiring statistical evidence,[70] it is far more common for courts to require statistical evidence. Indeed, Professor Sandra Sperino has observed that

> a plaintiff may proceed with a disparate impact case only after establishing that a particular . . . practice creates a disparate impact on a protected group. The primary way of making this showing is through the use of statistical evidence.[71]

Persons with print disabilities combatting the book famine would likely use the capacity to read standard print as the criterion to judge which group an individual would fall into. While this division might appear reasonably uncontroversial, similarly clear categories have been impugned by courts. For example, using skin colour as a criterion does not guarantee that the formulation of the groups will not confront difficulties. *Wards Cove* v. *Atonio* illustrates how interpreting statistics can create difficulties for courts.[72] The non-white workers (predominately native Alaskans and Filipinos) argued that Wards Cove was engaging in disparate impact by policies and practices that resulted in non-white workers being employed in seasonal, low-paid jobs, and white workers being employed in permanent, high-paying jobs. After losing in the District Court, the workers successfully argued their case before the United States Court of Appeals for the Ninth Circuit. The United States Court of Appeals for the Ninth Circuit accepted workers' evidence which demonstrated that a high percentage of non-white workers were employed in the seasonal unskilled jobs and a low percentage of non-white workers were employed in the permanent skilled jobs. The United States Supreme Court

Discrimination within the US, Canada, Australia, Great Britain and the Netherlands' (report, European Commission, 2004) 82.

[69] *Citadel T. Sablan* v. *A.B. Won Pat International Airport Authority, Guam* (D Guam, No. 10–013, 9 December 2011). Statistics, however, are not required in every situation. See Elaine W Shoben, 'Disparate Impact Theory in Employment Discrimination: What's Griggs Still Good For? What Not?' (2004) 42 *Brandeis Law Journal* 597, 606 ('Disparate impact is ordinarily proven by statistics, but there are cases in which the facts permitted proof without this step').

[70] For examples of where judicial notice has been accepted by the Australian courts see *Waters* v. *Public Transport Corporation* (1991) 173 CLR 349 and *Hickie* v. *Hunt and Hunt* [1998] HREOCA 8. In the United Kingdom see *Islington London Borough Council* v. *Ladele* [2009] EWCA Civ. 1357.

[71] Sandra F Sperino, 'The Sky Remains Intact: Why Allowing Subgroup Evidence Is Consistent with the *Age Discrimination in Employment Act*' (2006) 90 *Marquette Law Review* 227, 260.

[72] *Wards Cove Packing Co., Inc.* v. *Atonio*, 490 US 642 (1989).

argued, however, that the Court of Appeal incorrectly identified the statistical comparison. The United States Supreme Court held that the correct analysis should be to compare the percentage of non-white workers in permanent, high-paying positions with the percentage of the available labour pool that was non-white and had the appropriate skills to perform those jobs. The case was remanded back to the Court of Appeals to perform the correct statistical analysis.

Obviously, the boundaries of established disability categories can be utilised to set the boundaries of a group. Analysing these groups, however, involves statistical interpretation. Lord Walker in *Secretary of State for Trade and Industry* v. *Rutherford (No 2)* observed that the statistical data in an indirect discrimination claim produces startlingly different results depending on whether the comparison focuses on advantage-led (proportions of advantaged people with and without the attribute) or disadvantage-led (proportions of disadvantaged people with and without the attribute).[73] Provided that persons with print disabilities carefully plead groups and are rigorous in their use of statistics, then establishing a simple group comparison is relatively easy. Proving that this comparison is associated with sufficient detriment to justify legal intervention is far more difficult.

SECTION IV THERE MUST BE UNFAVOURABLE TREATMENT THAT IS DETRIMENTAL: WHAT LEVEL OF DISADVANTAGE ENLIVENS INDIRECT DISCRIMINATION AND DISPARATE TREATMENT?

The concept of what level of disadvantage should enliven anti-discrimination laws goes to the heart of the issue of the struggle for substantive equality. This chapter thus far has analysed how the comparator groups are formulated and where different treatment will occur. This chapter now turns to analyse where the different treatment caused by the practice causes sufficient harm to qualify for indirect discrimination and disparate impact protection.

Whether or not a practice causes actionable disadvantage is analysed from the disabled person's perspective and from the alleged discriminator's perspective. This chapter will first analyse the issue from the disabled person's perspective and then analyse where the law deems the existence of harm as reasonable. This chapter will now analyse how anti-discrimination laws operate on the premise that inequalities are acceptable and that persons with

---

[73] *Secretary of State for Trade and Industry* v. *Rutherford (No 2)* [2006] UKHL 19.

disabilities are expected to cope with reasonably high levels of discrimination before such conduct is held to be unlawful.

Coping with Disadvantage and the Convention on the Rights of Persons with Disabilities

To require a person with a disability to prove that they have suffered a certain level of harm to have their denial of rights labelled as discrimination operates on the premise that persons with disabilities are not entitled to exercise their rights on an equal basis with others. Essentially, this legislative approach provides that it is not discrimination unless the denial of rights cannot be overcome by the person with a disability. The analysis below demonstrates that the United States adopts the approach which most strongly rejects the notion that persons with disabilities should cope with disadvantage in society. The Australian and United Kingdom positions, in contrast, expect persons with disabilities to be substantially disabled by society before indirect discrimination provisions are enlivened.

Requiring a person with a disability to prove harm, and requiring them to prove they are sufficiently unable to cope with breaches of their human rights, violates the concept of equality posited in the CRPD. The focus here is not on what it is reasonable to expect the duty holder to do to enable access, but instead on what harm is acceptable. Put another way: the question is what denial of human rights is acceptable.

The requirement for a person with a disability to suffer a certain level of harm to qualify for protection is not reflected in the CRPD.[74] The definition of disability discrimination in Article 2 of the CRPD provides that any distinction based on disability that reduces a person's capacity to fully exercise their human rights constitutes discrimination:

> Discrimination on the basis of disability means any distinction, exclusion or restriction on the basis of disability which has the purpose or effect of impairing or nullifying the recognition, enjoyment or exercise, on an equal basis with others, of all human rights and fundamental freedoms in the political, economic, social, cultural, civil or any other field.

There is arguably no justification for including hardship as a requirement for establishing whether or not disability discrimination has occurred.[75]

---

[74] Sarah Fraser Butlin, 'The UN Convention on the Rights of Persons with Disabilities: Does the *Equality Act 2010* Measure up to UK International Commitments?' (2011) 40(4) *Industrial Law Journal* 428.

[75] Anna Lawson, 'Disability and Employment in the Equality Act 2010: Opportunities Seized, Lost and Generated' (2011) 40(4) *Industrial Law Journal* 359.

There is a limit to the resources of the state and private actors. The CRPD recognises that there is a limit on what can be done to reduce disability discrimination in society. States are required to combat discrimination that reduces the capacity of persons with disabilities to exercise their economic, social and cultural rights 'to the maximum of [their State's] available resources'.[76] The assessment of what expenditure and steps are reasonable should consider the degree of harm experienced by persons with disabilities as one factor in determining what it is reasonable to expect of duty holders. Harm in itself should not be elevated to a requirement of enlivening the disparate impact doctrine.

A legislative approach that performs the reasonableness test only where a disabling practice causes substantial harm seems to provide that it is reasonable to adopt discriminatory practices if the harm is calculated as slight or moderate. The approach in the CRPD does not expect states to devote substantial resources to reduce a very small barrier. The approach in the CRPD, however, would expect states to adopt laws which compel duty holders to remove disabling barriers that create moderate harm, where the removal of such barriers requires insignificant cost or effort. The problem with elevating harm caused by the practices to a threshold issue potentially means that many disabling barriers which could easily be removed remain as a cause of inequality, as the focus is not on removing barriers but on what harm should be endured.

Coping with Disadvantage in the United States

Disparate impact in the United States arguably focuses less on the extent of suffering and capacity to cope than the equivalent statutes in Australia and the United Kingdom. In the United States, a person with a disability would identify the policy they seek to impugn, specify the protected class which has been disproportionately impacted and explain the adverse effect caused by the practice.[77] In some situations the requirement to prove disadvantage can be established simply by relying upon statistical exclusion. The Equal Employment Opportunity Commission has developed the four-fifths rule, which provides that a selection rate of any protected group that is below 80 per cent is evidence of adverse impact.[78] No such rule exists in Australia or the United Kingdom.

The disparate impact doctrine in the United States arguably does not require proof of an inability to cope, or substantial hardship, to successfully

---

[76] CRPD, art. 4(2).   [77] 42 USC § 2000e-2(k) (2006).   [78] 29 CFR § 1607.4(D) (2014).

impugn a practice. *Enyart v. National Conference of Bar Examiners* involved a candidate for the bar exam who was legally blind.[79] Enyart requested accommodations to how she sat the bar exam to enable her to use her adaptive technology (screen reader and screen magnification). The California Bar Association accepted that these requests would not alter the substance of the exam; however, the National Conference of Bar Examiners refused to provide the exam in a digital format. The National Conference of Bar Examiners was not concerned with the requested accommodations altering the content of the exam or that the adjustments would provide an unfair advantage to Enyart. Instead, the National Conference of Bar Examiners provided Enyart the options of sitting the exam using a human reader or an audio recording of the exam. Either of these options was offered in addition to the use of closed-circuit television for text magnification.[80] Considering that lawyers with vision impairments primarily operate using digital versions of documents and rarely, if ever, use live readers or recorded books for work purposes,[81] it is not surprising that Enyart rejected these options. Enyart asserted that live readers and audio recordings were not effective and would not enable her to complete the exam in an efficient manner. The Ninth Circuit Court of Appeals upheld Enyart's case and held that entities must provide individuals with disabilities 'an equal opportunity to demonstrate their knowledge or abilities to the same degree as non-disabled people'.[82] The court does not ask whether the person with a disability would be able, 'despite extreme discomfort and disability-related disadvantage, to pass the relevant exams'.[83] While Enyart could possibly have coped with completing the bar exam using other accommodations, the court did not focus on what Enyart could cope with, but instead on what would provide an equal opportunity.

Coping with Disadvantage in the United Kingdom

The *Equality Act 2010* (UK) will only impugn practices where it causes a sufficient amount of harm. In respect to persons with print disabilities attempting to access the written word, the approach in Australia and the

---

[79] 630 F 3d 1153 (9th Cir., 2011).

[80] *Enyart v. National Conf. of Bar Exam'rs*, 630 F 3d 1153, 1156–7 (9th Cir., 2011).

[81] Jack Bernard et al., 'The Transition to Law School' in Stephanie L Enyart, Carrie A Basas and Rebecca S Williford (eds), *Lawyers, Lead On: Lawyers with Disabilities Share their Insights* (2011) American Bar Association, ch. 1; Ron McCallum, 'Participating in Political and Public Life: A Challenge for We Persons with Sensory Disabilities' (2011) 36(2) *Alternative Law Journal* 80.

[82] *Enyart v. National Conf. of Bar Exam'rs*, 630 F 3d 1153, 1166 (9th Cir., 2011).

[83] Ibid., 1157.

United Kingdom would only assess whether it was reasonable to expect an educator, employer, provider of goods and services or other duty holder to take any steps once the court was satisfied that the digital disablement caused sufficient harm.

The harm analysis in the United Kingdom focuses on the practices that are alleged to disable the person with an impairment. The *Disability Discrimination Act* 1995 (UK) previously adopted the tests of 'substantial disadvantage' for employment,[84] and for the provision of a service, 'impossible or unreasonably difficult'.[85]

The *Equality Act* 2010 (UK) replaced these different tests with a single approach, which first asks whether the practice puts, or would put, persons within the identified group 'at a particular disadvantage when compared with persons' outside this group.[86] After ascertaining that the practice causes particular disadvantage to the group generally, the second step is to analyse whether the practice disadvantages the particular plaintiff within this broader group. This second stage asks whether the practice puts, or would put, the person with a disability at the 'particular disadvantage' experienced by the wider group.

While there is a need for particular disadvantage, it appears that the level of harm required will not result in significant numbers of actions being unsuccessful. The guidance to the Equality Bill 2010 illustrates how the particular disadvantage test operates:

> A woman is forced to leave her job because her employer operates a practice that staff must work in a shift pattern that she is unable to comply with because she needs to look after her children at particular times of the day, and no allowances are made because of those needs. This would put women (who are shown to be more likely to be responsible for childcare) at a disadvantage, and the employer will have indirectly discriminated against the woman unless the practice can be justified.

It is also relevant to note that the level of disadvantage for indirect discrimination provisions is lower than the required disadvantage to entitle a person with a disability to demand a reasonable adjustment. A duty holder is only required to make a reasonable adjustment where there is a substantial disadvantage.[87] The disadvantage test will assist individuals who are significantly disadvantaged by practices of exclusion. For example, a requirement that persons with print disabilities use standard print means they, or people on their behalf, must expend money and/or effort converting material into an

---

[84] *Disability Discrimination Act* 1995 (UK) s 6(1).   [85] Ibid., s 21(1).
[86] *Equality Act* 2010 (UK) s 19(2)(b).   [87] Ibid., s 20(3).

accessible format. If practices utilise digital platforms which are not accessible with screen readers, then this prevents persons with disabilities from operating the system. The problem is that some barriers to access may not be readily identified as a disadvantage. A duty holder that includes the use of an E-Library that includes its own audio reader would argue that this feature is enabling. What about if the E-Books are only readable by the E-Library's own reader? This would exclude disability-specific adaptive technologies that people with print disabilities may be accustomed to utilising, and that are substantially more efficient. Whether or not such an E-Library is disabling or enabling could create evidential difficulties for a person with a print disability.

The problem in establishing disadvantage under the *Equality Act 2010* (UK) is complicated by the concept of group disadvantage. While it might be relatively easy for an individual to establish that they have suffered harm from a practice, it is evidentially more complex to establish that a particular group has suffered harm. Initially it was thought it was necessary to prove disadvantage for a particular group and for the individual.[88] In the *Eweida* litigation, the Court of Appeal upheld a finding that a policy prohibiting the wearing of a visible cross did not put Christians as a group at a particular disadvantage, in part because wearing the cross was not a requirement of the faith.[89] The European Court of Human Rights disagreed with the Court of Appeal and found that there was no need to prove disadvantage for a group and for the individual.[90] Group disadvantage is no longer a threshold requirement for indirect discrimination;[91] rather the existence of group disadvantage now forms part of the analysis of whether the practice is reasonable.[92]

Indirect discrimination already includes mechanisms to factor in the disadvantage experienced by the practice. The indirect discrimination provisions enable a duty holder to defend their conduct if the practice constitutes a 'proportionate means of achieving a legitimate aim'.[93] Where the practice concerns discrimination based upon disability, then the *Equality Act 2010* (UK) provides additional balancing between the impact on persons with disabilities and the impact on the duty holder in the reasonable adjustment provisions analysed below.[94] Requiring persons with disabilities to prove they have suffered sufficient disadvantage arguably introduces an unnecessary test into the shield against disabling practices.

---

[88] See generally Malcom Sergeant, *Discrimination and the Law* (2003) Routledge, ch. 8.

[89] *Eweida* v. *British Airways plc* [2010] IRLR 322, 324 (Sedley LJ).

[90] *Eweida* v. *United Kingdom* [2013] EqLR 264.

[91] *Mba* v. *London Borough of Merton* [2014] EqLR 51.   [92] Hepple, *Equality*, 85–6.

[93] *Equality Act 2010* (UK) s 19(2)(d).

[94] See below discussions and, in particular, *Equality Act 2010* (UK) s 19(5).

Coping with Disadvantage in Australia

The Australian position, arguably, is the approach which least reflects the notion of equality posited in the CRPD. Whereas the United Kingdom position focuses on how the practices in society disadvantage and disable people with impairments, the Australian approach turns the focus onto how the person who has been disabled by the practice manages to cope with that barrier to equality. A practice will only breach Australian indirect discrimination laws where the person with a disability is sufficiently unable to cope with the denial of their human rights.

The coping test has resulted in negative outcomes for persons with disabilities in Australia. The test has reduced the capacity of students with print disabilities to obtain essential readings in the formats that best promote equality. For example, in *Hinchliffe* v. *University of Sydney*, the coping test was applied to a university student with a print disability desiring to access essential course readings.[95] The university provided the student with the reading material in a printed format which only provided her with partial access. The university remedied their error and provided the student with the material in the required format after class had commenced. In assessing whether the university had breached the indirect discrimination provisions, the court considered whether the student coped with the disadvantage. In this case, the student scanned papers and obtained assistance from her mother and grandmother to read documents onto tape. The court held that '[g]enerally, it was possible for the applicant to comply with the university's requirement. She could make use of course material provided to her in a standard format by converting it to a different format'.[96] As the student had some eyesight, a strong support network and was prepared to work exceptionally hard, the court held there was insufficient harm caused to amount to a breach of the indirect discrimination provisions.

The coping test essentially authorises any practice that causes discriminatory harm, providing that a person with a disability can find a strategy to sufficiently cope with that harm. This requires courts to decide when coping strategies are sufficiently unsuccessful to enliven protection. The Full Court of the Federal Court of Australia performed such an analysis in *Hurst* v. *State of Queensland*.[97] In this case, a student was fluent in one form of sign language, but was required to receive education in another form of sign language that she was less familiar with. Even though the student received reasonable grades, she was not able to function to her full potential. The court held that

---

[95] *Hinchliffe* v. *University of Sydney* [2004] FMCA 85.   [96] Ibid., [115].
[97] *Hurst* v. *State of Queensland* [2006] FCAFC 100.

'[a] hearing impaired child may well be able to keep up with the rest of the class, or "cope", without Auslan. However, that child may still be seriously disadvantaged if deprived of the opportunity to reach his or her full potential and, perhaps, to excel.'[98]

Courts accept that students with disabilities will experience disablement, but that this often does not constitute sufficient harm to justify intervention. In *Clarke* v. *Catholic Education Office*, the court held that an inability to comply was held to require a 'serious disadvantage', with the result that the student could not 'meaningfully participate in classroom instruction' without the accommodation.[99] On appeal the Full Court adopted a similar approach through holding that the question of whether or not a student could comply should be decided by asking whether the student was 'able to receive the full benefit of [their] education'.[100] The Full Court of the Federal Court of Australia has accepted that persons with disabilities have a right to access education, but no equivalent right to access employment.[101] Accordingly, the level of disadvantage that a person with a disability is expected to cope with outside the educational sector is significantly higher.

There are arguably many situations where persons with print disabilities can cope with reading disablement through the support of friends and family and expenditure of resources. There is a substantial gap between coping with reading disablement and the equality envisaged by the *CRPD*. In the United States case of *Enyart* v. *National Conference of Bar Examiners*, the capacity to cope was not addressed. If *Enyart* v. *National Conference of Bar Examiners* was brought in Australia under the *Disability Discrimination Act 1992* (Cth), then it is possible the court would have determined that Enyart could have sufficiently coped with the disadvantage such that she had no remedy. The coping test means that discrimination in society is deemed not to amount to disability discrimination simply because persons who are disabled by barriers find mechanisms to cope with inequalities. Coping with disadvantage is a long way from the capacity to exercise rights on an equal basis with others, as envisaged by the *CRPD*.

---

[98] Ibid., [125].

[99] *Clarke* v. *Catholic Education Office and Anor* (2003) 202 ALR 340, 340. This decision was affirmed on appeal in *Catholic Education Office* v. *Clarke* (2004) 81 ALD 66. Tamberlin J concurred with the joint judgment of Sackville and Stone JJ.

[100] *Catholic Education Office* v. *Clarke* (2004) 81 ALD 66, 69.

[101] *Devers* v. *Kindilan Society* (2010) 116 ALD 239.

SECTION V THE DISPARATE IMPACT CANNOT BE JUSTIFIED: THE BUSINESS CASE FOR EXCLUSION

Capacity to Justify Social Exclusion as a Matter of Course

Facially neutral practices that are found to discriminate against persons with disabilities and create disadvantage can be legitimised under the anti-discrimination regimes in Australia, the United Kingdom and the United States. Despite the disadvantage and the inability to cope, the law will only hold such conduct to be discriminatory where, in Australia, it is held to be unreasonable;[102] in the United Kingdom, where it is held not to be a proportionate means of achieving a legitimate aim;[103] and in the United States, where the barriers are unnecessary and have no business justification.[104]

The capacity to justify social exclusion as a matter of course is a significant distinction between the disparate treatment and impact doctrines. Lady Hale has explained this difference: '[t]he main difference between … [the forms of discrimination] is that direct discrimination cannot be justified. Indirect discrimination can be justified if it is a proportionate means of achieving a legitimate aim.'[105]

The test to determine whether discriminatory practices can be justified adopts separate tests from the tests for reasonable accommodation and reasonable adjustment for direct discrimination and disparate treatment.[106] To determine if discrimination is justified, the proportionality analysis in Australia, the United Kingdom and the United States considers if there is a legitimate aim for the treatment, that the means for achieving this aim are appropriate or necessary, and that this justification is objectively reasonable.

To establish that a discriminatory practice is justified does not always require duty holders to consider equality issues. A duty holder who ensures that their practice has a strong business case could defend their conduct, even

---

[102] *Disability Discrimination Act 1992* (Cth) s 6(3).

[103] *Equality Act 2010* (UK) s 19(2)(d). This reasonableness test is permitted under European Union laws, and variations of the reasonable adjustment model appear expressly or implicitly in the anti-discrimination laws of all twenty-eight European Union States and Norway. See European Network of Legal Experts in Gender Equality and Non-Discrimination, *Reasonable Accommodation for Disabled People in Employment Contexts: A Legal Analysis of EU Member States, Iceland, Liechtenstein and Norway* (2016) European Commission, 56 <www.equalitylaw.eu/downloads/3724-reasonable-accommodation-for-disabled-people-in-employment-contexts> (accessed 18 November 2016).

[104] Michelle A Travis, 'Equality in the Virtual Workplace' (2003) 24(2) *Berkeley Journal of Employment and Labor Law* 283, 322.

[105] *Regina (E)* v. *Governing Body of JFS and another (United Synagogue and others intervening)* [2010] 2 AC 728, 757.

[106] Weber, 'Unreasonable Accommodation and Due Hardship', 1135.

if they have not considered if an alternative approach was available that would ensure improved equality outcomes.[107] Professor Sandra Fredman argues that

> in order to advance the transformational goal of equality, justification defences should be subject to a high level of scrutiny before being accepted. Most importantly, the respondent should be required to consider ways of modifying the discriminatory practice better to accommodate the excluded class.[108]

While Fredman's position appears to be logical and to support the objectives of human rights conventions, at the moment such steps are often not required.

Where Anticipatory Conduct to Promote Equality Is Required

There are some situations where the disparate impact doctrine requires anticipatory conduct from duty holders.[109] The nature of these anticipatory duties will depend on the nature of the relationship. While employers attract some positive obligations,[110] educators attract far higher obligations.[111] Educators have anticipatory obligations to ensure that students with disabilities are not at a substantial disadvantage compared with the wider student cohort.[112] While educators have the highest duty, even this has limits. Professor Peter Blanck explains that '[i]t is one thing to provide digital web content for class materials as an ADA accommodation, but it may be quite another to require that an entire library be digitised to be equivalently enjoyed by that same individual.'[113]

While educators are generally not expected to digitise entire collections of books, they would be expected to provide already digitised books in formats that are accessible. The educator generally does not have copies of digitised books, but rather has a licence to access E-Books through an externally run E-Library. Educators are not expected to download E-Books and render them accessible. While the latter might be reasonable for a small number of

---

[107] Susan Grover, 'The Business Necessity Defense in Disparate Impact Discrimination Cases' (1996) 30 *Georgia Law Review* 387, 387–9.

[108] Fredman, *Discrimination Law*, 181–2.   [109] Hepple, Equality, 96–7.

[110] Michael Connolly, *Townshend-Smith on Discrimination Law: Text, Cases and Materials*, 2nd edn (2004) Routledge, 237–8.

[111] Marshall J compared the right to access education involving substantive obligations on educators to the lesser right not to be excluded from education in *Devers* v. *Kindilan Society* [2009] FCA 1392, [26], upheld on appeal in *Devers* v. *Kindilan Society* (2010) 116 ALD 239. The High Court of Australia denied leave to appeal in *Devers* v. *Kindilan* [2011] HCASL 18.

[112] *Equality Act 2010* (UK) sch. 13; see also the Explanatory Notes for the Equality Bill 2009 (UK) [898].

[113] Blanck, *Equality*, ch. 8.

prescribed readings, it would not be reasonable to expect an educator to download tens of thousands of books. The question is whether it is reasonable to require an educator to find a way for students with print disabilities to access E-Book libraries. While this is arguably reasonable, to date no court has imposed such a duty upon an educational institution. Essentially, the disparate impact doctrine can reduce the impact of barriers in society, but it is not a substitute for structural changes in society that have the possibility of achieving equality.[114]

The Retrofitting Focus of Anti-Discrimination Laws

One of the primary limitations with the disparate impact doctrine in Australia, the United Kingdom and the United States is the capacity of duty holders to pay scant attention to equality issues when adopting practices.[115] Once a practice has been created, it may be difficult to make the environment accessible, thus enabling the duty holder to justify the existence of the inequality. Even if macro issues were considered, the reasonable accommodation model responds after systems are created. The exceptionalist approach does not challenge the imbalances of power or discourse of dominance. Under this paradigm, the underlying disabling structures in society which lead to exclusion remain in place. Discussing the United States regime, Dr Beth Ribet has criticised how anti-discrimination laws ignore employers' conduct in creating barriers to employment: '[t]he culpability of the employer or entity in the production of the disability itself is not conceived within the terrain of the law, when considering or weighing what its burden should be.'[116] Similarly, Professor Sandra Fredman observes that the current approach to reasonable accommodations 'assumes that the individual should fit the job, rather than that the job should be adjusted to fit the worker'.[117] The retrofitting focus of anti-discrimination laws means many barriers to inclusion are created which anti-discrimination laws do not require to be removed.

---

[114] Selmi, 'Was the Disparate Impact Theory a Mistake?'.

[115] Anna Lawson, 'Challenging Disabling Barriers to Information and Communication Technology in the Information Society: A United Kingdom Perspective' (2010) 2 *European Yearbook of Disability Law* 131, 138–9.

[116] Beth Ribet, 'Emergent Disability and the Limits of Equality: A Critical Reading of the UN Convention on the Rights of Persons with Disabilities' (2011) 14(4) *Yale Human Rights and Development Law Journal* 155, 169.

[117] Sandra Fredman, 'Disability Equality: A Challenge to the Existing Anti-Discrimination Paradigm?' in Anna Lawson and Caroline Gooding (eds), *Disability Rights in Europe: From Theory to Practice* (2005) Hart Publishing, 199, 204.

It is often difficult or impossible to retrofit systems to render them accessible. Arguably, a system which focuses on retrofitting will not create an accessible society. The *CRPD* calls upon states to promote universal design where possible. Under this approach, reasonable adjustments and accommodations operate where it is difficult or expensive to implement universal design. This chapter argues that relying on systems that permit barriers to be created and then seeking to retrofit access can reduce many barriers to inclusion, but it is a considerable distance from creating equality. Equality can only be achieved where states do more to promote universal design, and embrace reasonable accommodations and adjustments where inclusive design is impractical.

CONCLUSION

The bifurcated approach to prohibiting discrimination in Australia, the United Kingdom and the United States focuses on enabling persons with disabilities to operate in a disabling society. While these laws prohibit the worst forms of overt discrimination, anti-discrimination duties leave the causes of reading disablement undisturbed. Domestic laws largely enable duty holders to develop systems that exclude persons with disabilities. Rather than requiring duty holders to promote inclusion, the anti-discrimination laws in Australia, the United Kingdom and the United States focus on retrofitting disabling systems once they are operational. Once created, many systems are difficult to retrofit.[118]

The highly legalistic and technical approach to reducing discrimination does not just assess whether or not it is reasonable to expect a duty holder to create an inclusive environment. In Australia and the United Kingdom, in particular, the duty holder is not subject to indirect discrimination provisions unless the person with a disability suffers a particular disadvantage or is unable to cope with the denial of their rights. Even if the person with a disability has satisfied all the foregoing elements of the disparate impact doctrine, then the duty holder is still able to justify their conduct if there is a sufficient business case or if it is reasonable to deny persons with disabilities their human rights.

The anti-discrimination provisions in Australia, the United Kingdom and the United States have enabled many persons with print disabilities to gain

---

[118] For an example of arguments pertaining to the expense of retrofitting railway cars, see *Council of Canadians with Disabilities v. Via Rail Canada, Inc.* [2007] 1 SCR 650. For discussion of this Canadian Supreme Court judgment see David Baker and Sarah Godwin, 'All Aboard!: The Supreme Court of Canada Confirms that Canadians with Disabilities Have Substantive Equality Rights' (2008) 71 *Saskatchewan Law Review* 39, 59.

access to readings for educational, employment and cultural purposes. These laws, however, are drafted to regard disability access as the exception to the norm. The anti-discrimination prohibitions contain very few proactive obligations on duty holders, and are content to operate within a society that disables people with different abilities. While anti-discrimination laws have helped persons with disabilities to operate during the book famine, these laws do not have the capacity to tackle the root causes of the famine itself and so reverse digital inequalities.

9

Introducing Positive Duties in Promoting Equality Outcomes for Persons with Disabilities: The United Kingdom Public Sector Equality Duty Reducing Digital Disablement

INTRODUCTION

This chapter analyses how the emergence of positive duties in anti-discrimination laws can help reduce digital disablement for persons with print disabilities. Chapter 6 analysed the threshold definitions to determine who qualifies as disabled in Australia, Canada, the United Kingdom and the United States. Chapters 7 and 8 then analysed the coverage and operation of traditional anti-discrimination duties in Australia, the United Kingdom and the United States. The anti-discrimination duties in Australia, the United Kingdom and the United States prohibit discrimination in certain situations and require very little proactive conduct from duty holders. Beyond reasonable accommodations and adjustments, these duties are constructed as prohibitions or negative duties. While these duties assist in reducing the instances of discrimination, they fall far short of achieving equality. Prohibitions and reasonable accommodations and adjustments do not unsettle existing disabling practices.

The realisation that a new approach was required to advance the struggle for equality resulted in calls for new regulatory approaches. Where the traditional anti-discrimination model largely required duty holders to refrain from conduct, positive duties focus on duty holders taking proactive action to reduce the creation of inequalities in society. Positive duties do not focus on attributing blame, but on identifying which parties in society can help reduce inequalities and requiring them to take action.[1] As will be analysed in the first section of this chapter, positive duties embrace a significantly different

---

[1] Sandra Fredman, 'Evolutions in Antidiscrimination Law in Europe and North America: Breaking the Mold: Equality as a Proactive Duty' (2012) 60 *The American Journal of Comparative Law* 265, 266.

regulatory approach than that reflected in traditional negative duties. This
different approach has arguably resulted in improved equality outcomes.

All the jurisdictions analysed in this monograph have some form of legislative positive duties. In the United States positive duties are not found in
disability anti-discrimination laws, but instead in specialist regimes that are
analysed in Chapter 11 of this monograph. The Canadian approach contains
positive duties in both its anti-discrimination regime and its human rights
jurisdiction. The interaction between the human rights and anti-
discrimination jurisdictions has resulted in a unique system. The Canadian
disability human rights framework and positive duties are analysed separately
in Chapter 10.

Positive duties are also found in traditional anti-discrimination regimes,
where proactive obligations operate alongside the existing duties that were
analysed in Chapters 6, 7 and 8. This approach is adopted to a very limited
extent in Australia and, to a much greater extent, in the United Kingdom.
Part 3 of Australia's *Disability Discrimination Act 1992* (Cth) enables duty
holders to prepare disability action plans and lodge them with the Australian
Human Rights Commission. These action plans are voluntary, but can be
used in evidence to help defend a suit of discrimination.[2] More exciting
positive duties can be found in Victoria, which is one of Australia's six state
jurisdictions.[3] Victoria has enacted far-reaching positive voluntary duties in
Part 3 of the *Victorian Equal Opportunity Act 2010* (Vic).[4] The Victorian Act
requires people who attract duties not to discriminate or harass, and to take
'reasonable and proportionate measures to eliminate that discrimination,
sexual harassment or victimisation as far as possible'.[5] While these provisions
appear exciting, in fact they are entirely voluntary as, following the *Equal
Opportunity Amendment Act 2011* (Vic), all enforcement provisions for the
positive duties have been removed from the Act. As a consequence, there is
now no capacity for an aggrieved party to lodge a complaint with the Victorian
Equal Opportunity and Human Rights Commission or to bring a judicial
review, and there is no scope to request the Attorney-General or another

---

[2] For example, where a defendant is claiming unjustifiable hardship under the *Disability Discrimination Act 1992* (Cth) s 11(1)(e).

[3] For a discussion of positive duties in Australia that target disabilities and those that target other attributes, see for discussion: Neil Rees, Simon Rice and Dominique Allen, *Australian Anti-Discrimination Law*, 2nd edn (2014) Federation Press, ch. 5.

[4] Dominique Allen, 'Victoria Paves the Way to Eliminating Discrimination' (2010) 23(4) *Australian Journal of Labour Law* 318; Paul Harpur, 'A Proactive Duty to Eliminate Discrimination in Victoria' (2012) 19(4) *Australian Journal of Administrative Law* 180.

[5] *Equal Opportunity Act 2010* (Vic) s 15. The relevant duties which enliven s 15 are found in parts 4, 6 and 7.

agency to consider performing an investigation for a breach of the positive duties found in Part 3 of the *Equal Opportunity Act 2010* (Vic). In contrast to Australia, the *Equality Act 2010* (UK) has introduced duties on public sector agencies to give due regard to achieving equality and has enabled judicial review of such decisions. Due to the national nature and improved levels of enforcement, this chapter will use the public sector equality duty found in the United Kingdom as a case study of how positive duties in anti-discrimination laws can help promote digital equality in the area of information communication technologies.

SECTION I INTRODUCING THE CONCEPT OF POSITIVE DUTIES

The Perverse Effect Doctrine and Unintended Consequences

The concern of unintended consequences is a risk inherent in any regulatory intervention. Similar to any intervention, anti-discrimination laws can have perverse effects and unintended consequences. Some scholars have argued that traditional disability discrimination laws have had the unintended consequences of reducing the employment rates of persons with disabilities in the United States.[6] Some scholars have argued that there is insufficient evidence to link reductions in employment and the *Americans with Disabilities Act of 1990*.[7] Others have identified that the introduction of disability anti-discrimination laws may have a short-term negative impact, but that the long-term net effects of such laws will be positive.[8] While it is beyond this chapter to devote considerable attention to the perverse effect doctrine, this chapter will analyse evidence which suggests that the positive duty in the *Equality Act 2010* (UK) is achieving some of its purposes without any significant unintended consequences.

---

[6] Andrew J Houtenville and Richard V Burkhauser, 'Did the Employment of People with Disabilities Decline in the 1990s, and was the ADA Responsible? A Replication and Robustness Check of Acemoglu and Angrist (2001) – Research Brief' (Employment and Disability Institute Collection No. 91, Cornell University ILR School, 2004); Daron Acemoglu and Joshua D Angrist, 'Consequences of Employment Protection? The Case of the *Americans with Disabilities Act*' (2001) 109 *Journal of Political Economy* 915; Thomas DeLeire, 'The Wage and Employment Effects of the *Americans with Disabilities Act*' (2000) 35(4) *Journal of Human Resources* 693.

[7] Peter Blanck, Susan Schwochau and Chen Song, 'Is it Time to Declare the ADA a Failed Law?' in David C Stapleton and Richard V Burkhauser (eds), *The Decline in Employment of People with Disabilities: A Policy Puzzle* (2003) Institute for Employment Research, 301.

[8] Samuel R Bagenstos, 'Review Essay: Has the *Americans with Disabilities Act* Reduced Employment for People with Disabilities? The Decline in Employment of People with Disabilities: A Policy Puzzle' (2004) 25 *Berkeley Journal of Employment and Labor Law* 527, 563.

Command and Control

The anti-discrimination laws analysed in Chapters 6, 7 and 8 command duty holders not to engage in acts of discrimination. These prohibitions are supported by weak enforcement mechanisms, as analysed in Chapter 12. These laws attempt to achieve their ends by drawing from the command-and-control regulatory model. Command-and-control models focus on commanding regulated parties not to engage in certain conduct, and on encouraging compliance by the threat of punishment.[9]

Command-and-control regulation is especially effective where the command and regulated parties are easily identifiable.[10] A good example of this is traffic regulations that require all motorists to drive below a prescribed speed limit. Command-and-control models, however, struggle to achieve desired outcomes where it is difficult to create a command that will achieve the desired outcome. To be effective, command-and-control models must target people who can influence the desired result, require those parties to take the necessary steps to achieve the desired outcome, and avoid unintended consequences.[11]

Limitations of Relying on Command-and-Control Regulation to Combat Digital Disablement

There are three primary limitations of using a command-and-control model to reduce the causes of digital disablement in society. First, the parties regulated are not always the best parties to reduce the causes of disablement. Second, even if the regulated parties followed the command not to discriminate, the passive nature of the prohibition means that many barriers in society will be created which are difficult to retrofit. The third limitation is difficulties associated with control. As will be analysed in Chapter 12, anti-discrimination laws have a history of being poorly enforced. Moreover, individuals in organisations can be motivated by their subjective perceptions of sanctions, including the probability of detection by the state, and the reaction of their own organisation and supervisors.[12] People can also be driven by their

---

[9] Lisa Heinzerling, 'Selling Pollution, Forcing Democracy' (1995) 14 *Stanford Environment Law Journal* 300, 302; Cass R Sunstein, 'Problems with Rules' (1995) 83 *California Law Review* 953, 1019.

[10] Louis Kaplow, 'Rules Versus Standards: An Economic Analysis' (1992) 42 *Duke Law Journal* 557, 560.

[11] Paul Harpur, 'From Universal Exclusion to Universal Equality: Regulating Ableism in a Digital Age' (2013) 40(3) *Northern Kentucky Law Review* 529, 541.

[12] Sally S Simpson and Melissa Rorie, 'Motivating Compliance: Economic and Material Motives for Compliance' in Christine Parker and Vibeke Lehmann Nielsen (eds), *Explaining Compliance: Business Responses to Regulation* (2011) Edward Elgar, 59.

own moral code or a range of other internalised motivations to comply, and the existence of legal sanctions may negatively alter compliance responses.[13] In addition to this problem, the adversarial nature of civil litigation can result in access issues being managed by risk-averse lawyers rather than by parties who are focused on promoting equality. Accordingly, the traditional command-and-control anti-discrimination model does not always achieve the best equality outcome and should be only one arm in the struggle to promote an inclusive society.

Positive Duties and Management-Based Systems

The resilience of inequalities has led to a body of scholarship which argues that positive duties are required to enable everyone in society to fully exercise their human rights.[14] How these positive duties should be operationalised has attracted a rich body of scholarship. Professor Susan Sturm has argued that a structural approach is required to reduce more subtle forms of discrimination.[15] Sturm argues that the structuralism approach requires a regulatory 'approach that encourages the development of institutions and processes to enact general norms in particular contexts'.[16] Professor Sandra Fredman has argued that equality laws should focus on all parties who impact on inclusion rather than focusing on defined relationships.[17] The concept of positive duties reflects a market-based management response to addressing inequalities in society.

Arguably one of the most effective processes to achieve continuous change is through management systems. In their seminal work, Professors Cary Coglianese and David Lazer explained the regulatory criteria for effective systems-based regulation.[18] An effective management-based process will

[13] Tom R Tyler, 'The Psychology of Self-Regulation: Normative Motivations for Compliance' in Parker and Nielsen (eds), *Explaining Compliance*, 78.
[14] Frank Dobbin and Alexandra Kalev, 'Multi-Disciplinary Responses to Susan Sturm's *The Architecture of Inclusion*: The Architecture of Inclusion: Evidence from Corporate Diversity Programs' (2007) 30 *Harvard Journal of Law and Gender* 279; Sandra Fredman, 'Breaking the Mold: Equality as a Proactive Duty' (2012) 1 *American Journal of Comparative Law* 265; Samuel R Bagenstos, 'The Structural Turn and the Limits of Antidiscrimination Law' (2006) 94 *California Law Review* 1.
[15] Susan Sturm, 'Second Generation Employment Discrimination: A Structural Approach' (2001) 101 *Columbia Law Review* 458.
[16] Ibid., 463.
[17] Sandra Fredman, 'Combating Racism with Human Rights' in Sandra Fredman (ed.), *Discrimination and Human Rights: The Case of Racism* (2001) Oxford University Press, 27.
[18] Cary Coglianese and David Lazer, 'Management-Based Regulation: Prescribing Private Management to Achieve Public Goals' (2003) 37 *Law and Society Review* 691, 694.

contain processes to identify hazards, processes to mitigate the hazards identified, procedures for monitoring and correcting problems, training policies for implementation, and measures for evaluating and refining the system.[19] As will be seen throughout this chapter, legislative reforms and scholarship that embrace positive duties to combat inequalities in society embrace the concept that the regulatory focus should move away from the state prohibiting conduct, and instead turn to finding vehicles to empower and motivate parties to find strategies to achieve equality outcomes.

An effective equality intervention should find strategies to motivate regulated parties to be actively involved with increasing levels of compliance.[20] Once the cause of disablement is identified, then the question should be who has the capacity, directly or indirectly, to help reduce that barrier. Traditional anti-discrimination duties prohibit parties in prescribed relationships from engaging in discrimination. While these duties required duty holders to make reasonable adjustments to enable access once systems were established, Chapter 8 identified that this did not always result in equal access.

Under the management-based approach equality issues are not addressed after a system is created, but instead during the planning, implementation and operation of the system. This means that duty holders are more likely to identify and manage barriers to equality throughout the process. For example, suppose there were two E-Book platforms which provided access to the same titles for the same cost, but one embraced universal design and the other was not accessible for persons with disabilities. Under the traditional anti-discrimination model, a duty holder generally could purchase either system and would then need to consider disability access once the system was in place. The management-based approach, in contrast, would include disability accessibility as a factor in the decision-making process when determining which E-Book platform to purchase. While this process will not guarantee equality, there is an increased probability that the E-Book platform which embraced universal design would be purchased.

The CRPD Recognises the Importance of Positive Duties

The United Nations *Convention on the Rights of Persons with Disabilities* (CRPD) recognises the need for positive duties to ensure that persons with disabilities can exercise their civil, economic and social rights.[21] Chapter 2 of

---

[19] Ibid.

[20] Fiona Haines, *The Paradox of Regulation: What Regulation Can Achieve and What It Cannot* (2011) Edward Elgar, 10–20.

[21] CRPD, opened for signature 30 March 2007, 2515 UNTS 3 (entered into force 3 May 2008).

this monograph analysed how the CRPD transformed how disability human rights are constructed under international human rights laws, and cemented the disability human rights paradigm. This has resulted in a paradigm shift with respect to rights to access and notions of equality generally. Some of these positive duties directly impacted on the capacity of persons with print disabilities to use information communication technologies, such as E-Libraries and E-Book readers, and were analysed in Chapter 2. Chapter 2 analysed how the CRPD has enshrined a right to access information communication technologies, which requires positive conduct by states to promote the uptake of universal design and to introduce laws to require duty holders to make reasonable accommodations to enable access. Chapter 2 then analysed how the CRPD created proactive obligations on state signatories to facilitate the access of persons with disabilities to information communication technologies when exercising their rights to education, work, freedom of expression, recreation and participation in the cultural life of the community. This duty requires the state to ensure that non-state actors respect these rights.[22]

Speaking on the right to participation in cultural life, recreation, leisure and sport found in article 30, Professors Michael Stein and Janet Lord explain that to discharge the duty of implementing the inclusive development requirement in the realm of sport and recreation, it is required 'that national human rights institutions are proactively monitoring and seeking to promote such rights for disabled persons'.[23] Arguably, this requires states to implement measures that impact on non-state actors in order to help enable persons with disabilities to exercise their right to access information communication technologies, such as digital books and E-Readers.

General Comments Issued by the United Nations Committee on the Rights of Persons with Disabilities and Positive Duties

The CRPD recognises the importance of positive duties and embraces them in order to promote the new international paradigm that requires positive conduct from states. The first two general comments issued by the United Nations Committee on the Rights of Persons with Disabilities illustrate just how far the

---

[22] Steve Estey and Janet E Lord, 'The Potential Role of National Human Rights Institutions and Disabled People's Organizations in Implementing the Right to Sport, Recreation, Play and Leisure in the UN Disability Convention' in Eli A Wolff, Mary A Hums and Elise C Roy (eds), *Sport in the United Nations Convention on the Rights of Persons with Disabilities* (2007) International Disability in Sport Working Group, 20.

[23] Janet E Lord and Michael Ashley Stein, 'Social Rights and the Relational Value of the Rights to Participate in Sport, Recreation, and Play' (2009) 27 *Boston University International Law Journal* 249, 280.

CRPD has embraced positive duties. The first general comment concerned the right to equal recognition before the law under *CRPD* article 12.[24] The general comment on article 12 went much further than merely requiring states not to bar persons with disabilities from justice because of their disability. The general comment required substantial action from states, both to abolish substituted decision-making processes, and to replace them with supported decision-making regimes as far as possible. Critically, the general comment noted that the nature and type of support will vary depending on the needs of the individual.[25] People have different abilities, genders, education, financial status, emotional strength, support networks and so on. These factors will impact on how each supported decision-making process is operationalised.[26]

The change from substituted to supported decision making is much more than a mere change in nomenclature. Substituted decision making embraces the medicalisation of disability and involves a guardian speaking for and on behalf of the person with a disability in all economic, legal and medical matters.[27] The guardian determines the objective best interest of the disabled individual and acts on that basis. This approach allows a guardian to act in a manner contrary to the desires of the person whose interest they are charged with 'guarding'.

In contrast to substituted decision making, supported decision making recognises that impairment is a part of diversity and involves mechanisms to empower persons with disabilities to exercise their own will and preferences.[28] Supported decision-making processes take into consideration individual concerns, trauma, experiences with legal systems and levels of literacy.[29] After factoring in all these considerations, communication barriers need to be identified and measures implemented to enable the voice of the person with a disability to be heard.[30] Accordingly, the move from substituted to supported decision making will require substantial effort from state and private actors.

---

[24] Committee on the Rights of Persons with Disabilities, *General Comment No. 1 (2014): Article 12: Equal Recognition before the Law*, 11th sess., UN Doc. CRPD/C/GC/1 (19 May 2014).

[25] Ibid., [18].

[26] Heather Douglas and Paul Harpur, 'Intellectual Disabilities, Domestic Violence and Legal Engagement' (2016) 31(3) *Disability and Society* 305.

[27] Eilionoir Flynn and Anna Arstein-Kerslake, 'The Support Model of Legal Capacity: Fact, Fiction, or Fantasy?' (2014) 32 *Berkeley Journal of International Law* 134, 135–8.

[28] Committee on the Rights of Persons with Disabilities, *General Comment No. 1 (2014): Article 12: Equal Recognition before the Law*, 11th sess., UN Doc. CRPD/C/GC/1 (19 May 2014) 24.

[29] Irma H. Mahone et al., 'Shared Decision Making in Mental Health Treatment: Qualitative Endings from Stakeholder Focus Groups' (2011) 25(6) *Archives of Psychiatric Nursing* 27, 35.

[30] Penelope Weller, *New Law and Ethics in Mental Health Advance Directives: The Convention on the Rights of Persons with Disabilities and the Right to Choose* (2013) Routledge, 143–7.

The second general comment issued by the Committee on the Rights of Persons with Disabilities concerns the right to access in article 9.[31] This general comment is highly relevant in enabling persons with print disabilities to access the written word, and was discussed in Chapter 2 of this monograph. To protect the right to access of persons with disabilities, the general comment explains that states are required to introduce positive duties into laws. These positive duties 'should incorporate and be based on the principle of universal design, as required by the Convention (art. 4, para. 1(f)). It should provide for the mandatory application of accessibility standards and for sanctions, including fines, for those who fail to apply them.'[32] In addition to sanctioning parties for failing to embrace universal design, states are required to ensure that their procurement policies require only accessible universally designed services and facilities.[33] Mandating the uptake of universal design involves requiring research into how design can disable and enable persons with disabilities, and then designing 'products, environments, programmes and services to be usable by all people, to the greatest extent possible, without the need for adaptation or specialized design'.[34] It is clear that the human rights paradigm introduced by the CRPD involves considerable positive obligations on states. This chapter will now analyse how positive duties have been introduced into United Kingdom equality laws, and will consider how these duties might promote the right to read of persons with print disabilities using information communication technologies.

SECTION II POSITIVE DUTIES IN ACTION: THE PUBLIC SECTOR EQUALITY DUTY IN THE *EQUALITY ACT* 2010 (UK)

From the Emergence of Positive Duties in the UK to the Public Sector Equality Duty

The United Kingdom has a hesitant, uneven and incomplete trajectory history of expanding the operation of positive duties.[35] The *Fair Employment (Northern Ireland) Act* 1989 (UK) imposed positive duties on large employers to reduce tensions between Catholic and Protestant communities by achieving fair participation at work.[36] The *Northern Ireland Act* 1998 (UK) extended employers' positive duties to promote equality in

---

[31] Committee on the Rights of Persons with Disabilities, *General Comment No. 2 (2014): Article 9: Accessibility*, 11th sess., UN Doc. CRPD/C/GC/2 (22 May 2014).

[32] Ibid., 28.   [33] Ibid., 32.   [34] *CRPD*, art. 2.

[35] Linda Dickens, 'The Road Is Long: Thirty Years of Equality Legislation in Britain' (2007) 45(3) *British Journal of Industrial Relations* 463.

[36] Kevin A Burke, 'Fair Employment in Northern Ireland: The Role of Affirmative Action' (1994) 28 *The Columbia Journal of Law and Social Problems* 1.

respect of religion, age, disability, race, sex, marital status and sexual orientation.[37]

The actual and potential impact of positive obligations in, inter alia, the Northern Ireland regime, led to calls for the expansion of such duties.[38] One of the most influential studies which called for the expansion of positive duties was published by Professors Bob Hepple, Mary Coussey and Tufyal Choudhury.[39] Hepple, Coussey and Choudhury performed considerable case studies of employers across the United Kingdom and United States to understand the operation of inequalities and various remedial interventions. They recognised the limitations of traditional anti-discrimination duties and recommended a structural approach to ensuring equality. These authors argued that laws should create four new duties upon parties:

(1)   a positive duty on public authorities to advance equality;
(2)   proactive duties on private sector employers to achieve employment equity or fair participation;
(3)   proactive duties on employers to introduce pay equity schemes; and
(4)   the use of contract and subsidy compliance as a sanction and incentive.[40]

The study published by Hepple, Coussey and Choudhury led directly to a private member's bill by Lord Lester of Herne Hill QC, which was not enacted into law.[41] Seven years later, however, a less transformational version of the 2003 private member's bill was enacted into law, becoming the *Equality Act 2010* (UK).

The *Equality Act 2010* (UK) includes limited positive duties in the public sector equality duty in Part 11, Chapter 1.[42] This chapter will now analyse the extent to which the public sector equality duty has and will reduce digital disablement created by inaccessible information communication technologies.

---

[37]   Eithen McLaughlin, 'From Negative to Positive Equality Duties: The Development and Constitutionalisation of Equality Provisions in the UK' (2007) 6 *Social Policy and Society* 111.

[38]   Christopher McCrudden, 'Procurement and the Public Sector Equality Duty: Lessons for the Implementation of the *Equality Act 2010* from Northern Ireland?' (2011) 11(1–2) *International Journal of Discrimination and the Law* 85.

[39]   Bob Hepple, Mary Coussey and Tufyal Choudhury, *Equality: A New Framework* (2000) Hart Publishing, 56–85.

[40]   Ibid., 127.

[41]   Anthony Lester, 'Foreword' in Bob Hepple, *Equality*, 2nd edn (2011) Hart Publishing.

[42]   Becci Burton, 'Neoliberalism and the *Equality Act 2010*: A Missed Opportunity for Gender Justice?' (2014) 43(2) *Industrial Law Journal* 122.

Introducing the Public Sector Equality Duty in the Equality Act 2010 *(UK)*

The public sector equality duty is one of the primary means to strengthen the law to support progress on equality in the United Kingdom.[43] In addition to complying with direct and indirect discrimination provisions, public authorities must comply with the public sector equality duty, found in s 149 of the *Equality Act 2010* (UK). The public sector equality duty requires public authorities, in the exercise of their functions, to 'have due regard to the need to:

(a) eliminate discrimination, harassment, victimisation and any other conduct that is prohibited by or under [the *Equality Act 2010* (UK)];

(b) advance equality of opportunity between persons who share a relevant protected characteristic and persons who do not share it;

(c) foster good relations between persons who share a relevant protected characteristic and persons who do not share it.

As the name suggests, the public sector equality duty is focused on promoting equality in the exercise of public functions. As the focus is on the discharge of public functions, s 149(2) extends the operation of the duty to private actors, in situations where a private actor 'exercises public functions'. When exercising those public functions, the private actor 'must, in the exercise of those functions, have due regard' to equality in the same way as a public sector authority in the same position would have due regard.

What, then, is a 'public function'? The *Equality Act 2010* (UK) s 150(5) explains that a public function is a function of a public nature for the purposes of the *Human Rights Act 1998* (UK). The *Human Rights Act 1998* (UK) ss 6(3)(b) and 6(5) combined provide that any person whose functions are of a public nature will be a public authority. Core public authorities are bodies whose functions are entirely public, such as the police and government departments.[44]

Hybrid public authorities engage in a mix of public and private activities and are only 'public authorities when engaging in activities of a public nature'. There has been substantial judicial and scholarly debate about when a function of a potential hybrid public authority becomes a public one.[45] The House of Lords held in the Aston case that a parochial church council was

---

[43] Sandra Fredman, 'The Public Sector Equality Duty' (2011) 40(4) *Industrial Law Journal* 405.

[44] *YL v. Birmingham City Council* [2007] UKHL 27, [37] (Baroness Hale) (*YL*).

[45] Alexander Williams, 'Public Authorities' in David Hoffman (ed.), *The Impact of the UK Human Rights Act on Private Law* (2011) Cambridge University Press, 48.

not exercising a function of a public nature when making building repairs.[46] The House of Lords held in the YL case that publicly funded care provided by a private nursing home to an elderly patient was not a public function.[47] The government provided submissions in the YL case arguing that the provision of private nursing care that was funded by the state was a public function. Following this case, the *Health and Social Care Act 2008* (UK) s 145 reversed the impact of the YL precedent by providing that private health care that has some state funding is a public function. The House of Lords' judgments support the approach that focuses on the nature of the task being performed rather than on the institution's overall nature. Using this approach, Professor Richard Stone argues that it appears likely that educational institutions, such as universities, are funded partially by the state and therefore are of a public nature and are public authorities.[48] Almost all Scottish further and higher educational providers, grant-aided schools and transport partnerships have accepted that they are public authorities and bound by the public sector equality duty and reporting obligations.[49] While there remains some uncertainty over what functions are public, it is clear that libraries that are public or associated with educational providers almost certainly can be regarded as exercising public functions in relation to decisions around what digital services they offer.

The Duty to Give Due Regard

The requirement to advance equality and foster good relations requires actual positive conduct from public authorities.[50] Merely engaging in a public relations exercise or box ticking will not discharge the duty. Courts will look to the substance of the conduct and require genuine engagement with equality issues.[51] The duty is drafted to include a proportionality requirement.[52] To give 'due regard' is something different from 'simple regard' or just 'regard'.

---

[46] *Parochial Church Council of the Parish of Aston Cantlow and Wilmcote with Billesley, Warwickshire v. Wallbank and another* [2003] UKHL 37.

[47] *YL v. Birmingham City Council* [2007] UKHL 27.

[48] Richard Stone, *Textbook on Civil Liberties and Human Rights*, 9th edn (2012) Oxford University Press, 38.

[49] Equality and Human Rights Commission, 'Measuring Up? Performance: A Report of Public Authorities' Performance in Meeting the Scottish Specific Equality Duties' (report, Equality and Human Rights Commission Scotland, September 2015).

[50] Aileen McColgan, *Discrimination, Equality and the Law* (2014) Hart Publishing, 7, 8.

[51] *R (Domb) v. London Borough of Hammersmith* [2009] EWCA Civ. 941 [52].

[52] Sandra Fredman, 'Addressing Disparate Impact: Indirect Discrimination and the Public Sector Equality Duty' (2014) 43(3) *Industrial law Journal* 349.

To give something due regard means the matter at hand has had due consideration and attention.[53]

The Bracking and Brown Principles are the leading authority on what a public authority must do to satisfy its obligation to give 'due regard'.[54] The Bracking and Brown Principles were established in two leading cases. In the first of these cases, *R (Brown)* v. *Secretary of State for Work and Pensions*, the court held:

- Due regard is fulfilled before and at the time a particular policy that will or might affect people with protected characteristics is under consideration, as well as at the time a decision is taken.
- Due regard involves a conscious approach.
- The duty cannot be satisfied by justifying a decision after it has been taken.
- The duty must be exercised in substance, with rigour and with an open mind in such a way that it influences the final decision. It is not a question of 'ticking boxes'.
- The duty is a continuing and a non-delegable one.[55]

Subsequently, in *Bracking* v. *Secretary of State for Work and Pensions* the Court of Appeal approved the Brown Principles and added further principles:

- The duty is upon the decision maker personally. What matters is what they took into account and what they knew.
- A public authority must assess the risk and extent of any adverse impact and the ways in which such risk may be eliminated before the adoption of a proposed policy.
- A public authority should have enough evidence to demonstrate that it has discharged the duty.[56]

Courts will scrutinise the actual conduct of public authorities, as well as their public statements, to determine whether the public sector equality duty has been satisfied.[57] A deficient equality impact assessment is evidence that the public authority has not given due regard.[58]

---

[53] Aileen McColgan, 'Litigating the Public Sector Equality Duty: The Story So Far' (2015) 35(3) *Oxford Journal of Legal Studies* 453.
[54] Irene Henery, 'The Public Sector Equality Duty: Are Employers "Measuring Up"?' (2015) 126 *Employment Law Bulletin* 4.
[55] *R (Brown)* v. *Secretary of State for Work and Pensions* [2008] EWHC 3158, [90]–[96].
[56] *Bracking* v. *Secretary of State for Work and Pensions* [2013] EWCA Civ. 1345.
[57] *R (Hajrula)* v. *London Councils* [2011] EWHC 448, [68].
[58] *Foreign National Prisoners* [2010] EWHC 147, [55] and [56].

Regulations under the Public Sector Equality Duty Providing Guidance on 'Due Regard'

The content of the public sector equality duty was provided with clarity through the introduction of specific duties in regulations. The change of government following the 2010 general election in the United Kingdom resulted in a divergence between the position in England and that in Scotland and Wales. The change from a Labour government to a Conservative government, with an emphasis on austerity, heralded a reduction in the focus on human rights issues. Prime Minister David Cameron desired to reduce bureaucracy and move away from a process-driven approach to transparency.[59] The ideological opposition to requiring public authorities to take equality action resulted in the *Draft Equality Act 2010 (Specific Duties) Regulations 2011* (UK) not being adopted for England.[60]

The constitutional structure of the United Kingdom meant that the reluctance to ensure equality in England did not impact on the capacity of Scottish and Welsh lawmakers.[61] Accordingly, parliaments in these jurisdictions respectively adopted the *Equality Act 2010 (Specific Duties) (Scotland) Regulations 2012* and the *Equality Act 2010 (Statutory Duties) (Wales) Regulations 2011*.

The *Equality Act 2010 (Specific Duties) (Scotland) Regulations 2012* and the *Equality Act 2010 (Statutory Duties) (Wales) Regulations 2011* impose a range of specific positive duties on public authorities in their respective jurisdictions. Section 3 of both the Scottish and Welsh regulations require public authorities to report progress on mainstreaming the public sector equality duty. These regulations require public authorities to report on the progress they have made towards making the equality duty integral to the exercise of their functions, so as to better perform the duty. Section 4 of both the Scottish and Welsh regulations also require public authorities to publish equality impact assessments and equality outcomes. Of course, the public authority could report that it has not acted to implement the public sector equality duty; however, this could be politically difficult. Section 5 of the Scottish regulations creates a duty on public authorities to assess and review policies and practices. Similarly, ss 5 and 13 of the Welsh regulations require public authorities to review, engage and consult with people with protected characteristics on the authority's equality activities. To create a benchmark of employment equality,

---

[59] Government Equalities Office, '*Equality Act 2010*: The Public Sector Equality Duty Reducing Bureaucracy' (policy review paper, 17 March 2011) 1.

[60] Hepple, *Equality*, 167–8.

[61] Mark Ryan and Steve Foster, *Unlocking Constitutional and Administrative Law*, 3rd edn (2014) Routledge, 361–2, 367–78

s 6 of the Scottish regulations requires public authorities to gather and use employee information. Section 7 of the Welsh regulations has a broader obligation that requires public authorities to make arrangements for collection of information about compliance with equality obligations. To encourage public discourse, s 10 of the Scottish regulations and s 7 of the Welsh regulations require public authorities to publish reports in accessible formats. The combination of the public sector equality duty and the associated regulations creates a comprehensive management system approach to equality for public authorities in Scotland and Wales.

Will the Duty to Give 'Due Regard' Result in All Attributes Being Considered?

The public sector equality duty requires considerable effort from public authorities. This chapter will now consider how the public sector equality duty can improve the capacity of persons with disabilities to access information communication technologies. The *Equality Act 2010* (UK) protects a large number of attributes, including age, disability, gender reassignment, pregnancy and maternity, race, religion or belief, and sex and sexual orientation.[62] Disability is just one aspect and each attribute has numerous issues which impact upon equality. With so many equality issues and attributes, this section analyses whether public authorities are required to, and whether they do, give due regard to issues concerning persons with disabilities.

The *Equality Act 2010* (UK) requires public authorities to consider issues relating to all protected characteristics.[63] This means that all public authorities must consider how their conduct will impact on persons with disabilities. Section 149(4) explains that '[t]he steps involved in meeting the needs of disabled persons that are different from the needs of persons who are not disabled include, in particular, steps to take account of disabled persons' disabilities'. If a public authority cancelled or purchased a licence to use an E-Book library, and did not give due regard to whether or not the platform is accessible for persons with print disabilities, this would not give due regard to the impact of the decision on persons with disabilities.

The operation of the duty to give regard to all characteristics can be illustrated by the judgment in *R (Brown)* v. *Secretary of State for Work and Pensions*.[64] In *R (Brown)* v. *Secretary of State for Work and Pensions* the Court held that the decision to close a post office without considering the impact on disabled persons was not giving due regard to the needs of persons with such an

[62] *Equality Act 2010* (UK) s 149 (7).   [63] Ibid., s 149 (7).   [64] [2008] EWHC 3158.

attribute. This meant the public sector equality duty was not satisfied and the decision to close the post office needed to be reconsidered. The requirement to consider disability issues is even more significant under the specific duties regulations in Scotland and Wales. Section 4(3) of the Scottish regulation, for example, requires the public authority to explain how it is discharging its duty for every attribute, or explain why it is not addressing the equality issues impacting on persons with that attribute. Clearly public authorities need to include equality issues concerning persons with disabilities in discharging the public sector equality duty.

How Are Public Authorities Approaching their Equality Duties?

The previous section determined that public authorities have a duty to specifically address the rights of persons with disabilities to discharge the public sector equality duty. This section will consider whether public authorities are in fact considering persons with disabilities. The following section will then analyse whether the due regard to persons with disabilities is likely to promote the capacity of persons with disabilities to access digital information on the same basis as the wider public.

While English public authorities do not need to publish equality impact assessments, a number have adopted this practice. According to Professor Bob Hepple, the voluntary nature of this step, combined with increasing cost pressures, has led to 'some English public bodies ... abandoning monitoring and impact assessments and are not consulting interested persons, trade unions and equality representatives or involving disabled persons'.[65] While there is limited evidence on the extent to which English public authorities are discharging the public sector equality duty, the specific duty regulations mean there is more evidence of levels of compliance in Scotland and Wales.

The Equality and Human Rights Commission has performed two in-depth sets of reviews on the documentation published by Scottish public authorities. The first set of reviews analysed documents published between May and June 2013 by Scottish public authorities. The 2013 review resulted in three reports. The first 2013 report analysed the extent to which Scottish public authorities were discharging their duty to report progress on mainstreaming the equality duty, and publishing reports on equality outcomes, progress, gender pay information and employment according to attribute.[66]

[65] Hepple, *Equality*, 167.
[66] Equality and Human Rights Commission, 'Measuring Up? Monitoring Public Authorities' Performance against the Scottish Specific Equality Duties' (report, Equality and Human Rights Commission Scotland, June 2013).

The second report analysed whether public authorities were gathering and using employee information records for the composition, recruitment and retention of employees by reference to their relevant protected characteristics.[67] The final 2013 report involved an in-depth analysis of each public authority's equality outcomes.[68]

Building on the 2013 reports, the Equality and Human Rights Commission analysed the conduct of the 239 Scottish public authorities between May and June 2015, which resulted in two reports presenting different data. The Practice Report provides a qualitative analysis including some best-practice examples.[69] The Performance Report considers how public authorities have met their duties under the *Equality Act 2010 (Specific Duties) (Scotland) Regulations 2012*.[70] The Performance Report does not consider the detail or the quality of conduct or publications. The Performance Report found that almost all Scottish public authorities were engaging to some extent with their equality obligations:

- 96% of listed authorities published a mainstreaming report;
- 96% of listed authorities reported on progress made to achieve their equality outcomes;
- 95% of required listed authorities published gender pay gap information;
- 89% of assessed listed authorities published some employee information.

Public authorities are clearly active in publishing on their equality activities.

The equality activities engaged in by Scottish public authorities are benefiting persons with disabilities. Public authorities with more than 150 employees need to report on recruitment, retention and training by attribute. While information on some attributes was not reported on, disability, as well as age, sex and race, was one of the four protected characteristics most frequently reported on. Throughout the Performance Report, this hierarchy of protected attributes was manifested. The table below illustrates the theme of how protected characteristics were reported upon. This table is modified from

---

[67] Equality and Human Rights Commission, 'Measuring Up? Report 2: Monitoring Public Authorities' Performance of the Employment Duties' (report, Equality and Human Rights Commission Scotland, September 2013).

[68] Ibid.

[69] Equality and Human Rights Commission, 'Measuring Up? Report 4: Practice: A Report of Public Authorities' Practice in Meeting the Scottish Specific Equality Duties' (report, Equality and Human Rights Commission Scotland, September 2015).

[70] Equality and Human Rights Commission, 'Measuring Up? Performance: A Report of Public Authorities' Performance in Meeting the Scottish Specific Equality Duties' (report, Equality and Human Rights Commission Scotland, September 2015).

the reporting on staff development by reference to protected characteristics contained within the Performance Report:

Protected characteristic	%
Race	43%
Sex	42%
Disability	38%
Age	37%
Religion or belief	26%
Sexual orientation	24%
Gender reassignment	12%
Pregnancy and maternity	6%

This table illustrates that collecting data and reporting on disability is a high priority for most Scottish public authorities.

While the Performance Report demonstrates that Scottish public authorities are collecting data on disability, it does not show the nature of the interventions. The Practice Report provides some limited examples on how public authorities are promoting the rights of persons with disabilities.[71] The Practice Report considers all issues related to all protected attributes and only provides a snapshot of some best practices.

Due to length, a large number of examples of best practices are not included in the report. As many equality practices are not mentioned in the Practice Report, the fact that access to digital technologies or libraries is not mentioned does not indicate a lack of attention to these issues. The Practice Report does provide some examples of interventions which benefit persons with disabilities. For example, the University of Edinburgh has reportedly introduced schemes to improve the admission rate for persons with disabilities. The University of Stirling has implemented a range of measures to raise awareness and develop a supportive workplace.

The Performance Report and the Practice Report demonstrate that Scottish public authorities are promoting equality interventions benefiting persons with disabilities. This chapter will next analyse how public authorities determine how to devote equality resources to different issues.

---

[71] Equality and Human Rights Commission, 'Measuring Up? Report 4: Practice: A Report of Public Authorities' Practice in Meeting the Scottish Specific Equality Duties' (report, Equality and Human Rights Commission Scotland, September 2015).

How Public Authorities Determine How to Devote Resources

The previous section has demonstrated that public authorities are considering issues impacting on persons with disabilities and are actively implementing some measures to promote ability equality. With so many protected characteristics and equality issues, how should public authorities distribute resources? The *Equality Act 2010* (UK) and regulations require a range of positive conduct from public authorities, but these instruments do not explain how public authorities should determine how to allocate resources between different equality issues. There was a possibility that using a socio-economic criteria might have been required by the *Equality Act 2010* (UK); however, despite being proposed, 'socio-economic factors' is not a protected characteristic under the statute.[72] Public authorities have limited resources to devote to equality interventions, and implementing a measure to assist one group may result in people with another protected characteristic not benefiting from support. This section will consider how public authorities should approach the conflict over equality resources.

Professor Ayelet Shachar has argued that there is a paradox of multicultural vulnerability where protecting the interests of some minority groups can result in the interests of different minority groups being sacrificed.[73] Conflicts between respecting rights can arise in various situations.[74] The main conflict that is relevant to ensuring that persons with disabilities can access information communication technologies is over resource distribution. Public authorities generally have the discretion to determine how to distribute resources between equality issues.

While public authorities have significant discretion in how they devote equality resources, they are required to consider the implications of their decisions on different characteristics. Courts retain the power to review how a public authority has distributed resources. In *R (Luton BC) v. Secretary of State for Education*, the termination of a programme on budgetary grounds was open to challenge.[75] The public authority in Luton had not made any equality impact assessment, which meant the case did not turn on the content of a budgetary assessment. In *R (Rotao Rahman) v. Birmingham City Council*, the Court firmly accepted the notion that the public sector equality duty

---

[72] Sandra Fredman, 'New Horizons: Incorporating Socio-Economic Rights in a British Bill of Rights' (2010) *Public Law* 297; Kay Wheat, 'Mental Health and Stigma: How Best to Protect Workers from Discrimination' (2013) 34 *Windsor Review of Legal and Social Issues* 1, 23.

[73] A Shachar, 'On Citizenship and Multicultural Vulnerability' (2000) 28 *Political Theory* 64, 65.

[74] A Shachar, 'Group Identity and Women's Rights in Family Law: The Perils of Multicultural Accommodation' (1998) 6(3) *Journal of Political Philosophy* 285.

[75] *R (Luton BC) v. Secretary of State for Education* [2011] EWHC 217.

required public authorities to perform equality impact assessments when distributing resources:

> Even where the context of the decision-making was a local authority's limited financial resources, that did not excuse compliance with the public sector equality duties and indeed there was much to be said for the proposition that in straightened times the need for clear, well-informed decision-making when assessing the impacts on less-advantaged members of society was as great, if not greater.[76]

As a consequence, decisions by public authorities on resource distribution can be reviewed. Public procurement decisions can have a significant impact on disability access to information communication technologies within the community.[77] As mentioned in Chapter 1 of this monograph, some E-Book platforms are not accessible. If a public authority decided to utilise an E-Book platform that was not accessible for persons with print disabilities, then the public authority might be asked to explain why this platform was adopted rather than an equivalent platform that was accessible.

If a public authority decided to purchase a licence to use an E-Library that was not accessible for persons with print disabilities when there was an equivalent library that was accessible, then this decision would seem to go against the objective of the public sector equality duty. Before a decision-maker can assess the equality impact, they will need to perform some research. How much effort does a public authority need to make? Based upon research by the author and Suzor on the E-Book library platforms subscribed to by a major Australian university, most platforms were accessible to some extent.[78] No library platform stated that it denied or restricted levels of access for persons with print disabilities, and all platforms had good corporate citizen statements. Arguably, however, it would not be sufficient to rely on statements by suppliers alone.

Courts have determined that there needs to be a degree of rigour about the efforts to give due regard.[79] Whether this is sufficiently rigorous to discharge the public sector equality duty has not been tested. The court in *Williams and Anor, R (on the application of)* v. *Surrey County Council* did provide that

---

[76] *R (Rotao Rahman)* v. *Birmingham City Council* [2011] EWHC 944, [46].

[77] Dónal Rice, 'Public Procurement as a Means to Achieving Social Gains: Progress and Challenges in European Legislation and Standards for Accessible Information and Communication Technology' (2015) 29(2/3) *International Review of Law, Computers and Technology* 162.

[78] Paul Harpur and Nicolas Suzor, 'The Paradigm Shift in Realising the Right to Read: How E-Book Libraries Are Enabling in the University Sector' (2014) 29(10) *Disability and Society* 1658.

[79] *R (Luton BC)* v. *Secretary of State for Education* [2011] EWHC 217, [62].

a public library needed to consider the implications of reducing staff on people who have the protected characteristics of age and disability.[80] The public library was required to have performed some data gathering when making an assessment. It is relatively easy to obtain some data on accessibility on high-profile information communication technology devices. For example, significant accessibility issues with the Amazon Kindle Reader have attracted advocacy and scholarly attention at the time of writing this monograph.[81] A simple search on Google asking, 'Is the Kindle accessible for persons with disabilities?' provided eight hits on the first page which high-lighted serious concerns with this platform. One of the hits concerned a major disability person organisation and provided a contact person.

While the technical reasons why an E-Book platform might not be acces-sible might be difficult to ascertain, identifying that there are some accessi-bility difficulties can be relatively easy and requires no expertise. Information provided on blogs or disability person organisations' websites, however, might not be sufficient for a public authority to alter its practices. It would seem that a public authority that is deciding where to devote substantial financial resources would be required to take some effort to determine if an E-Book platform is accessible for persons with disabilities or not. If a public authority determines that there are reports about accessi-bility difficulties, then at a minimum that authority would need to consult with stakeholders, including inviting the supplier to respond to the reported accessibility concerns. If an information communication technology is not accessible for persons with disabilities, then the public authority is required to consider whether the technology can be rendered accessible or whether there are equivalent technologies that are accessible to everyone, regardless of their abilities.

CONCLUSION

This chapter has analysed how the emergence of positive duties in anti-discrimination laws can help reduce digital disablement relating to E-Book information communication technologies. This chapter was divided into two sections. The first section explained the regulatory approaches that underpin traditional and positive anti-discrimination duties. Traditional anti-discrimination duties reflect the command-and-control approach to regulation. Command-and-control models focus on commanding regulated parties not

---

[80] *Williams and Anor, R (on the application of)* v. *Surrey County Council* [2012] EWHC 867.
[81] See for discussion Chapter 1 of this monograph.

to engage in certain conduct, and encouraging compliance by threat of punishment.

This chapter argued that command-and-control models by themselves have failed to combat inequalities. Traditional anti-discrimination laws do not clearly articulate a command that will sufficiently reduce disablement in society. Lawmakers have also struggled to identify sufficient strategies to ensure sufficient control to motivate compliance with the prohibition not to discriminate.

Recognising the problems with the command-and-control model, positive duties have been promoted by scholars and partially adopted into law in some jurisdictions. Unlike traditional anti-discrimination duties which rely upon prohibitions, positive duties require parties to seek out and identify the causes of disablement in society and find vehicles to promote equality. Positive duties encourage parties to consider equality issues while creating systems rather than focusing on retrospectively adjusting disabling systems. Where command-and-control approaches attract legal sanctions, positive duties often have softer enforcement and a wider regulatory capture. The importance of positive duties has been recognised by the CRPD, which requires states and private actors to take positive conduct to reduce the causes of disablement in society.

Section II of this chapter then analysed the lead-up, implementation and application of the public sector equality duty in the United Kingdom. The public sector equality duty requires core and hybrid public authorities to give due regard to a range of equality outcomes. The duty to give due regard requires public authorities to actively consider equality issues when developing systems. The extent of this duty is clarified and extended for public authorities in Scotland and Wales by regulations introduced by those jurisdictions' lawmakers.

The public sector equality duty across the United Kingdom requires public authorities to give due regard to disability access when making any decisions in relation to information communication technologies, whether it be with regard to storing, retrieving, manipulating, transmitting or receiving information in digital forms. The obligation to consider how digital disablement can be increased or reduced by decisions does not mean that the public authority has to adopt the approach that increases equality. The public sector equality duty requires public authorities to give regard to disability access in making its decision. While this process may not always result in a reduction in digital disablement, the fact that equality issues are being discussed increases the probability that public authorities will identify strategies to promote inclusion and will seek to procure information communication technologies that embrace universal design. The public sector equality duty accordingly increases the attention given to disability digital access in public authorities and with those who supply products and services to those authorities. The public sector equality duty will not remove all barriers to digital equality, but it will make a significant contribution to promoting a more inclusive society.

10

The Right to Digital Equality in Action: Protections under the *Canadian Charter of Human Rights and Freedoms* and Human Rights Acts

INTRODUCTION

After analysing who was entitled to claim protection under anti-discrimination laws in Chapter 6 of this monograph, Chapters 7 and 8 analysed the anti-discrimination regimes in Australia, the United Kingdom and the United States. Chapter 9 then analysed how limited positive duties have been introduced in the United Kingdom. This chapter turns the analysis to Canada, and analyses how Canadian laws protect persons with print disabilities.

There are significant differences between the laws protecting the right to digital equality of persons with print disabilities in Canada and Australia, the United Kingdom and the United States. The fact that Canadian laws recognise digital equality as a human right and embrace positive duties distinguishes this jurisdiction from most states across the globe.

Equality Constitutional Protection in Australia, the United Kingdom and the United States

Australian and United States constitutional law has not been utilised to provide persons with print disabilities with human rights protection to any notable extent. Australia has no relevant federal constitutional rights protections and there is no federal charter of rights. While two Australian jurisdictions have rights charters,[1] these instruments have not been utilised by persons with disabilities to ensure economic rights.[2] Largely, these instruments provide no protection for the right to read. The limited exception to this position

---

[1] *Human Rights Act 2004* (ACT); *Charter of Human Rights and Responsibilities Act 2006* (Vic).

[2] For a discussion of litigation under these instruments see Andrew Byrnes, Hilary Charlesworth and Gabrielle McKinnon, *History, Politics and Law* (2009) University of New South Wales Press, 73–86 and 108–38; see also George Williams, 'The Victorian *Charter of Human Rights and Responsibilities*: Origins and Scope' (2006) 30 *Melbourne University Law Review* 880.

is the right to be free from discrimination in education found in the *Human Rights Act 2004* (ACT) s 27A(3)(a).

While the United States does have a bill of rights, these rights, in particular the equal protection clause,[3] have not been significantly utilised by disability rights advocates since the United States Supreme Court's decision in *City of Cleburne* v. *Cleburne Living Center, Incorporated*.[4]

United States constitutional protections aimed at protecting persons with disabilities have been interpreted in ways that perpetuate negative stereotypes and reinforce oppression.[5] Professor Michael Waterstone has argued that United States constitutional law has the capacity to offer an alternative legal avenue to protect the rights of persons with disabilities; however, Professor Waterstone, along with Professors Michael Stein and David Wilkins, have found that at present such advocacy is not on the agenda of disability cause lawyers.[6]

When compared to Australia and the United States, the United Kingdom, through its involvement in the European Union, has an active disability constitutional rights discourse. As a signatory to the *European Convention on Human Rights*, United Kingdom laws are subject to rulings by the European Court of Human Rights.[7] The European Court of Human Rights has handed down a range of judgments which concern the rights of persons with disabilities to communication and access. For example, in *Jasinskis* v. *Latvia* the Court found there had been a violation of human rights where police failed to give a deaf and mute person any means of communicating, in a situation where injuries sustained while in custody

---

[3] The Fourteenth Amendment to the United States Constitution contains the Equal Protection Clause. The Equal Protection Clause provides that no state shall deny to any person within its jurisdiction 'the equal protection of the laws'. For a detailed discussion of the Equal Protection Clause, see William D Araiza, *Enforcing the Equal Protection Clause* (2016) New York University Press.

[4] 473 US 432 (1985). The case struck down a zoning ordinance as infringing the equal protection rights of individuals with mental retardation, but held the disability classification was only entitled to rational basis scrutiny.

[5] Anita Silvers and Michael Ashley Stein, 'Disability, Equal Protection, and the Supreme Court: Standing at the Crossroads of Progressive and Retrogressive Logic in Constitutional Classification' (2001) 35 *University of Michigan Journal of Law Reform* 81, 112.

[6] Michael E Waterstone, 'Disability Constitutional Law' (2014) 63 *Emory Law Journal* 527, 531; Michael Waterstone, Michael Ashley Stein and David Wilkins, 'Disability Cause Lawyers: Relentless Pragmatism in the Shadow of the Supreme Court' (2012) 53(4) *William and Mary Law Review* 1287, 1318.

[7] Peter Bartlett, Oliver Lewis and Oliver Thorold, *Mental Disability and the European Convention on Human Rights* (2006) Brill, 7; Alexandra Timmer, 'A Quiet Revolution: Vulnerability in the European Court of Human Rights' in Martha Albertson Fineman and Anna Grear (eds), *Vulnerability: Gender in Law, Culture, and Society* (2013) Ashgate, 147.

proved fatal.[8] The Court, however, has not read the right to access broadly. The Court has recognised a right to disability access where the person with a disability is detained by the state. In *Price v. The United Kingdom* the Court found there was a violation of human rights when a female prisoner with a disability was forced to sleep in her wheelchair and receive help from untrained male guards to go to the toilet.[9] The Court has been less willing, however, to recognise the right to access where the denial is related to a cultural pursuit. In *Botta v. Italy* the absence of wheelchair-accessible lavatories and ramps to the beach was held not to be a breach of human rights.[10]

Unlike Australia, the United Kingdom and the United States, Canadian human rights jurisprudence has recognised the right to digital accessibility as a right protected by the *Canadian Charter of Human Rights and Freedoms (Charter)*.[11] Section 1 of this chapter will analyse how the *Charter* interacts with domestic anti-discrimination laws, and will analyse how the *Charter* has been read to provide a right to read. Secondly, this chapter will analyse how Canadian anti-discrimination laws, referred to as human rights Acts, have adopted a dynamic approach to defining disability that includes positive duties. The rejection of an overly legalistic way to defining discrimination, combined with positive duties, means Canadian laws are comparatively better positioned to protect the right to read of persons with print disabilities than the equivalent regimes in Australia, the United Kingdom and the United States.

SECTION I THE RIGHT TO EQUALITY UNDER THE
CHARTER OF HUMAN RIGHTS AND FREEDOMS

The right to equality is recognised in the *Charter* in article 15:

(1)   Every individual is equal before and under the law and has the right to the equal protection and equal benefit of the law without discrimination

---

[8] *Jasinskis v. Latvia* (European Court of Human Rights, Chamber, ECHR Application No. 45744/08, 21 December 2010); Anna Lawson, 'Disability Equality, Reasonable Accommodation and the Avoidance of Ill-Treatment in Places of Detention: The Role of Supranational Monitoring and Inspection Bodies' (2012) 16(6) *International Journal of Human Rights* 845.

[9] *Price v. The United Kingdom* [2001] VII Eur Court HR 153; David Weissbrodt et al., 'Applying International Human Rights Standards to the Restraint and Seclusion of Students with Disabilities' (2012) 30 *Law and Inequality: A Journal of Theory and Practice* 287.

[10] *Botta v. Italy* [1998] I Eur Court HR; Maria Liisberg, 'Accessibility of Services and Discrimination Concentricity, Consequence, and the Concept of Anticipatory Reasonable Adjustment' (2015) 15(1–2) *International Journal of Discrimination and the Law* 123.

[11] The *Charter of Human Rights and Freedoms* appears in Part I of the *Constitution Act 1982* being Schedule B to the *Canada Act 1982* (UK).

and, in particular, without discrimination based on race, national or ethnic origin, colour, religion, sex, age or mental or physical disability.

(2)   Subsection (1) does not preclude any law, program or activity that has as its object the amelioration of conditions of disadvantaged individuals or groups including those that are disadvantaged because of race, national or ethnic origin, colour, religion, sex, age or mental or physical disability.

The Canadian Supreme Court has adopted various tests to determine whether there has been a breach of the equality guarantee found in article 15.[12] It is possible to distil these tests into a two stage test:

(1)   Does the law create a distinction based on an enumerated or analogous ground?

(2)   Does the distinction create a disadvantage by perpetuating prejudice or stereotyping?[13]

Question 1: Does the Law Create a Distinction Based on an Enumerated or Analogous Ground?

The *Charter*'s jurisdiction extends to all laws made in Canada, as well as regulations and policies created under such laws. This means that the *Charter* applies to whether or not the implementation of laws and policies enable persons with disabilities to access them.[14] How then does the *Charter* interact with federal and provincial anti-discrimination laws and policies? Anti-discrimination laws in Canada are found in the federal and provincial human rights Acts. While both the *Charter* and human rights Acts enshrine rights, the *Charter* has primacy as part of the *Canadian Constitution Act 1982* and protects more fundamental rights.[15] Accordingly, the *Charter* can have a direct impact on the human rights Acts.

Whereas the human rights Acts regulate defined relationships, the *Charter* binds all legislative and executive activities.[16] As a consequence, the *Charter* can be used to strike down aspects of the human rights Acts. In *Vilven* v. *Air Canada*, a pilot challenged an exemption in the then section 15 of the *Canadian Human Rights Act*.[17] Section 15(1)(c) at the time authorised discriminatory Acts if they were following industry standards. In this case,

---

[12]   *Andrews* v. *Law Society (British Columbia)* [1989] 1 SCR 143; *Law* v. *Canada (Minister of Employment and Immigration)* [1999] 1 SCR 497.

[13]   *Canada (Attorney General)* v. *Jodhan* [2012] FCA 161, [53] (Nadon J).

[14]   *Eldridge* v. *British Columbia (Attorney General)* [1997] 3 SCR 624.

[15]   Marni Tolensky and Stephen Lavender, *The 2014–2015 Annotated Canadian Human Rights Act* (2015) Thomson Reuters Canada, 2.

[16]   *Laessoe* v. *Air Canada* [1996] 27 CHRR D/1.   [17]   *Vilven* v. *Air Canada* [2009] CHRT 24.

a collective agreement required a pilot to be retired when he reached a particular age. The Canadian Supreme Court held that this exemption was contrary to rights found in the *Charter* and struck out the provision.

Unlike constitutional rights in Australia and the United States,[18] the Canadian Federal Parliament has the power to pass legislation to override a human rights determination that strikes down a law. This has not been exercised to protect disability digital accessibility or analogous disability rights and is beyond the scope of this chapter.

Question 2: Does the Distinction Create a Disadvantage by Perpetuating Prejudice or Stereotyping?

When considering whether or not a distinction has created a disadvantage by perpetuating prejudice or stereotyping, the Canadian Supreme Court requires positive conduct from the state.[19] To the extent possible, the benefit of law offered to the public must be as inclusive as possible to persons with disabilities. Once a state has entered the field, then the state attracts a duty to ensure equality.[20]

The *Charter* equality guarantee may not require the state to provide an entirely new service, but if the state does provide a service to the wider public, then that service should be provided in a way that does not discriminate based upon disability.[21] For example, in *Eldridge* v. *British Columbia (Attorney General)*, the Canadian Supreme Court found that health services needed to be provided to all Canadians in a way that provided for equality.[22] The failure to provide sign language interpretation to deaf patients seeking hospital services meant the service was not provided on an equal basis, and thus violated deaf patients' equality rights. Article 15 mandates that laws and policies are not discriminatory, but could the *Charter* be read to advance the right to read?

The Right to Digital Accessibility and the Jodhan *Litigation*

A Canadian with a print disability, Donna Jodhan, experienced reading disablement and successfully used article 15 of the *Charter* to protect her

[18] J Hiebert, 'A Hybrid Approach to Protect Rights? An Argument in Favour of Supplementing Canadian Judicial Review with Australia's Model of Parliamentary Scrutiny' (1998) 26(1) *Federal Law Review* 115; Kent Roach, *The Supreme Court on Trial: Judicial Activism or Democratic Dialogue* (2001) Irwin Law, 59.

[19] *Facilities Subsector Bargaining Assn.* v. *British Columbia* [2007] 2 SCR 391.

[20] Cara Wilkie and Meryl Zisman, 'Positive and Negative Rights under the *Charter*: Closing the Divide to Advance Equality' (2011) 30 *Windsor Review of Legal and Social Issues* 37.

[21] *Nova Scotia (Workers' Compensation Board)* v. *Martin* [2003] 2 SCR 504.

[22] *Eldridge* v. *British Columbia (Attorney General)* [1997] 3 SCR 624.

right to read.[23] Jodhan argued that there was a system-wide failure by government to ensure that its websites provided information in a way that was accessible to persons with print disabilities. To illustrate the systemic nature of the problem, Jodhan provided five examples:

1. Jodhan explained that in September 2004 she experienced difficulty applying for employment at www.jobs.gc.ca and had to complete the application with assistance by phone. This was followed by failure to access information on the site between March and June 2007.

2. She was unable to create an online profile at www.jobs.gc.ca because pop-up windows, which blind users cannot navigate, kept popping up. She had to complete her online profile on the website with sighted assistance.

3. She alleged significant accessibility issues when trying to access information on Statistics Canada and Service Canada websites between March and June 2007, since the information was only available in PDF format, which is not accessible to screen reader technology.

4. The 2006 online Census return was only available to people with print disabilities by way of expensive adaptive technologies, and not by the cheaper adaptive technology used by Jodhan. Furthermore, Jodhan alleged that the form of the Census did not meet the World Wide Web Consortium (W3C) standards for accessibility.

5. Jodhan explained that she experienced difficulty accessing www.servicecanada.gc.ca in June 2007 to obtain information on the Canada Pension Plan and employment programmes.[24]

Jodhan pleaded that the above five barriers to digital equality constituted a breach of article 15 of the *Charter*. As the below analysis illustrates, Jodhan's right to digital equality was unanimously recognised by all judges who heard the case; in the Federal Court by Justice Kelen and on appeal by Justices Nadon, Sharlow and Dawson.[25]

Was there a Law that Resulted in Digital Reading Disablement?

Jodhan argued that the federal *Financial Administration Act* supported practices which violated her article 15 *Charter* right.[26] Section 7 of the *Financial*

---

[23] *Jodhan v. Attorney General of Canada* [2011] 2 FCR 355; *Canada (Attorney General) v. Jodhan* [2012] FCA 161.
[24] *Canada (Attorney General) v. Jodhan* [2012] FCA 161, [9]–[14].
[25] *Jodhan v. Attorney General of Canada* [2011] 2 FCR 355; *Canada (Attorney General) v. Jodhan* [2012] FCA 161.
[26] RSC 1985, c F-11.

Administration Act empowered the Treasury Board to develop the Communications Policy of the Government of Canada. The Communications Policy was used to regulate all communications made by the federal public service. The Communications Policy recognised that information must be made available in multiple online formats to ensure equal access. Jodhan argued that the Communications Policy was not being implemented in a way that protected the equality rights of persons with print disabilities.

The Canadian Attorney-General argued that the Communications Policy could not be used to support the first limb of the article 15 test with respect to digital equality. The Attorney-General argued that effective access to government information and services, not online access, is the true benefit of the law. Access could be obtained through alternative means, such as attending government agencies or ringing call centres. The Attorney-General argued that providing substantially inferior levels of digital access and limiting or denying people the benefit of the internet was not inconsistent with providing meaningful access.

Justice Nadon rejected the Attorney-General's position that providing substantially inferior and fundamentally different services to people with disabilities was offering them services on an equal basis as people without disabilities:

> I have great difficulty understanding how the benefit of access to government information and services can be truly enjoyed or exercised, in the present day, without access to that information by way of the Internet. In other words, depriving a person of access to government information and services by the use of one of the most important, if not the most important, tool ever designed for accessing not only government information and services, but all types of information and services, cannot constitute, in my respectful opinion, the provision of effective access to that information and those services.[27]

Justice Nadon continued:

> The thrust of the Attorney General's submission is that effective access to government information and services is attained when the information is accessed by a person irrespective of the means used to obtain the information. I understand the Attorney General to be saying that as long as the sought-after information and services are obtained, irrespective of the time lag and inconvenience encountered, there has been effective access and thus the same benefit has been received. In other words, if one person can access information online within a matter of minutes and another person can access the same information by traveling to a government office, waiting for his or

[27] *Canada (Attorney General)* v. *Jodhan* [2012] FCA 161, [129].

her turn and then meeting with a government employee to obtain the same information, there has been effective access in both cases and thus both persons have received the same benefit of the law. I cannot agree with the Attorney General's position. In my view, one of the above two persons has not received the same benefit. They have not been treated equally.[28]

Accordingly, where the government utilises the internet to provide services, then those online platforms must be accessible for persons with print disabilities.

Did the Denial of Digital Equality Create a Disadvantage by Perpetuating Prejudice or Stereotyping?

All justices in the *Jodhan* litigation agreed that the operation of government websites that were not accessible for persons with disabilities caused disadvantage.[29] To avoid this disadvantage requires positive conduct from the state.[30] Once it is determined what steps could be taken to ensure substantive equality, the inquiry then turns to considering justifications as to why such measures were not adopted. The duty to remove barriers to equality is not absolute. The duty requires the state to accommodate people with disabilities within 'reasonable limits'.[31]

The Attorney-General did not seek to defend the failure to provide for digital equality. Rather than attempting to defend the existence of barriers to digital equality, the Attorney-General argued that alternative means were available so online access was acceptable. The position of the Attorney-General was rejected by all justices in this case, with Justice Nadon concluding:

As I indicated earlier, I have difficulty with the proposition that equal access to government information and services can be attained without access to online information and services. In the present matter, no evidence has been offered by the Attorney General to the effect that there is any impediment to moving forward and enabling the visually impaired to readily access government information and services online. Consequently, I also have difficulty with the proposition that alternative formats and channels meet the goal of substantive equal treatment. Where not possible for technological, cost, or other reasons, I readily accept that the visually impaired would have to access government information and services through alternative formats or channels. Thus, to the extent possible, the benefit of law offered to the public must be as inclusive as possible.[32]

[28] Ibid., [130]. [29] Ibid., [61]. [30] Ibid. [31] Ibid., [151]. [32] Ibid., [151].

Accordingly, article 15 of the *Charter* entitles all Canadians to full access to government information and online services unless it would create an undue hardship to provide this level of access. Persons with print disabilities have the right to equal digital access. Providing alternative inferior means of access infringes the equality guarantee in the *Charter*.

Outcome and Impact of the Jodhan Case

The immediate impact of the *Jodhan* case is limited to the parties named in the litigation as defendants. The Treasury Board supervises 106 departments under the Communications Policy. Jodhan only filed suit against the Public Service Commission of Canada, Statistics Canada and the Attorney-General of Canada. Accordingly, the *Jodhan* judgment only bound the named parties and not all 106 departments bound by the Communications Policy. This judgment, however, does require the Treasury Board to enforce its Communications Policy over the 106 departments within a reasonable period of time. A reasonable period of time was held to be within fifteen months of the final orders.[33]

While the *Jodhan* case was limited to the named defendants, the impact of this case has significant implications for all digital communications that are connected with the implementation of Canadian laws. Any website that is involved with the implementation of a Canadian law must now ensure that persons with print disabilities are accommodated within the ambit of reasonable limits. The failure to take proactive action to ensure inclusive communications amounts to a breach of article 15 of the *Charter*.

The *Jodhan* case enshrines a right to inclusive digital communication that extends a right to read certain E-Books. Where an E-Book library is utilised to give effect to a policy under a legislative scheme, then the state has a duty to take reasonable steps to ensure that the digital format is accessible to persons with print disabilities. The breadth of this equality right can be illustrated by recalling that public libraries and educational institutions, from kindergarten to university, are all now utilising E-Books. Public libraries, kindergarten, schools and universities are all regulated by legislative regimes.[34] As the first limb of article 15 applies to digital communications connected with furthering

---

[33] Ibid., [185].

[34] For examples of legislation regulating public libraries see: *Libraries Act*, RSA 2000, c L-11; *Public Libraries Act*, RSQ 1964, c B-3; *Public Libraries Act*, RSN 1998, c P-40; *Public Libraries Act*, SPEI 1998, c 46. For examples of legislation regulating K-12 see: *Education Act*, SS 1995, c E-0.2; *Schools Act*, RSA 2000, c S-3. For examples of legislation regulating universities see: *Higher Education Foundation Act*, RSNB 2011, c 169; *University Foundations Act*, SO 1992, c 22; *University of Saskatchewan Act*, SS 1995, c U-6.1.

legislative purposes, arguably the equality guarantee applies to all libraries that are connected with the furtherance of a legislative regime, whether it be providing Canadians with a right to read books for pleasure, education or employment.

Applying the right to digital equality to E-Books, E-Libraries and E-Readers is potentially more problematic. All of the impugned websites in the *Jodhan* litigation, as far as can be determined, owned the copyright in the information that was not presented in an inclusive manner. They presumably did not own the copyright in the software used to display the information, but it appears the software could have been designed in an inclusive manner and that the ultimate cause of the barrier was the state. Educators and public libraries generally do not own the copyright in E-Books or E-Libraries. What, then, do public libraries and educators need to do to discharge their *Charter* article 15 obligations?

Article 15 requires duty holders to take proactive action to understand the barrier to equality and act within reasonable limits to remove such barriers. At a minimum, this requires public libraries and educators to contact E-Libraries to offer their E-Publications in formats that are accessible to the print-disabled. If rights-holders refuse to provide E-Books in accessible formats, then public libraries and educators, subject to contractual terms, are not in a position to force them to provide equal access. Public libraries and educators, however, do have a duty to explore options to determine if E-Libraries exist that do provide access and to consider whether contracting with the accessible E-Library is viable.

The significance of article 15 litigation, culminating in the *Jodhan* case, cannot be overemphasised. Article 15 requires duty holders to disrupt practices that create barriers to digital reading equality for persons with print disabilities. Where settled practices of digital exclusion are unsettled, article 15 provides an avenue for persons with print disabilities to seek redress and demand an equal right to read.

SECTION II CANADIAN ANTI-DISCRIMINATION LAWS LEADING THE WAY TO EQUALITY

This section will analyse how Canadian anti-discrimination laws protect the right to read of persons with print disabilities. While Canadian anti-discrimination laws emerged from similar legal roots as the Australian, United Kingdom and United States laws,[35] over the last few decades the Canadian approach has diverged markedly in how it constructs duties not to discriminate.

---

[35] Rosemary C Hunter and Elaine W Shoben, 'Disparate Impact Discrimination: American Oddity or Internationally Accepted Concept?' (1998) 19 *Berkeley Journal of Employment and Labor Law* 108, 119–20.

This section is divided into two parts. First, this section will analyse how Canadian anti-discrimination laws do not adopt a bifurcated approach to defining discrimination, but instead utilise a unified definition. Secondly, this section will analyse how anti-discrimination laws in Australia, the United Kingdom and the United States largely rely on negative duties not to discriminate. Canadian anti-discrimination laws, in contrast, require positive action from duty holders. Canadian laws already required extensive positive conduct from duty holders. Arguably, recent *Charter* article 15 judgments will extend what positive conduct is required from duty holders. This section concludes that the Canadian approach to constructing equality duties has greater capacity to reduce digital disablement than the equivalent regimes in Australia, the United Kingdom and the United States.

How Canadian Anti-Discrimination Laws Construct Discrimination

Prior to the 1999 Canadian Supreme Court judgment in *British Columbia (Public Service Employee Relations Commission)* v. *BCGSEU (Fire Fighters' Case)*, discrimination was constructed through a bifurcated approach similar to that adopted currently in Australia, the United Kingdom and the United States.[36] In the *Fire Fighters' Case* Justice McLachlan questioned whether constructing discrimination through two separate approaches was helpful. Her Honour acknowledged that the adverse impact doctrine advanced how law constructed discrimination:

> The conventional analysis was helpful in the interpretation of the early human rights statutes, and indeed represented a significant step forward in that it recognized for the first time the harm of adverse effect discrimination.[37]

Justice McLachlan noted that the law had advanced so that constructions of discrimination recognised both disparate impact and disparate treatment. The bifurcated approach, according to Justice McLachlan, had served its purpose and was now hindering the fight against discrimination in society.

One of the greatest limitations with the bifurcated approach to constructing discrimination is the need to categorise the discriminatory act within one of two separate tests. The requirement to neatly categorise the act of discrimination within one of these tests has evolved into an unnecessary legal barrier to identifying whether or not unequal treatment has occurred. Justice McLachlan provided an example in the *Fire Fighters' Case* to illustrate the

---

[36] *Fire Fighters' Case* [1999] 3 SCR 3.   [37] Ibid., 17.

limitations with the bifurcated approach.[38] Her Honour noted that a rule requiring all workers to attend work on Fridays could be cast as an intentional act to injure workers who were unable to work on Fridays due to their religious beliefs. The same act could also be framed as a neutral rule that had an indirect discriminatory impact on a few workers who had certain religious beliefs. Requiring a plaintiff to construct the discrimination they have experienced within a direct discrimination/disparate treatment or indirect/disparate impact created an unnecessary legal hurdle to combatting the underlying inequality.

Rejecting the bifurcated approach, Justice McLachlan introduced a three-step unified test to determine if unlawful discrimination has occurred. This unified test asks:

(1) whether the duty holder adopted the challenged standard for a purpose rationally connected to the performance of the job;
(2) whether the duty holder chose the standard in an honest and good faith belief that it was required to fulfill the work related purpose; and
(3) whether the standard is reasonably necessary in that it would be impossible to accommodate an individual with a protected attributed without imposing undue hardship upon the duty holder.[39]

The three-step unified test is now the settled test to determine if discrimination has occurred in Canada.[40]

The three-step unified test to defining discrimination substantially transforms how discrimination is constructed.[41] The Canadian Supreme Court explains that it:

(1) avoids the problematic distinction between direct and adverse effect discrimination;
(2) requires employers to accommodate as much as reasonably possible the characteristics of individual employees when setting the workplace standard; and
(3) takes a strict approach to exemptions from the duty not to discriminate, while permitting exemptions where they are reasonably necessary to the achievement of legitimate work-related objectives.[42]

---

[38] Ibid., 18.   [39] Ibid., 32–3.
[40] Sandra Fredman, *Discrimination Law* (2011) Oxford University Press, 212–14.
[41] Colleen Sheppard, 'Of Forest Fires and Systemic Discrimination: A Review of *British Columbia (Public Service Employee Relations Commission) v. B.C.G.S.E.U.*' (2001) 46 *McGill Law Journal* 533.
[42] *Fire Fighters' Case*, 30–1.

Whereas the anti-discrimination laws in Australia, the United Kingdom and the United States prohibit duty holders from adopting facially neutral practices that have a discriminatory impact, the Canadian approach requires duty holders to actively seek out and reduce the barriers to equality in practices that disable persons with impairments.[43] The imposition of positive duties to reasonably accommodate people with disabilities in Canada arguably improves the capacity to combat digital disablement.

The Duty to Accommodate Persons with Disabilities under the Canadian Three-Step Unified Test

This part will now analyse in detail how the duty to accommodate persons with disabilities operates in Canada. Originally, Canadian jurisprudence drew from the development of the disparate impact doctrine in the United States.[44] Similar to Australia, the United Kingdom and the United States, the failure to accommodate in Canada is only actionable where discrimination has arisen within one of a range of prescribed relationships.[45] As analysed in Chapter 7 of this monograph, the prescribed relationships that attract anti-discrimination duties in Canada are similar to those found in the anti-discrimination regimes in Australia, the United Kingdom and the United States. For example, people offering goods, services, facilities or accommodations,[46] and employers,[47] attract anti-discrimination duties in Canada. What sets Canada apart from other jurisdictions is what is required from duty holders within these

---

[43] Marilyn Ginsburg and Catherine Bickley, 'Accommodating the Disabled: Emerging Issues under Human Rights Legislation' (1992) 1 *Canadian Labour Law Journal* 72.

[44] Ravi Malhotra, 'The Legal Genealogy of the Duty to Accommodate American and Canadian Workers with Disabilities: A Comparative Perspective' (2007) 23 *Washington University Journal of Law and Policy* 1, 5.

[45] *Moore* v. *Canada Post Corp.* [2007] CHRD No. 31.

[46] *Canadian Human Rights Act*, RSC 1985, c H-6, s 5; *Human Rights Act*, RSA 2000, c A-25.5, s 4; *Human Rights Code*, RSBC 1996, c 210, ss 8, 9 and 10; *The Human Rights Code*, SM 1987–88, c 45, s 13; *Human Rights Act 2011* (New Brunswick) s 6; *Human Rights Act*, SN 2010, c H-13.1, ss 12 and 13; *Human Rights Act*, SNWT 2002, c 18, s 11; *Human Rights Act*, RSNS 1989, c 214, s 5(1)(a); *Human Rights Act*, SNu 2003, c 12, s 12; *Human Rights Code*, RSO 1990, c H-19, s 1; *Human Rights Act*, RSPEI 1988, c H-12, s 2(1)(b); *Charter of Human Rights and Freedoms*, Cqlr, c C-12, s 12; *The Saskatchewan Human Rights Code*, SS 1979, c S-24.1, s 12; *Human Rights Act*, RSY 2002, c 116, s 9(a).

[47] *Canadian Human Rights Act*, RSC 1985, c H-6, s 7; *Human Rights Act*, RSA 2000, c A-25.5, s 8; *Human Rights Code*, RSBC 1996, c 210, s 13; *The Human Rights Code*, SM 1987–88, c 45, s 14; *Human Rights Act 2011* (New Brunswick) s 4; *Human Rights Act*, SN 2010, c H-13.1; *Human Rights Act*, SNWT 2002, c 18, s 7; *Human Rights Act*, RSNS 1989, c 214, s 5(1)(d); *Human Rights Act*, SNu 2003, c 12, s 9; *Human Rights Code*, RSO 1990, c H-19, s 5; *Human Rights Act*, RSPEI 1988, c H-12, s 6; *Charter of Human Rights and Freedoms*, Cqlr, c C-12, s 16; *The Saskatchewan Human Rights Code*, SS 1979, c S-24.1, ss 9 and 16; *Human Rights Act*, RSY 2002, c 116, s 9(b).

prescribed relationships. When compared to Australia, the United Kingdom and the United States, the Canadian duty is far more generous towards persons with disabilities.[48]

In Australia, the United Kingdom and the United States, the duty to make accommodations or adjustments for persons with disabilities arises after the system is created and often when a person with a disability has requested the change. The duty in Canada unsettles the processes of disablement. The Canadian approach disrupts the systems and practices that lead to the creation of barriers in the first place. Canadian anti-discrimination laws require duty holders to seek out and remove barriers to inclusion during the design and implementation stages of product and systems development. As illustrated in the Canadian Supreme Court judgment in *Council of Canadians with Disabilities* v. *Via Rail Canada Inc.*,[49] discrimination law in Canada seeks to get in at the development stage and requires duty holders to avoid creating barriers that disable people with impairments.[50]

The factual basis that resulted in the Canadian Supreme Court judgment in *Council of Canadians with Disabilities* v. *VIA Rail Canada Inc.* started in 2000.[51] In 2000, the Canadian national passenger provider, VIA, was provided with funding to purchase new passenger cars for its fleet. This would increase the number of rail passenger cars across the national network by a third. The Canadian government stated that the new passenger cars, unlike the then aging fleet, would be accessible for persons with disabilities.[52] VIA decided to purchase Renaissance Rail Cars on the basis that they were significantly cheaper than the alternative models. As the Renaissance Rail Cars were not accessible for persons with various mobility impairments, they were not able to be purchased by rail providers in a number of jurisdictions. VIA was aware of the inaccessible nature of the Renaissance Rail Cars, both by information available to the public and by submissions by disability groups in 2000. VIA determined to press ahead with the purchase regardless of the disabling barriers and fought disability rights advocates all the way to the Canadian Supreme Court, culminating in a 2007 judgment.

---

[48] Kay Wheat, 'Mental Health and Stigma: How Best to Protect Workers from Discrimination' (2013) 34 *Windsor Review of Legal and Social Issues* 1, 19. The article compares Canada to the United Kingdom and the United States.

[49] [2007] 1 *SCR* 650.   [50] Ibid.

[51] David Baker and Sarah Godwin, 'All Aboard! The Supreme Court of Canada Confirms that Canadians with Disabilities Have Substantive Equality Rights' (2008) 71 *Saskatchewan Law Review* 39, 48–50.

[52] See Affidavit of Laurie Beachall (3 August 2004) at [8] from proceedings in *VIA Rail Canada Inc.* v. *National Transportation Agency* [2005] 4 *FCR* 473 cited in Baker and Godwin, 'All Aboard!', 48.

The Canadian Supreme Court held that VIA was discriminating both by purchasing passenger cars which denied persons with mobility impairments access, and for failing to alter those cars to render them accessible. The Canadian Supreme Court held that persons with mobility impairments have the human right to use wheelchairs as a mobility aid on public transport.[53] VIA argued that persons with mobility impairments were able to find alternative means to move between the destinations served by the rail network. The Canadian Supreme Court strongly rejected this argument: '[i]t is the rail service itself that is to be accessible, not alternative transportation services such as taxis. Persons with disabilities are entitled to ride with other passengers, not consigned to separate facilities'.[54] The Canadian Supreme Court rightly rejected the notion that segregated or separate, inferior and, in many cases, far more expensive and slower, services are not equal services.

The concept of equality adopted by the Canadian Supreme Court was one of equal access and not one of segregation. The duty to avoid barriers to inclusion arose at the design stage, and the Court held there was no requirement to wait for the barrier to be in existence before anti-discrimination laws applied.[55] The Canadian Supreme Court explained: 'while human rights principles include an acknowledgement that not every barrier can be eliminated, they also include a duty to prevent new ones, or at least, not knowingly to perpetuate old ones where preventable'.[56] The duty of reasonable accommodation required VIA to consider removing barriers to equality throughout the process and not just once the passenger cars had been purchased and were in use.

Similar to the duty to make reasonable accommodations and adjustments in Australia, the United Kingdom and the United States, the duty in Canada is limited to what is reasonable. The Canadian Supreme Court in *Eldridge v. British Columbia (Attorney General)* has recognised that the duty to take 'positive action' is subject to the principle of reasonable accommodation.[57]

The Canadian duty to accommodate requires a duty holder to do everything required to remove barriers to equality to the point of undue hardship. In *Council of Canadians with Disabilities* v. *VIA Rail Canada Inc.*, the Canadian Supreme Court held that undue hardship recognises that there are situations where the hardship in accommodating someone's disability means the accommodation is not reasonable, 'but unless that hardship imposes an undue or unreasonable burden, it yields to the need to

[53] *Council of Canadians with Disabilities* v. *VIA Rail Canada Inc.* [2007] 1 SCR 650, [162].
[54] Ibid., [175].   [55] Ibid., [118].   [56] Ibid., [186].
[57] *Eldridge* v. *British Columbia (Attorney General)* [1997] 3 SCR 624, [79].

accommodate'.[58] The fact that the duty in Canada is positive substantially transforms how the undue hardship assessment operates.

As the duty in Canada is constructed as a positive duty, the duty is enlivened at the time of establishing the disabling system. The positive duty of reasonable accommodation should not factor in costs that the duty holder has created by breaching their human rights obligations at the design stage.

If duty holders could breach their human rights obligations and avoid the duty to render the system accessible because it was expensive, then this would encourage duty holders to breach their human rights obligations in ways that were prohibitively expensive to remedy. The Canadian Supreme Court refused to permit VIA to argue that they should be free from removing expensive barriers to equal access that they adopted rather than embracing inclusive design from the outset:

> Neither the Rail Code, the Canada Transportation Act, nor any human rights principle recognizes that a unique opportunity to acquire inaccessible cars at a comparatively low purchase price may be a legitimate justification for sustained inaccessibility. In the expansion and upgrading of its fleet, VIA was not entitled to ignore its legal obligations and public commitments. The situation it now finds itself in was preventable in a myriad of ways.[59]

Whether or not the costs on VIA were undue could not be determined by the Court. The Court noted VIA had failed to adduce sufficient evidence for them to raise undue hardship, and accordingly this defence was not available to them.[60]

The *Council of Canadians with Disabilities* v. *VIA Rail Canada Inc.* judgment has substantial implications for the removal of barriers in Canada. If a duty holder purchased access to an E-Book or E-Library that they knew was not accessible, then this would deny persons with a print disability the capacity to read on an equal basis with others. Arguably, the situation now is that duty holders, such as educational institutions and libraries, have a duty not to purchase access to E-Libraries that do not enable persons with print disabilities acceptably high levels of access.

CONCLUSION

The expansive approach to rights recognition in Canadian law distinguishes Canada from other jurisdictions. The combination of the *Charter's* recognition of the right to read, the application of positive duties under the *Charter*

---

[58] *Council of Canadians with Disabilities* v. *VIA Rail Canada Inc.* [2007] 1 SCR 650, [120]–[122].
[59] Ibid., [164].   [60] Ibid., [226].

and anti-discrimination laws means that Canadian law provides persons with disabilities substantially more protection than the equivalent regimes in Australia, the United Kingdom and the United States. It is often expensive or impossible to retrofit disabling systems once they are created. Canadian laws do not wait for disabling barriers to be created before enlivening equality duties. Canadian *Charter* and anti-discrimination duties require duty holders to be proactive in considering disability access at the design stage. At the design stage, it is much easier to reduce or avoid creating disabling barriers in the first place.

The right to read arguably has robust protection under Canadian *Charter* jurisprudence. The *Jodhan* litigation provides strong support for the right to read and the right to be free from digital disablement. The interaction between the *Charter* and anti-discrimination laws in Canada means that anti-discrimination laws must be read in a way that complies with the *Charter*. Article 15 of the *Charter* has been read widely to recognise a right to read online material. The wide reading of *Charter* article 15 reflects the expansive approach to reasonable accommodations under Canadian anti-discrimination laws. The Canadian Supreme Court has read the right to reasonable accommodations widely and requires inclusive design to be considered throughout the design and manufacture of systems. This broad approach to reasonable accommodation and equality has been continued by the Canadian Supreme Court.[61]

The broad approach to equality by Canadian law will advance the rights of persons with disabilities, but it will not ensure equality. While positive duties will help advance equality, there is no free-standing general duty to make reasonable accommodations in Canada.[62] As it stands, no duty to accommodate is imposed over designers and manufacturers who are not bound by existing duties. This weakens the transformational impact of the Canadian equality regime.

Despite this limitation, however, the operation of positive duties within the prescribed relationships will help reduce digital disablement. Libraries that provide services as a government entity or within education spheres attract a positive duty to reduce the creation of barriers to persons with disabilities. This duty requires libraries to consider how their E-Library platforms can be rendered accessible to persons with print disabilities. This will likely encourage libraries to pressure E-Library providers to enable disability access, and should also motivate libraries to seek out E-Libraries that are already fully

[61] Gwen Brodsky, '*Moore* v. *British Columbia*: Supreme Court of Canada Keeps the Duty to Accommodate Strong' (2013) 10 *Journal of Law and Equality* 85.

[62] *Moore* v. *Canada Post Corp.* [2007] CHRD No. 31.

accessible. Arguably, the combination of the recognition of the right to read under the *Charter* and the operation of the existence of this greater protection enhances the capacity of persons with disabilities to exercise their right to read. The broad protections in Canadian law represent one front in the war against inequalities in society. By itself it will not achieve equality,[63] but it is a strong step in the right direction.

[63] Ravi Malhotra, 'A Tale of Marginalization: Comparing Workers with Disabilities in Canada and the United States' (2009) 22 *Journal of Law and Social Policy* 79.

11

United States Regulatory Interventions Targeting
Disability-Inclusive Digital Environments

INTRODUCTION

This chapter analyses federal regulatory approaches in the United States which promote disability-inclusive digital environments.[1] The positive duties in the frameworks analysed in this chapter differ from the positive duties in Canada and the United Kingdom analysed in Chapters 9 and 10 of this monograph. The positive duties in Canada and the United Kingdom were not disability-specific and did not provide specifics on what is required to render digital spaces accessible to persons with disabilities. The three frameworks analysed in this chapter create duties on a wide range of parties to take specific steps to create a more disability-inclusive digital environment.

The first regulatory framework analysed is a disability standard created under the authority of existing anti-discrimination laws. The other two frameworks are novel and illustrate the imagination of United States disability advocates and lawmakers. The second section of this chapter will introduce and analyse the creation of a book repository where K-12 publishers are contractually required to provide copies of instructional materials in accessible formats. Building out of laws regulating disability education, the National Instructional Materials Access Center represents an exciting use of purchasing power to motivate publishers to help reduce the impact of the book famine on people with print disabilities. Finally, this chapter analyses a model that seeks to remove barriers to ability equality at the design and manufacturing stages of products. The *Twenty-First Century Communications and Video Accessibility Act of 2010* (*21st CVAA*) imposes duties upstream on designers and

---

[1] In addition to federal statutes, some state jurisdictions contain laws specifically targeting this area. See, e.g., Minnesota Statutes, *Accessible Electronic Information Services* (2011) ss 237.52, 248.061, 248.062.

manufacturers in order to help create a more inclusive digital environment.[2] Equal access to digital spaces is vital in order to enable persons with disabilities to socialise, transact business, find jobs and obtain an education.[3] The measures analysed in this chapter will help provide such access.

SECTION I INFORMATION COMMUNICATION TECHNOLOGY STANDARDS AND RULES

The *Rehabilitation Act of 1973* requires federal agencies to 'develop, procure, maintain, or use' information communication technologies in a way that ensures federal employees, and members of the public with disabilities, have comparable access to and use of such information and data relative to other federal employees, unless doing so would impose an undue burden.[4] Following the introduction of s 508 in 1986, *508 Standards* were promulgated. Since the original *508 Standards* there have been significant technological developments, and in 2006 the United States Access Board established the Telecommunications and Electronic and Information Technology Advisory Committee to review the *508 Standards* and make recommendations. This process has resulted in the release of proposed rules in 2015 – the version that is analysed in this section.[5] The Office of Information and Regulatory Affairs has announced that it is planned that the final rules will be released in October 2016, after this monograph has been submitted for publication.[6]

Who Is Bound by the 508 Standards? *Federal Agencies and Federal Contractors*

The *508 Standards* apply to information communication technology that is 'procured, developed, maintained, or used by' federal agencies.[7] Similar to most governments across the world, federal agencies regularly outsource state

---

[2] *21st CVAA*, Pub L No. 111–260, 124 Stat 2751 (codified in scattered sections of 47 USC).

[3] Brad Areheart and Michael Ashley Stein, 'Integrating the Internet' (2015) 83 *George Washington Law Review* 449.

[4] 29 USC § 794d.

[5] The Information and Communication Technology (ICT) Standards and Guidelines' proposed rule can be found at: <www.access-board.gov/guidelines-and-standards/communications-and-it/about-the-ict-refresh/proposed-rule/single-file-version> (accessed 18 November 2016).

[6] Office of Information and Regulatory Affairs, *Information and Communication Technology Standards and Guidelines* (2015) <www.reginfo.gov/public/do/eAgendaViewRule?pubId=201510&RIN=3014-AA37> (accessed 18 November 2016).

[7] *508 Standards*, E201.1.

activities to contractors.[8] Where a contractor acquires or develops information communication technologies as part of the government contract, they must comply with the 508 *Standards*. However, where information communication technologies are 'acquired by a contractor incidental to a contract', the contractor is not required to conform to the 508 *Standards*.[9] The 508 *Standards* have arguably missed an opportunity to further enshrine disability-inclusive information communication, whether or not the used technology was acquired specifically or incidentally for the government work.

Contract workers are more vulnerable to exploitation.[10] Contract workers can operate their own corporate entity or work for another corporate entity that contracts with the government. The corporate veil means that contract workers have either reduced or no legal rights against the host employer.[11] Contractors already attract anti-discrimination obligations for other attributes. For example, on 21 July 2014, President Barack Obama signed an executive order that prohibits the federal government and contractors from employment discrimination on the basis of gender identity.[12] Arguably, the 508 *Standards* should require federal contractors to comply with disability standards in all their information communication technology activities.

What Do the 508 Standards Require?

The 508 *Standards* apply to information communication technologies. Information communication technologies are used to consume digital content. If they are not accessible to persons with disabilities then this will adversely impact on their employment prospects and interaction with state services. Reflecting the importance of disability-inclusive information communication technologies, the 508 *Standards* require all regulated parties to

---

[8] Yu-Che Chen and James Perry, 'Outsourcing for E-Government: Managing for Success' (2003) 26(4) *Public Performance and Management Review* 404; H Brinton Milward and Keith Provan, 'Managing the Hollow State Collaboration and Contracting' (2003) 5(1) *Public Management Review* 1.

[9] 508 *Standards*, E202.3.

[10] Katherine Van Wezel Stone et al., 'Employment Protection for Atypical Workers: Proceedings of the 2006 Annual Meeting, Association of American Law Schools Section on Labor Relations and Employment Law' (2006) 10 *Employee Rights and Employment Policy Journal* 233, 234.

[11] Edwina Dunn, 'James Hardie: No Soul to Be Damned and No Body to Be Kicked' (2005) 27(2) *Sydney Law Review* 339; Susan Engel and Brian Martin, 'Union Carbide and James Hardie: Lessons in Politics and Power' (2006) 20(4) *Global Society* 475.

[12] *Executive Order No. 13,672*, 79 Fed. Reg. 42 971, §§ 1–2 (23 July 2014). See for discussion note, 'Exec. Order No. 13,672. Executive Order Prohibits Federal Government and Contractor Employment Discrimination on the Basis of Sexual Orientation or Gender Identity' (2015) 128(4) *Harvard Law Review* 1304.

'ensure that all functionality of . . . [information communication technology] is accessible to and usable by individuals with disabilities, either directly or by supporting the use of assistive technology'.[13]

> When agencies procure, develop, maintain or use ICT they shall identify the business needs of users with disabilities affecting vision, hearing, color perception, speech, dexterity, strength, or reach to determine:
> (a) How users with disabilities will perform the functions supported by the ICT; and
> (b) How the ICT will be installed, configured, and maintained to support users with disabilities.[14]

There are situations where complying with the *508 Standards'* inclusive requirement may impose an undue burden on or may require a fundamental alteration in the nature of the information communication technology.[15] In such circumstances, persons with disabilities must be provided access to the information and data by alternative means. If disability-inclusive information communication technologies cannot be provided for, for whatever reason, then the regulated party must document in writing:

> (a) the non-availability of conforming ICT, including a description of market research performed and which provisions cannot be met, and
> (b) the basis for determining that the ICT to be procured best meets the requirements in the *508 Standards* consistent with the agency's business needs.[16]

The *508 Standards* motivate the federal government, contractors and those seeking to sell products to such parties to embrace universal design. Previous *508 Standards* and other regulatory standards have had a positive impact on creating disability-inclusive products.[17] The existence of inclusive design has had a positive impact on federal employees with disabilities.[18]

One limitation is that procurement officers in federal agencies, as well as contractors, are not always able to determine easily the extent to which information communication technologies are accessible for persons with disabilities. Designers and suppliers of information communication technologies are not obliged to research or provide information on the extent to which

---

[13] *508 Standards*, E203.1.   [14] Ibid., E203.2.   [15] Ibid., E202.5.3.   [16] Ibid., E202.6.1.
[17] Yeliz Yesilada et al., 'Understanding Web Accessibility and its Drivers' (paper presented at Proceedings of the International Cross-Disciplinary Conference on Web Accessibility, New York, 16–17 April 2012).
[18] Peter Blanck et al., 'Employment of People with Disabilities: Twenty-Five Years Back and Ahead' (2007) 25 *Law and Inequality* 323, 333.

their products comply with inclusive design principles. Arguably, requiring designers and suppliers to provide such information would assist procurement officers to understand the extent to which the products they are ordering include or disable persons with print disabilities. While this may not guarantee disability-inclusive federal spaces, it would enhance the capacity of procurement officers to understand the implications of their decisions on persons with disabilities. Considering the fact that product warnings and product information statements have become the norm, whether it be in relation to the health content of food,[19] the risks from substances consumed[20] or products used in the workplace, requiring designers and suppliers of information communication technologies aimed to be sold to agencies and contractors to provide disability-inclusive information is arguably a reasonable requirement.

SECTION II THE RIGHT TO EDUCATION BEING USED TO PROMOTE THE RIGHT TO READ EDUCATIONAL MATERIALS: THE *INDIVIDUALS WITH DISABILITIES EDUCATION ACT* AND THE NATIONAL INSTRUCTIONAL MATERIALS ACCESS CENTER

United States laws have a long history of recognising the right to education.[21] During the nineteenth century the United States was a world leader in providing free public education to some of its citizens.[22] The desire to educate young Americans, however, did not extend to many minority groups, including persons with disabilities.[23] As recently as the 1970s, students were prohibited from public schools because they were deaf, blind, emotionally disturbed or mentally handicapped.[24]

---

[19] Julie Caswell and Eliza M Mojduszka, 'Using Informational Labeling to Influence the Market for Quality in Food Products' (1996) 78(5) *American Journal of Agricultural Economics* 1248.

[20] Karen Graves, 'An Evaluation of the Alcohol Warning Label: A Comparison of the United States and Ontario, Canada in 1990 and 1991' (1993) 21 *Journal of Public Policy and Marketing* 1, 19; Janett D Pateiro, 'Pharmaceutical Companies Engaging in Direct-to-Consumer Advertising Must Provide Consumers with Adequate Warnings' (1999) 25 *American Journal of Law and Medicine* 4, 574.

[21] Sonja Ralston Elder, 'Enforcing Public Educational Rights via a Private Right of Action' (2009) 1 *Duke Forum for Law and Social Change* 137, 138.

[22] William J Reese, *America's Public Schools: From the Common School to 'No Child Left Behind'* (2005) John Hopkins University Press, 45.

[23] US Department of Education, *Thirty-Five Years of Progress in Educating Children with Disabilities through IDEA* (2010) 3.

[24] Megan McGovern, 'Least Restrictive Environment: Fulfilling the Promises of IDEA' (2015) 21 *Widener Law Review* 117, 118.

Not all school districts excluded children with disabilities from education. Where children with print disabilities were educated, it was recognised at a very early time that access to books was essential to enable students to exercise their right to education. In the USA, K-12 students' right to obtain textbooks in alternative formats was first enshrined in 1879. Educational institutions were required to provide students with Braille, raised-letter or large-print books.[25] The first systematic off-campus production of alternative textbooks started in 1948, when the non-profit association Recording for the Blind was established.[26]

The National Instructional Materials Access Center Transforming the Provision of K-12 Books to the Print-Disabled: The IDEA *in 2004*

One of the most significant developments in the provision of textbooks to students with print disabilities occurred with the reauthorisation of the omnibus disability education statute, the *Individuals with Disabilities Education Act 2004 (IDEA)*.[27] As will be analysed below, the 2004 reforms introduced a legislative regime which created a repository of educational materials which can be provided to students with print disabilities as required. Earlier versions of this legislation did not contain this scheme.[28] The *IDEA* operates alongside existing anti-discrimination duties.[29] Accordingly, compliance with the National Instructional Materials Access Center (NIMAC) scheme will not necessarily discharge a regulated party's duties under existing anti-discrimination duties.

NIMAC was established by *IDEA* s 674(e)(1), which provided that the secretary will establish and support the American Printing House for the Blind to develop and operate the National Instructional Materials Access Center. NIMAC is the national repository for educational materials uploaded in the National Instructional Access Standard (NIMAS) format.[30] As analysed

---

[25] See for a discussion of the *Act to Promote the Education of the Blind*: Margret A Winzer, *The History of Special Education: From Isolation to Integration* (1993) Gallaudet University Press, 9.

[26] This institution subsequently changed its name to include other print disabilities, becoming Recording for the Blind and Dyslexic.

[27] Pub L No. 101–476, 104 Stat 1142 (1990). The *IDEA* was reauthorised by the *Individuals with Disability Education Improvement Act of 2004*, Pub L No. 108–446, 118 Stat 2647 (2004).

[28] *Education of the Handicapped Act Amendments of 1990*, Pub L No. 101–476, 104 Stat 1103. For a discussion of the former statute see Mark C Weber, 'Common-Law Interpretation of Appropriate Education: The Road Not Taken in Rowley' (2012) 41(1) *Journal of Law and Education* 95, 98–9.

[29] Mark C Weber, 'A New Look at Section 504 and the ADA in Special Education Cases' (2010) 16 *Texas Journal on Civil Liberties and Civil Rights* 1.

[30] National Instructional Materials Access Center, 'Frequently Asked Questions: Teachers, Parents, Students' <www.nimac.us/faq_teachers.html#what> (accessed 18 November 2016).

below, NIMAC is provided with NIMAS-formatted files by publishers, and then distributes them free of charge to support the educational needs of American K-12 students.[31] NIMAC supports the work of educational providers and charities, such as the American Printing House for the Blind, Bookshare and Learning Ally,[32] to provide accessible versions of books to students.[33] Students, however, are not able to approach NIMAC directly and obtain accessible copies of books. Students must approach their educational institution or a recognised charity to source the books on their behalf.

NIMAS format is a specialised format that is used as a source file to convert digital content into Braille, large print, audio or another format for students with print disabilities. The NIMAS files generally require a human agent to insert computer code into a file so that formatting, tables and other formatting can be easily converted into a usable format.[34] Even a predominately text-based book will include tables, paragraph spacing and formatting that will require some coding.[35] The coding that is required for a book containing significant complex tables, graphics or other visual representations can be substantial. This coding has been developed so that all the content required for a student to read and understand the textbook can be rapidly provided by simply printing the NIMAS format file in the desired alternative format, whether it be Braille or large print.[36]

Who Provides NIMAS-Formatted Books to NIMAC?

The provision of NIMAS-formatted digital books to NIMAC requires positive conduct from a human agent, and could impact on copyright laws. The *IDEA* does not alter copyright; rather it operates within the existing copyright regime. Publishers hold copyright in the books and are the parties best able

[31] It does so under s 674(e)(2) of the *IDEA*.

[32] American Printing House for the Blind <www.aph.org> (accessed 18 November 2016); Bookshare <www.bookshare.org> (accessed 18 November 2016); Learning Ally <www.learningally.org> (accessed 18 November 2016).

[33] National Instructional Materials Access Center, 'Frequently Asked Questions: Teachers, Parents, Students' <www.nimac.us/faq_teachers.html#what> (accessed 18 November 2016).

[34] National Center on Accessible Educational Materials, 'National Instructional Materials Accessibility Standard (NIMAS)' <aem.cast.org/creating/national-instructional-materials-accessibility-standard-nimas.html> (accessed 18 November 2016).

[35] National Center on Accessible Educational Materials, 'Accessibility Standards, Specifications and Guidelines' <aem.cast.org/creating/accessibility-standards-specifications-guidelines.html> (accessed 18 November 2016).

[36] National Center on Accessing the General Curriculum, *National Instructional Materials Accessibility Standard Report – Version 1.0 (National File Format)* (2004) National Center on Accessible Educational Materials <aem.cast.org/about/publications/2004/ncac-nimas-report-national-file-format.html> (accessed 18 November 2016).

to provide digital copies of books. For this reason the *IDEA* uses contractual relationships to pressure publishers to provide NIMAS-formatted books to NIMAC.

The *IDEA* does not directly impose duties on publishers to provide NIMAS files to NIMAC. The *IDEA* enlists the contractual power of the United States educational sector to alter how the market responds to access to books for all students. The *IDEA* links each state's eligibility for federal government financial assistance for students with disabilities to those states' provision of textbooks in accessible formats.[37] The *IDEA* reauthorisation provides states with two options of providing students with accessible textbooks.

The first option requires the state to obtain e-texts or accessible textbooks in a 'timely manner'.[38] While states could operate inefficient systems and argue they have complied with their duties, adopting this approach still requires more effort from schools than embracing the second option. The second option requires very little from the state and significant effort on behalf of publishers.

The second option under s 612(23) of the *IDEA* utilises the purchasing power of the educational sector to motivate publishers to provide NIMAS-formatted files to NIMAC. Section 612(23)(c) provides that states can assure their funding by participating with NIMAC.[39] Under s 612(23)(c), states are required to include in all their procurement contracts or adoption processes a requirement that the publishers:

(i) prepare and, on or before delivery of the print instructional materials, provide to the National Instructional Materials Access Center electronic files containing the contents of the print instructional materials using the National Instructional Materials Accessibility Standard;[40] or

(ii) purchase instructional materials from the publisher that are produced in, or may be rendered in, specialised formats.

While publishers may refuse to enter into sales contracts on such terms, if all K-12 educational institutions require such terms in contracts, then publishers

---

[37] *IDEA*, s 612. These obligations are extended to the local educational agency by s 613.

[38] *IDEA*, s 612(23)(a) and (b).

[39] For more information on NIMAC see the Center's informational website: <www.nimac.us> (accessed 18 November 2016).

[40] NIMAS is defined in s 674(e)(3)(A) of the *IDEA*. The specifications of NIMAS were published as a regulation in Appendix C to Part 300 of NIMAS, published on 14 August 2006. For future developments on the Standard see CAST (the US Department of Education's Office of Special Education Programs awarded CAST funding to establish two national centres to further develop and implement NIMAS): <aem.cast.org> (accessed 18 November 2016).

that refuse to agree to such terms will be unable to participate in the increasingly competitive billion-dollar education textbook market.[41]

The duty on state school districts and publishers to facilitate access to textbooks differs substantially from existing anti-discrimination laws. While both the ADA and IDEA aim to promote equality, how this objective is realised differs significantly.[42] The ADA strives to enable persons with disabilities to have the same opportunities as people without disabilities, whereas the IDEA strives to enable students with disabilities to receive the same educational opportunities as the wider student cohort.[43] Essentially, the ADA seeks to reduce instances of discrimination subject to a reasonableness test, whereas the IDEA seeks to ensure equal access to education. These different regulatory focuses have resulted in significantly different duties. Unlike the ADA, the IDEA contains extensive and specific procedural requirements that require considerable positive action to achieve equal access.[44]

The establishment of the National Instructional Materials Access Standard and Center was regarded as a massive leap forward in respect of students' access to alternative format textbooks.[45] NIMAC is an important scheme that is having a positive impact on the capacity of schools to provide students with print disabilities access to books in a timelier manner.[46]

NIMAC should result in students with disabilities being able to access instructional materials used in class in a timelier manner. NIMAC, however, has a more limited role in creating a library of instructional materials to be used for research or as extra readings. Although the NIMAC scheme requires school districts to keep the pressure on publishers to comply with their contractual duties, it will not ensure access to a vast number of educational books. In January 2013, NIMAC had 32,727 file sets, and in January 2014, 36,572.[47] When compared with the millions of books available on Google

[41] United States Government Accountability Office, 'College Textbooks: Students Have Greater Access to Textbook Information' (report to congressional committees, June 2013).

[42] Angela Estrella-Lemus, 'An *IDEA* for Special Education: Why the *IDEA* Should Have Primacy over the *ADA* in Adjudicating Education Claims for Students with Disabilities' (2014) 34 *Journal of the National Association of Administrative Law Judiciary* 405, 408.

[43] Scott B MacLagan, 'Right of Access: How One Disability Law Enabled Another' (2010) 26 *Touro Law Review* 735, 743.

[44] *K.M. v. Tustin Unified Sch. Dist.*, 725 F 3d 1088, 1096 (9th Cir., 2013). Cert. denied 134 Sup Ct 1493 (2014).

[45] Scott Abel, 'XML Levels Educational Playing Field for Blind and Visually Impaired' (8 February 2005) <thecontentwrangler.com/2005/02/08/xml_levels_educational_playing_field_for_blind_and_visually_impaired> (accessed 18 November 2016).

[46] NIMAC, 'NIMAC User Survey Results' (March 2012) <www.nimac.us/ppt/final_NIMAC March2012surveyresult.pptx> (accessed 18 November 2016).

[47] National Instructional Materials Access Center, 'NIMAC Update to the NIMAS Board' (January 2014).

E-Books or the HathiTrust, it is apparent that the NIMAC scheme plays an important, but limited role in combatting the book famine.

SECTION III TARGETING DIGITAL DISABLEMENT AT ITS SOURCE: THE *TWENTY-FIRST CENTURY COMMUNICATIONS AND VIDEO ACCESSIBILITY ACT*

Recognising that persons with disabilities were not fully benefiting from technological advancements, United States lawmakers enacted the *21st CVAA*. This law does not alter the anti-discrimination duties analysed in Chapters 6, 7 and 8 of this monograph. In effect, the *21st CVAA* creates a new regulatory regime to further promote equality. This section will analyse the operation of this dynamic law, and examine the potential for increased accessibility created by expanding the regulatory pie by placing performance duties on certain designers and manufacturers.

Communications Access: 21st CVAA *Title* I

The duties in the *21st CVAA* are contained in two broad titles. Title I enshrines universal design with respect to communication devices for the deaf, blind and generally for persons with disabilities. Except for s 106 of the *21st CVAA*,[48] all the other provisions in Title I amend the *Communications Act of 1934*.

Two of the amendments in Title I focus on communications between human agents rather than improving access to digital content. The *21st CVAA* s 102 amended the *Communications Act of 1934* s 710(b), (c), (e) and (h) to enhance the inclusive design of telephones and other audio devices held to the ear. These amendments require that such telephone devices are compatible with hearing aids. These provisions expand on the existing protection already contained in the *Hearing Aid Compatibility Act of 1988*. To improve relay services, the *21st CVAA* ss 103 and 105 amended the *Communications Act 1938* s 225 and inserted s 719. Relay services are 'telephone transmission services that provide the ability for an individual who is deaf, hard of hearing, deaf-blind, or who has a speech disability to engage in communication by wire or radio with one or more individuals'.[49] The amendments introduced by the *21st CVAA* ss 103 and 105 modify who must contribute to the fund to support relay services, and facilitate rule-making about such services.

---

[48] *21st CVAA*, s 106 provides for the creation of an emergency Access Advisory Committee.
[49] Ibid., s 103; *Communications Act of 1934*, s 225(a)(3).

The provisions from Title 1 that will be analysed in most detail in this chapter are ss 116, 117 and 118 of the *Communications Act of 1934*, which were introduced by s 104 of the *21st CVAA*. These provisions impose obligations on manufacturers and service providers of devices that can be used to access digital content. The devices that are captured by these amendments include equipment used for advanced communications services, including end-user equipment, network equipment and software.[50]

The term 'advanced communication services' is defined by s 3(53) of the *Communications Act of 1934*, which was introduced by s 101 of the *21st CVAA*. This new definition defines advanced communication services to include 'voice over internet protocol' services that are interconnected and unconnected electronic messaging services and inter-operable video-conferencing services. These provisions also apply to mobile phones which have internet browser capacity.[51] These duties extend to multi-purpose devices and equipment.[52] Critically for the capacity to access the written word, these provisions bind E-Readers, although they do have a temporary waiver from the Advanced Communication Services Rules at the time of writing.[53] This chapter will now analyse how the *21st CVAA* Title 1 enhances inclusive design on these devices.

The amended *Communications Act of 1934* s 716 requires both manufacturers and providers of advance communication services to 'ensure that the equipment and software shall be accessible to and usable by individuals with disabilities, unless the requirements of this subsection are not achievable'.[54] Manufacturers and providers can ensure usability by either:

[50] Ibid., s 104; *Communications Act of 1934*, s 716.

[51] Ibid., s 104; *Communications Act of 1934*, s 718.

[52] Consumer and Governmental Affairs Bureau, 'Biennial Report to Congress as Required by the *Twenty-First Century Communications and Video Accessibility Act of 2010*' (Federal Communications Commission, 5 October 2012) 33 <apps.fcc.gov/edocs_public/attachmatch/ DA-12-1602A1.doc> (accessed 18 November 2016); 47 USC § 617(h)(1); 47 CFR § 14.5. The Commission also adopted general outcome-oriented performance objectives that define 'accessible', 'usable' and 'compatible'. See 47 CFR § 14.21. Consideration of more specific performance objectives is deferred until the Access Board adopts final guidelines for ss 255 and 508. See Federal Communications Commission, *Implementation of Sections 716 and 717 of the Communications Act of 1934, as Enacted by the Twenty-First Century Communications and Video Accessibility Act of 2010; Amendments to the Commission's Rules Implementing Sections 255 and 251(a)(2) of the Communications Act of 1934, as Enacted by the Telecommunications Act of 1996; In the Matter of Accessible Mobile Phone Options for People Who Are Blind, Deaf-Blind, or Have Low Vision* (Report and Order and Further Notice of Proposed Rulemaking, FCC 11-151, 7 October 2011) [212] <apps.fcc.gov/edocs_public/attach match/FCC-11-151A1.pdf> (accessed 18 November 2016).

[53] An exemption for E-Readers exists for the time being, but will be bound in the future.

[54] *21st CVAA*, s 104; *Communications Act of 1934*, s 716(a)(1) and (b)(1).

1. ensuring that the equipment that such manufacturers offer or services that such providers offer are 'accessible to and usable by individuals with disabilities without the use of third party applications, peripheral devices, software, hardware, or customer premises equipment'; or

2. if such manufacturers or service providers choose, 'using third party applications, peripheral devices, software, hardware, or customer premises equipment that is available to the consumer at nominal cost and that individuals with disabilities can access'.[55]

The proactive duty under s 716 has the potential of removing many barriers to digital equality before products are offered for sale to customers. This focuses the attention on the parties who have the greatest resources to implement universal design. This expansion of regulatory attention cannot be overemphasised and, if enforced, is likely to result in a significant uptake of universal design, and consequently a substantial impact on the lives of persons with disabilities.

The scope of the duties contained in the amended *Communication Act* ss 716 and 718 are clarified by guidelines and rulings. The *Communications Act of 1934* s 255 empowers the Access Board to issue guidelines, and the *21st CVAA* s 104 amended the *Communications Act* s 716(e), and s 718(c) and (d), to empower the Federal Communications Commission (FCC) to create rules. Accordingly, it is necessary to consider this additional material to understand the impact of Title I of the *21st CVAA* on reducing the book famine.

In October 2011, the FCC released a report and order adopting rules to implement ss 716 and 717 of the amended *Communications Act*.[56] These rules required manufacturers and service providers regulated by these provisions to consider accessibility during the design and implementation of their products and services as of January 2012. From 2013, this duty was increased.[57] Following this date, covered entities must fully implement s 716 by ensuring that products and services are accessible to and usable by individuals with disabilities, or compatible with assistive technology, unless not achievable.[58] There are a range of means to discharge this duty. For example, web-based email services

---

[55] Ibid., s 104; *Communications Act of 1934*, s 106(a)(2), (b)(2) and s 718(b).

[56] Federal Communications Commission, *Report and Order of 7 October 2011*. The rules adopted in the Report and Order are codified in 47 CFR Pt 14. See also Section III(C) of this Report (summarising other actions taken by the Commission with respect to the implementation of ss 716 and 717 of the Act).

[57] Consumer and Governmental Affairs Bureau, 'Biennial Report to Congress as Required by the *Twenty-First Century Communications and Video Accessibility Act of 2010*' (Federal Communications Commission, 8 October 2014) 10–13 <apps.fcc.gov/edocs_public/attach match/DA-14-1470A1.doc> (accessed 18 November 2016).

[58] Federal Communications Commission, 'Report and Order of 7 October 2011', [110].

could discharge their duty under these rules by ensuring their services are coded to web accessibility standards.[59]

In April 2013, the FCC adopted rules that implement s 718.[60] These rules require manufacturers and providers of mobile phones with built-in internet browsers to comply with the Commission's accessibility requirements.[61] While these rules apply specifically to s 718, they also apply to mobile phones and other hand-held digital devices that are regulated under s 716.[62] While ss 716 and 718 overlap, s 718 deals specifically with the needs of people who are blind or vision-impaired 'to address a special class of browsers for a specific subset of the disabilities community because of the unique challenges of achieving non-visually accessible solutions in a mobile phone and the relative youth of accessible development for mobile platforms'.[63] The FCC adopts a functional approach to determine whether the hardware or software is accessible or not.[64] Similar to the test for functional accessibility under s 716,[65] the functional requirement under s 718 focuses on practical accessibility and usability.

Rendering Television and Digital Video Accessible: The 21st *CVAA Title* ɪɪ

The *21st CVAA* Title ɪɪ focuses on increasing the access of persons with disabilities to television and digital video programming. Traditional books

[59] Ibid., [85].

[60] Consumer and Governmental Affairs Bureau, 'Biennial Report to Congress as Required by the *Twenty-First Century Communications and Video Accessibility Act of 2010*' (Federal Communications Commission, 8 October 2014) 14 <apps.fcc.gov/edocs_public/attachmatch/DA-14-1470A1.doc> (accessed 18 November 2016).

[61] Federal Communications Commission, *Implementation of Sections 716 and 717 of the Communications Act of 1934, as Enacted by the Twenty-First Century Communications and Video Accessibility Act of 2010; Amendments to the Commission's Rules Implementing Sections 255 and 251(a)(2) of the Communications Act of 1934, as Enacted by the Telecommunications Act of 1996; and In the Matter of Accessible Mobile Phone Options for People Who Are Blind, Deaf-Blind, or Have Low Vision* (Second Report and Order, FCC 13–57, 29 April 2013) <apps.fcc.gov/edocs_public/attachmatch/FCC-13-57A1.pdf> (accessed 18 November 2016). The Second Report implements s 718 and part of s 716 of the Act to ensure that people with disabilities have access to emerging and innovative advanced communications technologies. See also Section ɪᴠ of this Report (summarising Commission actions with respect to the implementation of s 718 of the Act).

[62] Federal Communications Commission, 'Second Report and Order of 29 April 2013', [10].

[63] Federal Communications Commission, 'Report and Order of 7 October 2011', [293].

[64] Federal Communications Commission, 'Second Report and Order of 29 April 2013', [11].

[65] Federal Communications Commission, *Implementation of Sections 255 and 251(a)(2) of the Communications Act of 1934, as Enacted by the Telecommunications Act of 1996; Access to Telecommunications Service, Telecommunications Equipment and Customer Premises Equipment by Persons with Disabilities* (Report and Order and Further Notice of Inquiry, FCC 99–181, 29 September 1999) [22] <transition.fcc.gov/Bureaus/Common_Carrier/Orders/1999/fcc99181.pdf>; Federal Communications Commission, *Report and Order of 7 October 2011*, [93]–[94].

are printed on paper and rarely have any video programming directly linked to the text. E-Books are born digital and increasingly include multimedia,[66] utilising digital video programming as part of the text. In such E-Books, the video programming is integral to the content of the book. For example, in a medical text video content can illustrate a procedure; in an engineering book it can illustrate a mechanical fault; in a law text it can provide a case study for tutorial questions.

Even though video content in E-Books is increasingly used in education, in many cases this content is not captioned. The lack of captioning can have a negative impact on people with disabilities who cannot consume video and audio content in the same way as the wider public; for example, people who have hearing impairments.[67] The fact that much of this video content is not captioned is the basis of an ongoing *ADA* lawsuit filed by the National Federation of the Deaf against Harvard University and MIT.[68] While the *21st CVAA* Title II will not alter parties' *ADA* requirements,[69] it will improve access to video content for people with disabilities. Accordingly, the *21st CVAA* Title II is relevant to ensuring that persons with print disabilities have access to those parts of E-Books that include multimedia.

Ensuring Video Programming Can Be Consumed by Persons with Disabilities

Title II of the *21st CVAA* contains provisions which focus on ensuring content and devices that play video programming are accessible. There are two provisions which focus on ensuring that video content is rendered accessible. The *21st CVAA* s 201 provides for the formation of a Video Programming and Emergency Access Advisory Committee. While important, s 201 has limited relevance for ending the book famine. The *21st CVAA* s 202, in contrast, will improve access to persons with hearing impairments to video content. The *21st CVAA* s 202 significantly reinstates video description rules

---

[66] Chris Gibson, 'An Evaluation of Second-Generation E-Book Readers' (2011) 29(3) *The Electronic Library* 303.

[67] Virginia Wooten, 'Waiting and Watching in Silence: Closed Captioning Requirements for Online Streaming under *National Association for the Deaf* v. *Netflix, Inc.* and the *21st Century CVAA*' (2012) 14 *North Carolina Journal of Law and Technology* 135.

[68] *National Association of the Deaf et al.* v. *Harvard University et al.* (D. Mass., Civ. No. 3:15-cv-30023-MGM, 9 February 2016); *National Association of the Deaf et al.* v. *Massachusetts Institute of Technology* (D. Mass., Civ. No. 3:15-cv-300024-MGM, 9 February 2016). Both actions are discussed in Marc Charmatz, 'Department of Justice Files Statements of Interest in Captioning Cases against Harvard and MIT' (2015) 21(2) *Disability Compliance for Higher Education* 2, 3.

[69] *National Association of the Deaf, et al.* v. *Netflix, Inc.*, 869 F Supp 2d 196, 199 (D. Mass., 2012).

that were adopted in 2000, but were vacated by the US Court of Appeals for the District of Columbia Circuit in *Motion Picture Association of America, Inc., et al.* v. *Federal Communications Commission and United States of America.*[70]

The *21st CVAA* s 202 amends s 713 of the *Communications Act of 1934* to improve video description and closed captioning. The new s 713 expands the regulation of video accessibility to cover video content transmitted by both television and digital formats, but not over live or mirror broadcasting. The amendments anticipate that the regulations will create a formula to explain who needs to provide accessible video and the amount of video they need to provide that is accessible. Rules have been created that mandate the amount of video description on standard television broadcasting.[71] Of increased relevance for information communication technology accessibility are the developments pertaining to internet-based video broadcasting, which are pending at the time of writing.

Ensuring Devices that Play and Read Content Embrace Inclusive Design

Ensuring that E-Books, video programming and other content embraces universal design is only half the struggle in achieving digital equality. Devices are required to consume digital content. This includes smart televisions, smart phones, E-Readers and standard computers. It is critical that devices used to consume digital content embrace inclusive design.

The *21st CVAA* reflects the impact devices can have on achieving digital equality. Section 203 of the *21st CVAA* inserted s 303(z) into the *Communications Act of 1934*, providing

> that, if technically feasible – (1) apparatus designed to receive or play back video programming transmitted simultaneously with sound, if such apparatus is manufactured in the United States or imported for use in the United States and uses a picture screen of any size – (A) be equipped with built-in closed caption decoder circuitry or capability designed to display closed-captioned video programming.

To ensure persons with disabilities can operate devices, the *21st CVAA* s 204 inserted s 303(aa) into the *Communications Act of 1934* to provide for disability-accessible user interfaces on digital apparatus.

---

[70] 309 F 3d 796 (DC Cir., 2002).
[71] See Federal Communications Commission, 'Video Description: Implementation of the Twenty-First Century Communications and Video Accessibility Act of 2010' (Report and Order, FCC 11–126, 25 August 2011) [2], [5] <apps.fcc.gov/edocs_public/attachmatch/FCC-11-126A1.pdf> (accessed 18 November 2016); 47 CFR § 79.3.

Section 205 of the *21st CVAA* also focused on interfaces by inserting s 303 (bb) into the *Communications Act of 1934*. Section 303(bb) provides

> that if achievable (as defined in section 716), that the on-screen text menus and guides provided by navigation devices (as such term is defined in section 76.1200 of title 47, Code of Federal Regulations) for the display or selection of multichannel video programming are audibly accessible in real-time upon request by individuals who are blind or visually impaired, except that the Commission may not specify the technical standards, protocols, procedures, and other technical requirements for meeting this requirement.

In January 2012 the Commission adopted rules to implement the amendments introduced by the *21st CVAA* ss 203 to 205.[72] All regulated devices must comply with functional display standards. These rules apply to the software and hardware on devices that can be used to consume video programming. This includes televisions, computers, tablets, smart phones and media players.[73] The only devices not regulated are those categorised as either professional equipment or display-only monitors.[74] Whether or not the device is regulated turns on its capabilities, rather than the intent of the manufacturer.[75]

Significance of the 21st CVAA *on Promoting Digital Equality*

The significance of the *21st CVAA* is that it adopts a universal design model to removing inequalities in society. The *21st CVAA* does not wait until a product is created to make reasonable adjustments. The *21st CVAA* operates on the basis that many of the barriers in society can be best removed by the people who create them at the design and manufacture stage. On signing this Act into law, President Obama observed that the *21st CVAA*

> will make it easier for people who are deaf, blind or live with a visual impairment to do what many of us take for granted from navigating a TV or

---

[72] Federal Communication Commission, 'Closed Captioning of Internet Protocol-Delivered Video Programming: Implementation of the Twenty-First Century Communications and Video Accessibility Act of 2010' (Report and Order, FCC 12–9, 13 January 2012) <apps.fcc.gov/edocs_pub lic/attachmatch/FCC-12-9A1.pdf> (accessed 18 November 2016). See also 47 CFR §§ 79.103 and 79.104.

[73] Ibid., [3]. But see [120], summarising the Commission's response to the CEA petition for reconsideration.

[74] Ibid., [3].

[75] Federal Communication Commission, 'Closed Captioning of Internet Protocol-Delivered Video Programming: Implementation of the Twenty-First Century Communications and Video Accessibility Act of 2010' (Order on Reconsideration and Further Notice of Proposed Rulemaking, FCC 13–84, 14 June 2013) [5]–[7] <apps.fcc.gov/edocs_public/attachmatch/FCC-13-84A1.pdf> (accessed 18 November 2016).

DVD menu to sending an email on a smart phone . . . set[ting] new standards so that Americans with disabilities can take advantage of the technology our economy depends on.[76]

The regulatory premise underpinning the *21st CVAA* is that society should attempt to avoid creating inequalities where it is economically reasonable to do so.

Research on the impact of the *21st CVAA* suggests that these amendments are having a positive impact. Section 717(b)(1)(A) of the *Communication Act* requires the Commission to assess levels of compliance with ss 255, 716 and 718. In preparation for the 2014 report, the FCC tentatively found that since the 2012 *21st CVAA* Biennial Report 'there has been an increase in the availability of telecommunications equipment with varying degrees of functionality and features, and offered at differing price points, that are accessible to individuals with disabilities'.[77] These tentative findings were supported by submissions to the FCC. The FCC concluded in its 2014 report that 'there is a greater selection of accessible telecommunications devices available to people with disabilities now than were available at the time that the Commission prepared its 2012 *CVAA* Biennial Report'.[78] Overall, the FCC found that industry was generally making efforts to comply and, despite accessibility gaps, there was a positive trend towards reducing digital disablement.

No regulatory scheme by itself can achieve digital equality for persons with disabilities. Despite the limitations of a single regulatory scheme in a single jurisdiction, the *21st CVAA* will have a substantial impact on moving society towards equality. As the United States digital market becomes more accessible, this creates a flow-on impact for digital products across the globe. It also increases the marketplace for inclusively designed products. The increased commercial attention in this area means that new businesses are being formed to take advantage of opportunities to provide accessibility expertise to

---

[76] Barack Obama, 'Remarks by the President at the Signing of the *21st Century Communications and Video Accessibility Act of 2010*' (media release, The White House, Office of the Press Secretary, 8 October 2010) <www.whitehouse.gov/the-press-office/2010/10/08/remarks-president-signing-21st-century-communications-and-video-accessib> (accessed 18 November 2016).

[77] Federal Communications Commission, 'Consumer and Governmental Affairs Bureau Seeks Comment on its Tentative Findings about the Accessibility of Communications Technologies for the 2014 Biennial Report under the *Twenty-First Century Communications and Video Accessibility Act*' (Public Notice, DA 14–1255, 28 August 2014) [21] <apps.fcc.gov/edocs_public/attachmatch/DA-14-1255A1.pdf> (accessed 18 November 2016).

[78] Consumer and Governmental Affairs Bureau, 'Biennial Report to Congress as Required by the *Twenty-First Century Communications and Video Accessibility Act of 2010*' (Federal Communications Commission, 8 October 2014) 40 <apps.fcc.gov/edocs_public/attachmatch/DA-14-1470A1.doc>.

technology entities that desire to comply with the *21st CVAA* and the overall trend towards inclusive design. The increased attention and money in the accessibility sector means that the digital disablement of persons with print impairments is being reduced. While there is a long way to go before digital disablement has been eradicated and the right to read is realised, there is a definite trend towards equality and there is light at the end of the tunnel.

CONCLUSION

Traditional anti-discrimination laws analysed in Chapter 8 of this monograph rely on prohibiting discrimination through the use of negative duties. Positive duties in Canada and the United Kingdom were introduced to achieve more substantive change. Unlike the positive duties analysed in Chapters 9 and 10 of this monograph, the United States regulatory frameworks analysed in this chapter created specific disability duties on various parties across the design, manufacture and purchase of technologies that enable persons with print disabilities to access content.

This chapter first analysed the *508 Standards* created under the *Rehabilitation Act of 1973*. These standards operated as an extension of existing anti-discrimination laws, and created increased obligations on federal agencies and contractors to design and purchase disability-accessible information communication technologies. This chapter then analysed the frameworks that sought to remove the barriers to inclusion by targeting upstream parties. NIMAC targeted book publishers, and the *21st CVAA* targeted designers and suppliers of certain digital technologies. Both of these measures sought to create digital spaces that do not disable people with impairments. While these measures will not guarantee digital equality, they represent a significant attempt to promote digital ability equality and, if enforced, will substantially improve the capacity of persons with print disabilities to access information and the written word.

1 2

The Enforcement of Legal Duties: Protecting Copyright or Promoting Reading Equality?

INTRODUCTION

The proceeding chapters in this monograph have analysed laws that create rights and responsibilities that impact on the severity of the book famine experienced by persons with print disabilities. Those chapters have focused on the content of the duties and have largely not analysed issues of compliance. The imposition of duties will only result in practical differences on the ground if regulated parties comply with their obligations. For this reason, monitoring and enforcement are said to be essential components in the effective operation of any regulatory system.[1]

The question of how to motivate parties to comply with their legal duties has generated a considerable body of scholarship, which will be touched on in this chapter. Regulatory enforcement is more complex where legal frameworks with competing objectives overlap. For example, the operation of laws is complicated where there is an overlap between laws which prohibit digital discrimination and promote access to information, and those which seek to restrict the use of information. This chapter will illustrate that the enforcement of anti-discrimination laws and laws which promote equality are generally weak. In contrast, copyright laws are robustly enforced with substantial sanctions for non-compliance. The interaction between these competing regimes arguably sends the message that protecting rights-holders' interests in controlling use of information is a higher priority than complying with anti-discrimination laws and laws which promote equal access to information.

This chapter argues that laws and institutions associated with enforcement are limiting the capacity of equality interventions to reduce the book famine. First, this chapter will briefly explain the theory behind the regulatory enforcement model adopted in the laws analysed in this monograph. This chapter will

[1] C Hood, H Rothstein and R Baldwin, *The Government of Risk* (2001) Oxford University Press, 23.

then analyse the strengths and weaknesses in how traditional anti-discrimination laws, analysed in Chapters 6, 7 and 8 of this monograph, are enforced. Thirdly, this chapter will analyse how the processes used to enforce the frameworks, analysed in Chapters 9, 10 and 11, that take proactive conduct to promote equality are enforced. Finally, this chapter will consider how the robust enforcement and significant sanctions associated with breaches of copyright laws (discussed in Chapters 4 and 5) can result in regulated parties focusing more on protecting copyright than promoting equality.

SECTION I MOTIVATING CORPORATE COMPLIANCE: THE ENFORCEMENT PYRAMID

Deterrence, economic rational acting, responsive regulation and behavioural psychology are all techniques that can be employed to control corporate conduct.[2] Rather than analysing all these models in detail, this chapter will focus on the primary technique employed to enforce laws which seek to promote human rights and equality: responsive regulation and the enforcement pyramid. The enforcement of equality laws draws from broader regulatory theories, in particular the concept of the enforcement pyramid.[3] Professors Ian Ayres and John Braithwaite have combined both incentives and punishments in their widely supported enforcement pyramid model.[4]

The regulatory enforcement pyramid model provides incentives for parties who attempt to comply with their duties, and punishment for those who intentionally or negligently fail to discharge their duties. The pyramid assumes that the majority of people will be at the bottom of the pyramid, voluntarily complying with their duties. In the middle of the pyramid are supportive schemes to assist people to comply with their duties. At the top of the pyramid are legal sanctions for the small number of people who fail to discharge their legal duties.

Responsive regulation is premised on the notion 'that escalating forms of government intervention will reinforce and help constitute less intrusive and

---

[2] See for discussion Christopher Hodge, *Law and Corporate Behaviour: Integrating Theories of Regulation, Enforcement, Compliance and Ethics* (2015) Hart Publishing.

[3] Paul Harpur, 'From Universal Exclusion to Universal Equality: Regulating Ableism in a Digital Age' (2013) 40(3) *Northern Kentucky Law Review* 529; Paul Harpur, 'Developments in Chinese Labour Laws: Enforcing People with Disabilities' Right to Work?' (2009) *Lawasia Journal* 26; Bob Hepple, Mary Coussey and Tufyal Choudhury, *Equality: A New Framework* (2000) Hart Publishing, 2.

[4] Ian Ayres and John Braithwaite, *Responsive Regulation: Transcending the Deregulation Debate* (1992) Oxford University Press, 19–53.

delegated forms of market regulation and social change'.[5] The enforcement pyramid represents an understanding that regulators should determine how effective parties are at regulating themselves prior to escalating interventions to impose legal sanctions.[6] The enforcement pyramid involves a carrot-and-stick approach, where the stick remains a crucial aspect of the model.[7] Professor Richard Johnstone argues:

> At the heart of the enforcement pyramid is a paradox – the greater the capacity of the regulator to escalate to the top of the pyramid, and the greater the available sanctions at the top of the pyramid, the more duty holders will participate in co-operative activity at the lower regions of the pyramid.[8]

While education and persuasion remain important means of promoting compliance,[9] the existence of monitoring and sanctions are critical aspects of regulatory enforcement.[10]

The sanctions at the top of the enforcement pyramid can be achieved through formal judicial orders or informal pressure from violating normative social standards.[11] Professors Robert Kagan, Neil Gunningham and Dorothy Thornton explain that natural persons' compliance with laws are influenced by the fear of detection and formal legal sanction, humiliation or disgrace from their community, or to comply with an internal sense of duty.[12]

A wide range of factors are involved in the creation of norms. The existence of laws influences the extent to which compliance with a norm is regarded as moral.[13] This occurs most effectively where the sanction reflects the

---

[5] Ibid., 3.

[6] John Braithwaite, *Restorative Justice and Responsive Regulation* (2002) Federation Press, 299; Richard Johnstone and Rick Sarre, 'Regulation: Enforcement and Compliance' (working paper, Australian Institute of Criminology, 2004) 11.

[7] Paul Teague, 'New Employment Times and the Changing Dynamics of Conflict Resolution Work: The Case of Ireland' (2006) 28 *Comparative Labor Law and Policy Journal* 587.

[8] Richard Johnstone, 'From Fiction to Fact – Rethinking OHS Enforcement' (Working Paper No. 11, ANU National Research Centre for Occupational Health and Safety Regulation, 2003) 17.

[9] Neil Gunningham, 'Occupational Health and Safety Regulation: Two Paths to Enlightenment' (1998) 19 *Comparative Labor Law and Policy Journal* 547, 571; Bob Hepple, 'Enforcing Equality Law: Two Steps Forward and Two Steps Backwards for Reflexive Regulation' (2011) 40(4) *Industrial Law Journal* 315.

[10] Belinda Smith, 'Not the Baby and the Bathwater: Regulatory Reform for Equality Laws to Address Work–Family Conflict' (2006) 28 *Sydney Law Review* 689, 706.

[11] Andrew Ashworth, 'Social Control and "Anti-Social Behaviour": The Subversion of Human Rights?' (2004) 120 *Law Quarterly Review* 263.

[12] Robert Kagan, Neil Gunningham and Dorothy Thornton, 'Fear, Duty, and Regulatory Compliance: Lessons from Three Research Projects' in Christine Parker and Vibeke Lehmann Nielsen (eds), *Explaining Compliance: Business Responses to Regulation* (2012) Edward Elgar.

[13] R A Duff, *Towards a Theory of Criminal Law?* (2010) Proceedings of the Aristotelian Society, Supp. Vol. LXXXIV, 1–28.

seriousness of the act.[14] Adopting this broad concept of sanction within the enforcement pyramid, this chapter will now analyse the extent to which equality and copyright laws are enforced, and consider the impact this has on removing barriers to persons with disabilities consuming books on an equal basis to others.

SECTION II ENFORCING ANTI-DISCRIMINATION DUTIES TO COMBAT THE BOOK FAMINE

This section introduces a range of factors which reduce the enforcement of disability discrimination laws. There are many factors which impact on the enforcement of disability discrimination laws.[15] This section does not attempt to analyse all the issues associated with enforcing anti-discrimination laws. Instead, this section adopts a more limited approach of focusing on the issues that have a significant impact on the prospects of enforcing anti-discrimination laws to combat the book famine. This section will first analyse the barriers to enforcement associated with the pre-litigious steps of a dispute, before analysing how complaints of discrimination are enforced. This section will then analyse how fear of victimisation and resource issues reduce the capacity of plaintiffs to utilise anti-discrimination laws.

Pre-Litigious Steps: Introducing the Naming, Blaming and Claiming Model

The decision not to take legal action to enforce disability discrimination laws requires consideration of pre-litigious stages.[16] Professors Richard Felstiner, William Abel and Austin Sarat argue that '[t]he sociology of law should pay more attention to the early stages of disputes and to the factors that determine whether naming, blaming, and claiming will occur'.[17] The naming, blaming and claiming model advanced by Felstiner, Abel and Sarat has been applied,

---

[14] Anthony Bottoms and A von Hirsch, 'The Crime-Preventive Impact of Penal Sanctions' in Peter Cane and Herbert Kritzer (eds), *The Oxford Handbook of Empirical Legal Research* (2010) Oxford University Press; Andrew Ashworth and Lucia Zedner, 'Defending the Criminal Law: Reflections on the Changing Character of Crime, Procedure, and Sanctions' (2008) 2 *Criminal Law and Philosophy* 21, 22.

[15] Jean R Sternlight, 'In Search of the Best Procedure for Enforcing Employment Discrimination Laws: A Comparative Analysis' (2004) 78 *Tulane Law Review* 1401.

[16] Paul Harpur, 'Naming, Blaming and Claiming Ablism: The Lived Experiences of Lawyers and Advocates with Disabilities' (2014) 29(8) *Disability and Society* 1234.

[17] William Felstiner, Richard L Abel and Austin Sarat, 'Emergence and Transformation of Disputes: Naming, Blaming, Claiming' (1980–81) 15 *Law and Society Review* 631, 636.

according to Google Scholar, in over 1,800 scholarly works, and can be applied to a dispute pertaining to disability discrimination.[18]

In their seminal work, Felstiner, Abel and Sarat observed that legal disputes are social constructs that involve three distinct stages before litigation commences.[19] The first stage of a dispute occurs when an unperceived injurious experience is perceived as an injurious experience. The capacity to name conduct as injurious can be confounded by a lack of information, internalised oppression and other anthropological variables.[20]

If an individual has named conduct as injurious, then the next stage towards litigation involves transforming the named injury into a grievance. To transform a named injury into a grievance involves an individual attributing blame to a particular party or parties. Once an individual has attributed blame in their own minds, then the third stage involves turning a grievance into a claim against the blamed party. The term 'claim' here refers to the act of approaching the blamed party to obtain redress for the individual's injury and should not be confused with the originating documents in civil litigation of the same name. If the blamed party expressly or implicitly refuses the claim of the individual, then a dispute exists. Following the above three stages, an individual may or may not commence legal proceedings.

Naming, Blaming and Claiming for Acts of Digital Disablement

In other research, using the naming, blaming and claiming model, the author has determined that there are three key factors which discourage persons with print disabilities from transforming their grievances into claims: the problem of the disconnect between the parties who cause disablement and those who attract duties under anti-discrimination laws, limited resources and fear of victimisation.[21] The disconnect between the coverage of anti-discrimination duties and the parties who cause digital disablement was analysed in detail in Chapter 7 of this monograph. This chapter will now analyse how limited resources and fear of victimisation impact upon the pre-litigious and litigious steps of disputes pertaining to digital disablement.

---

[18] Scott Burris et al., 'Disputing under the *Americans with Disabilities Act*: Empirical Answers, and Some Questions' (2000) 9 *Temple Political and Civil Rights Law Review* 237; Sharona Hoffman, 'Settling the Matter: Does Title 1 of the ADA Work?' (2008) 59(2) *Alabama Law Review* 305; Laura Nielson and Robert L Nelson, 'Rights Realized – An Empirical Analysis of Employment Discrimination Litigation as a Claiming System' (2005) *Wisconsin Law Review* 663.

[19] Felstiner, Able and Sarat, 'Emergence and Transformation of Disputes', 632.   [20] Ibid., 633.

[21] Harpur, 'Naming, Blaming and Claiming Ablism'.

Litigious Steps for Enforcing Traditional Anti-Discrimination Laws

A person with a disability who has experienced unlawful discrimination seeks redress for the wrong by first filing a complaint with a specialist commission. A full list of anti-discrimination and human rights agencies, commissions and tribunals appears as an appendix to this monograph. The federal commissions include the Australian Human Rights Commission, the Canadian Human Rights Commission, the British Equality and Human Rights Commission, which covers Britain, but not the entire United Kingdom, and the United States Equal Employment Opportunity Commission and Office for Civil Rights. All of these bodies have a role in determining if a complaint has sufficient merit to be accepted, and in providing alternative dispute resolution services to try to resolve the dispute. Unless there is a particular public interest aspect of the case, the respective commissions will not appear as an amicus curiae (friend of the court) before administrative or judicial tribunals.

If the complaint is not resolved in mediation or conciliation, then the complainant has the right to take their dispute to a hearing. These hearings can be heard in anti-discrimination or human rights tribunals coming within the administrative arm of the state, or in the courts under the judicial arm of the state. Administrative tribunals are less formal and provide a more accessible format to resolve these disputes.[22] The constitutional power to enable disputes to be heard by administrative bodies can be limited. For example, the High Court of Australia held that Chapter 3 of the *Australian Constitution* meant that the separation of power doctrine prevented federal anti-discrimination disputes being heard before administrative tribunals.[23] Whether the matter is heard before an administrative tribunal or court, both parties have the right to file appeals through the appellate courts to the highest courts in the land. While there are procedural differences, the issues complainants encounter are largely similar across jurisdictions. This chapter will now analyse two leading issues which hinder the ability of plaintiffs to enforce their rights under anti-discrimination laws.

Risk of Victimisation

Whistle-blowing occurs where a person observes a wrong being committed and makes a public interest disclosure.[24] This might occur if a worker is aware that

---

[22] Beth Gaze, 'The Costs of Equal Opportunity' (2000) 25(3) *Alternative Law Journal* 125, 127.
[23] *Brandy v. Human Rights and Equal Opportunity Commission* (1995) 183 CLR 245; Peter Johnston, 'Recent Developments Concerning Tribunals in Australia' (1996) 24(2) *Federal Review* 323.
[24] Transparency International, 'Alternative to Silence: Whistleblower Protection in 10 European Countries' (research paper, 2009).

their company is violating anti-discrimination laws and discloses this fact to an appropriate body. Such disclosures are protected where they come under the protection of whistle-blowing laws.[25] Informal discussions indicated that information was leaked to support the protests by disability groups in August 2015, when the New York City school system's Educational Policy Panel was considering entering into a $30 million contract, under which Amazon would construct an electronic storefront for New York City schools and become the primary provider of electronic textbooks and related educational materials for students. At the time of the protests, the Amazon platform did not comply with universal design and excluded students with a print disability from equal access.

Victimisation generally occurs where the person who makes the complaint is personally impacted by the wrong: i.e. they are experiencing discrimination.[26] Laws arguably fail to provide adequate protection to people who disclose wrongdoing, which impacts on rates of disclosures.[27] While whistle-blowing and victimisation have many similarities, this chapter will focus on victimisation, as this form of disclosure is more relevant to the enforcement of anti-discrimination laws.

The primary anti-discrimination laws in Australia, Canada, the United Kingdom and the United States contain protection for people who report discriminatory treatment.[28] Similar to whistle-blowing, the protections found in anti-discrimination laws arguably provide inadequate protection. A person who provides information in prescribed situations can gain protection under these regimes. Victimisation regimes generally provide inadequate protection.[29] The capacity of these laws to protect persons with disabilities who raise concerns about discrimination or make formal complaints is doubtful.

---

[25] Tom Devine, Paul Harpur and David Lewis, 'Civil and Employment Law Remedies' in A J Brown, David Lewis and Richard Moberly (eds), *International Handbook on Whistleblowing Research* (2014) Edward Elgar.

[26] Victimisation is also referred to by other names. In Australia, for example, victimisation is called 'discriminatory, coercive and misleading conduct' by the harmonised *Work Health and Safety Act 2011* (Cth) part 6; victimisation is also called 'adverse action' by the *Fair Work Act 2009* (Cth) Part 3-1.

[27] A J Brown and M Donkin, 'Introduction' in A J Brown (ed.), *Whistleblowing in the Australian Public Sector* (2008) ANU Press, 11; Paul Harpur, 'The Gap between Law and Practice when Workers Are Silent Witnesses to Workplace Violence: Evidence from the Health Sector' (2014) 30(1) *Journal of Health, Safety and Environment* 9; Ryan Russell, 'Exceptions to the Employment-at-Will Doctrine: The Relationship between the Common Law Tort of Retaliatory Discharge and the Tennessee "Whistle-Blower" Act' (2005) 6 *Transactions* 447.

[28] Australia and the United Kingdom describe this act as victimisation: *Disability Discrimination Act 1992* (Cth) s 42; *Equality Act 2010* (UK) s 27. Canada and the United States label this conduct as retaliation and coercion: *Canadian Human Rights Act*, RSC 1985, c H-6, s 14.1; 42 USC § 12203.

[29] Michael Connolly, 'Rethinking Victimisation' (2009) 38(2) *Industrial Law Journal* 149; Peter McTigue, 'Victimisation Discrimination' (2006) 15 *Nottingham Law Journal* 28.

Research indicates that fear of victimisation deters people from enforcing their rights in education and employment.[30] Persons with disabilities confront vulnerabilities that are particular to complainants with such attributes. People who view disability through a medical model lens regard impairment as the cause of disablement. Under this approach, there is an expectation that inequalities are the norm, and that persons with disabilities should be grateful for any efforts to improve their disabled lives.[31] While such an approach goes against the *Convention on the Rights of Persons with Disabilities* (CRPD) and the human rights paradigm, this approach arguably finds traction in certain sectors of the community.

Professor Lennard Davis has eloquently analysed how society constructs those who make any efforts to accommodate persons with disabilities as 'bending over backwards', even where these efforts fall short of obligations under anti-discrimination laws.[32] Persons with disabilities who desire to exercise their rights have been labelled as narcissists, and accused of excessive hyper-individuality, unreasonable self-focus and unjustly blaming the wider community for their sorrows.[33]

Under the disabling 'bending over backwards' paradigm, persons with disabilities are pressured to be grateful for the help they have received and strongly discouraged from taking any action to enforce their rights. Rather than being encouraged to fight for equality, persons with print disabilities are encouraged to be satisfied with sub-optimal and unequal treatment. Within this disabling paradigm, persons with disabilities are discouraged from arguing that educators, employers, publishers and others are not doing enough to combat the book famine. This pressure arguably deters and hinders persons with print disabilities who are seeking to file suit to redress the wrongs committed against them.

Persons with Disabilities Have Limited Resources to Combat Digital Disablement

Most of the population has limited emotional, financial and time resources to pursue every grievance they experience. People who are categorised as

---

[30] Harpur, 'Naming, Blaming and Claiming Ablism'; Paul M Secunda, 'Overcoming Deliberate Indifference: Reconsidering Effective Legal Protections for Bullied Special Education Students' (2015) *University of Illinois Law Review* 175.

[31] Tobin Siebers, *Disability Theory* (2008) University of Michigan Press, 34.

[32] Lennard J Davis, *Bending Over Backwards: Disability, Dismodernism, and Other Difficult Positions* (2002) New York University Press.

[33] Lennard J Davis, 'Bending Over Backwards: Disability, Narcissism, and the Law' (2000) 21(1) *Berkeley Journal of Employment and Labor Law* 193.

disabled have additional limitations as they are disabled by society. People with disabilities are often impoverished,[34] discriminated against in employment[35] and rely upon welfare.[36] Accordingly, people with disabilities are in the unfortunate position of having fewer resources to pursue grievances, while having more grievances that they need to pursue simply to have equal treatment.

The emotional strain on people with disabilities to continually fight for their rights has been described as advocacy fatigue. Dr Carrie Basas defines advocacy fatigue to mean 'the increased strain on emotional, physical, material, social, and wellness resources that comes from continued exposure to system inequities and inequalities and the need to advocate for the preservation and advancement of one's rights and autonomy'.[37] The intersection of limited resources, experiencing disablement and the traumas that come from reliving discrimination creates significant pressures on the decision to self-advocate for one's rights. Accordingly, persons with disabilities need to consider carefully what grievance they will devote their limited resources to pursuing.

The premise of the social model is that impairment is turned into disability by barriers in society. While other models have recognised that the causes of disablement are more complex, the notion that society has a significant disabling impact on persons with different abilities remains an unfortunate reality. Some barriers by themselves will have a significant impact on the person with an impairment, and in other situations the collective impact of many small barriers to equality, which, while individually are more irritating than disabling, when experienced together can have a significant disabling impact.

As discussed in Chapters 1 and 7, there are a range of parties who may contribute to the existence of digital content that is not usable by persons with disabilities. These parties include authors, publishers, libraries, designers and manufacturers of hardware, amongst others. The difficulty in determining who should be held legally responsible is illustrated by analysing the range of

---

[34] Jeanine Braithwaite and Daniel Mont, 'Disability and Poverty: A Survey of World Bank Poverty Assessments and Implications' (Discussion Paper 5, World Bank, 2008).

[35] Paul Harpur, 'Combating Prejudice in the Workplace with Contact Theory: The Lived Experiences of Professionals with Disabilities' (2014) 34(1) *Disability Studies Quarterly* 1; Paul Harpur and Ben French, 'Is It Safer without You? Analysing the Intersection between Work Health and Safety and Anti-Discrimination Laws' (2014) 30(1) *Journal of Health, Safety and Environment* 167; Anna Lawson, 'Disability and Employment in the *Equality Act 2010*: Opportunities Seized, Lost and Generated' (2011) 40(4) *Industrial Law Journal* 359, 363.

[36] Mark C Weber, 'Disability Rights, Welfare Law' (2011) 32 *Cardozo Law Review* 2483.

[37] Carrie Griffin Basas, 'Advocacy Fatigue: Self-Care, Protest, and Educational Equity' (2015) 33(2) *Windsor Yearbook of Access* 37.

parties who contribute to the barriers represented by multimedia content in an E-Book which does not include disability accessibility features. The creation of such an E-Book could occur where an author utilises information technology support at their university to assist them in designing the multimedia content. The author's publisher, who receives the E-Book, may decide not to embrace inclusive design as it might impact on the copyright of the author and others. This E-Book is then published and E-Libraries host the E-Book with multimedia content that is not accessible for persons with print disabilities. Finally, educational institutions purchase access to the E-Book, and their students, including those with print disabilities, consume the E-Book on university hardware. Some hardware devices can have software settings that reduce levels of disability accessibility. With so many parties contributing to their digital disablement, how does the person with a print disability decide who to request assistance from or who may have breached anti-discrimination duties? If a person with a disability does identify the main cause of their digital disablement, has there been a legal breach where there is sufficient evidence to put before a court?

The limitations with relying on victim enforcement to combat digital disablement can be demonstrated by analysing the application of anti-discrimination laws to the above hypothetical example of an E-Book with multimedia content. It is reasonable to assume that a student with a print disability would be aware that students without a disability can utilise all the features of E-Books, while such content is not accessible to persons with print disabilities. As this digital disablement can negatively impact on their education, it is probable that most students with print disabilities would identify that they have experienced an injury.

While a student (or their parents) with a print disability may name their treatment as an injury, accurately attributing blame and advocating for this injury is far more complex.[38] The blame attribution process requires a full understanding of the actual causes of the accessibility barrier. Most persons with print disabilities are not information technology experts and could not readily understand how different pieces of hardware and software interact to reduce disability access. Even if a person identified the access problem, they would need to attribute blame to a particular party who attracts a legal duty.[39] Establishing that technology has caused discrimination can be especially

---

[38] Erin Phillips, 'When Parents Aren't Enough: External Advocacy in Special Education' (2008) 117(8) *Yale Law Journal* 1802; Eloise Pasachoff, 'Special Education, Poverty, and the Limits of Private Enforcement' (2011) 86(4) *Notre Dame Law Review* 1413.

[39] Belinda Smith and Dominique Allen, 'Whose Fault Is It? Asking the Right Question to Address Discrimination' (2012) 37(1) *Alternative Law Journal* 31.

challenging.[40] An additional complication in the above example is that the author, copyright holder, publisher, E-Library and educational institution could all be in different jurisdictions, or even different countries, and might be difficult or impossible to contact (if the work is an orphan work).[41]

In addition to complicated evidential and legal issues, persons with disabilities are often vulnerable and may even require support to lodge a grievance.[42] Where a grievance is lodged, power relations can result in authorities discounting the voice of the person with a disability.[43] To effectively agitate for their rights, persons with disabilities often require support from an advocate with disability law expertise. It can, however, be difficult to obtain the assistance of a disability rights advocate.

Furthermore, the disability rights movement has been comparatively less effective in developing strategic litigation to agitate for rights. For example, Professors Michael Waterstone, Michael Ashley Stein and David Wilkins have identified the limited role of disability cause lawyers in taking key precedents to the United States Supreme Court.[44]

Disability rights advocacy is expensive. Lawyers are expensive and there is limited funding for individuals pursuing disability discrimination public interest law suits.[45] One avenue to reduce costs for individuals is to pursue a class action. It is, however, increasingly difficult to have class actions certified, which reduces the potential of this option for persons with disabilities.[46] Disability person organisations have a history of assisting in public interest litigation.[47]

---

[40] Solon Barocas and Andrew D Selbst, 'Big Data's Disparate Impact' (2016) 104 *California Law Review* 671; Mark Burdon and Paul Harpur, 'Re-Conceptualising Privacy and Discrimination in an Age of Talent Analytics' (2014) 37(2) *University of New South Wales Law Journal* 679.

[41] See Chapter 4 of this monograph for a discussion of orphan works.

[42] Eilionoir Flynn and Anna Arstein-Kerslake, 'The Support Model of Legal Capacity: Fact, Fiction, or Fantasy?' (2014) 32(1) *Berkeley Journal of International Law* 134, 135; Leslie Salzman, 'Guardianship for Persons with Mental Illness – A Legal and Appropriate Alternative?' (2011) 4 *Saint Louis University Journal of Health Law and Policy* 279, 284; Committee on the Rights of Persons with Disabilities, 'General Comment No. 1: Article 12: Equal Recognition before the Law', 11th sess., UN Doc. CRPD/C/GC/1 (19 May 2014) [28].

[43] Paul Harpur and Heather Douglas, 'Disability and Domestic Violence: Protecting Survivors' Human Rights' (2014) 23(3) *Griffith Law Review* 405.

[44] Michael Waterstone, Michael Ashley Stein and David Wilkins, 'Disability Cause Lawyers: Relentless Pragmatism in the Shadow of the Supreme Court' (2012) 53(4) *William and Mary Law Review* 1287; Michael Ashley Stein, Michael E Waterstone and David B Wilkins, 'Book Review: Cause Lawyering for People with Disabilities' (2010) 123 *Harvard Law Review* 1658.

[45] Gary Blasi, 'Framing Access to Justice: Beyond Perceived Justice for Individuals' (2009) 42 *Loyola of Los Angeles Law Review* 913.

[46] Michael Ashley Stein and Michael E Waterstone, 'Disability, Disparate Impact, and Class Actions' (2006) 56(3) *Duke Law Journal* 861.

[47] Michael Waterstone, 'A New Vision of Public Enforcement' (2007) 92 *Minnesota Law Review* 434.

Public interest litigation is also expensive and there is a trend to reduce public funding to support such litigation. Indeed, the seven-year battle against Canada's national passenger rail provider, VIA Rail, nearly bankrupted the national organisation representing Canadians with disabilities.[48] Following this litigation, the level of support for disability person organisations was reduced, which meant similar litigation would not be possible in the future.[49] Another option would be for the state anti-discrimination commissions to be provided with increased funding and to become more active. Such calls have been made before, though an increase in state enforcement has not materialised.[50]

SECTION III PRACTICAL EXAMPLES OF HOW ENFORCING ADA HAS COMBATTED THE BOOK FAMINE

Laws are intended to alter how regulated parties act.[51] Ideally, the existence of laws alters conduct without the need for any enforcement action. Where legal action is required, it is increasingly common to settle the dispute before reaching court. There is a trend in the United States which involves non-confidential settlements of disputes which require defendants to take various actions to combat the book famine. This chapter will now analyse publicly available settlement agreements between persons with print disabilities in the United States and E-Libraries, and with educators who use E-Libraries to critique the capacity of this enforcement option to combat the book famine.

Litigation Directly against E-Libraries

Chapter 1 discussed how the number and content of E-Libraries continues to increase at a prodigious rate. These vast digital resources afford persons with

---

[48] David Baker and Sarah Godwin, 'All Aboard!: The Supreme Court of Canada Confirms that Canadians with Disabilities Have Substantive Equality Rights' (2008) 71(1) *Saskatchewan Law Review* 39.

[49] Ibid., 72.

[50] Dominique Allen, 'Strategic Enforcement of Anti-Discrimination Law: A New Role for Australia's Equality Commissions' (2010) 36(3) *Monash University Law Review* 103; Paul Harpur, Ben French and Richard Bales, 'Australia's *Fair Work Act* and the Transformation of Workplace Disability Discrimination Law' (2012) 30 *Wisconsin International Law Journal* 190; Paul Harpur, Ben French and Richard Bales, 'Australia's Solution to Disability Discrimination Enforcement' (2011) 31 *Cornell HR Review* 1; Pauline T Kim, 'Panel v: Proving Discrimination: Addressing Systemic Discrimination: Public Enforcement and the Role of the EEOC' (2015) 95(3) *Boston University Law Review* 1133; Margo Schlanger, 'The Equal Employment Opportunity Commission and Structural Reform of the American Workplace' (2014) 91 *Washington University Law Review* 1519; Smith, 'Not the Baby and the Bathwater'.

[51] Cass Sunstein, 'On the Expressive Function of Law' (1996) 144 *University of Pennsylvania Law Review* 2021.

print disabilities the hope of turning the book famine into a book feast. However, persons with print disabilities can only benefit from this vast wealth of information if E-Libraries embrace universal design. In 2014, one of these E-Libraries, Scribd, was arguably not accessible, but through legal advocacy, a non-confidential settlement agreement was reached in November 2015 to provide equality of access to people with all abilities.

Scribd's E-Library provides users access to over a million E-Books.[52] Scribd's website explains that '[m]ovie lovers have Netflix, music lovers have Spotify, and book lovers have Scribd'.[53] As one of the world's leading E-Libraries, Scribd has the capacity to make a notable impact on reversing the book famine.

In 2014 it was alleged that Scribd did not embrace universal design and was not accessible for persons with print disabilities. A woman named Heidi Viens had a daughter with a print disability who was not able to utilise all aspects of the Scribd E-Library on the same basis as the wider public. In July 2014, with the support of the National Federation of the Blind, Heidi Viens filed suit against Scribd, alleging violation of the ADA.

In November 2015, Scribd settled the suit without admitting they had discriminated.[54] This public settlement does not focus on compensation, but on altering Scribd's E-Library to 'ensure that blind persons who use screen access software shall have effective and equal access to all of the various benefits sighted persons have in regards to the Website and related native mobile applications for iOS and Android'.[55] In this settlement deed, Scribd undertakes to take specific steps to ensure equality of access by 31 December 2017.[56]

To enable equal access to literary content, Scribd undertook to alter existing E-Books and to require publishers to provide new E-Books in accessible formats. To enable access to existing content, Scribd also undertook to 'reprocess all EPUB E-Books that it has received from publishers to ensure that they are accessible with screen access software according to the existing International Digital Publishing Forum standard'.[57] For new files, Scribd will require that publishers ensure E-Books meet this standard.[58] Scribd, however, did not undertake to provide descriptions of graphics beyond those provided by publishers. In addition, to help maintain continuing levels of

---

[52] Scribd, 'About Us' <www.scribd.com/about> (accessed 18 November 2016).

[53] Scribd, 'Home' www.scribd.com (accessed 18 November 2016).

[54] 'Settlement Agreement and Release' between National Federation of the Blind and Heidi Viens, and Scribd, Inc. (November 2015) National Federation of the Blind <nfb.org/images/photos/scribd%20settlement%20agreement%20and%20release.pdf> (accessed 18 November 2016).

[55] Ibid., Recitals.   [56] Ibid., Clause 3(b).   [57] Ibid., Clause 4(a).   [58] Ibid., Clause 4(b).

disability access, Scribd undertook to test for accessibility and to consult with disability person organisations prior to releasing alterations to its platform.[59]

The National Federation of the Blind, Viens and Scribd settlement does more than introduce technical requirements. It has helped to alter the stated vision of how Scribd constructs its service. The CEO of Scribd at the time of the settlement, Trip Adler, explained that Scribd is 'committed to building the library of the future and making it accessible to all. Our collaboration with the National Federation of the Blind is an important step in making this a reality, and we look forward to ensuring our technology is usable for the blind community.'[60] If more litigation against E-Libraries was commenced and settled on terms similar to the National Federation of the Blind, Viens and Scribd settlement, then the outcome in improved access would make a substantial contribution to reversing the book famine, and might even reverse it for those living in wealthy countries with the resources to access such E-Libraries. Of course, many persons with print disabilities do not have the financial resources to purchase E-Books from commercial E-Libraries, nor do they live in jurisdictions where such E-Book libraries are available.

Settling Cases against Educators to Pressure Publishers to Embrace Universal Design

Bringing suit directly against E-Libraries or manufacturers of E-Readers is a high-risk litigation choice. There remains uncertainty about the nature and extent of the application of anti-discrimination duties to publishers, E-Libraries and manufacturers of E-Readers. Chapter 7 analysed how a circuit split in the USA means that websites, and by extension E-Libraries, do not attract anti-discrimination duties for purely digital operations in every circuit. Rather than attempting the complicated task of suing for discrimination against the parties who create barriers to digital equality, and running the risk of adverse cost orders in jurisdictions where this is common, plaintiffs may elect to sue within more well-established relationships.

Plaintiffs who desire access to educational materials often adopt the easier legal road of demanding that their educational institution provides equal access to such materials. While educational institutions have limited capacity to alter how E-Libraries or E-Readers provide their services, educational

---

[59] Ibid., Clause 5.
[60] National Federation of the Blind, 'National Federation of the Blind and Scribd Agree to Collaborate to Make Reading Subscription Service Accessible to the Blind' (19 November 2015) <nfb.org/national-federation-blind-and-scribd-agree-collaborate-make-reading-subscription-service-accessible> (accessed 18 November 2016).

institutions can determine what service they purchase. If educators recognise that they have a duty to purchase disability-accessible educational materials, and if educators alter their purchasing practices, then this means E-Libraries and E-Readers that are not disability accessible run the risk of being shut out of a billion-dollar market.

Disability person organisations and students with print disabilities recognise the potential power of targeting educators to alter the conduct of other parties in the E-Book supply chain. One of the first cases of this nature followed the decision by Arizona State University to use the Kindle E-Book reader in a pilot educational programme.[61] The Kindle E-Book reader's interface was entirely visual, which prevented students with vision impairments from using functions, including selecting E-Books. Furthermore, E-Books were not able to be read once open due to the design of the E-Reader. The National Federation of the Blind and the American Council for the Blind sought a preliminary injunction against Arizona State University. Arizona State University settled the case by agreeing to offer students educational materials on E-Readers that were accessible to all students.[62]

Following the Arizona State University settlement, there has been a string of actions against educational providers where E-Books or E-Readers are used that are not accessible to students with print disabilities. This has resulted in a range of educational providers having legal proceedings commenced against educators for creating educational environments that involve information communication technologies that are not accessible to students with print disabilities. The educational providers range from large universities to community colleges, including Florida State University,[63] Louisiana Tech University,[64] Mesa Community College,[65] Pennsylvania

---

[61] Kel Smith, 'Accessibility and the Real World' in Kel Smith and Morgan Kaufmann (eds), *Digital Outcasts: Moving Technology Forward without Leaving People Behind* (2013) Morgan Kaufmann Publishers, 69–91.

[62] Peter Blanck, *Equality: The Struggle for Web Accessibility by Persons with Cognitive Disabilities* (2014) Cambridge University Press, ch. 8.

[63] *Christopher Shane Toth and Jamie Ann Principato* v. *The Florida State University Board of Trustees* (Complaint in the United States District Court for the Northern District of Florida (Tallahassee Division), 29 June 2011) National Federation of the Blind <nfb.org/images/nfb/documents/word/complaint_final_c.doc> (accessed 18 November 2016).

[64] 'Settlement Agreement between the United States of America, Louisiana Tech University, and the Board of Supervisors for the University of Louisiana System under the Americans with Disabilities Act' (22 July 2013) <www.ada.gov/louisiana-tech.htm> (accessed 18 November 2016).

[65] *Sebastian Ibanez and the National Federation of the Blind* v. *Mesa Community College and Maricopa Community College District* (Complaint in the United States District Court for the District of Arizona, 22 May 2012) National Federation of the Blind <nfb.org/images/nfb/documents/pdf/mesa%20teach.pdf> (accessed 18 November 2016).

State University,[66] University of California, Berkeley,[67] University of Montana,[68] Virtual Community School of Ohio,[69] and Youngstown State University.[70] Rather than taking these actions to court and judgment, many cases are being resolved by the parties on terms that would not be possible if the matter was resolved by a court order. Importantly for combatting the book famine, many educators are agreeing to offer educational materials only through digital platforms that are accessible to all students.

The settlement with Florida State University illustrates how litigation against educational providers is trending. Two Florida State University students with vision impairments encountered substantial discrimination. The software packages that were utilised in their programmes were not accessible to students with print disabilities.[71] This software was used for both learning and assessment purposes. In addition, the students were not provided with textbooks in accessible formats, exam scripts were not provided in accessible formats, clickers that were not accessible for students with print disabilities were used in class, and the students were victimised when they raised these concerns. The discrimination they experienced set them back years. Nine months after filing suit, Florida State University settled with the two students, agreeing to compensate them $75,000 each (being a total of $150,000). The University also agreed that future procurement of 'digital technology and digital instructional materials shall be accessible to the blind', and they agreed 'to take such steps, if any, as are necessary to remove accessibility barriers for blind students to the extent required by law so that

---

[66] 'Resolution Agreement between Pennsylvania State University and the National Federation of the Blind' (undated) National Federation of the Blind <nfb.org/images/nfb/documents/word/pennteach.rtf> (accessed 18 November 2016).

[67] 'Settlement between the University of California, Berkeley, and Disability Rights Advocates, David Jaulus, Brandon King, and Tabitha A Mancini' (6 May 2013) <dralegal.org/wp-content/uploads/files/casefiles/settlement-ucb.pdf> (accessed 18 November 2016).

[68] 'Resolution Agreement between the University of Montana and the US Department of Education, Office for Civil Rights' (10 March 2014) National Federation of the Blind <nfb.org/images/nfb/documents/pdf/agreement_university_of_montana_march_10_2014.pdf> (accessed 18 November 2016).

[69] 'Virtual Community School of Ohio Resolution Agreement: Compliance Review #15-11-5002' (30 September 2013) <www2.ed.gov/documents/press-releases/virtual-community-ohio-agreement.doc> (accessed 18 November 2016).

[70] Letter from United States Department of Education, Office for Civil Rights (Region XV) to James P Tressel (President, Youngstown State University), 12 December 2014 <www2.ed.gov/documents/press-releases/youngstown-state-university-letter.pdf> (accessed 18 November 2016).

[71] 'Final Settlement Agreement, Waiver and Release between the Florida State University Board of Trustees, and Christopher Shane Toth and Jamie Ann Principato' (February 2012) National Federation of the Blind <nfb.org/images/nfb/documents/pdf/fsu%20settlement%20agreement.pdf> (accessed 18 November 2016).

these students can access the content of the curriculum in an equally effective and integrated manner as their non-disabled peers'.[72] Interestingly, the university went further and agreed that by May 2012, it would make the 'My Student Body Alcohol Course accessible to the blind using screen access software or, alternatively, will not offer it to any student'.[73] This means that if the software providers do not render the package accessible to all students, the university will terminate its commercial relationship with the provider. Through pressuring educators to create inclusive educational environments, this litigation reduces the market for digital content that does not embrace universal design. If a critical mass of educational providers only purchased hardware and software that embraced universal design principles, then this commercial pressure would have a profound impact on designers, manufacturers and suppliers.

Using Settlement Agreements to Resolve Disputes and to Combat the Book Famine: Terms of Settlement and Potential for Systemic Change

Through alternative dispute resolution processes, parties are able to resolve disputes on their own terms. Rather than the win-and-lose outcomes that flow from a judicial ruling, alternative dispute resolution processes enable parties to seek more mutually beneficial outcomes.[74] Further, whereas courts are restricted by the remedies provided for in legislation, parties can agree to any terms that they desire to resolve the dispute. This process can result in more systemic change, as well as novel outcomes that can have more positive and long-term results.[75]

Plaintiffs and defendants often desire that the terms of their deeds of settlement remain confidential.[76] Plaintiffs may desire to resolve anti-discrimination litigation in a way that minimises the risks from victimisation

---

[72] 'Final Settlement Agreement, Waiver and Release between the Florida State University Board of Trustees, and Christopher Shane Toth and Jamie Ann Principato' (February 2012) National Federation of the Blind <nfb.org/images/nfb/documents/pdf/fsu%20settlement%20agreement .pdf> (accessed 18 November 2016).

[73] Ibid., Clause 1(j).

[74] Paul Harpur, 'The Financial Benefit for Insurers: Mediate in Personal Injuries Disputes' (2004) 2 *Australasian Dispute Resolution Journal* 70.

[75] Dominique Allen, 'In Defence of Settlement: Resolving Discrimination Complaints by Agreement' (2014) 14(4) *International Journal of Discrimination and the Law* 199.

[76] Jon Bauer, 'Buying Witness Silence: Evidence-Suppressing Settlements and Lawyers' Ethics' (2008) 87(2) *Oregon Law Review* 481; Minna Kotkin, 'Invisible Settlements, Invisible Discrimination' (2006) 84 *North Carolina Law Review* 927; Scott A Moss, 'Illuminating Secrecy: A New Economic Analysis of Confidential Settlements' (2007) 105(5) *Michigan Law Review* 867.

and potential harm to themselves. Defendants generally desire to have the terms of settlement agreements confidential to limit harm to their corporate brand. While keeping the terms of settlement agreements confidential may help the individual litigants, this approach can hinder the transformational change of the advocacy.

To enhance the transformational impact of resolving disputes, there is an increasing trend to make the terms of settlement deeds publicly available, in part or in full. Professors Michael Waterstone, Michael Ashley Stein and David Wilkins found that disability-cause lawyers generally focused on the wider impact of anti-discrimination disputes, and entered into agreements where the terms of the settlement are public, with the exception of confidential addendums.[77] One lawyer in the Waterstone, Stein and Wilkins study commented:

> All of our settlements are public. So what we're looking for is to create precedent so with the next company, we may not even file a suit we may just talk to them and they start to say well you know what we want is the definition of accessibility is XYZ we can say no here is what we've done, here's what we've done, here are the last 6 settlements we did in this area, this is the standard.[78]

To enhance the public impact of litigation, the cause lawyers would actively engage with media. They would publish media releases at each stage of the litigation, to help draw attention and inform the public about their legal duties.[79]

While alternative dispute resolution processes can achieve systemic change, these processes can also result in sub-optimal outcomes. Power imbalances and the personal interests of the parties can equally result in outcomes that fail to meet the needs of the specific plaintiff or of the wider disability community. For example, if the terms of an agreement are not carefully drafted, this might result in defendants failing to remedy the discrimination and thus requiring further enforcement action.[80]

Using Settlement Agreements to Resolve Disputes and Combat the Book Famine: The Time Taken to Resolve Disputes Is Problematic

Utilising alternative dispute resolution processes to settle systemic discrimination disputes, when compared with litigation, is comparatively more

---

[77] Waterstone, Stein and Wilkins, 'Disability Cause Lawyers'.   [78] Ibid., 1315.

[79] Ibid., 1327.

[80] Sonja Ralston Elder, 'Enforcing Public Educational Rights via a Private Right of Action' (2009) 1 *Duke Forum for Law and Social Change* 137, 138.

empowering for plaintiffs, as well as being a quicker and cheaper means of resolving disputes.[81] This is not to suggest that plaintiffs or the wider public would regard the reaching of such settlements as rapid or inexpensive. Indeed, most settlements take years to resolve. For example, in the Florida State University case discussed above, the barrier was first raised in August 2008 and resolved in February 2012, which is a period of forty-two months. In the Louisiana Tech University case, the barrier was first raised in March 2011 and settled in July 2013 – a period of twenty-eight months.[82] The time taken in reaching these settlements would have had intensely detrimental outcomes on the education and lives of the plaintiffs. Considering educational courses can last a few semesters for a certificate, a year for honours or a master of laws, and three years for many courses, a delay of weeks can be detrimental, a delay of months can be devastating, and a delay of years can be fatal to the educational experience.

SECTION IV ENFORCING LAWS WHICH SEEK EQUALITY RATHER THAN JUST PROHIBIT DISCRIMINATION

The previous section has analysed how traditional anti-discrimination duties are enforced through victim-led civil litigation. This section will analyse how laws that take a more proactive approach to resolving equality are enforced. While the positive duties in Canada and the United Kingdom can be enforced through litigation, as will be analysed below, the nature of this litigation is very different to that of traditional anti-discrimination laws. This section will analyse how these positive duties are enforced, and then analyse how the novel interventions in the United States introduced in Chapter 11 are enforced.

Enforcing Positive Duties in Canada

Positive duties in Canada, analysed in Chapter 10, appear within the anti-discrimination and constitutional jurisdictions. The positive duties sourced

---

[81] Rachel Field, 'Rethinking Mediation Ethics: A Contextual Method to Support Party Self-Determination' (2011) 22(1) *Australasian Dispute Resolution Journal* 8.

[82] *Christopher Shane Toth and Jamie Ann Principato v. The Florida State University Board of Trustees* (Complaint in the United States District Court for the Northern District of Florida (Tallahassee Division), 29 June 2011) National Federation of the Blind <nfb.org/images/nfb/documents/word/complaint_final_c.doc> (accessed 18 November 2016); 'Settlement Agreement between the United States of America, Louisiana Tech University, and the Board of Supervisors for the University of Louisiana System under the Americans with Disabilities Act' (22 July 2013) <www.ada.gov/louisiana-tech.htm> (accessed 18 November 2016).

within the *Canadian Human Rights Act 1985* are enforced in a similar way to the negative duties found in the anti-discrimination statutes in Australia, the United Kingdom and the United States discussed above. A complaint about a breach of negative or positive duties under the *Canadian Human Rights Act 1985* is first filed with the Canadian Human Rights Commission. If the complaint is not resolved before the commission, then the complaint can be heard before the Canadian Human Rights Tribunal. Appeals from this tribunal can be made to appellant courts. In most cases, the Canadian Human Rights Commission will not provide a complainant with any support before the tribunal or on appeal to the courts.

The *Canadian Charter of Rights and Freedoms* (*Charter*) enshrines constitutional rights involving positive obligations, which are enforced very differently in comparison to traditional anti-discrimination duties. Violations of *Charter* rights fall within the constitutional jurisdiction and are only enforceable by the courts. A person who has had their *Charter* rights violated can seek a declaration under the *Federal Courts Act 1985* s 18.1. This provides that an application for judicial review may be made by 'anyone directly affected by the matter in respect of which relief is sought'. Subsection 18.1(3) enables the Federal Court to make an order against any 'federal board, commission, or other tribunal', on any of the grounds listed in subsection 18.1(4). These orders include violations of positive *Charter* rights.[83] Constitutional litigation is expensive, very legalistic, and is generally far beyond the means of most members of the community.[84] Furthermore, persons with disabilities often have fewer resources than the wider public, which places judicial review further out of reach for members of this group.

Enforcing Positive Duties in the United Kingdom

As analysed in Chapter 9, the positive duties in the United Kingdom are sourced within the *Equality Act 2010* (UK). While these duties appear in an omnibus anti-discrimination statute, the public sector equality duty is enforced through an entirely separate process. Whereas traditional anti-discrimination duties are enforced through specialist tribunals, violations

---

[83] See for example *Canadian Association of the Deaf* v. *Canada* [2007] 2 FCR 323.
[84] Ian Brodie, 'Interest Group Litigation and the Embedded State: Canada's Court Challenges Program' (2001) 34(2) *Canadian Journal of Political Science/Revue Canadienne de Science Politique* 357; Vera Chouinard, 'Legal Peripheries: Struggles over DisAbled Canadians' Places in Law, Society and Space' (2001) 45(1) *Canadian Geographer* 187; Lisa Vanhala, 'Disability Rights Activists in the Supreme Court of Canada: Legal Mobilization Theory and Accommodating Social Movements' (2009) 42(4) *Canadian Journal of Political Science* 981.

of the public sector equality duty do not give rise to a personal right of action.[85]

There are several means of enforcing the public sector equality duty. There is a non-judicial means of monitoring, involving a declaration and public pressure to motivate compliance. This form of enforcement occurs where the Equality and Human Rights Commission investigates and makes a non-binding declaration that the public sector equality duty has been breached.[86] To motivate self-compliance there are also some reporting obligations under the public sector equality duty. The reporting obligations under the public sector equality duty have already been discussed in Chapter 9.

Judicial enforcement of the public sector equality duty is possible where a person has standing to bring judicial review. The judicial review can be filed by an individual who has standing, or alternatively by the Equality and Human Rights Commission where its declaration of non-compliance has been ignored by the public sector agency. If the courts find that the public sector equality duty has not been considered, then they have the power to require the public sector agency to remake the decision while factoring in the public sector equality duty.[87] This order does not require the public sector agency to alter its decision, but instead focuses on ensuring that all attributes are considered in the decision-making process. It is conceivable that the public sector equality duty is increasing the attention that public sector agencies pay to creating inclusive digital spaces.

The Individuals with Disabilities Education Act: *Enforcing Compliance with the National Instructional Materials Access Center and Standards*

Access to instructional materials is one small component of the broader agenda contained in the *Individuals with Disabilities Education Act (IDEA)*. The enforcement vehicles in the *IDEA* focus on the interaction of school districts and the educational experiences of students with disabilities. While students with disabilities can file a due process claim under the *IDEA* and benefit from mediation,[88] these processes are not likely to result in any meaningful outcome in relation to the interaction between school districts and NIMAC and publishers.

---

[85] Bob Hepple, *Equality*, 2nd edn (2014) Hart Publishing, 172.   [86] Ibid., 175.

[87] *Stuart Bracking & Ors v. Secretary of State for Work and Pensions* [2014] Eq LR 60, [69].

[88] 20 USC §1415(e) (Supp 2004); Andrea F Blau, 'Available Dispute Resolution Processes within the *Reauthorized Individuals with Disabilities Education Improvement Act* (IDEIA) of 2004: Where Do Mediation Principles Fit In?' (2007) 7(1) *Pepperdine Dispute Resolution Law Journal* 65; Demetra Edwards, 'New Amendments to Resolving Special Education Disputes: Any Good Ideas?' (2005) 5(1) *Pepperdine Dispute Resolution Law Journal* 137, 138.

Section 415(6)(a) of the *IDEA* provides students with disabilities (generally through their parents) the right to bring a complaint 'with respect to any matter relating to the identification, evaluation, or educational placement of the child, or the provision of a free appropriate public education to such child'. Such rights focus on the interaction between the school district and the student, and not on the interaction between the school district and third parties such as the National Instructional Materials Access Center or publishers. Furthermore, courts have repeatedly refused to order monetary damages for breaches of the *IDEA*, even where individual students have suffered quantifiable economic losses.[89] While school districts can technically have their federal funding restricted if they do not provide access to instructional materials,[90] in reality most school districts participate with NIMAC because it represents an efficient way for them to discharge their anti-discrimination duties.

There has been academic debate contending that private enforcement and damages should be available for a breach of the *IDEA*.[91] Candace Chun, for example, has argued that section 1983 should be available to provide monetary damages for a breach of the *IDEA*.[92] Section 1983 provides:

> Every person who, under color of any statute, ordinance, regulation, custom, or usage, of any State . . . subjects, or causes to be subjected, any citizen of the United States . . . to the deprivation of any rights, privileges, or immunities secured by the Constitution and laws, shall be liable to the party injured.[93]

Even though courts have read the situations to award damages extremely narrowly, Candace Chun has observed that 'many parents have turned to section 1983 seeking relief for the egregious violations of students' rights by schools'.[94]

---

[89] See for examples: *Gean v. Hattaway*, 330 F 3d 758, 774 (6th Cir., 2003); *Polera v. Bd. of Educ.*, 288 F 3d 478, 483–6 (2nd Cir., 2002); *Witte v. Clark County Sch. Dist.*, 197 F 3d 1271, 1275 (9th Cir., 1999); *Sellers v. Sch. Bd. of Manassas*, 141 F 3d 524, 526–7 (4th Cir., 1998); *Charlie F. v. Bd. of Educ.*, 98 F 3d 989, 991 (7th Cir., 1996); *Heidemann v. Rother*, 84 F 3d 1021, 1033 (8th Cir., 1996).

[90] 20 USC §1412(1) (2000).

[91] Rebecca Bouchard, 'Education Law: The Relationship between the *Individuals with Disabilities Education Act* and Section 1983: Are Compensatory Damages an Available and Appropriate Remedy?' (2003) 25(2) *Western New England Law Review* 301; Terry Seligmann, 'A Diller, A Dollar: Section 1983 Damage Claims in Special Education Lawsuits' (2001) 36 *Georgia Law Review* 465.

[92] Candace Chun, 'The Use of § 1983 as a Remedy for Violations of the *Individuals with Disabilities Education Act*: Why It Is Necessary and What It Really Means' (2009) 72 *Albany Law Review* 461, 465.

[93] 42 USC § 1983 (2003).

[94] Chun, 'The Use of § 1983 as a Remedy for Violations of the *Individuals with Disabilities Education Act*', 476.

While some circuits prohibit section 1983 claims for breaches of the *IDEA*,[95] other circuits permit such claims.[96] Even where a section 1983 claim was available, a student would only be able to quantify damages where they have been denied access to instructional materials, and a denial of such material is already actionable under the more plaintiff-friendly *ADA*. Essentially, there is no means of compelling school districts to participate with NIMAC.

Enforcing the Twenty-First Century Communications and
Video Accessibility Act of 2010

Section 104 of the *Twenty-First Century Communications and Video Accessibility Act of 2010 (21st CVAA)* introduced ss 717 and 718 into the *Communications Act of 1934*. The new s 717 contains the *21st CVAA* enforcement and record-keeping obligations. Pursuant to the enforcement regime established under s 717 of the *Communications Act of 1934*, consumers can make formal and informal complaints to the Federal Communications Commission (FCC). Different rules apply to informal and formal complaints. Before filing an informal complaint, rules introduced in 2013 require aggrieved consumers to first submit a 'request for dispute assistance' (RDA) to the Disability Rights Office of the Consumer and Governmental Affairs Bureau of the Federal Communications Commission, for help in resolving the consumer's accessibility problem with a telecommunications or advanced communications service provider or equipment manufacturer.[97] Formal complaints can be filed without this process with the Enforcement Bureau at the FCC.

After receiving a complaint, the FCC can 'direct the manufacturer or service provider to bring the service, or in the case of a manufacturer, the next generation of the equipment or device, into compliance with requirements of those sections within a reasonable time established by the Commission in its order'.[98] Where the breach pertains to internet browsers built into telephones, the Enforcement Bureau of the FCC can hand down a forfeiture penalty for non-compliance of 'not more than $100,000 for each violation or each day of a continuing violation, except that the amount

---

[95] *Blanchard* v. *Morton Sch. Dist.*, 504 F 3d 771, 774–5 (9th Cir., 2007); *A.W.* v. *Jersey City Pub. Sch.*, 486 F 3d 791, 806 (3rd Cir., 2007); *Diaz-Fonseca* v. *Puerto Rico*, 451 F 3d 13, 29 (1st Cir., 2006); *Padilla* v. *Sch. Dist. No. 1*, 233 F 3d 1268, 1274 (10th Cir., 2000); *Sellers* v. *Sch. Bd. of Manassas*, 141 F 3d 524, 525 (4th Cir., 1998).

[96] *Marie O.* v. *Edgar*, 131 F 3d 610, 611–12 (7th Cir., 1997); *Mrs. W.* v. *Tirozzi*, 832 F 2d 748, 750 (2nd Cir., 1987).

[97] See 47 CFR §§ 14.32 (consumer dispute assistance), 14.34–14.37 (informal complaints), 14.38–14.52 (formal complaints).

[98] *Communications Act of 1934*, s 717(3)(b)(1).

assessed for any continuing violation shall not exceed a total of $1,000,000 for any single act or failure to act'.[99] Even though the provider or manufacturer might receive an order and a forfeiture penalty, the aggrieved consumer is not entitled to any damages. Arguably, the *21st CVAA* enforcement framework combines cooperation with industry and stakeholders with the threat of significant legal sanctions for non-compliance. This enforcement model, combined with the transformational approach of targeting the causes of digital disablement discussed in Chapter 11, arguably makes the *21st CVAA* one of the most transformational equality interventions enacted into law.

SECTION V STRONG COPYRIGHT ENFORCEMENT OBSTRUCTS THE DEVELOPMENT OF UNIVERSAL AND DISABILITY-ACCESSIBLE E-LIBRARIES

Chapters 3, 4 and 5 argued that copyright restricts the free flow of information and significantly contributes to the continuation of the book famine. If copyright laws focused less on restricting access and instead on rewarding creativity, this would create a regulatory space where universal libraries could flourish. As analysed in Chapters 4 and 5 of this monograph, domestic copyright laws restrict sharing of information and tightly restrict unauthorised access for special cases. If existing copyright laws are robustly enforced, this will hinder the creation of universal libraries and will negatively impact on compliance and above-compliance responses to anti-discrimination duties.

Chapters 6, 7 and 8 illustrated that traditional anti-discrimination duties do not require regulated parties to enable persons with print disabilities to read books on an equal basis with others. Anti-discrimination duties require a much lower level of access that is bounded by what is reasonable in each situation. In such a legal environment, the book famine experienced by persons with print disabilities will only be addressed through above-compliance activities. This section will argue that it is possible that the combination of restrictive copyright laws and a high level of enforcement reduces the willingness of parties to engage in certain above-compliance activities.

How Non-Compliance Is Constructed: Pirates Versus Ableism

The normative discourse pertaining to breaching copyright restrictions is arguably much stronger than that relating to protecting the rights of persons

---

[99] *21st CVAA*, s 104; *Communications Act of 1934*, s 718(c).

with disabilities. This means there is greater normative social pressure to restrict the free flow of information than normative social pressure to ensure everyone in the community can gain access to information. Until recently, denying persons with disabilities human rights was the norm and was regarded as acceptable conduct.[100] As illustrated by the discussion of Professor Lennard Davis's work on 'bending over backwards' above, discrimination against persons with disabilities continues to be defended by many in the community. The challenges in constructing disability discrimination as something un-acceptable are arguably aggravated by the lack of an appropriate label to describe this wrong.[101] Disability rights scholars have proposed the use of 'ableism' and 'disablism'; however, these terms are not widely employed and do not carry the same normative social power as analogous terms such as 'sexism' and 'racism'.[102]

Unlike disability rights, the normative social pressure protecting copyright has a long history and is well-settled. Since the advent of the fifteenth century, copyright holders have sought to restrict access to books.[103] Part of this process has been to promote the notion that copying book content without permission from the author should be regarded as theft. The use of information that is restricted by copyright without permission is labelled as piracy, and the people who make unauthorised use of information as pirates.[104] The notion that unauthorised sharing of copyright-restricted information is piracy is supported by dominant discourses of legal authorities, rights-holders and their lobby groups.[105] These powerful and wealthy interests have been successful historic-ally at minimising the voices of the counter-discourses led by copyright activist groups and disabled person organisations. This process has resulted in persons with disabilities being regarded as special cases and exceptions to the over-arching approach of restricting sharing information and knowledge. Through this discourse, people who breach copyright restrictions to share information are not constructed as Robin Hoods, but instead as socially undesirable pirates. Beyond limited exceptions, the overarching norm is to elevate the commercial

---

[100] See in particular the discussion in this monograph on eugenics and the medical model in Chapter 2.

[101] Paul Harpur, 'From Disability to Ability: Changing the Phrasing of the Debate' (2012) 27(3) *Disability and Society* 325.

[102] Paul Harpur, 'Sexism and Racism, Why Not Ableism? Calling for a Cultural Shift in the Approach to Disability Discrimination' (2009) 34(3) *Alternative Law Journal* 163.

[103] Adrian Johns, *Piracy: The Intellectual Property Wars from Gutenberg to Gates* (2010) University of Chicago Press, ch. 4.

[104] Sebastian Haunss, *Conflicts in the Knowledge Society* (2013) Cambridge University Press, 200.

[105] Jessica Reyman, *Intellectual Property: Copyright Law and the Regulation of Digital Culture* (2010) Routledge, 26.

interests of rights-holders to maintain information monopolies over the human rights of persons with disabilities.

Responses to Differences in Enforcement: Protecting Copyright Is More Important than Avoiding Discrimination

In contrast to anti-discrimination laws, copyright laws are strongly enforced by powerful groups in society, and non-compliance is enforced through civil and criminal sanctions.[106] International law requires that states criminalise unauthorised exploitation of copyright-restricted works. Article 61 of the TRIPS agreement provides:

> Members shall provide for criminal procedures and penalties to be applied at least in cases of wilful trademark counterfeiting or copyright piracy on a commercial scale. Remedies available shall include imprisonment and/or monetary fines sufficient to provide a deterrent, consistently with the level of penalties applied for crimes of a corresponding gravity.[107]

The copyright laws in Australia, Canada and the United Kingdom have criminalised non-compliance with copyright laws, and the conduct attracts substantial fines and imprisonment.[108]

The robust enforcement of copyright laws has resulted in file-sharing services being criminally liable for facilitating the distribution of restricted knowledge.[109] The conviction of the founders of the Pirate Bay file-sharing service is a good example of the extent of sanctions for breaching copyright restrictions.[110] The founders were both sentenced to twelve months'

---

[106] Christopher Buccafusco and Jonathan S Masur, 'Innovation and Incarceration: An Economic Analysis of Criminal Intellectual Property Law' (2014) 87 *Southern California Law Review* 275.

[107] *Marrakesh Agreement Establishing the World Trade Organization*, opened for signature 15 April 1994, 1867 UNTS 3 (entered into force 1 January 1995) annex 1C (*Agreement on Trade-Related Aspects of Intellectual Property Rights*), clause 61; Xuan Li and Carlos M Correa, 'Towards a Development Approach on IP Enforcement: Conclusions and Strategic Recommendations' in Xuan Li and Carlos M Correa (eds), *Intellectual Property: Enforcement International Perspectives* (2009) Edward Elgar, 207.

[108] The longest terms of imprisonment for violating copyright in Australia and Canada are five years including fines, and in the United States, ten years including fines. In the United Kingdom it is two years including fines and sanctions. See *Copyright Act 1968* (Cth) s 132(2); *Copyright Act*, RSC 1985, c C-42, s 2.1; *Copyright, Designs and Patents Act 1988* (UK); 18 USC § 2319.

[109] Benton Martin and Jeremiah Newhall, 'Criminal Copyright Enforcement against Filesharing Services' (2013) 15(1) *North Carolina Journal of Law and Technology* 101.

[110] Stefan Larsson, 'Metaphors, Law and Digital Phenomena: The Swedish Pirate Bay Court Case' (2013) 21(4) *International Journal of Law and IT* 354.

imprisonment and ordered to pay tens of millions of euros.[111] The criminalisation of sharing information has resulted in significant attention from founders, operators and users of file-sharing services.[112]

Beyond criminal sanctions, copyright laws have adopted a range of vehicles to restrict the use of copyright-protected information. Civil proceedings can be commenced which can result in significant monetary orders.[113] Then there are measures that seek to block traffic to offending sites. For example, the Australian *Copyright Amendment (Online Infringement) Act 2015* (Cth) enables rights-holders to apply to the Federal Court to have foreign websites blocked that infringe copyright restrictions. The Federal Court will perform a primary purpose test to determine if the primary purpose of the offending website is to infringe copyright restrictions or to facilitate infringements. If the primary purpose is found to be infringement or facilitating infringement, the Federal Court will order all Australian internet service providers to block their clients from accessing the online location where the infringement occurred.

Whereas anti-discrimination laws are enforced by groups with limited resources, many rights-holders have significant resources. Indeed, many of the copyright enforcement tactics reflect the power of the copyright lobby. For example, to protect digital copyright interests, some copyright holders have retained agents who send threatening emails to people without first checking if they have even breached the law, in order to pressure compliance and compensation.[114] Rights-holders and their lobbyists use aggressive civil and criminal litigation to close down and discourage people from unauthorised sharing of information. Considering that the sanctions involve extremely high monetary awards and imprisonment, corporate and natural persons are more likely to be motivated to avoid non-compliance with copyright laws than non-compliance with human rights principles or anti-discrimination laws.

While performing research in 2009 and 2010, the author experienced how the fear of copyright-related sanctions can restrict the access of university students with print disabilities to textbooks.[115] After determining that university students were experiencing substantial and damaging delays in accessing

---

[111] Stockholm District Court, Case No B 13301-06 (17 April 2009); Svea Hovratt (appellate court), Case No B 4041-09 (26 November 2010).

[112] Graham Reynolds, 'Case Comment: Pirate Bay on English Bay? BitTorrent File Sharing and Copyright Infringement in the Supreme Court of British Columbia' (2012) 43(1) *U.B.C. Law Review* 193.

[113] Annemarie Bridy, 'Is Online Copyright Enforcement Scalable?' (2011) 13(4) *Vanderbilt Journal of Entertainment and Technology Law* 695.

[114] Sean B Karunaratne, 'Case against Combating BitTorrent Piracy through Mass John Doe Copyright Infringement Lawsuits' (2012) 111(2) *Michigan Law Review* 283.

[115] The 2009 and 2010 research was supported by a grant: Queensland University of Technology, Division of Technology, Information and Learning Support Grant, 'providing students with

books,[116] the author and some of the research team proposed starting a database similar to Bookshare. As a pilot, this database would only provide access to university students at a small number of Australian universities. During consultations to establish this database, the author found that students who had textbooks in accessible formats were contractually bound not to share books provided to them. Some students were prepared to share materials they had personally scanned. University librarians were nervous about sharing materials they had scanned on this database and university administrators were concerned about potential copyright liabilities. The university accepted it had duties under anti-discrimination law to provide access, and as a former student I knew they provided an extremely good service; however, the fear of copyright sanctions removed support for creating a database. Ultimately, the idea of starting a database to enhance the access of university students with print disabilities to textbooks was dropped. As a result, fear of copyright laws directly reduced the capacity of students with print disabilities to obtain textbooks in accessible formats.

CONCLUSION

The interaction between the enforcement of laws which promote access to information for persons with print disabilities and copyright laws which seek to restrict access to information is contributing to the continuation of the book famine. The analysis in this chapter commenced by explaining how the enforcement pyramid is the model which best explains how the legal duties analysed in this monograph are enforced.

Secondly, this chapter analysed how traditional anti-discrimination laws are enforced. This discussion included an analysis of the pre-litigious and litigious steps involved in suing for discrimination, the risk of victimisation and the impact of resource limitations on enforcement. Thirdly, this chapter analysed how laws which promote equality are enforced. This included analysing the enforcement of positive duties in Canada and the United Kingdom, along with weak enforcement under the *IDEA* and more effective enforcement under the *21st CVAA*. Finally, this chapter analysed the robust enforcement

---

vision impairment print material in an accessible electronic format: identifying barriers in the current model'.

[116] Paul Harpur and Rebecca Loudoun, 'The Barrier of the Written Word: Analysing Universities' Policies to Include Students with Print Disabilities and Calls for Reforms' (2011) 33(2) *Journal of Higher Education Policy and Management* 153; Paul Harpur, 'Providing Students with Vision Impairment Print Material in an Accessible Electronic Format: Identifying Barriers in the Current Model' (Final Report, Queensland University of Technology Division of Technology, Information and Learning, QUT Library and Law School, 2010).

of copyright laws along with the substantial penalties which flow from non-compliance.

Laws and their enforcement both convey messages.[117] Arguably, the message conveyed by the enforcement of anti-discrimination, equality and copyright laws on the whole is that substantial changes from the existing status quo are not required. Traditional anti-discrimination laws and the positive duties in Canada and the United Kingdom rely on sporadic and weakly enforced individual enforcement. The probability of being found liable by a court for breaching anti-discrimination and equality duties is reasonably low. This might send the wrong signal to regulated parties, such as employers and educators. Copyright laws, in contrast, are aggressively enforced with significant punishments. Copyright laws send the message that there is a reasonably high risk that a breach of these laws will result in detection and substantial punishment. The interaction between these competing regimes means that regulated parties are more likely to devote more resources to complying with copyright laws, rather than duties under anti-discrimination laws or laws which promote equality. The impact of copyright laws is even more acute when parties may be considering engaging in above-compliance activities to promote access to information for persons with print disabilities. While such above-compliance activities would further the rights of persons with print disabilities, the enforcement of copyright laws is likely to suppress the formation of interventions that would help combat the book famine.

---

[117] Sandra Fredman, *Discrimination Law*, 2nd edn (2011) Oxford University Press, 280.

Closing Thoughts and New Options to Reduce Digital Disablement

Arguably, new enforcement options are required that more fairly balance the interests of rights-holders with the human rights of persons with print disabilities. Research demonstrates that many parties fail to comply with their regulatory obligations due to inattention or miscalculation, and not because key actors have actively decided not to comply with the law.[1] Enabling persons with print disabilities to consume E-Books and digital content is a technical process, which harried line managers may devote inadequate resources to in order to ensure compliance. There are, however, situations where parties intentionally deny access. The analysis of the Amazon Kindle reader in Chapter 1 is an example of a rational and lawful decision to deny access to persons with print disabilities. In contrast, Chapter 1 also identified that a significant number of publishers are actively seeking to reduce the book famine by working with Bookshare to provide books to print-disabled readers. There is no doubt that sanctions remain a vital tool in the regulatory framework; however, moving forward, regulators should continue to seek additional strategies to achieve desired targets.

There is arguably great scope for disability rights scholars to engage further with regulatory theory to craft new vehicles to promote equality. Professors Robert Baldwin, Martin Cave and Martin Lodge have identified the key regulatory models which can be used to craft interventions.[2] These options include:

[1] R A Kagan and J Scholz, 'The "Criminology of the Corporation" and Regulatory Enforcement Styles' in K Hawkins and J Thomas (eds), *Enforcing Regulation* (1984) Kluwer Nijhoff Publishing, 67–9; D Spence and T Malloy, 'Regulation, Compliance and the Firm' (2003) 76 *Temple Law Review* 451.

[2] Robert Baldwin, Martin Cave and Martin Lodge, *Understanding Regulation: Theory, Strategy, and Practice*, 2nd edn (2011) Oxford University Press, 106.

1. To command – where legal authority and the command of law are used to pursue policy objectives.
2. To deploy wealth – where contracts, grants, loans, subsidies or other incentives are used to influence conduct.
3. To harness markets – where governments channel competitive forces to particular ends (for example, by using franchise auctions to achieve benefits for consumers).
4. To inform – where information is deployed strategically (e.g. so as to empower consumers).
5. To act directly – where the state takes physical action itself (e.g. to contain a hazard or nuisance).
6. To confer protected rights – where rights and liability rules are structured and allocated so as to create desired incentives and constraints (e.g. rights to clean water are created in order to deter polluters).[3]

The majority of strategies analysed in this monograph rely on a variant of the command-and-control model. Enforcement often relies upon a survivor of ableism to carry the burden of enforcing the laws. State support and enforcement will help combat the worst forms of ableism; however, commands and sanctions are only one regulatory option. Civil rights laws continue to play a vital role in promoting equality, although more regulatory options need to be explored.

A theme throughout this monograph has been that the parties who attract legal obligations are not always the parties in the best position to remedy the inequality. Rather than imposing anti-discrimination duties on every party in the product life cycle who can impact upon disablement, perhaps incentivising equality activities may be an option that would be easier to enforce and more politically acceptable. Enforcing incentives is much easier than imposing sanctions, as incentivised parties do all the legwork to demonstrate that they are entitled to the reward. Provided there is sufficient community benefit to the incentive scheme,[4] the absence of compulsion means there should be less reluctance from the business community about the introduction of the scheme.

There are already incentive schemes surrounding disability employment in the form of tax credits.[5] Tax credits could foreseeably be granted for the research, development and adoption of disability-inclusive digital

---

[3] Ibid.

[4] Edward L Rubin, 'Images of Organizations and Consequences of Regulation' (2005) 6 *Theoretical Inquiries in Law* 347, 348.

[5] Lennard J Davis, 'Bending Over Backwards: Disability, Narcissism, and the Law' (2000) 21(1) *Berkeley Journal of Employment and Labor Law* 193, 203.

spaces.[6] Where there is a disabling digital environment, persons with disabilities currently experience harm in their cultural, educational, economic, employment and general lives. Rather than requiring persons with disabilities to carry the cost of disabling spaces, incentives would shift part of the burden onto the state and encourage equality activities from parties who can make digital spaces disability-inclusive.

[6] Delia Ferri, 'Does Accessible Technology Need an "Entrepreneurial State"?: The Creation of an EU Market of Universally Designed and Assistive Technology through State Aid' (2015) 29(2–3) *International Review of Law, Computers and Technology* 137.

Appendix: List of Anti-Discrimination and Civil Rights Laws and Tribunals/Commissions Impacting on Disability in the Federal and State/Province Jurisdictions in Australia, Canada, the United Kingdom and the United States

State/Province	Legislation	Complaint agency/commission/tribunal	URL of agency/commission/tribunal
Australia			
Federal	Disability Discrimination Act 1992 (Cth)	Australian Human Rights Commission	www.humanrights.gov.au
New South Wales	Anti-Discrimination Act 1977 (NSW)	Anti-Discrimination Board of New South Wales	www.lawlink.nsw.gov.au/adb
Queensland	Anti-Discrimination Act 1991 (Qld)	Anti-Discrimination Commission Queensland	www.adcq.qld.gov.au
South Australia	Equal Opportunity Act 1984 (SA)	Government of South Australia Equal Opportunity Commission	www.eoc.sa.gov.au
Tasmania	Anti-Discrimination Act 1998	Equal Opportunity Tasmania, Office of the Anti-Discrimination Commissioner	www.antidiscrimination.tas.gov.au
Victoria	Equal Opportunity Act 2010 (Vic)	Victorian Equal Opportunity and Human Rights Commission	www.humanrightscommission.vic.gov.au
Western Australia	Equal Opportunity Act 1984 (WA)	The Government of Western Australia Equal Opportunity Commission	www.eoc.wa.gov.au
Australian Capital Territory	Discrimination Act 1991 (ACT)	Australian Capital Territory Human Rights Commission	www.hrc.act.gov.au
Northern Territory	Anti-Discrimination Act 1996 (NT)	Northern Territory Anti-Discrimination Commission	www.adc.nt.gov.au
Canada			
Federal	Canadian Human Rights Act, RSC, 1985, c. H-6	Canadian Human Rights Commission	www.chrc-ccdp.gc.ca/eng
Alberta	Human Rights Act, RSA 2000, c A-25.5	Alberta Human Rights Commission	www.albertahumanrights.ab.ca

(continued)

(continued)

State/Province	Legislation	Complaint agency/commission/tribunal	URL of agency/commission/tribunal
British Columbia	British Columbia Human Rights Code, RSBC 1996, c 210	British Columbia Human Rights Tribunal	www.bchrt.bc.ca; www.canlii.org/en/bc/laws/stat/rsbc-1996-c-210/46440/rsbc-1996-c-210.html
Manitoba	Human Rights Code, CCSM c H175	The Manitoba Human Rights Commission	www.manitobahumanrights.ca/yourhumanrights.html
New Brunswick	Human Rights Act, RSNB 1973, c H-11	New Brunswick Human Rights Commission	www.gnb.ca/hrc-cdp/index-e.asp
Newfoundland and Labrador	Human Rights Act, 2010, SNL 2010, c H-13	Newfoundland and Labrador Human Rights Commission	www.justice.gov.nl.ca/hrc/index.html
Nova Scotia	Nova Scotia Human Rights Act, RSNS 1989, c 214	Nova Scotia Human Rights Commission	humanrights.gov.ns.ca
Ontario	Accessibility for Ontarians with Disabilities Act, 2005; Ontario Human Rights Code, RSO 1990, c H.19	Ontario Human Rights Commission	www.ohrc.on.ca/en/about-commission
Prince Edward Island	Human Rights Act, RSPEI 1988, c H-12	Prince Edward Island Human Rights Commission	www.gov.pe.ca/humanrights
Quebec	Quebec Charter of Human Rights and Freedoms, CQLR.txt	Commission des droits de la personne et des droits de la jeunesse, Québec	www.cdpdj.qc.ca/en/commission/Pages/default.aspx
Saskatchewan	Saskatchewan Human Rights Code, SS 1979, c S-24.1	Saskatchewan Human Rights Commission	saskatchewanhumanrights.ca
Northwest Territories	Human Rights Act, SNWT 2002, c 18	Northwest Territories Human Rights Commission	nwthumanrights.ca

Jurisdiction	Legislation	Commission	Website
Nunavut Territories	Nunavut Human Rights Act, SNu 2003, c 12	Nunavut Human Rights Tribunal	www.nhrt.ca/splash.html
Yukon Territories	Yukon Territory Human Rights Act, RSY 2002, c 116		canlii.ca/t/8j8z
United Kingdom			
United Kingdom	Equality Act 2010 (UK)	Equality and Human Rights Commission	www.equalityhumanrights.com
Northern Ireland	Human Rights Act 1998 (UK)	Equality Commission for Northern Ireland and Northern Ireland Human Rights Commission	www.equalityni.org/AboutUs; www.nihrc.org/about-us
Scotland	Scottish Commission for Human Rights Act 2006 (Scotland); The Equality Act 2010 (Specific Duties) (Scotland) Amendment Regulations 2015 (Scotland)	Scottish Human Rights Commission	www.scottishhumanrights.com
Wales	The Equality Act 2010 (Statutory Duties) (Wales) Regulations 2011	Equality and Human Rights Commission	www.equalityhumanrights.com/about-us/devolved-authorities/commission-wales/about-commission-wales
United States of America			
Federal	Americans with Disabilities Act of 1990; Rehabilitation Act of 1973	US Equal Employment Opportunity Commission; US Department of Transportation; Federal Communications Commission; The United States Department of Justice	www.eeoc.gov; www.dot.gov; www.fcc.gov; www.usdoj.gov

(continued)

(continued)

State/Province	Legislation	Complaint agency/commission/tribunal	URL of agency/commission/tribunal
Alabama	Handicapped Persons Code	Alabama Department of Human Resources, Equal Employment & Civil Rights	dhr.alabama.gov/directory/Equal_Emp_Civil_Rts.aspx
Alaska	Alaska Human Rights Law, AS 18.80.200	Alaska State Commission for Human Rights	humanrights.alaska.gov
Arizona	Arizona Code of Ordinances, Chapter 15,28: Arizonans with Disabilities Act	Arizona Attorney General, Civil Rights Division	www.municode.com/library/az/safford/codes/code_of_ordinances?nodeId=TIT15BUCO_CH15.28ARDIAC; www.azag.gov/civil-rights
Arkansas	Arkansas Civil Rights Act of 1993, Chapter 123, Subchapter 1	Little Rock Area Office of the US Equal Employment Opportunity Commission; Fair Housing Commission	law.justia.com/codes/arkansas/2010/title-16/subtitle-7/chapter-123/subchapter-1; www.eeoc.gov/field/littlerock/index.cfm; www.fairhousing.arkansas.gov
California	Unruh Civil Rights Act	Attorney General's Office – Civil Rights Division	oag.ca.gov/civil
Colorado	Uniform Duties to Disabled Persons Act	Colorado Civil Rights Division, Department of Regulatory Agencies	www.colorado.gov/pacific/dora/civil-rights
Connecticut	Connecticut Fair Employment Practices Act	Commission on Human Rights and Opportunities; Office of Protection and Advocacy for Persons with Disabilities	www.state.ct.us/chro; www.ct.gov/opapd/site/default.asp
Delaware	Delaware Fair Housing Act; Delaware Equal Accommodations Law	Delaware Department of State, Division of Human Relations	statehumanrelations.delaware.gov/index.shtml

State	Law	Agency	Website
Florida	Florida Civil Rights Act of 1992	Florida Commission on Human Relations	fchr.state.fl.us
Georgia	Georgia Fair Employment Practices Act of 1978; Georgia Fair Housing Law	Georgia Commission on Equal Opportunity	www.gceo.state.ga.us
Hawaii	Hawaii Administrative Rules (Title 12, Chapter 46), Subchapter 9 – Disability Discrimination; HRS Chapter 378 (Hawaii Employment Practices Act, Part 1); HRS Chapter 489 (Discrimination in Public Accommodations); HRS Chapter 515 (Discrimination in Real Property Transactions)	Hawaii Civil Rights Commission	labor.hawaii.gov/hcrc
Idaho	Title 67, Chapter 59 of the Idaho Code	Idaho Commission on Human Rights	humanrights.idaho.gov/law.html
Illinois	Illinois Civil Rights Act of 2003; Illinois Human Rights Act	Illinois Attorney General – Civil Rights	www.illinoisattorneygeneral.gov/rights/civilrights.html
Indiana	Indiana Civil Rights Law	Indiana Civil Rights Commission	www.in.gov/icrc
Iowa	Iowa Civil Rights Act of 1965	Iowa Civil Rights Commission	icrc.iowa.gov
Kansas	Kansas Act against Discrimination	Kansas Human Rights Commission	www.khrc.net

(continued)

(continued)

State/Province	Legislation	Complaint agency/commission/tribunal	URL of agency/commission/tribunal
Kentucky	Kentucky Civil Rights Act	Kentucky Commission on Human Rights	kchr.ky.gov/Pages/default.aspx
Louisiana	Uniform Duties to Disabled Persons Act	Louisiana Commission on Human Rights	www.blancogovernor.com/HumanRights/howthecommissionworks.htm
Maine	Maine Human Rights Act; Use of Genetic Information for Employment Purposes	Maine Human Rights Commission	www.state.me.us/mhrc/index.shtml
Maryland	Code of Maryland	State of Maryland Commission on Civil Rights	mccr.maryland.gov
Massachusetts	Massachusetts Civil Rights Act; Law Prohibiting Discrimination against Medicare Beneficiaries	Massachusetts Commission against Discrimination	www.mass.gov/mcad
Michigan	Elliott-Larsen Civil Rights Act	Michigan Department of Civil Rights	www.michigan.gov/mdcr
Minnesota	Uniform Duties to Disabled Persons Act; 2015 Minnesota Statutes 471.471 Access Review Board, Accessible Electronic Information Services, 237.52, 248.061, 248.062	Minnesota Department of Human Rights	www.humanrights.state.mn.us
Mississippi	Public Welfare Code	Mississippi Department of Employment Security	mdes.ms.gov
Missouri	Missouri Human Rights Act	Department of Labor & Industrial Relations, Missouri Commission on Human Rights	labor.mo.gov/mohumanrights

330

State	Act/Law	Commission/Agency	Website
Montana	Montana Human Rights Act (Title 49); Montana Governmental Code of Fair Practices	Montana Department of Labor & Industry, Human Rights Commission	erd.dli.mt.gov/human-rights/human-rights-commission
Nebraska	Nebraska Age Discrimination in Employment Act; Nebraska Fair Employment Practice Act	Nebraska Equal Opportunity Commission	www.neoc.ne.gov
Nevada	Nevada Fair Employment Practices Act	Nevada Department of Employment, Training and Rehabilitation, Nevada Equal Rights Commission	detr.state.nv.us/nerc/NERC_index.htm
New Hampshire	Law against Discrimination	New Hampshire Commission for Human Rights	www.nh.gov/hrc/index.html
New Jersey	Law against Discrimination	Department of Law & Public Safety, New Jersey Division on Civil Rights	www.nj.gov/oag/dcr/index.html
New Mexico	Uniform Duties to Disabled Persons Act	Office of the Governor, Human Rights Commission	governor.state.nm.us/Human_Rights.aspx
New York	Human Rights Law	New York State, Division of Human Rights	www.dhr.ny.gov
North Carolina	North Carolina Persons with Disabilities Protection Act	Human Relations Commission	www.doa.state.nc.us/hrc
North Dakota	North Dakota Human Rights Act; Uniform Duties to Disabled Persons Act	North Dakota Department of Labor and Human Rights, Human Rights Division	www.nd.gov/labor/human-rights
Ohio	Ohio Revised Code 4112; Ohio Administrative Code 4112; Uniform Duties to Disabled Persons Act	Ohio Civil Rights Commission	crc.ohio.gov

(continued)

(continued)

State/Province	Legislation	Complaint agency/commission/tribunal	URL of agency/commission/tribunal
Oklahoma	Oklahoma Anti-Discrimination Act; Uniform Duties to Disabled Persons Act	Oklahoma Human Rights Commission	www.okdrs.org/guide/oklahoma-human-rights-commission
Oregon	Oregon Revised Statutes, Chapter 659 – Miscellaneous Prohibitions Relating to Employment and Discrimination	State of Oregon, Civil Rights Division	www.oregon.gov/BOLI/CRD/Pages/index.aspx
Pennsylvania	Pennsylvania Human Relations Act; Pennsylvania Fair Educational Opportunities Act	Pennsylvania Human Relations Commission	www.phrc.pa.gov/About-Us/Pages/About-PHRC.aspx#.VsNaq_N_Z5
Rhode Island	Rhode Island Commission for Human Rights Rules and Regulations, Accessibility to Persons with Disabilities	Rhode Island Commission for Human Rights	www.richr.ri.gov
South Carolina	Equal Enjoyment and Privileges to Public Accommodations Act; South Carolina Bill of Rights for Handicapped Persons; South Carolina Fair Housing Law	South Carolina Human Affairs Commission	www.eeoc.gov/field/greenville/fepa.cfm
South Dakota	South Dakota Codified Law Chapter 20, section 13	South Dakota Department of Labor & Regulation, Human Rights Commission	dlr.sd.gov/human_rights/commission.aspx

State	Law	Agency	Website
Tennessee	Tennessee Human Rights Act	Tennessee Disability Act; Tennessee Human Rights Commission	www.tn.gov/humanrights
Texas	Workforce Innovation and Opportunity Act	Texas Workforce Commission	www.twc.state.tx.us/commissioners
Utah	Utah Antidiscrimination Act; Utah Employment Selection Procedures Act; Utah Fair Housing Act	State of Utah Labor Commission, Utah Antidiscrimination & Labor Division	laborcommission.utah.gov/divisions/Anti discriminationAndLabor/index.html
Vermont	The Parental and Family Leave Act; Vermont Fair Employment Practices Act; Vermont Fair Housing and Public Accommodations Act	State of Vermont Human Rights Commission	hrc.vermont.gov
Virginia	Virginia Human Rights Act	Office of the Attorney General, The Division of Human Rights	www.ag.virginia.gov/index.php/programs-initiatives/human-rights
Washington	The Washington Law against Discrimination, Chapter 49.60 RCW	Washington State Human Rights Commission	www.hum.wa.gov
West Virginia	West Virginia Human Rights Act; West Virginia Fair Housing Act	West Virginia Human Rights Commission	www.hrc.wv.gov/Pages/default.aspx
Wisconsin	Fair Employment (Sections 111.31–111.397, Wisconsin Statutes, Chapter DWD 218 Wisconsin Administrative Code); Open Housing (Section 106.50, Wisconsin Statutes, Chapter DWD 220);	State of Wisconsin Department of Workforce Development, Civil Rights Bureau	dwd.wisconsin.gov/er/discrimination_civil_rights/how_to_file_cr_complaint.htm

(continued)

(continued)

State/Province	Legislation	Complaint agency/commission/tribunal	URL of agency/commission/tribunal
	Public Accommodations & Amusements (Section 106.52, Wisconsin Statutes, Chapter DWD 221 Wisconsin Administrative Code); Family & Medical Leave (Section 103.10, Wisconsin Statutes, Chapter DWD 225 Wisconsin Administrative Code); Post Secondary Education (Section 106.56, Wisconsin Statutes)		
Wyoming	Wyoming Fair Practices Act of 1965	Wyoming Department of Workforce Services	www.wyomingworkforce.org

Note: All URLs accessed 6 December 2016.

Index